Civil Society
History and Possibilities

S0-BCG-429

'Civil society' is one of the most used – and abused – concepts in current political thinking. In this important collection of essays, the concept is subjected to rigorous analysis by an international team of contributors, all of whom seek to encourage the historical and comparative under-standing of political thought. The volume is divided into two parts: the first section analyses the meaning of civil society in different theoretical traditions of Western philosophy. In the second section, contributors consider the theoretical and practical contexts in which the notion of civil society has been invoked in Asia, Africa and Latin America. These essays demonstrate how an influential Western idea like civil society is itself altered and innovatively modified by the specific contexts of intellectual and practical life in the societies of the South.

SUDIPTA KAVIRAJ is Reader in the Department of Political Studies, School of Oriental and African Studies, University of London. He is the author of *The Unhappy Consciousness* (1995) and editor of *Politics in India* (1998).

SUNIL KHILNANI is Professor of Politics in the School of Politics and Sociology, Birkbeck College, University of London. His publications include *Arguing Revolution: The Intellectual Left in Postwar France* (1993) and *The Idea of India* (1997).

Civil Society

History and Possibilities

Edited by

Sudipta Kaviraj
and
Sunil Khilnani

CAMBRIDGE
UNIVERSITY PRESS

PUBLISHED BY THE PRESS SYNDICATE OF THE UNIVERSITY OF CAMBRIDGE
The Pitt Building, Trumpington Street, Cambridge, United Kingdom

CAMBRIDGE UNIVERSITY PRESS
The Edinburgh Building, Cambridge CB2 2RU, UK
40 West 20th Street, New York, NY 10011–4211, USA
10 Stamford Road, Oakleigh, VIC 3166, Australia
Ruiz de Alarcón 13, 28014 Madrid, Spain
Dock House, The Waterfront, Cape Town 8001, South Africa

http://www.cambridge.org

© in this collection Cambridge University Press 2001

This book is in copyright. Subject to statutory exception and to the provisions of relevant collective licensing agreements, no reproduction of any part may take place without the written permission of Cambridge University Press.

First published 2001

Printed in the United Kingdom at the University Press, Cambridge

Typeset in Times 10/12pt   System 3b2   [CE]

A catalogue record for this book is available from the British Library

Library of Congress Cataloguing in Publication data

Civil society: history and possibilities / edited by Sudipta Kaviraj and Sunil Khilnani.
    p.   cm.
Includes bibliographical references and index.
ISBN 0 521 63344 3 – ISBN 0 521 00290 7 (pb.)
1. Civil society. I. Kaviraj, Sudipta. II. Khilnani, Sunil, 1960–
JC337.C563 2001 301–dc21   00–065176

ISBN 0 521 63344 3 hardback
ISBN 0 521 00290 7 paperback

Luis Castro Leiva
In memory

Contents

List of contributors   *page* ix

Introduction: Ideas of civil society   1

Part I : *Theoretical traditions in the West*   9

1 The development of civil society   11
   SUNIL KHILNANI

2 Concepts of civil society in pre-modern Europe   33
   ANTONY BLACK

3 The contemporary political significance of John Locke's
   conception of civil society   39
   JOHN DUNN

4 Civil society in the Scottish Enlightenment   58
   FANIA OZ-SALZBERGER

5 Enlightenment and the institution of society: notes for a
   conceptual history   84
   KEITH MICHAEL BAKER

6 Hegel and the economics of civil society   105
   GARETH STEDMAN JONES

7 Civil society and the Marxist tradition   131
   JOSEPH FEMIA

Part II : *Arguments in the South*   147

8 Civil society in an extra-European perspective   149
   JACK GOODY

9 On civil and political society in post-colonial democracies   165
   PARTHA CHATTERJEE

10 Civil society and the fate of the modern republics of Latin
    America   179
    LUIS CASTRO LEIVA and ANTHONY PAGDEN

11 The Western concept of civil society in the context of
    Chinese history   204
    THOMAS A. METZGER

12 Civil society, community, and democracy in the Middle East   232
    SAMI ZUBAIDA

13 Mistaking 'governance' for 'politics': foreign aid, democracy,
    and the construction of civil society   250
    ROB JENKINS

14 The promise of 'civil society' in the South   269
    GEOFFREY HAWTHORN

15 In search of civil society   287
    SUDIPTA KAVIRAJ

Index   324

Contributors

KEITH MICHAEL BAKER, Anthony P. Meyer Family Professor and Director, Stanford Humanities Centre, Stanford University.

ANTHONY BLACK, Professor in the History of Political Theory, University of Dundee.

PARTHA CHATTERJEE, Professor and Director, Centre for Studies in Social Sciences, Calcutta, and Professor, Department of Anthropology, Columbia University.

JOHN DUNN, Professor of Political Theory, and Fellow of King's College, University of Cambridge.

JOSEPH FEMIA, Reader in Political Theory, University of Liverpool.

JACK GOODY, Emeritus Professor of Social Anthropology, and Fellow of St John's College, University of Cambridge.

GEOFFREY HAWTHORN, Professor of International Politics, and Fellow of Clare Hall, University of Cambridge.

ROBERT JENKINS, Senior Lecturer in Politics, Birkbeck College, University of London.

SUDIPTA KAVIRAJ, Reader in Politics, School of Oriental and African Studies, University of London.

SUNIL KHILNANI, Professor of Politics, Birkbeck College, University of London.

LUIS CASTRO LEIVA, was Professor at IIDEA, Caracas, and held the Edward Larocque Tinker Chair at the University of Chicago until his death in 1999.

THOMAS A. METZGER, Senior Fellow, Hoover Institution, Stanford University.

FANIA OZ-SALZBERGER, Lecturer in History, University of Haifa.

ANTHONY PAGDEN, Professor of Political Theory, Johns Hopkins University.

GARETH STEDMAN JONES, Professor of Political Science, and Fellow of King's College, University of Cambridge.

SAMI ZUBAIDA, Reader in Sociology, Birkbeck College, University of London.

Introduction: ideas of civil society

The idea of civil society has made a dramatic return recently. In discussions about politics in the most diverse settings, analysts and theoretical thinkers speak about civil society – its lack, its decline, its promise and possibility. Yet such diverse popularity itself creates a problem of indeterminacy. Does the idea mean the same thing in all these different contexts? Are supporters of 'civil society' in the West, in the former Communist societies, in the Third World, all trying to achieve the same ideal? Secondly, exactly what sort of thing is the idea of civil society? Is it a descriptive term for a certain type of social structure, mode of social behaviour, or political ideal? What does the 'realization' of civil society imply in countries where it is set up as an ideal? What are the conditions of its possibility and existence? Such questions are raised in this volume.

The discussion to be found here is not meant to take a partisan position in the debate for and against 'civil society' – it seeks, rather, to clarify. We started in an enquiring and agnostic spirit: it seemed that the debate about 'civil society' was both fascinating and unclear. It was unclear because both individuals and distinguishable strands in the literature used the idea with substantially different meanings; at times, the ambiguity was not just that there were several meanings, but that the meaning was radically unclear. Yet what was arresting about this discussion was that despite such ambiguities and difficulties, serious political groups and scholars kept coming back to it, and chose to express their specific political unhappiness or ambition through this phrase instead of others. Both these reasons seemed to us to require an exercise in clarification – of the theoretical semantics and of the historical contexts.

There are at least three clearly identifiable strands in the contemporary discussions about civil society, or, more precisely, discussions in which the idea of civil society figures significantly. In some theoretical contexts, as in intellectual debates about what the organization of society and its relation to the state in post-Communist societies should be, the notion is used with great theoretical seriousness. Communist systems invariably overextended the legal jurisdiction and effective control of state institutions, such as the bureaucracy, over nearly all spheres of social life. After the collapse of those kinds of states, there was a need, it was argued, for encouraging the flourishing of institutions of 'civil society' outside the legal jurisdiction of the state. There are at least two strands of current leftist political thought in the West which are also keen to revive the idea of a civil society, for reasons which are only partially comparable. Some radical theorists, after the disillusionment with the ideas of socialism and its distinct soiling by Communist experience, wish to radicalize the idea of democracy by re-invoking notions of civil society. At times, writers who are critical of the retreat of the welfare state through the years of neo-conservative reaction in the 1980s have concluded that while it is impossible for socialists to revive the older tradition of trade-union militancy and statism, equally the conservative atomization of society is unacceptable. Some within these strands of thought have argued forcefully, at times invoking the British pluralist tradition, that what is required is a revival of the associative initiatives of non-state organizations in civil society. Evidently, there is a similarity between the post-Communist argument and the associational one; but the direction of critical enterprise is strikingly different. The first is directed at the excesses of Communist statism, the second at those of capitalist atomization. Another strand of current thinking in the West also concerns civil society: the arguments about new social movements. Again, there is a strong affinity between the associational argument and the idea that the new social movements, which are quite distinct from classical working-class movements in interest and form, are the carriers of radical democratic aspirations.

The chapters collected here are not intended to comment on or gloss all three current discussions, but only one of them: the contemporary discussion about the 'Third World' or the 'South' and the invocation of civil society in that context. To clarify that debate, we decided to follow an unconventional strategy. We felt that the theoretical difficulties arose because of ambiguities on two sides. First, because the contexts in which civil society was invoked varied a great deal between various Third World societies. In some cases, it meant modern forms of sociability based on interest, which could be begun and ended without embarrassment or further obligation. In some others, it simply emphasized the need for a secure, reliable, predictable legal order. In still other cases – for example, in India, where stable democratic institutions have worked for half a century – authors sometimes expressed their dissatisfaction with the social consequences of democracy and the failures of its party system by having recourse to the concepts of civil society.

However, the contextual distinctions between political institutions and practices was not the only source of confusion. The idea of a civil society was not entirely singular in its connotations in the history of Western thought either. Some of the ambiguities in the contemporary Third World discussions arose because of the multiple meanings of the term in the Western tradition itself. Thus, when faced with theoretical ambiguity in the Third World debate, it was not enough simply to say that those who used the idea did not look carefully at *the* Western concept. There was no single or simple Western concept to study and emulate. We therefore concluded that greater clarity could be achieved if we looked at precisely what the idea sought to convey in distinct European traditions. The structure of this volume is organized around this contrast.

If the European tradition of thinking about 'civil society' is disaggregated, it reveals at least three different strands, with individual thinkers imparting subtle and distinctive inflexions to the theoretical use of the concept. In this book, these traditions are analysed separately in essays dealing with the Scottish Enlightenment, French Enlightenment thought, and the German strand running through Marx and Hegel. However, some individual thinkers seemed of particular importance in the Western traditions, because they introduced either a specific formulation of the problem, or a special conceptual development. There are thus specific analyses of Locke's thought because he turns the more traditional contractarian dichotomy between 'the state of nature' and 'civil society' towards the new distinction between 'civil society' and the state (although in his work this dichotomy is not used explicitly). Hegel's intervention in the discussions on civil society is considered crucial by most interpreters, because of his new interpretation of the idea as *bürgerliche Gesellschaft*; accordingly, he is given separate analytical treatment here.

It is widely accepted that development of theoretical thinking on politics occurs within two types of contexts. The first is an intellectual and cultural context of received 'languages' through which individual writers think about their societies. Their performances are both enabled and constrained by the contents of this received conceptual language, or intellectual tradition. Secondly, political theorizing happens under the pressure of historically specific predicaments, particularly intense problems faced by generations of people who think their way through them by analysing them theoretically. Political theory is thus often produced under the pressure and demands of political practice. It is this historical urgency and pressure that often elicits highly original uses of received doctrine or conceptual resources. Political thinking is thus at times an act of intellectual desperation, not of calm and orderly intellectual introspection. It is not surprising, therefore, that once the idea of civil society gains a certain currency, it would be pressed into service by authors desperately seeking solutions to their specific historical problems in Third World contexts. To purely academic tastes, their uses might look like misapplication; but this is inevitable; and, paradoxically, this precisely confirms the historicity of political thinking.

What is the connection between the European discourses of 'civil society' and its historical entry into non-Western political discourse? First, it is essential to note that the idea of a 'civil society' passed into the political literature of European colonies in the nineteenth century; it is wrong to think of this concern as being expressed only in relatively recent times. The reasons for the first engagement with the ideas of 'civil society' are also not difficult to gauge. European political rule brought in institutions which had a certain type of discursive field associated with them. If colonial political structures had to be visualized conceptually as a 'state', this immediately brought in an implicit distinction from civil society. The idea entered colonial discourses about politics in two rather obvious ways. Colonial administrations themselves explicitly used it to justify their patterns of intervention or non-intervention in societies under their control, to claim sometimes that some matters were those of the 'civil society' and thus out of the jurisdiction of the colonial state. Secondly, modern elites in colonies often absorbed Western influences and emulated forms of behaviour based on these distinctions. The analysis of the Indian and Chinese political traditions provides examples of this kind of absorption.

But there was probably a more general reason as well. Introduction of the modern state everywhere disrupted and transformed earlier distributions and arrangements of social power. With the arrival of European colonialism, the state became an undeniable, unavoidable part of the business of social living; and the institutional organization of the modern state invites a discourse in terms of a state/civil society distinction. If the state is considered too powerful and invasive, people must search for a concept that gives a collective definition to the spheres that are or ought to be left out of its control. European cultural influence always delivered this discourse, with this conceptual distinction at its centre, to the colonial intelligentsia. Thus, it is hardly surprising that with the coming of the modern state – with its enormous potentialities of collective action and equally vast dangers – this conceptual language began to be used outside the West.

The historical result has been a strange paradox – which political scientists analysing non-Western societies cannot ignore. Actual political processes in the Third World are mostly very different from political life in the West; yet strangely, the language used to describe, evaluate and express the experiences of politics are the same everywhere. For historical reasons, nearly all societies of the Third World speak, as far as politics is concerned, a Western language. It is a language which identifies states and civil societies, speaks of bureaucracies, political parties, parliaments, expresses political desires for the establishment of liberal, Communist or socialist political forms, and evaluates political systems in terms of democracy and dictatorship. Yet it is common knowledge that these words do not denote objects which behave in the same way as in the West, where this language originated. The existence of a bureaucracy does not mean the untroubled operation of Weberian rules of rationalization; operation of democracy does not necessarily mean a secure understanding of inviolable rights of individuals or respect for minorities. Political institutions taken from the West are introduced into societies which have embedded forms of sociability that are very different from the common individualistic forms of the modern West. The actual manner of operation and historical effects of those political institutions are sometimes startlingly different. Another compelling reason for the use of this political language to describe a different kind of social world lies in the nature of intellectual traditions. Many non-Western societies have intellectual cultures of great antiquity and sophistication. Often, however, these intellectual traditions did not have a pronounced attention to the sphere of 'politics' in the modern sense, and therefore do not have a highly developed vernacular tradition to draw upon and develop. As a result, their historical entanglement with the modern state – the expression of its entirely novel structure of historical experience, dealing with its concentrated power, its ability to affect people's lives on an unprecedentedly large scale – has to rely at least initially on the language that comes from the West, the habitual, standard language of conveying and reflecting on this experience. However, over the longer historical term, as these historical state trajectories and the human experiences associated with them come to diverge from Western forms, inevitably new elements emerge. To pursue those themes is not the main purpose of this volume, though this question lies at the heart of most of the chapters dealing with civil society in the South.

Analysis of politics and history of ideas about societies of the South therefore have to be comparative. But there is also an additional reason for such exercises. Analysis of Third World politics is carried out inescapably in the language of present-day political science. If we accept, however, that these analytical languages are historically indexed and structured, this might suggest a subtle problem of applicability. Third World societies face large historical processes as problems which are much more similar to what Western societies faced in the nineteenth century – the re-organization of social life around a modern sovereign state, conflicts generated by early industrialization, contradictions arising out of secularization of state forms against resistance from universalistic claims of traditional religion to control all aspects of social life. These historical processes are no longer central facts of modern Western life; and therefore contemporary Western social thought is not directed towards intellectually grasping such processes. In the early modern thought of the West, however, these historical problems are absolutely central. In the tradition of thought stretching from Locke to Marx, these questions constitute the main objects of analysis. Contemporary engagement with Third World societies thus might have a great deal to gain from a careful, critical reading of early modern Western political thought. The idea of a 'civil society' was in any case fashioned by this tradition in all its theoretical complexity.

In this period of intellectual globalization, such conceptual questions are becoming increasingly urgent for another reason. Parallel to indigenous reflection on the historical effects of re-organizing societies around the power of the modern state, there is now a large and insistent discourse emerging from development institutions and lobbies. International donor agencies, Western governments providing aid, non-governmental organizations (NGOs) working on development issues, each has increasingly focused on the social conditions necessary for the successful functioning of democratic institutions. Historical experience of the last half century has shown that the democratic impulse is irreversible, but uncertain in its consequences. In nearly all societies, authoritarian or repressive governments face challenges to their unrestricted power, but the popular desire for democracy is not easy to translate into stable responsible government. It is not simply a matter of the formal constitutional or institutional form: these forms, introduced on a wide scale after de-colonization, crumple and collapse with astonishing rapidity when faced with a recalcitrant sociology. It is widely acknowledged now that successful functioning of democracy requires more than legal artifice; it requires sociological and historical conditions to operate and to take root. But that leads to the further vexed question about whether such structures of modern sociability can be fashioned by external pressure. These problems are discussed in some of the chapters in part II.

We hope, through the example of this volume, to suggest that much more research is required in the comparative history of ideas – which would require bringing together, in a comparative frame, historical studies of ideas from the West and the contemporary Third World. If globalization is to produce benevolent results, it is essential to build bridges through the understanding of such problems.

Acknowledgements

In putting together this collection, we have received generous help from many friends. We thank the contributors for their support and great patience through long delays. John Dunn helped us at all stages of the project, from its original conception to its final stages, by giving advice and encouragement. We are grateful for the support and advice we have received at various stages from Geoffrey Hawthorn. He, with John Dunn, also helped us organize a workshop at King's College, Cambridge. The Nuffield Foundation gave a grant for the workshop. The Departments of Politics at the School of Oriental and African Studies (SOAS) and of Politics and Sociology at Birkbeck College have given us support through the seminars. The Research Committee at SOAS and the Department of Politics and Sociology gave us an initial grant, and the SOAS research office a small grant for final word-processing. Richard Fisher at Cambridge University Press has been much tried by the process of assembling this book for publication and we are grateful to him for his understanding and patience. Thanks too are due to Jean Field, for her alert copy-editing. Sadly, during the course of the project we lost one of our most vital and intellectually engaging colleagues, Luis Castro Leiva. We dedicate this volume to his memory.

Theoretical traditions in the West

1   The development of civil society

Sunil Khilnani

Fugitive in its senses, the idea of civil society infiltrates all efforts to assess the possibilities and threats revealed by the glacial political shifts at the turn of the century. In a period of rising political animosities and mistrust, it has come to express a political desire for greater civility in social relations.[1] More ambitiously, in light of the mounting unintelligibility of the politically created world, it names a desire for analytically more appropriate categories of understanding. Invoked at the same time as the diagnosis and as the cure for current ills, deployed by conservatives, liberals, and radical utopians alike, by oppositional movements and by international aid donors, civil society has become an ideological rendezvous for erstwhile antagonists. It is championed across the globe as '*the* idea of the late twentieth century'.[2]

In the West, disillusion with the given 'boundaries' of politics and with the restrictions of what are seen as the increasingly decrepit processes of party politics, has provoked interest in civil society as a means of rejuvenating public life.[3] In the East, the term has come more narrowly to mean – besides political and civil liberties – simply private property rights and markets.[4] In the South, the collapse of the theoretical models that

---

This chapter seeks to sketch the broad parameters of recent discussions of civil society. As such, it draws freely on a host of published studies, as well as on the papers and discussions of the Civil Society seminar held jointly by the School of Oriental and African Studies and Birkbeck College, University of London. I am especially grateful to Sudipta Kaviraj for his help in thinking about the subject, and to Emma Rothschild for her initial suggestion that I should tackle it.

[1] Cf. V. Havel, 'Politics, Morality, and Civility', *Summer Meditations* (London: Faber, 1992).

[2] National Humanities Center, *The Idea of a Civil Society* (Humanities Research Center, Research Triangle Park, North Carolina, 1992), p. 1.

[3] See C. Maier (ed.), *The Changing Boundaries of the Political* (Cambridge: Cambridge University Press, 1987); J. Keane, *Democracy and Civil Society* (London: Verso, 1988); J. Cohen and A. Arato, *Civil Society and Political Theory* (Cambridge, Mass.: MIT Press, 1992); and for a somewhat different use of the idea of civil society, see P. Hirst, *Associative Democracy* (Cambridge: Polity Press, 1993).

[4] See P. G. Lewis (ed.), *Democracy and Civil Society in Eastern Europe* (Basingstoke: Macmillan); E. Hankiss, *Eastern European Alternatives* (Oxford: Oxford University Press,

dominated post-Second World War understandings of politics there has given new currency to the idea of civil society: intellectuals in India and in Latin America, in the Middle East and in China, Africa and South East Asia, are all infusing new and complex life into the category.[5] International agencies and lenders too have turned their attention to this idea. In an effort to accelerate and increase the efficiency of development tasks, they now seek ways to by-pass the central state and to assist directly what they identify as the constituents of civil society: private enterprises and organizations, church and denominational associations, self-employed workers' co-operatives and unions, and the vast field of NGOs, all have attracted external interest. They have come to be seen as essential to the construction of what are assumed to be the social preconditions for more accountable, public, and representative forms of political power.[6] To all who invoke it, civil society incarnates a desire to recover for society powers – economic, social, expressive – believed to have been illegitimately usurped by states.

Although central to classical Western political theory, the concept of civil society was largely moribund during the days when models of state-led modernization dominated both liberal and Marxist conceptions of social change and development. It was recovered during the late 1970s and 1980s, as these models disintegrated. Civil society seemed to promise something better and available: it was democracy and prosperity, autonomy and the means to exercise it. Yet, in those regions that have emerged from authoritarian rule or from close political regulation of the economy – that is, in regions which seemed to have created what were assumed to be the preconditions for the emergence of a civil society – the picture has been much darker. The common pattern has been the appearance of a multiplicity of non-negotiable identities and colliding self-righteous

1990); C. Kukathas, D. W. Lovell, and W. Malay, *Transition from Socialism* (Melbourne: Longman Chesire, 1991): R. Rose. 'Eastern Europe's Need for a Civil Economy' (unpublished MS, 1992).

[5] See M. A Garreton, 'Political Democratisation in Latin America and the Crisis of Paradigms', in J. Manor (ed.), *Rethinking Third World Politics* (Harlow: Longmans, 1991). See also, for the Indian case, the work of Rajni Kothari: *State Against Democracy* (Delhi: Ajanta Publications, 1988); for the Middle East, see Zubaida's chapter in this volume; for a discussion of the Southern African case, see T. Ranger, 'Civil Society in Southern Africa', paper presented to Civil Society seminar, Birkbeck College and SOAS, London; for Sub-Saharan Africa, see the Introduction and J.-F. Bayart, 'Civil Society in Africa', in P. Chabal (ed.), *Political Domination in Africa* (Cambridge: Cambridge University Press, 1986).

[6] See G. Hawthorn, 'Sub-Saharan Africa', in D. Held (ed.), *Prospects for Democracy* (Cambridge: Polity Press, 1993), pp. 343 and 354: see also World Bank, *The Social Dimensions of Structural Adjustment in Sub-Saharan Africa* (Washington: World Bank, 1989), cited by Hawthorn, 'Sub-Saharan Africa'.

beliefs, not a plural representation of malleable interests. Civil society remains as distant and precarious an ambition as ever.

Is it a coherent and possible one? As commonly understood today, is it an idea that may usefully guide and influence strategies designed to accomplish 'transitions'? In the burgeoning literature on transitions, two models dominate: on the one hand, a 'shock-therapy' model, which advocates the sudden institution of, for example, free markets in goods and services, and on the other hand, a 'gradualist' model, which stresses the importance of maintaining stable political structures and which emphasizes the unintended results of actions.[7] The very notion of 'transition' has, however, itself lost much of its coherence: it implies a determinate end-state, yet at no time since the establishment of the professional social sciences has there been a weaker and more indeterminate conception of what exactly populations and their territories are changing *to*, or can reasonably hope for.[8] Can the category of 'civil society' serve – as Ralf Dahrendorf claimed – as the conceptual and practical 'key' to such transitions?[9] Do the disparate uses of the term amount to a determinate normative ideal? More importantly, are there resources within the concept's history, which can, for current conditions, relevantly specify the causal agencies and capacities needed to achieve and maintain this ideal? Finally, does 'civil society' name a systemic entity, an institutional package, or is it most appropriately used to describe a particular set of human capacities and modes of conduct, always only contingently available (even in places where it does, at present, happen to exist)?

In contemporary discussions, there is no agreement about the proper location of the sources of civil society, sources which ought to and actually can restrain and moderate the state. One response, which for convenience might be called a 'liberal' position, sees the effective powers of civil society as basically residing in the economy, in property rights and markets where such rights may be freely exchanged. Another view, a 'radical' position, locates civil society in a 'society' independent of the economic domain and the state, where ideas are publicly exchanged,

---

[7] Both of these models can be found in Adam Smith's *An Inquiry into the Nature and Causes of the Wealth of Nations* (1776), the classic analysis of the processes of transition from pre-commercial to commercial society.

[8] Despite exhortations such as F. Fukuyama, *The End of History and the Last Man* (New York: Free Press, 1991).

[9] R. Dahrendorf, *Reflections on the Revolution in Europe* (London: Chatto, 1990), p. 93. Cf. also J. Cohen and A. Arato, *Civil Society and Political Theory*, p. 2: 'if we are to understand the dramatic changes occurring in Latin America and Eastern Europe in particular, the concept of civil society is indispensable [especially] if we are to understand the stakes of these "transitions to democracy" as well as the self-understanding of the relevant actors'.

associations freely formed, and interests discovered. Finally, a 'conservative' position prefers to see it as residing in a set of cultural acquisitions, in historically inherited manners of civility which moderate relations between groups and individuals: unlike the previous two positions, adherents of this view do not see these acquisitions as being necessarily universally available.[10] Each of these domains – economy, society, culture – is portrayed by its respective advocates as a domain of special authenticity and efficacy which ought to limit the state, and which can accomplish more effectively what states have tried, often with pathetic success, to do for themselves.

Historical pedigrees may be found for each of these views concerning the development of civil society, yet each also betrays a historical partiality and thinness. The purpose of this chapter is to sketch some of the general themes of this book, which hope to caution against such thinness and partiality, and to urge a richer historical sense upon all current efforts directed at the development of civil societies. The first part briefly considers three decisive moments in the historical development of the concept: John Locke, the Scottish theorists of commercial society, and Hegel. Each had distinct (if in some respects overlapping) visions, and each had a causal account of how their vision might be secured. Their assumptions may today appear implausible; but contemporary advocates of the idea of civil society must at the very least match these causal ambitions. The second part of the chapter considers the significance of the category of civil society, both as an analytic tool and as a critical, regulative principle for the politics of the South. Taken at its boldest, the idea of civil society embodies the epic of Western modernity: as such, it raises questions about the significance of the historical experience of Western politics for societies that possess their own cultural and historical logics, yet which have by no means remained untouched by the peculiar Western saga. Is the combination of liberal democracy and civil society a necessary fate for inhabitants of the modern West, but of little or no relevance to the East or the South?[11] In what respects might the experience of the West be relevant to these regions? The point is not one about the replicability of institutions and practices, in the manner that modernization theory once assumed was possible, but about the possibility of identifying a common set of goals and purposes, perhaps

---

[10] Cf. F. Mount, *Times Literary Supplement*, 15 October 1993: 'the grammar of civility has been neglected . . . it is the absence of this moral conversation – and the habitual acceptance of personal obligations arising out of it – which we lament in the ex-Communist states of Central and Eastern Europe: the way we put it is that "they lack civil society"'.

[11] J. Gray, *Post-Liberalism* (London: Routledge, 1993), chs. 14 and 20; and see my review article, *The Political Quarterly*, 64, no. 4 (1993), pp. 481–4.

best described by the idea of political accountability.[12] Attempts to strengthen 'democratization' and political accountability have assumed that this can be accomplished through the introduction of constitutions, competitive political parties, and markets and property rights. These are taken to constitute a coherent and stable mix for securing autonomy and prosperity, the modern liberty that Benjamin Constant characterized as the liberty to live as one pleases.[13] But the category 'civil society' can introduce a new complexity and sharpness to assessments of the difficulties facing democracy in the South, both in establishing preconditions and dealing with consequences.

I

In the early post-Second World War decades, the concept of civil society received no significant attention in the West. It played no structural role in the arguments during the 1950s of liberal political theorists like Isaiah Berlin, Jacob Talmon, or Karl Popper, all of whom were defenders of liberal values and of individual liberty and all of whom wished to specify the proper sphere and limits of political authority. Berlin, for example, in his classic essay, 'Two Concepts of Liberty', insisted that 'a frontier must be drawn between the area of private life and that of public authority': likewise Talmon, in distinguishing the liberal from the totalitarian conception of democracy, claimed that the former 'recognizes a variety of levels of personal and collective endeavour, which are altogether outside the sphere of politics'.[14] Both vividly portrayed the dangers of 'absolute politics', and both sought to circumscribe the boundaries of politics: yet neither felt any particular need to invoke the idea of civil society. During the same period, critics of the Left likewise found the term of little interest. Marxists, both orthodox and dissident, used it negatively: it was identified with 'bourgeois society', a realm of contradiction and mystification sustained by relations of power. Civil society, understood as bourgeois society, was seen as the sphere of needs, inextricably linked to the productive base of capitalist society, and in need of constant police and regulation by the state. Members of the Frankfurt School, influenced

---

[12] See J. Lonsdale, 'Political Accountability in African History', in P. Chabal (ed.), *Political Domination in Africa* (Cambridge: Cambridge University Press, 1986).

[13] See B. Constant, 'The Liberty of the Ancients Compared with that of the Moderns', in *Political Writings*, trans. and ed. by B. Fontana (Cambridge: Cambridge University Press, 1988).

[14] I. Berlin, 'Two Concepts of Liberty' (1958), in *Four Essays on Liberty* (Oxford: Oxford University Press, 1969), p. 124: and cf. p. 127, J. Talmon, *The Origins of Totalitarian Democracy* (1952) (London, 1972 edn), p. 1.

by Lukács's interpretation of Hegel, saw the concept as a prism through which the contradictions and conflicts of capitalism were refracted. The term played no role in critiques of Left totalitarianism which stressed the distortions produced by unbridled state power: Herbert Marcuse, for example, made no use of the category in his influential study of *Soviet Marxism.*

A serious revival of the term did, however, begin on the Left. In the late 1960s, it gained popularity among radicals disaffected with Marxism. The existing structures of Left politics (dominated by Communist Parties) were rejected, in favour of 'social movements' – these were seen as more authentic embodiments of social demands and interests. Equally, the recovery of Antonio Gramsci's work was a vital spur: his modification of the arrangements of Marx's schema of base and superstructure gave the concept of civil society – applied to Western Europe – a wholly novel centrality.[15] The consequence of Gramsci's relocation of civil society, at the level of the superstructure, along with the state, and his claim that it was the site of decisive struggle for hegemony, provoked a reorientation towards cultural critique. The term finally went into orbit during the late 1970s and 1980s, after its adoption by groups and intellectuals agitating against the authoritarian states and regimes in Eastern Europe (especially Poland) and Latin America. Most recently, the idea of civil society has appealed to those who wish to sustain the project of a 'post-modern utopianism', to reconcile socialism and democracy. In these usages, 'civil society' is employed to designate a conception richer than 'constitutional representative democracy': it is seen as a supplement – and not a substitute – to the perceived illegitimacies of this system. Conversely, it is also seen as a means of establishing a more integrated relationship between socialism and democracy.[16] From this perspective, civil society is understood as a term that identifies the sociological underpinnings of modern democracy. It follows that the historic inability of socialism to find a democratic form for itself has come implicitly to be explained as largely a consequence of its theoretical ignorance of and practical antagonism towards civil society. For Left radicals, it has thus become a handy term which at once both helps them to acclimatize to liberal political theory, and allows them to revive doctrines of popular sovereignty.

---

[15] See N. Bobbio, 'Gramsci and the Conception of Civil Society', in *Which Socialism?* (Cambridge: Polity Press, 1987).

[16] Cf. Keane, *Democracy and Civil Society*; Cohen and Arato, *Civil Society and Political Theory*; and C. Mouffe (ed.), *Dimensions of Radical Democracy* (London: Verso, 1992), which claims that such categories as civil society and citizenship can produce 'a radicalization of the modern democratic tradition' (p. 1).

These rediscoveries of the idea of civil society obscure its historical depth. A typical example of such oversight is manifest in Jean Cohen and Andrew Arato's large volume on the subject, which gives barely seven pages (out of nearly 800) to consideration of the pre-Hegelian idioms which bear on the idea of civil society.[17] However, as the following chapters make clear, the languages of Roman law, classical republicanism, Pufendorf and the natural law tradition, Locke, Montesquieu, the theorists of commercial society, as well as Hegel and the nineteenth-century traditions of civil associations and guild socialism, are all essential components of any historically informed understanding of the idea. These different historical strands often cut against one another rather than combining into a single continuous conceptual history. Restrictions in historical perspective have often promoted confusion in contemporary understanding, which instinctively tends to define civil society in opposition to the state, and to propose a misleading zero-sum relation between the two. Civil society is not a new, post-Hegelian concept. It is a much older term, which entered into English usage via the Latin translation, *societas civilis*, of Aristotle's *koinonia politike*. In its original sense, it allowed no distinction between 'state' and 'society' or between political and civil society: it simply meant a community, a collection of human beings united within a legitimate political order, and was variously rendered as 'society' or 'community'.[18] It was Hegel who first bifurcated the concept, but in a way whereby state and civil society functioned in his account as redescriptions of one another.[19]

If civil society is defined in opposition to the 'state' then, as Norberto Bobbio has noted, 'it is difficult to provide a positive definition of "civil society" because it is a question of listing everything that has been left over, after limiting the sphere of the state'. But such attempts to substantialize definitions of civil society are unhelpful. Civil society is not best thought of as the theoretical specification of a substantive model, which actual societies must then strive to approximate. Historically, the term has been defined in opposition to several antonyms. In the Anglo-Scottish and French idioms that surround the term, civil society (along with cognate terms) was generally opposed to the condition of despotism and barbarism, or to natural society.[20] In these traditions, the problem of

---

[17] Cohen and Arato, *Civil Society and Political Theory.*
[18] See A. Black, this volume; and N. Bobbio, 'Civil Society', in *Democracy and Dictatorship* (Cambridge: Polity Press, 1989).
[19] Hegel himself ignored the pre-modern and natural law history of the concept, as well as its place in Aristotle's *Politics*: see M. Reidel ' "State" and "Civil Society": Linguistic Context and Historical Origin', in *Between Tradition and Revolution* (Cambridge: Cambridge University Press, 1984), pp. 133–4.
[20] Cf. J. Starobinski, 'Le Mot Civilisation', *Le Remède dans le mal* (Paris: Gallimard, 1989).

the appropriate boundaries between political and civil authority, between public and private, has tended to be discussed in a number of political languages: rights, constitutionalism, mixed government, the rule of law, markets, and the division of labour (all of which may be taken to provide part of the content of civil society). In the German tradition, on the other hand, civil society has generally been situated in opposition either to community or to the state.[21]

Three moments in the historical development of the term have been of particular significance: the ideas of John Locke, the Scottish theorists of commercial society, and Hegel. For Locke, the fundamental contrast defining a civil society was the state of nature: a predicament in which deeply held individual beliefs about how to act collided, and where there could be no authoritative answer to the question, 'who will be judge?'. A civil society was one purged as effectively as possible of this condition.[22] Locke made no separation between civil society, and political society – in no sense was civil society conceived of as distinct from an entity termed 'the state'. Rather, a civil society was a term accorded to a benign state, a legitimate political order. Locke, in John Dunn's words, 'distinguished sharply between true civil societies in which governmental power derives in more or less determinate ways from the consent of their citizens, and political units which possess at least equivalent concentrations of coercive power but in which there is neither the recognition nor the reality of any dependence of governmental power upon popular consent'.[23] The Lockean conception of a legitimate political order, however, was vastly different from our own post-Hobbesian conception of the state as an impersonal structure of authority. Committed to a strongly individualist conception, Locke saw political legitimacy as founded upon unbroken chains of personal trust. A legitimate political society was one in which the modality of human interaction was trust: trust was not a variably chosen strategy, contingent upon circumstances, but the very premise of such an order. Both rulers and ruled conceived of governmental power as a trust, *and* the psychic relation between ruled and rulers was governed by relations of trust. As Dunn has emphasized, what must strike us about Locke's conception was his willingness to entangle two issues which modern traditions of political understanding commonly treat as radically disparate: 'the psychic and practical relations between individual citizens

---

[21] Ferdinand Tönnies, *Gemeinschaft und Gesellschaft* (Leipzig, 1887), is the classic statement of this distinction. See J. Samples, 'Kant, Tönnies and the Liberal Idea of Community in German Sociology', *History of Political Thought*, vol. 8, no. 2 (1987), pp. 245–62.

[22] J. Dunn, this volume.

[23] J. Dunn, 'Trust and Political Agency', in D. Gambetta (ed.), *Trust* (Oxford: Blackwell, 1988), p. 83.

across the space of private life, and the structural relations between bureaucratic governments and the subjects over whom they rule'.[24] He wished above all to resist the depersonalization and demoralization of political authority which he saw as characteristic of his times.

In contrast to the state of nature, Locke understood civil society as a condition where there exist known standing laws, judges, and effective powers of enforcement. Such a condition was necessarily a skilled and precarious political achievement: it did not in any way represent the truth of a developmental process or a theoretical system. For Locke, 'a civilized society was not an essentially systemic entity: it was simply an aggregation of civilized human beings', that is, a society of human beings who had succeeded in disciplining their conduct.[25] If there was to be any possibility of securing a civilized society, certain minimal conditions were clearly necessary: these included a representative political order, a system of private property rights, and toleration of freedom of worship (although this did not, for Locke, extend to freedom of speech or to toleration of atheism).[26] The creation of such a civilized habitat could also, no doubt, in part be helped by processes of socialization, by the inculcation of a 'penal conception of the self'.[27] But such processes could never be comprehensive or entirely successful, for Locke 'saw no reassuring array of automatic mechanisms, either within the individual human psyche, in a human society at large, or in the organization of people's productive activities, that ensured the provisions of such benefit'.[28] Unlike many later theorists, Locke gave no primacy to some special mechanism – for example, the market or the division of labour – which could engender and sustain a civilized society. Furthermore, such a society was not one where individuals were at liberty to live as they pleased: rather, it was a space where individuals could fulfil the injunctions of the Christian God. What ultimately held human beings together

---

[24] Ibid., pp. 83–4.

[25] J. Dunn, ' "Bright Enough For All Our Purposes": John Locke's Conception of a Civilized Society', *Notes and Records of the Royal Society*, 43 (1980), pp. 133–53.

[26] For a discussion of what to us must appear as Locke's restrictive conception of toleration, see J. Dunn, 'The Claim to Freedom of Conscience: Freedom of Speech, Freedom of Thought, Freedom of Worship?', in O. P. Grell, J. I. Israel, and N. Tyacke (eds.), *From Persecution to Toleration: The Glorious Revolution and Religion in England* (Oxford: Oxford University Press, 1991), pp. 171–93: also J. Tully, 'Locke', in J. H. Burns and M. Goldie (eds.), *The Cambridge History of Political Thought 1450–1700* (Cambridge: Cambridge University Press, 1991), esp. pp. 649–52.

[27] See the interpretation of Locke in J. Tully, 'Governing Conduct', in E. Leites (ed.), *Conscience and Casuistry in Early Modern Europe* (Cambridge: Cambridge University Press, 1988), pp. 12–71.

[28] Dunn, ' "Bright Enough For All Our Purposes" ...'

in the form of a civil society, a community, was this shared conviction of their terrestrial purposes.

A more secular response to the problem of civil society conceived of as a moral community was proposed by the theorists of commercial society. The language of commercial society emerged during the eighteenth century, as an attempt to resolve the mounting difficulties confronting the Christian answer to the problem of community.[29] It claimed to show how those very processes within modern societies which critics of commercial society assumed would undermine the hope for a virtuous community were in fact creating new solidarities, which enabled a new form of society. This was a form of human association held together by interdependencies of need – the fundamental modality of human interaction here was not trust, but need. The nature of these interdependencies established the necessity of society and the dynamics of this process was now captured by the concept of 'civilization', which described a progressive development of human capacities and 'manners'. Crucial to the viability of such a society was a commitment to an effective system of justice, embodied in law and upheld by political authority. This governed the possibility of effective markets, which both fulfilled existing needs while continually generating new ones, and whose dynamism allowed a steady refinement of civility.

However, as the early theorists of this view were careful to insist, a commercial society was not held together simply by relations of utility and rational self-interest. In fact it produced and sustained a realm of human interaction and relationship which precisely was not governed by *necessitudo*, need. This was the realm of private friendship and free interpersonal connections, of morals, affections, and sentiments. Contrary to later critics who bemoaned the destructive effects of commerce and exchange upon 'community', in the view of the theorists of commercial society human association was actually enriched by the introduction of voluntariness and choice, which enabled persons to come together in an arena freed from the grip of dependencies of need. For Adam Smith, for example, in pre-commercial societies all human social relations were pervaded by exchange relationships: it was only commercial societies that had successfully instituted a distinction between the realms of market exchange and personal relations. According to Smith, commercial societies at once circumscribed the realm of need, consigning it to the market, and simultaneously created a sphere of non-instrumental human relations, governed by 'natural sympathy', the moral affections. Commercial

---

[29] See I. Hont and M. Ignatieff (eds.), *Wealth and Virtue: The Shaping of Political Economy in the Scottish Enlightenment* (Cambridge: Cambridge University Press, 1983).

societies thus made possible a higher form of human association, based not upon exclusive and non-voluntary relations (like fictitious kinship bonds or patron–client relations – both forms of human relation typical of pre-commercial societies). In such trading societies, strangers were no longer imponderable and threatening presences: instead, one found here 'authentically indifferent co-citizens – the sort of indifference that enables one to make contracts with all'. The dispersed existence of such 'indifferent strangers' defined the new moral order as a generalized civil society and reinforced (rather than weakened) it, functioning in this way like the market in the economy.[30] The dissolution of older, more intense and exclusive ties by the universalism of sympathy was vital to the movement from barbarity and rudeness to politeness and polish, and it was essential to the creation of the new moral sense required by the emergent commercial society.[31] Commercial society was thus at once a social and economic order as well as a moral order – both being the products of the unintended collective outcome of private actions. This model of universal sociability was able to generate an independent social self-cohesiveness and consistency, collectively beneficial and self-regulating, which could serve to replace the forms of governance associated with pre-commercial social institutions. But it was vital to Smith's purposes to stress that the practical achievement of this model was an unintended outcome of human actions. The point has been well put by Allan Silver:

[T]he moral order, like the wealth of nations, is continuously created by an indefinitely large number of acts as people encounter each other in a field defined not by institutions or tradition, but their own interactions. The causal texture of both branches of Smith's theory, the economic and the social, is identical: desirable aggregate outcomes are the unintended result of an infinity of small-scale exchanges and interactions by ordinary persons. In both, the outcome is other and 'better' than those intended by ordinary persons. Self-interest in the market increases the wealth of all: sociability sustains a universal morality from which all benefit.[32]

For the theorists of commercial society, social practices and institutions – from the intimate connections of marriage and the family, to the wider web of property, and government – were to be understood not purely in terms of utility, of their social function, but of the sentiments which animated them. In place of the Christian conception of a universal community held together by fear of what the afterlife may bring, the eighteenth-century Scottish theorists substituted a wholly secular model

[30] A. Silver, 'Friendship in Commercial Society: Eighteenth-Century Social Theory and Modern Sociology', *American Journal of Sociology*, vol. 95, no. 6 (1990), pp. 1474–504, at pp. 1482–3.
[31] Ibid., p. 1488.   [32] Ibid., p. 1492.

of the moral order, which saw it 'as created by natural social interactions'.[33]

Commercial society, by enabling the emergence of this new type of relationship governed by natural sympathy, integrated individuals into larger societies, and connected them successively to more inclusive groups. Only in such societies could friendship potentially become a universal relation that might connect all: impersonal markets thus had the unintended but beneficial moral effect of allowing private social relations to be formed, free from the imperatives of rational self-interest and utility.[34] From this perspective the existence of 'strong' and intense social ties as opposed to 'weak' ones, which often appear in locations where the state is weak and ineffective (for example, among the contemporary urban poor), might be viewed as a retreat towards exclusive and involuntary relations based on need: that is to say, as relations characteristic of pre-commercial societies rather than of a civil society.

A distinct point, which follows from the conception of social relations in commercial societies as possessed of a voluntary dimension, manifest in the bond of friendship, is relevant here. The consequences of the commercial society model for political loyalty and allegiance was seen early by Montesquieu, in his discussion of the special character of individual liberty in England.[35] According to Montesquieu, the spirit of independence and individual liberty, characteristic of commercial societies produced not isolation and social solipsism, but a new type of public *moeurs*: it enabled a filigree of relations between individuals to emerge, which endowed social relations with an independent consistency. This social self-cohesiveness could act as a restraining barrier on political power. It produced (and here Montesquieu cited by way of example the English structure of party politics) a self-equilibrating system, which allowed no single party or branch of government to gain enduring dominance. This system was founded on the idea of the mutability of political loyalties: 'as each individual, always independent, would largely follow his own caprices and fantasies, he would often change parties: he would abandon one and leave all his friends in order to bind himself to another in which he would find all his enemies: and often, in this nation, he could forget both the laws of friendship and those of hatred'.[36] This portrayal of the agitation of social interaction within a commercial society, and of the regular reconfiguration of political groups into diverse

---

[33] Ibid., p. 1493.   [34] Ibid., p. 1494.

[35] Montesquieu, *Spirit of the Laws* (Cambridge: Cambridge University Press, 1989), bk. 19, ch. 27. See B. Manin, 'The Typologies of Civil Society', paper presented to Civil Society seminar, SOAS and Birkbeck College, University of London.

[36] Montesquieu, *Spirit of the Laws*, p. 326.

and transient majorities, carries an important contemporary lesson, of special relevance to those countries of the South where majoritarian conceptions of democracy, based on permanent and therefore indefeasible majorities, threaten to undermine the very point of democratic politics.

Hegel is the pivotal figure in shaping contemporary understandings of the idea of civil society. Hegel's question, recognizably continuous with that of Locke and the theorists of commercial society, concerned the possibility of creating and sustaining a community under modern conditions. It was in response to this problem that he introduced the distinction between the 'state' and 'civil society'. His solution tried to integrate the individual freedoms specified by the natural law tradition (from Hobbes to Rousseau and Kant) with a rich vision of community, existing under conditions of modern exchange. Influential interpreters such as Manfred Riedel have emphasized the novelty of Hegel's redefinition of civil society: he no longer used it as a synonym for political society, but defined it on the one hand as distinct from the family, and on the other (and most crucially) from the state.[37] Riedel has claimed that for Hegel civil society was the realm of instrumental relations between atomized and isolated individuals, an arena governed by utility. This was a realm devoid of moral qualities, which required management by external principles: the corporations, and the 'police'. Yet, as Gareth Stedman Jones argues, such an interpretation misses Hegel's purposes.[38] For Hegel, civil society was not the object of criticism and antagonism, nor was it one which required external management. On the contrary, it embodied an intrinsically valuable acquisition: it was the space where the higher principle of modern subjectivity could emerge and flourish. But what was lacking, and what Hegel sought to provide, was an adequate conceptualization of this sphere, one which was richer than that found in the natural law tradition, which to Hegel gave too much prominence to the instrumentalities embodied in the contract.

Hegel's conception of civil society derived from the attempt to incorporate what he saw as valuable in modern natural law – above all, the conception of modern liberal individual freedoms – with a vision of moral and political life, the *Sittlichkeit* of community. He arrived at his conception by two means: a revaluation of the concept of labour, whereby he came to emphasize its expressive rather than instrumental significance: and a revaluation of individual subjectivity, which he came to see as based on the dynamics of mutual recognition. Contrary to the

---

[37] See M. Riedel, *Between Tradition and Revolution: The Hegelian Transformation of Political Philosophy* (Cambridge: Cambridge University Press, 1984).

[38] G. Stedman Jones, this volume.

assertions of natural law theorists, civil society was not the product of the social institution of natural drives and instincts (for Hobbes, this was the instinct for self-preservation; for Rousseau it was natural inclination). For Hegel, civil society was not merely the system of needs, but equally the sphere of recognition. It was a horizontally rather than a vertically organized model. It enabled the possibility of identification between persons, and enabled connections of mutuality, based on rights and duties: it embodied rationally grounded norms which determined conduct and which required active inculcation. The rational self that inhabited civil society was not, for Hegel, a natural given (as natural law theorists tended to assume), nor could it be engendered as a simple by-product of the instrumental relations of the market and contract. It could only emerge through institutionally mediated cultural and historical processes of interaction, through, above all, processes of social recognition. It was community itself that was the source – and not the outcome – of self-conscious rational being. The system of possession, property, and exchange, universalized across civil society, was an instantiation of this web of recognition, and this universality was made explicit and itself recognized in the state. The state was thus not an externally imposed construct, but rather the ratification of a pre-existing entity.[39] In this way, Hegel proposed a solution to the Christian problem of community: he claimed to have produced a political equivalent of the Christian community, united not by fear of God but by belief in the divinity of the political community itself (like Locke, Hegel too ruled out the possibility of atheism: all had to profess some belief).

II

From this brief and hasty preview of some of the arguments to be found in this volume, some lines of inquiry relevant to current efforts to develop civil societies suggest themselves. These may help to recognize what conditions or capacities are necessary to reduce the chances of a complete breakdown of civility, a reversion to the state of nature. First, civil society is not best thought of as a substantive category, as embodying a set of determinate institutions which exist distinct from or in opposition to the state, and which might be supposed to possess causal independence from the state. An historical perspective should serve to warn against all theoretical models which, for example, posit 'civil society' as a distinct entity that throws up 'inputs' or 'demands' that the state must then service and accommodate (failing which, a 'crisis of governability' is said

[39] Ibid.

to occur).[40] Second, a necessary association between civil society and a specific political form – for example, liberal democracy – cannot be assumed. It may well be that a viable liberal democratic political order is not possible in the absence of a civil society; but, as the East Asian cases make clear, civil societies can live without liberal democracy.[41] Third, it follows that civil society is most usefully thought of as identifying a set of human *capacities*, moral and political. There is little reason to think that we can have a theoretical model which explains retrospectively and guides prospectively the 'transition' to a situation where human beings may have such capacities. Understood thus, civil society is not a determinate end-state, nor can it ever be a secure acquisition for any group of human beings. This provokes a fourth point, which concerns the notion of unintendedness. For the Scottish theorists of the eighteenth century, the emergence of commercial society could be explained as the unintended outcome of numerous individual actions, undertaken for different purposes.[42] 'Every step and every movement of the multitude', Adam Ferguson wrote, 'even in what are termed enlightened ages, are made with equal blindness to the future: and nations stumble upon establishments, which are indeed the result of human actions, but not the creation of human design'.[43] For any prospective inquiry which seeks to specify conditions and actions which could effectively produce a 'transition' to a particular desired outcome (elsewhere originally produced unintentionally), there is a difficulty here which may be logically insurmountable. It is impossible to replicate the initial conditions of action: we now know the outcome desired, and we now act intentionally to bring it about. However, the consequence of such present actions, intended towards a specific end, may in fact produce yet another unintended outcome (alternatively, we may pretend to act unintentionally; but this too cannot replicate precisely the initial conditions).[44]

Nevertheless, are there certain preconditions or prerequisites relevant

---

[40] For an account which brings out something of the historical specificity of this way of conceiving the relations between state and society, see A. Silver, '"Trust" in Social and Political Theory', in G. D. Suttles and M. N. Zald (eds.), *The Challenge of Social Control* (Norwood, N.J.: Ablex, 1985), pp. 52–67. This perspective on state–society relations, characteristic of 'systems theory', is implicit in much of the political science literature on development: see, for example, A. Kohli, *Democracy and Disorder: India's Crisis of Governability* (Cambridge: Cambridge University Press, 1990).

[41] Cf. J. Gray, *Post-Liberalism* (London: Routledge, 1993), p. 203: 'Civil society may exist and flourish under a variety of political regimes, of which liberal democracy is only one'; Gray, however, sustains this point with an argument different from mine.

[42] See A. O. Hirschman, 'Rival Views of Market Society', *Rival Views of Market Society and Other Essays* (New York: Viking, 1986).

[43] A. Ferguson. *An Essay on the History of Civil Society* (Edinburgh, 1768, 2nd edn), p. 187.

[44] I am indebted for this formulation of the point to Sudipta Kaviraj.

to the development of the human capacities associated with civil society? What follows is a tentative and provisional set of considerations (made in awareness of Albert Hirschman's warning against the pitfalls of trying to fasten on immutable preconditions and prerequisites).[45] First, civil society presupposes a concept of 'politics': a conception which both specifies the territorial and constitutional scope of politics, and recognizes an arena or set of practices which is subject to regular and punctual publicity, which provides a terrain upon which competing claims may be advanced and justified. That is, it presupposes a conception of politics that embodies a common sense of its purposes, a sense of what it is that individuals and groups are *competing for*, of why they have associated and agreed to compete and disagree. This need not exclusively take the form of, say, participation in the electoral practices of representative democracy, premised on the expansion of a conception of the citizenry. It can involve different and 'informal' ways of entering and acting within the arena of politics.[46] In this respect, even in situations of great social heterogeneity, politics can function not simply to entrench social division, but it can act as a cohesive practice.[47] A conception of politics held in common can encourage potential antagonists to become participants in a common 'game', and require them to justify their claims and demands: a point well demonstrated by A. C. Milner, who in his study of politics in Malaysia has argued that 'politics, perhaps quite unintentionally as far as its practitioners are concerned, may possibly be promoting an element of unity in a much divided society'.[48]

Where such conceptions are unavailable, or where there are deeply divided beliefs about the point of politics, the possibility of civil society is endangered. An example of the first kind is sub-Saharan Africa.[49] Here

[45] See A. O. Hirschman, 'The Search for Paradigms as a Hindrance to Understanding', *World Politics* 32 (April 1970), 329–43.

[46] For interpretations which give centrality to the formation and expansion of a citizenry, through the incorporation of larger and larger numbers into electoral practices, see for example E. Morgan, *Inventing the People: The Rise of Popular Sovereignty in England and America* (London: Norton, 1988): and the articles on Europe and Latin America in *Quaderni storici*, no. 69 (1988). For a quite different argument, which stresses the importance of 'informal' means, such as the expansion of the press and proliferation of associations, in constituting a 'public sphere', see H. Sabato, 'Citizenship, Political Participation, and the Formation of the Public Sphere in Buenos Aires 1850s–1880s', *Past and Present*, no. 136 (1992), pp. 139–63.

[47] For an illuminating theoretical discussion of this point, see A. Pizzorno, 'On the Individualistic Theory of Social Order', in P. Bourdieu and J. Coleman (eds.), *Social Theory for a Changing Society* (Boulder: Westview Press, 1991) esp. p. 225.

[48] A. C. Milner, 'Inventing Politics: The Case of Malaysia', *Past and Present*, no. 132 (1991), pp. 104–29, at p. 104.

[49] See J.-F. Bayart, 'Civil Society in Africa', in P. Chabal (ed.), *Political Domination in Africa* (Cambridge: Cambridge University Press, 1986).

states and their politics have been deeply unstable, and the people who live in these areas seem caught in cycles of authoritarian and despotic rule. As interpreted by Jean-François Bayart, the fundamental explanation of this is the absence of any 'organization principle' for a civil society. 'There is', Bayart notes, 'no common cultural frame of reference between dominant and dominated, and sometimes not even among the dominated'.[50] In the absence of such shared conceptual maps (the lack of which Bayart blames in part on the evasions of African intellectuals), the possibility of devising unitary political capabilities is precluded. But to some, the fact that there are indeed many particular social actors – peasantries and so on – who remain outside politics provides also a glimmer of hope: it is precisely the local forms of association, and the 'cultures of accountability' which exist among such actors, which may provide possible sources for advance towards democracy.[51]

Some have pointed to an analogous difficulty – the absence of a common conceptual map – in the Indian case, though it has arisen by a very different process. Here the point is not that such a common frame of reference never existed; it is, rather, that rival conceptions have entered into lethal confrontation. To construct and sustain such a common frame of reference is evidently a constant and effortful task, and some have laid the blame for the abdication of this task on the shoulders of the Nehruvian elite which dominated the Indian state during the decades immediately after independence.[52] In the Indian case too, an intellectual and conceptual failure has been identified as explaining the breakdown of domestic civility. The consequences of this conceptual neglect have become most apparent in recent decades. The rapid and large-scale entry of agrarian groups into state and national-level politics during the 1980s has had a massive impact on the conduct of parliamentary politics in India.[53] It has highlighted the chasm which exists between elite and vernacular universes of discourse, and it questions the possibility of creating an Indian civil society. An initial condition for a civil society, then, is the availability of a shared conceptual map which describes a collectivity (constituted by, say, 'citizens') and provides them with comprehensible (and plausible) conceptual categories which they can use

---

[50] Ibid., p. 117.
[51] Hawthorn, 'Sub-Saharan Africa', esp. pp. 344–5.
[52] Cf. S. Kaviraj, 'On State, Society and Discourse in India', in J. Manor (ed.), *Rethinking Third World Politics* (Harlow: Longman, 1991), pp. 90–1: 'In retrospect, [the Nehruvian elites'] basic failure seems to have been the nearly total neglect of the question of the cultural reproduction of society . . . it neglected the creation of a common thicker we-ness (something that was a deeper sense of community than merely common opposition to the British) and the creation of a single political language for the entire polity.'
[53] See A. Sen, 'The Threats to Secular India', *The New York Review of Books*, 8 April 1993.

to shape their dealings with one another ('rights', 'duties', 'parties', 'interests', 'secularism', 'law', and so on). Here one might adopt the distancing gaze of Michel Foucault (although it does not follow that one need share all his suspicions), and think of civil society as a set of practices which renders human beings governable: that is, as a technique of governance.[54]

A second precondition that a civil society appears to require is the presence of a particular type of self: one that is mutable, able to conceive of interests as transient, and able to change and to choose political loyalties and public affiliations. Such a self must possess the capacity of being open to discursive persuasion and deliberation, and be able to see his or her interests not as pre-given and pre-defined.[55] It must, that is, be a corrigible self, one that can conceive of a distinction or gap between its own identity and its interests. This is not necessarily a liberal conception of the individual self (although it is obviously not unrelated to such a conception). In liberal conceptions, civil society seems to require the presence of a particular type of individual, a rational and interest-maximizing being, who possesses pre-given economic interests which await release and fulfilment. Yet this view of a self or individual guided by rational self-interest is excessively reductive: it would be more useful to speak of a self that is constituted and guided by 'civilized self-interest' – a conception which values restraint. The intimate link between the idea of civil society and individualism which liberal political theory insists upon remains in fact a profoundly unstable relation, since individualism is itself one of the sources which can threaten and undermine the possibility of civil society.

On the other hand, the loyalties of traditional communities can also threaten and undermine. In the non-liberal societies of the South, where individualism is not developed and where family and community struc-ture have only rarely and intermittently enabled the construction of a private self, a central difficulty facing the possibility of civil society is the presence of identitarian solidarities of a sub-national character: that is, solidarities whose primary purpose is to secure recognition of identity, and whose claims are hence absolute and indivisible. Here the category of citizenship is conventionally introduced, despite the fact that modern political theory and practice has repeatedly highlighted the incoherence and instability of this notion. On the one hand the supposed advantages and qualities of citizenship are undermined by individualism.[56] Jean Leca

---

[54] See M. Foucault, *Résumé des cours 1970–1982* (Paris: Le Seuil, 1989), pp. 112–13.
[55] See B. Manin, 'On Legitimacy and Political Deliberation', *Political Theory* 15 (1987), pp. 338–68.
[56] Cf. A. Seligman, *The Idea of Civil Society* (New York: Free Press, 1992), esp. chapter 3.

has summarized the common account of how this happens as follows: the individual, whatever his or her origins, is recognized as of value, and so citizenship is extended to all who live within a territory: as a claim to control, especially over the spheres of private and cultural life, it prompts the individual citizen to make more claims and so extends the scope of citizenship. However, this widening of scope, combined with the development of impersonal mechanisms and abstract trust systems like the market, money, large organizations, and bureaucracy, induces feelings of impotence and encourages the decline of public sense among citizens. Unable to understand collective mechanisms and withdrawing from civic participation, the individual citizen now gives priority to one demand over all else and all others, and pursues satisfaction of it: 'from being a vision of the destiny of the city, the political becomes the system of mediation of the most divergent social demands, and the private takes precedence over the public as the goal of citizenship activity, as the public takes precedence over the private as a mode of resource allocation'.[57]

On the other hand, widening the scope of citizenship can corrode the quality of civility (distinct from 'civic sense'), a quality vital in situations of social heterogeneity. Civility allows a degree of mutual recognition between individuals of different social groups. But as Leca puts it, 'Civility, which is essential to citizenship, can, paradoxically, be better maintained when citizenship itself does not exist' – that is, when different competitive logics exist. Take the case of India, with its peculiar form of social pluralism. Prior to the emergence of a unitary state, and the requirement that this be constituted by particular types of individual, by 'citizens', society here was constituted by groups (defined by complex permutations of religious belief, caste position, and so on). These were situated in positions of adjacency to one another, pursuing different goals by different logics.[58] This was a distinctive, non-liberal form of pluralism. But the intensifying struggle for goods and resources which are dispensed by the state and are linked to citizenship (such as secure state employment, education, and so on), within a nation which has very differentiated social groupings and great economic disparities, can destroy civility, as it disaggregates existing groups and reconstitutes them as political agents. In such situations civility is maintained either where groups retain their separate identities and the ability to pursue their own purposes by their own logics, or where ideological forms such as nationalism can create political communities that are culturally homogeneous (or at least elites who share a political imagination).

[57] J. Leca, 'Individualism and Citizenship', in P. Birnbaum and J. Leca (eds.), *Individualism* (Oxford: Oxford University Press, 1990), pp. 161–2.
[58] S. Kaviraj, 'On State, Society and Discourse'.

A third, equally problematic, precondition is an institutionalized dispersal of social power. This is usually accomplished by means of a legal structure of property rights, and a system of markets where such rights can be exchanged, as well as by legal recognition of political associations and voluntary agencies. But there is a double exigency here, since in order to achieve such a dispersal of power, a strong and effective state is also needed: one that has precisely the capacity neutrally to enforce law and to regulate social interaction. Indeed, such a *Rechtstaat* or legal-constitutional state might in some capacity wish – and need – to regulate the accumulations of social power which markets can also encourage.

This range of divergent requirements embodies a dilemma that faces all those states in both the East and the South which seek to negotiate 'transitions' to democratic and market systems – which hope to establish both democracy and capitalism. In the South, 'civil society' has come almost exclusively to mean all those forces and agencies which oppose the state and its efforts at regulation: it has been used to describe agents and practices which wish to 'recapture' areas of life from the state. Yet, as the contributions to this volume make clear, this stark opposition between civil society and state is not the most helpful one. If conceived in this way, as naming a kind of spontaneous order set apart from the structures of the state, then civil society drifts towards political indeterminacy. It may, for example, be used to affirm a conception of a liberal *Rechtstaat* which can act to restrain what are taken to be pernicious aspects and practices of the state itself. But, besides this secular and liberal view, it can also be appropriated by those wishing to legitimate distinctly non-liberal goals and practices. Indeed, in this manner the appeal to civil society may be nothing less than a demand that the state be subordinated to a civil society which is proposed as a terrain of authenticity and special intimacy, one uncontaminated by government and located outside its regulation. As Sami Zubaida shows in his discussion of Egypt, for instance, two drastically opposed conceptions of civil society circulate in critical intellectual discourse, a 'secular-liberal' and an 'Islamic-communal' one: and they do not stand in a symmetrical relation to democratic politics.[59] The first presses the case for legal recognition of voluntary civil associations (political parties, unions, pressure groups). The second delimits as 'civil society' a space of practices and activities unregulated by the 'legal-constitutional' state, but which conforms to interpretations of Islamic tenets: it wishes to develop a rich system of

---

[59] See S. Zubaida, this volume.

religious, communal, and business networks, an 'Islamic sector' of the economy and society.

New states have had enormous demands placed on them simultaneously: to ensure their own security, to legitimate themselves through the practices of modern democratic politics, and to tend to the welfare of their citizens. In older states, such demands have been lodged sequentially, not simultaneously. On occasion, new states have been altogether extinguished by the weight of these demands or, more usually, they have succumbed to despotic ambitions. States in the South are characterized by a political oddity: although they may be accorded all the trappings of fully sovereign states, they are often unable to exercise control and command over their own populations and territories: domestically, they are deeply ineffective.[60] To its original historical exponents, civil society represented a moral community, a legitimate political order. In situations where many states in the South are 'quasi-states', modelling relations between state and civil society in terms of an opposition between the two can be misleading, obscuring the ways in which civil society, far from designating a world of spontaneous arrangements, is in fact constitutively intermeshed with the state. In many such locations, it is precisely the absence of an effective state that leaves human beings in what are approximations to the state of nature. In the South, it is certain capacities of the state which simultaneously require both development and moderation: they require development precisely in ways which are self-moderating, self-limiting. The extent and kind of civil society which one is likely to find in such areas – whether religious and communal or secular, whether constituted by groups seeking inclusion in or separation from the state – will as Geoffrey Hawthorn has argued, directly vary with and depend on the nature and success of the state in question.[61]

To focus, for example, on 'social movements' which exist outside 'high politics' and the party system as the crucial agent for the creation of a civil society and 'democratization' yields an overly partial perspective. Political legitimacy under current conditions is usually accorded to states where the chance to exercise state powers is decided by periodic electoral competition between political parties. Modern political parties, although they have generally shown little success in being able to maintain themselves as durable structures of trust, are a crucial point of articulation between civil society and the state. They have an amphibious status, existing on both terrains: they represent each to the other. Classical ideas

---

[60] See R. H. Jackson, *Quasi-states: Sovereignty, International Relations, and the Third World* (Cambridge: Cambridge University Press, 1990).
[61] G. Hawthorn, this volume.

of civil society contained a conception of how it was represented politically, and this must remain essential to any plausible modern versions of the idea. Corporations, associations, political parties – all are units which aggregate individuals, which achieve unitary political form, and which possess unitary political capabilities. Yet recent advocates of the idea of civil society altogether eschew discussion of political parties, in favour of an exclusive focus on social movements.[62] Although this is perhaps a perspective peculiar to American radicals, it is by no means restricted to them, and it avoids questions about the abilities of social movements to secure both stable and durable institutional form and to embody self-limiting properties: if they are to govern, what governs them?

Current understandings of civil society invariably see it as essentially a category of domestic political space. The term is used to identify and privilege agencies – markets, social movements, cultures – whose effective political causality is heavily local. Yet every local and domestic space, every nation-state, is today rocked by causalities which escape its bounds and which condition the possibility of its continuing viability as a habitat for civil human relations. In the task of developing viable and durable democratic politics in the South, the idea of civil society is hardly a self-sufficing one, let alone a fundamental 'key'. It is best thought of as a complicating term, one that embodies a range of historical idioms intended to establish a legitimate political order. Recovering its rich and unshapely forms in the history of Western political thinking can help to clarify why the project of constructing and sustaining democracy today is so vexed, why it can never be merely a question of introducing forms of competitive politics, or of establishing markets. Attention to the historical development of the concept of civil society identifies a host of requirements (not specified merely in institutional terms), precariously available at the best of times, which are necessary to develop and sustain civil human relations in developing societies.

[62] See Cohen and Arato, *Civil Society and Political Theory.*

2 Concepts of civil society in pre-modern Europe

Antony Black

One must distinguish categorically between the term 'civil society' in pre-modern or pre-Hegelian Europe and the mental and social phenomena associated with the term 'civil society' today. The term *societas civilis* was derived by pre-modern Europeans from Cicero's definition of the state (*civitas*) as a partnership in law (*societas*) with equality of legal status, but not of money or talent, among its members.[1] It became a generic term for a secular legal and political order, as distinct from a primitive society, or again from ecclesiastical society.

There is evidence that what *we* understand by civil society – a nexus of relatively free individuals and groups without reference to the state – did exist in Europe from (at the very latest) the twelfth century, in people's language, preferences and behaviour, especially in towns. It was an aspiration expressed in both popular consciousness and academic writing. When researching the guild mentality, I found to my surprise expressions of civil society alongside this and in the same social milieux. In fact in learned writings civil society vastly predominated, and collectivist values were expressed only in a religious context. First there was the aspiration for personal security or freedom from unlawful violence; next security of property, land, house, goods, from arbitrary seizure. Both depended on the value ascribed to law, lawful procedures, and lawful authority, as sustaining and promoting justice – the primary virtue (Plato) and the divinely ordained model of society (Augustine). Law was also Christian society's instrument for protecting the weak against the strong, and securing the personal rights of the poor and defenceless.

The most authoritative expression of law was the Roman legal system, glossed with Stoic *humanitas* and appeals to natural reason. Much of its

---

[1] 'Quare cum *lex sit civilis societatis vinculum*, ius autem legis aequale, quo iure *societas civium* teneri potest cum par non sit *condicio civium*? Si enim pecunias aequari non placet, si ingenia omnium paria esse non possunt, iura certe paria debent esse eorum inter se qui sunt cives in eadem republica. Quid enim est civitas nisi iuris societas?': Cicero, *De Republica* I, xxxii, 49. For a full survey of meanings of 'civil society (*bürgerliche Gesellschaft*)', see O. Brunner, W. Conze and R. Koselleck (eds.), *Geschichtliche Grundbegriffe* (Stuttgart: Klett, 1972–).

spirit and some of its provisions entered into the law of the church and of particular nations or states. Its values were driven by natural right, conceptually distinct from religious revelation and intended as a standard to which all human authorities should adhere.

This applied to the security of one's own house, family life, and personal possessions. Roman law regulated relations between persons and in respect of property in such a way as to make individual ownership secure and transferable by defined legal procedures, and so to make property relations in general predictable and property itself subject to rational exploitation. It suggested relatively free-floating relationships in which people were involved in buying, selling, contracting, marrying, and entering partnerships.[2]

The legitimacy of commerce and the opportunity to trade were inherent in the system. Similarly, papal legates could insist (1249) that those who obey the Roman church be granted 'the liberty of the sons of god: that is, be permitted to buy any goods from any persons, and what they have bought to keep for themselves and pass to their legitimate heirs, that they may freely spend, give, buy and do whatever they wish with mobile property . . . freely contract marriage with any legitimate persons'; in other words they should be given 'complete personal liberty'.[3] This idea of a society based on exchange and reciprocity was justified by the division of labour which binds people together into a single society through the mutual exchange of benefits. This was articulated by Althusius, writing in the early 1600s, using a combination of Aristotle, Cicero, and Christian thought.

God has distributed his gifts in diverse ways among men . . . so that I should need what you have and you should need what I have. Thus arose the necessity of sharing what was needful and useful, and this intercourse (*communicatio*) could only take place in socio-political life . . . For if one person did not require another's aid, what society, reverence, order, reason, humanity would there be? This was why villages and cities were built, academies founded and why many farmers, craftsmen . . . were joined together through their diversity in civil unity and society (*unitate et societate civili*) as so many members of the same body.[4]

Civilian solidarity (*Communicatio / Consociatio civilis*) is the result of *commercia*.

The socio-political culture of pre-modern Europe was distinguished

---

[2] Antony Black, *Guilds and Civil Society in European Political Thought from the Twelfth Century to the Present* (London: Methuen, 1984), p. 35.

[3] Peace of Christburg in Philippi (ed.), *Preussisches Urkundenbuch*, vol. I, part 1 (Berlin, 1882), pp. 158–61.

[4] J. Althusius, *Politica* (1603), edited by C. J. Friedrich (Cambridge, Mass.: Harvard University Press, 1932), ch. 1.

from Greco-Roman, Byzantine and Islamic culture in its admiration for and articulation of liberty. Free status was prized. Social mobility, or the promise of it, attracted many into the towns, and was saluted by the entrepreneurial renaissance: true nobility is not inherited but acquired through effort (Cicero). The corporate towns asserted and celebrated the free status of their inhabitants. 'If any man has resided free for a year and a day in a town under town law, he will more easily retain liberty for himself and his kin. No one can reduce him to servitude. All who dwell in a town are subject to one law of the freed.'[5] Here Germanic, Christian, and Roman values concurred. Cicero and St Paul conspired to make liberty a mark of virtue, civility, and grace. Liberty is necessary to virtue (John of Salisbury); social mobility and career freedom are incentives necessary to civic virtue and political success (Leonardo Bruni).[6] There is no need here to posit a spurious distinction between negative and positive liberty, for freedom from arbitrary or seigneurial coercion meant precisely freedom to marry, work, trade, join the clergy, and so on.

One can hardly overestimate the social importance of freedom to choose one's own spouse. One may see some connection between individual liberty and the nuclear family, which developed precociously in Europe, since this increased the self-determination of the individual householder and couple.[7]

Personal freedom was interdependent with the rule of law and with equality of persons, regardless of status, before the law. This was made explicit both in Germanic and in Renaissance discourse. Equality under the law was persistently upheld as a mark of good government both in guild towns and in humanist Florence. 'Equality of conditions' was praised in much the same sense by Cicero, the jurist Christophorus Porcius, Salamanio, and later by Rousseau and de Tocqueville.[8] Machiavelli saw social equality as the key to a truly free polity.[9] But medieval *moeurs* agreed precisely with Renaissance discourse in rejecting any extension of equality into the economic sphere. Equality was, on the other hand, significantly extended by Luther when he applied it to all callings.

There was a tension between civil ideas and what used to be called feudalism: the seigneur–vassal relationship, involving serfdom together with a view of society as essentially hierarchical with, in practice, inherited status. It would be more helpful to contrast civil values with *any*

[5] A. von Daniels and F. von Gruben (eds.), *Sachsische Weichbildrecht* (Berlin, 1858), p. 66.
[6] Black, *Guilds*, pp. 41, 98–103.
[7] Philippe Aries and George Duby (eds.), *A History of Private Life*, vol. II (Harvard University Press, 1988).
[8] Black, *Guilds*, p. 37; A. Black, 'Juristic Origins of Social Contract Theory', *History of Political Thought* 14 (1993), p. 74.
[9] *Opere* (Milan–Naples, n.d.), pp. 487–92.

system of patronage. This is a contrast between ideal types which, on the ground, almost always co-exist in a great variety of proportions. Patronage is a personal relationship, a system of informal networks operating outside open legal systems, distributing – or redistributing – power and resources as personal favours. As such it is the antithesis of civil values and in particular of equality before the law and the *carrière ouverte aux talents*. The contrast between feudalism and capitalism is particularly artificial, indeed obscurantist, glossing over key issues such as the exploitation of land for profit and the personal, often hereditary, powers of barons of commerce.[10]

There was a perception of *civilitas*, based upon respect for *ius civile*, and extending into urbanity and 'culture'. Both scholastics and humanists praised the way of life they called civil, urbane, political. Egidio Romano referred to 'civil life (*vita civilis*)' in which one 'lives as a man'. Bruni's highest praise for Florence was that her citizens were 'industrious, liberal, . . . affable and above all urbane'.[11] The contrast to this whole nexus of values was seen as bestiality, barbarity, tyranny. It also precluded the redistribution of property, communism, and millenniarism. The civil ideology was facilitated by Latin Christendom's official distinction between ecclesiastical and civil spheres or powers.

There was also no suggestion of ethnicity; rather *civilitas* was an internationalizing concept in so far as it was consciously related to qualities regarded as essentially human. This found expression in Dante's perhaps unique statement of *umana civiltà*.[12] It clearly shows the Greco-Roman genius present in European civilization. In contrast to the *umma* of the Islamic Middle East, there was an explicitly secular dimension to the conception of society. Indeed secularization was perhaps implicit in Christianity.

Freedom was claimed for groups as well as individuals; the rich turbulence of associational life in Europe from the twelfth century onwards was a clear mark of the emergence of what is now called civil society. Whole sets of collective projects emerged, some independent of the institutions of political and ecclesiastical authority, some subordinate, some in an unstructured relationship. Distinguishing (as law then did) between personal and territorial groups, we find, first, religious communities and craft guilds;

---

[10] This is charmingly illustrated by Jason de Maino (1435–1519) when he argues that a fief may change hands according to the rules of buying and selling: 'Si princeps in concessione feudi reciperet pretium, licet uteretur verbis "indulgemur", tamen cum sit venditio . . . per consequens erit contractus irrevocabilis, et non habebit naturam feudi; immo non privabitur ex causis ex quibus alias vasalli privari solent': *In secundum Digesti veteris commentaria* (Lyons, 1540), fol. 136r, nn. 12–14. Cf. Susan Reynolds, *Fiefs and Vassals: The Medieval Evidence Reinterpreted* (Oxford: Oxford University Press, 1994).
[11] Black, *Guilds*, pp. 37, 104–5.
[12] Michael Wilks, *The Problem of Sovereignty in the Later Middle Ages* (Cambridge: Cambridge University Press, 1963), pp. 103, 105.

secondly, village and town communities. Guilds generally claimed the right to spontaneous corporate existence in pursuit of economic rights, but were obliged to seek recognition from city authorities; this situation was recognized by jurists, but they insisted that corporate legitimacy depended on fulfilling legal criteria rather than on the ruler's will.[13]

The church, far from being a monolithic community, included a great variety of religious communities which sprang up in response to particular needs or aspirations, especially in the towns. Such communities, lay and clerical, comprised an important category of life choices for those who could not or would not adopt their parents' profession and status. The lawyer–pope Innocent IV, writing in the mid-thirteenth century, gave the clearest possible statement of the right to freedom of association on behalf of craft guilds.[14] Towns claimed, or were granted, liberties and privileges as corporate bodies, entailing a range of independence from economic rights to self-government. Self-determination for the individual and the group were often two sides of the same coin, especially in economic terms.[15]

In the universities, secular and ecclesiastical academic pursuits were conducted side by side. These too, provided they carried out the legal obligations indicated by the Digest, were *collegia licita*. Pre-modern liberty did not contain any calculated move towards toleration in religious matters. On the other hand, it was articulated without explicit reference to religious adherence; and the universities, sometimes regarded as a third component of Christendom alongside kingdom and priesthood, created a public space within which intellectual questions of most kinds could be debated relatively openly, provided official doctrine was not directly denied and the populace was not directly approached.

Government was an integral part of this civil ideology, which also prescribed the characteristics which a proper civil government should have. The earliest statement of the European city-state was also a precise statement of civil values:

A city is called the liberty of citizens or the immunity of inhabitants . . . for that reason walls were built to provide help for the inhabitants . . . 'City' means 'you dwell safe from violence (*Civitas, id est "Ci(tra) vi(m) (habi)tas"*)'. For residence is without violence, because the ruler of the city will protect the lowlier men lest they suffer injury from the more powerful. (John of Viterbo, *c.* 1250)[16]

Some went further and said that the only form of government appropriate to cities is the *regimen politicum*, in which rulers' powers are strictly

---

[13] Black, *Guilds*, pp. 16–23.
[14] *Super Decretalibus* (Turin, 1581), on x 5.31.14.
[15] A. Harding, 'Political Liberty in the Middle Ages', *Speculum* 55 (1980), pp. 423–33.
[16] *Liber de Regimine Civitatum* (*c.* 1250), ed. C. Salvemini, A. Gaudentius (ed.), *Bibliotheca Juridica mediae aevi*, vol. III (Bologna, 1901), c.1, p. 217.

delimited by law. In general, however, it was thought that civil values could be upheld under oligarchy or monarchy. The function of government is to suppress violence and uphold law. Legal equality of status may, perhaps should, extend to the relationship between ruler and ruled. These are 'of the same kind (*eiusdem generis*)'. Such government 'does not remove the subjects' liberty' (Aquinas); the true king rules 'as a man over men as free over the free' (Erasmus).[17] All this was implicit in the concept of *societas* (partnership), a relationship among equals. A logical outcome was to say that government, like a business partnership, was based upon and limited by contract.[18] Equal access to public office was a burgher–artisan demand as well as a Ciceronian *topos*.

These civil values and practices belonged to a society which arose in a highly specific cultural milieu, combining Germanic, Greco-Roman, and Judeo-Christian influences. This mixture goes far towards explaining why the outcome of European history was different from that of other histories. What we have uncovered is a unique set of values in a unique society. It is, therefore, unlikely that civil society (in the modern sense) can be used as an analytical tool for understanding other pre-modern societies or their pasts.

There were of course elements of civil society, free-floating individuals and groups, often with still less reference to the state, in other civilizations. But what gave pre-modern European civil society its peculiar attractiveness, force, and ideological basis – the religion–culture divide, the pluralism of attitudes invited by the Greco-Roman heritage, and a belief, sanctioned by law, in associational freedom – was partly or wholly absent. There is no reason why, under certain conditions, other societies may not now acquire as many features of civil society as modern Europe. But the evidence of this chapter clearly indicates that this would need, as one of its preconditions and perhaps the most difficult, the adoption of favourable cultural norms. The actual prospects will be explored later in this volume.

---

[17] Black, *Guilds*, pp. 79, 105.

[18] Black, 'Juristic Origins', pp. 57–76. As Mario Salamonio put it, writing in 1512: 'P(hilosophus): Inequalitas conditionum societatem disrumpit . . . Si nihil aliud est *civitas quam civilis quaedam societas*, contrahiturne ulla societas sine pactionibus? . . . Estne societas antequam ineatur? . . . Inirene potest antequam socii de conditionibus conveniant? . . . Ad esse ergo civitatis leges sunt necessarie . . . Sicut *pactum in societate negociali, ita lex in civili ordinatio* est . . . Socius sociali negotiationi praepositus, numquid ob id quod praepositus est, desinit esse socius? (J)urista: Minime. P: Et socialibus legibus solutus? J: Absit. P: Cur non idem in civili societate dicendum?' (De *Principatu*, ed. M. D'Addio (Milan, 1954), pp. 12, 28–9.

3   The contemporary political significance of John Locke's conception of civil society

John Dunn

What exactly is a civil society? This is not as easy a question to answer as one might trustingly suppose. Let me take two examples at random from a relatively recent issue of the *Financial Times*. On the front page on Tuesday 27 September 1994 ('Clinton lifts US sanctions on Haiti') no less an authority than President Clinton assures us that the United States has 'no desire to be the world's policeman, but we will do what we can to help civil societies emerge from repression'. On page 6 of the same issue ('Counting on the Americans') the less reassuring figure of Mr Gregory Mevs, one of the most powerful businessmen in Haiti – whose family monopolized sugar trade and production, along with the manufacture of shoes, plastics and detergents, and owned a huge petrol storage and port facility, gratefully utilized by the American occupying force – explains carefully that Haiti will only be in a position to seize the economic opportunities furnished by its longstanding comparative advantage if 'the institutions of the state' are 'made compatible with civil society'.

In the Haitian case, the institutions of the state have a certain immediacy to them; and it is instructive to note which features of their performance Mevs himself singles out as requiring adjustment. A civil service of sinecures must be replaced with a functioning bureaucracy. The economy must be secured to allow for a democratization of capital. 'A democratization of capital' sounds an impeccable objective, and one for which Haiti is palpably long overdue. But I take the point of the formula to indicate that it is not to be seen in contrast to the protection of the existing holdings of the Mevs family. What we have here is Robert Nozick's entitlement theory, shorn of any trace of the principle of rectification.[1] As a phrase, 'civil society' has travelled a long way since it left the senatorial pen of Marcus Tullius Cicero. How far can it still hope

The first draft of this chapter was prepared for a conference in Jerusalem at the Israel Academy of Sciences to celebrate the work of the late Professor Nathan Rotenstreich. This version was published by the Academy in their volume *Myth, Memory and History* (Jerusalem 1996) and in *Iyyun* (*The Jerusalem Philosophical Quarterly*), 45 (July 1996).

[1] Robert Nozick, *Anarchy, State and Utopia* (Oxford: Basil Blackwell, 1974).

to serve as a reliable instrument for understanding anything – let alone as a reliable instrument for understanding virtually everything of importance in the domestic politics of the modern world?

We need not linger over the question of how it might readily fail to provide reliable understanding. To serve as an effective instrument for enhancing understanding a term needs principally clarity of structure, and determinacy and stability of meaning. It is not difficult to use the term civil society so loosely and equivocally as to carry no meaning whatsoever. But the important question is whether, when used with sufficient care and precision, when used optimally, it can in principle provide firm intellectual purchase on the domain of modern politics. This is what I wish to call into question.

Over a relatively short span of time, and through a readily intelligible sequence of intellectual and political experience, the term itself has come to be used very widely indeed to analyse political possibility and to demarcate pathological from normative conditions, both in politics and in the life of a society at large. It is a term, as now used, of extreme vagueness. The question I propose to press is whether, at least in relation to the understanding of politics, that vagueness may simply be irremediable. For analysing political possibility or demarcating benign from pathological conditions in polity or society, if there is one thing worse than terms of extreme vagueness, it must be terms of irremediable vagueness. To judge whether the vagueness genuinely is beyond remedy, a promising approach is to look carefully at how the term has been used to express a powerful strategic analysis of politics.

At least two genuinely great political thinkers have used the term 'civil society' (or a term in another language standardly rendered into English by it) as a central device for expressing their understanding of the nature and practical significance of modern politics: namely Locke and Hegel. Each of these stood firmly within the European natural law tradition, Locke more or less in the middle and Hegel relatively determinedly at the end. Both, therefore, were profoundly concerned with the implications of Christianity (or at least of the Christianization of Europe) for an understanding of politics, in their own day, and in the future in so far as they could imagine it. And because they were so concerned they were also perforce, if perhaps slightly less self-awarely, concerned with the implications of the religious experience of the Jewish people for the understanding of that politics. I propose to approach this taxing challenge to modern political understanding by an analysis of the role which the phrase and the theoretical conception for which it stands play in the political thinking of John Locke.

Locke was a theocentric thinker for whom the truth of the Christian religion (as he understood this) was an indispensable major premise of a scheme of practical reason within which most human beings had sufficient motivational grounds for behaving as (in his view) they ought.[2] This judgement placed considerable strain upon his understanding of the political significance of the Law of Nature. To locate these strains, we may consider two questions. Firstly: how did Locke think about the Law of Nature, and about the grounds and character of the rights which human beings hold and the duties to which they are subject under that Law? And secondly: how exactly did the way in which he thought about the Law of Nature articulate with and inform the way in which he thought about politics – about the nature and scope of legitimate political authority and about the political agency of the human subjects or objects of such authority, whether legitimate or otherwise? Each of those questions is quite difficult to answer. But they are particularly puzzling when taken together and in relation to one another.[3] What can we say with some confidence in answer to these two questions? What remains comparatively obscure about them, and how far does this residual obscurity matter? There are technical difficulties in answering either with

[2] This is no longer seriously disputed by scholars who have taken the trouble to inquire carefully into the matter: see, for example, John Dunn, *The Political Thought of John Locke* (Cambridge: Cambridge University Press, 1969); John Dunn, *Locke* (Oxford: Oxford University Press, 1984); John Dunn, ' "Bright Enough For All Our Purposes": John Locke's Conception of a Civilized Society', *Notes and Records of the Royal Society*, 43 (1989), pp. 133–53; John Dunn, *Interpreting Political Responsibility* (Cambridge: Polity Press, 1990) John Dunn, 'Freedom of Conscience: Freedom of Speech, Freedom of Thought, Freedom of Worship?', in O. P. Grell, Jonathan Israel, and Nicholas Tyacke (eds.), *From Persecution to Toleration* (Oxford: Clarendon Press, 1991), pp. 171–93; Ian Harris, *The Mind of John Locke* (Cambridge: Cambridge University Press, 1994); John Marshall, *John Locke: Resistance, Religion and Responsibility* (Cambridge: Cambridge University Press, 1994); James Tully, *A Discourse on Property* (Cambridge: Cambridge University Press, 1980); James Tully, *An Approach to Political Philosophy: John Locke in Contexts* (Cambridge: Cambridge University Press, 1993); David Wootton, *John Locke: Writings on Politics* (Harmondsworth: Penguin, 1993).

[3] Not all these difficulties can be fully resolved even in principle. There are real obscurities as to what Locke himself believed he was doing at different points in his intellectual life, some of which are unlikely ever to be fully illuminated. We know immensely more about the development of his thinking than we do about that of virtually any other major intellectual figure of the seventeenth century (cf., for example, Thomas Hobbes, *The Correspondence*, ed. Noel Malcolm, 2 vols. (Oxford: Clarendon Press, 1994)). But knowing more does not always mean understanding better. It often means exchanging a distant and essentially historical bafflement at the innerness of a dramatically alien cultural world for much more sharply demarcated puzzles of ultimate understanding which we lack the cognitive resources to resolve even under the supposedly ideal visibility conditions of our own day (cf. Dunn, *Political Thought* and *Locke*). Following the researches of the last half century, what we do not ultimately understand about the development of Locke's political, moral, and epistemological thought is much the same in character (if naturally somewhat different in content) as what we do not ultimately understand about the determinants of ultimate imaginative commitment or theoretical choice in our own case, or in those of our most intimate friends or cherished enemies.

complete confidence, deriving from two principal sources. In the first place, Locke thought and wrote about the status and content of the Law of Nature and its implications for political action over a very long period of time – nearly half a century from the late 1650s to the beginning of the first decade of the eighteenth century when he was working away at his last major book, *A Paraphrase and Notes on the Epistles of St Paul*.[4] Not only did he think and write about each of these topics over a very long period, he also changed his mind quite elaborately about both in the course of that period. Secondly, and I think quite distinctly, he also had strong grounds over much of this time, both external incentives and purely personal motives, for expressing some aspects of his views about each in public with considerable care and discretion; for presenting them with less than perfect frankness.

To take only the most spectacular example of this second point, the two greatest works in which he expressed his views about each, the *Essay concerning Human Understanding* and the *Two Treatises of Government*, both published late in the year 1689, were issued by him with considerable care in a form in which one of them could not readily be held against the other. The *Essay* bore his own name and social rank proudly on its title page and it carried a lengthy, and obviously pre-sanctioned, dedication to one of England's leading noblemen. It was an eminently open and official publication: a fully public act. But the *Two Treatises*, by contrast, was issued anonymously and almost surreptitiously; and Locke himself went to very considerable lengths in the decade and a half before his death to avoid acknowledging his authorship of it on paper, even in private correspondence with his closest friends, and did not in fact formally acknowledge it anywhere, as far as we know, until his last will and testament.

What makes this careful (and clearly in this case politically motivated) evasion of analytical, and not merely biographical, importance is the notorious fact that the epistemological doctrines of the *Essay* are not readily reconcilable with (and may even be flatly contradictory of) the view of the emphatic presence and political force of the Law of Nature set out in the *Two Treatises*.[5] The second of these difficulties, that posed by Locke's compulsive discretion in the expression of some features of his views, must just be negotiated as best we can. But the first, that posed by

---

[4] John Locke, *A Paraphrase and Notes on the Epistles of St Paul*, ed A. P. Wainwright, 2 vols. (Oxford: Clarendon Press, 1987).

[5] Cf. Dunn, *Political Thought*; Dunn, *Locke*; Dunn, "Bright Enough for All Our Purposes"; Michael Ayers, *Locke*, 2 vols. (London: Routledge, 1991); John Colman, *John Locke's Moral Theory* (Edinburgh: Edinburgh University Press, 1983); A. John Simmons, *The Lockean Theory of Rights* (Princeton: Princeton University Press, 1992); Wootton, *John Locke*; Harris, *The Mind of John Locke*.

the timespan over which he considered both the Law of Nature and the grounds for political action, and the degree to which he changed his mind over each of these, needs to be faced explicitly at the outset. To underline the point, I shall simply list the major texts which register his changing views on one or other issue over this timespan, ignoring the huge range of briefer or more informal texts which also cast light on the evolution of his thinking. At a minimum, an adequate view of the development of Locke's conception of the character and status of the Law of Nature and its implications for politics would have to take in his youthful *Two Tracts on Government*, the extended explorations of the *Essays on the Law of Nature*, the successive preliminary drafts of the *Essay concerning Human Understanding*, the *Two Treatises of Government*, the *Letter on Toleration* and its polemical successors, the *Essay concerning Human Understanding* itself and a number of major revisions in its successive editions, the *Reasonableness of Christianity*, and a number of crucial passages even in *A Paraphrase and Notes on the Epistles.*[6]

It was, however, the *Two Treatises*, and more especially the *Second Treatise*, which made Locke into a political thinker of major importance; and it is the view of the practical presence of the Law of Nature within the human historical world, and of the political implications of that presence set out in the *Second Treatise*, which lies at the core of his political thinking as a legacy to the generations that have followed him.

The *Second Treatise* begins with the question of how legitimate political power can be distinguished from effective coercion: from force and violence. There is no single chapter of the *Second Treatise* devoted to the Law of Nature as such; and its effective historical presence is assumed rather than argued for. But the single most illuminating chapter of the entire book for an understanding of how Locke conceived that historical presence is the second chapter of the *Second Treatise*, which deals with the State of Nature. The State of Nature is a jural field of freedom and equality amongst the members of a single species. It is not a counterfactual sociological hypothesis about how human beings would have behaved, or must have behaved, or would behave in future, in the absence of effective governmental coercion, but a theoretical analysis of the fundamental relations of right and duty which obtain between human beings, relations which are logically prior to the particular historical

---

[6] For an early sketch of the pattern of development see Dunn, *Political Thought*, and more briefly Dunn, *Locke*; and for an important amendment see Dunn, "Bright Enough for All Our Purposes". For major recent treatments see, in very different modes, Ayers, *Locke*; Simmons, *The Lockean Theory of Rights*; Harris, *The Mind of John Locke*; Marshall, *John Locke*; and, more informally, Wootton, *John Locke*.

situations within which all actual human beings always in fact find themselves. It is the normative framework within which human history occurs, not some poorly lit and fantastical projection of a prehistoric phase in human social evolution. What defines it as this common framework is the joint subjection of all the members of the human species to the overwhelming power and authoritative purposes of their divine Creator. It is a condition, as Locke puts it,[7] 'of perfect freedom to order their actions, and dispose of their possessions, and persons as they think fit, within the bounds of the law of nature, without asking leave, or depending upon the will of any other man. A state also of equality, wherein all the power and jurisdiction is reciprocal, no one having more than another.' And, as he goes on:

That law, teaches all mankind, who will but consult it, that being all equal and independent, no one ought to harm another in his life, health, liberty, or possessions. For men being all the workmanship of one omnipotent, and infinitely wise Maker; all the servants of one sovereign master, sent into the world by his order and about his business, they are his property, whose workmanship they are, made to last during his, not one another's pleasure.[8]

These two statements express, and express accurately, the fundamental normative premises of Locke's understanding of human politics.

Nature as a whole is subject to God's power. But human beings are uniquely related to that power, in that, as well as being wholly under the effective control of their Creator (like all other created entities) and rightfully subject to his power (again like all other aspects of his Creation), they are also bound, as intelligent agents, to obey his commands, his Law: to act as that Law requires them to do. The Law of Nature, for Locke as for Thomas Aquinas, is the Law of Nature's God, as well as being the principle on which Nature operates when it operates as its God intended it to do. As intelligent agents, human beings can in principle understand that Law: can ascertain what it requires, grasp why they are obliged to obey it, and choose accordingly to do so. But as real agents, uniquely amongst natural creatures within this world, they can also fail to understand it: can misjudge what it requires, and fail too to recognize why they are obliged to obey it, and choose for these or other reasons to act in direct and profound conflict with its requirements. As free and intelligent agents, they are, at least potentially, responsible for each and every deviation from the recognition and performance of their natural duties. To be a particular individual person – as Locke famously argued in the chapter on personal identity which he added to a later

---

[7] John Locke, *Two Treatises of Government*, ed. Peter Laslett (Cambridge: Cambridge University Press, 1988), II, para. 4.

[8] Locke, *Two Treatises of Government*, II, para. 6 *passim*.

edition of his *Essay*[9] – was precisely to be capable of a law, to be responsible for one's own actions and their merits and faults, and to be so because one could always have acted differently.

How then can human beings know their duties under the Law of Nature? And how can they really be responsible, not just for deliberately flouting the requirements of this Law when they correctly grasp its demands, but also for their own authentic and plainly unintentional misjudgements of what these demands really are? Locke's answers to both of these questions are of great importance. But his answer to the first is decidedly more conventional, as well as more offhand and perfunctory, than his answer to the second.

Human beings can (and should) know their duties under the Law of Nature through the exercise of their Reason. The Law of Nature is a codification of reason. Reason, which is that Law, teaches all mankind who will but consult it, what the Law of Nature requires. To observe the Law of Nature is to observe the conclusions of valid (and pertinent) reasoning. To flout the Law of Nature is to pursue your desires or interests, not within the limits prescribed by reason but through the exercise of force, the way, as Locke expresses it, of beasts: creatures who lack rational powers, cannot recognize their place within the created order of Nature, cannot choose how to act in accordance with such recognition, and hence have no responsibility for the ways in which they do in fact behave.

But Reason can (and does) teach only those amongst mankind who do consult it. And very few human beings consult it as painstakingly and honestly as they should. Locke's official epistemological thesis in the *Two Treatises*, reiterated at the beginning of the *Essay* itself, is that Reason is sufficient for men to judge their duties under the Law of Nature accurately. As he says in the *Essay*: 'The candle which is set up in us shines bright enough for all our purposes.'[10] Especially, it shines bright enough for all our practical purposes: 'Our business here is not to know all things, but those which concern our conduct.'[11]

The thesis that Reason gives sufficient guidance on human duties under the Law of Nature is not merely Locke's official thesis in his three great works of 1689, it is also the position which he adopts in his longest single piece of systematic analysis of the character and accessibility of that Law, the comparatively juvenile work, now called the *Essays on the Law of Nature*, which he delivered as lectures at Christ Church, Oxford,

[9] John Locke, *An Essay concerning Human Understanding*, ed. Peter Nidditch (Oxford: Clarendon Press, 1975), Bk II, xxvii, esp. pp. 9, 18, 26: 335, 341–2, 346.
[10] Ibid., Bk I, 1, 5.
[11] Ibid., Bk I, 1, 6.

in the early 1660s.[12] In that work he was at pains to reject a number of the conventional mid-seventeenth-century English views on how human beings can know the Law of Nature; notably the theses that they can have knowledge of its content and obligatory force from the traditions of the society to which they belong, or from the universal consent of mankind at large. He rejected the first because of the variety of human traditions and the lack of any clear justification for believing anything to be true from the mere fact that other human beings had so believed it before you. He rejected the second, with greater asperity, because of the very evident absence of any such universal consent amongst human societies over which acts are appropriately permitted or forbidden, and over why they should in fact be so.

The *Essays on the Law of Nature* do, however, offer an explanation of how human beings can and should know the content of the Law of Nature. They can and should do so, it argues, by exerting their reason on the materials provided by their own sensory experience: by rational inference from the data furnished by their senses. When Locke maintained in the *Essay* that reason, the candle of the Lord, shines bright enough for all our purposes, he plainly did not mean that reason was a sufficient endowment for every historical human individual in fact to apprehend both what the Law of Nature required of them and why they had sufficient reason to observe its requirements. He simply meant that every historical human individual who satisfied the condition of being a person, a responsible agent, at all, had counterfactually, if only they had chosen or now chose to exercise them, the natural cognitive powers to grasp how they ought to act within the natural world in which they lived. Whether they in fact elected to use those powers as they should was a historical and not a natural matter: a question of choice in time, not of sheer transtemporal causal capability.

The epistemic foundations of the Law of Nature, as Locke understood these, lay in natural theology: in the judgements about divine power and purpose which could, in his view, be validly inferred from the properties of the natural world. In the *Essays on the Law of Nature* in the early 1660s he treated this structure of inference pretty cursorily. But with his increasing concern for, and increasing sophistication over, questions of epistemology from 1671 onwards, it became steadily harder to sustain the view that valid inferences from the properties of the natural world to the content of divine purposes and then back again to the terms of God's law for his wilful natural creature Man, could in fact be carried through to a

[12] John Locke, *Essays on the Law of Nature*, ed. Wolfgang Von Leyden (Oxford: Clarendon Press, 1954).

clear and compelling conclusion. It is clear that this imposed very severe strains on the fundamental structure of his moral and political thinking.

The best statement of the dangers to which it exposed him comes in the lengthy draft of a structure of demonstrative ethics which he wrote while composing the *Essay concerning Human Understanding*, and which he probably intended to serve, in a more complete form, as a conclusion to that work:

Law: The original and foundation of all Law is dependency. A dependent intelligent being is under the power and direction and dominion of him on whom he depends and must be for the ends appointed him by that superior being. If man were independent he could have no law but his own will no end but himself. He would be a god to himself and the satisfaction of his own will the sole measure and end of all his actions.[13]

Locke, then, considered as the fundamental existential condition of human beings just two possibilities. Either they are independent and gods to themselves, or they are dependent and under the direction of the God on whom they depend. He believed firmly that they are the second rather than the first: that their most fundamental characteristic is that they are dependent intelligent beings. What he needed to demonstrate epistemologically in his major mature works was that they are both dependent, and capable through their own intelligence of ascertaining exactly what God has directed them to do. After the publication of the *Essay* in 1689 a substantial number of commentators, both close friends (then or earlier) like James Tyrrell and William Molyneux and bitter theological or political enemies, pressed him to show how his account of human cognitive powers could explain just how human beings could in fact know what God's directives were (or even that there actually was a God concerned to direct human actions through the workings of human intelligence at all). Locke never attempted to meet this challenge in print; and we do not really know that he was ever confident that he could meet it. But what we do know is that he composed and published a few years later, in the *Reasonableness of Christianity* in 1695, an account of how they could know His directives not by natural theological inference but by direct acquaintance with divine revelation itself, through the texts of the Christian gospels, validated by the historical miracles of Jesus Christ.

Not only did Locke explain in this work how even very dim and undereducated human beings could know how God wished them to behave; he also acknowledged that even in the most sophisticated episodes in human intellectual history, amongst the great philosophers of the ancient world and the scientific geniuses of his own day, no human

---

[13] Ethica B: Bodleian MS Locke C 28, p. 141: Dunn, *Political Thought*, p. 1.

being had ever in fact succeeded in developing a full demonstrative account of the grounds and content of the Law of Nature on the basis of unaided natural reason (the task at which, it might be thought, Locke himself had tried so hard and so long but at which in the end he could not see how to succeed). What the Christian revelation revealed was an authoritative law which showed firmly that all human beings are indeed dependent, and that they do have compelling reason to satisfy a will profoundly other than, and in many respects often sharply at odds with, their own.

Locke's conception of what a law is was firmly in the voluntarist tradition of medieval natural law thinking that goes back particularly to William of Ockham: an authoritative command backed by an effective sanction. Without a cogent natural theology, and without the direct assistance furnished by revelation, it was relatively easy for human beings to see rational grounds for co-operative mutual inhibition in the terms that Hobbes, for example, had indicated. But it was impossible for them to see any ultimate reason for disciplining themselves to follow ends wholly external to their own will. Natural law without divine sanctions could be a systematization of human practical rationality. But it was quite unclear (to echo Hobbes's formulation) how it could properly be called a Law at all,[14] and equally unclear how it could confront any human agent with a genuinely external authority. It was the cognitive accessibility of the structure of effective sanctions required to lend real authority to the Law of Nature which Locke could not see how to demonstrate. And in his final work, the *Paraphrase and Notes on the Epistles of St Paul*, he at last openly acknowledged that key aspects of this structure of sanctions not only were not known in historical fact but actually could not have been known without the specific aid of revelation: that they lay simply beyond the reach of men's natural cognitive powers:[15] 'it was by the positive law of God only that men knew that death was certainly annexed to sin as its certain and unavoidable punishment.'[16] Throughout the historical era which had preceded the Christian revelation, therefore, men could not know God's positive law. And 'without a positive revelation of god their Soverain they could not tell at what rate God taxed their trespasses against the rule of their nature, reason, which dictated to them what they ought to doe'.[17] They could not know – and in fact did not even suspect – that the penalty for sin was to

---

[14] Thomas Hobbes, *Leviathan*, ed. Richard Tuck (Cambridge: Cambridge University Press, 1991), pt I, ch. 16, p. 111.

[15] Dunn, "Bright Enough for All Our Purposes".

[16] Locke, *A Paraphrase*, vol. II, p. 524 n. 13.

[17] Ibid., vol. II, p. 524 n. 13.

be death itself. The Law of Nature and requirements of reason were in fact secured as a law by the effective sanctions which enforced them. Human beings could get a shrewd sense of its content just by exercising their natural reason with a modicum of attention. What they could not know simply by exercising their natural cognitive powers was how strong and decisive were the sanctions by which God enforced that content. They could not know these merely by their reason because the sanctions could not, in Locke's own ultimate and explicit judgement, be validly inferred simply from the properties of the natural world.

What Locke called rectitude and pravity, right and wrong conduct, could by contrast in his view be validly inferred by the exercise of reason from the practical relations between human beings – and many aspects of them were quite effectively captured in the psychological and categorical structures of mutual human approval and disapproval (what he called, in the *Essay*, the law of opinion, reputation, or fashion), as well as in the ancient philosophical theories of the nature of right conduct. But what made rectitude and pravity decisively important for human agents was not their rational contours[18] but the pressing reasons for human agents to conform to rectitude and eschew pravity. What made these reasons stably and decisively sufficient to guide human conduct was in the end in Locke's eyes just one thing: the punishments and rewards of the Deity Himself. The taking away of God, as he said in the *Letter concerning Toleration*, though but even in thought, dissolves all.[19] It disrupts, that is to say, the entire apparatus of practical reason which he deployed to analyse all the major issues of political authority and political agency on which he attempted to pronounce.

In the field of politics this potential fissure between the rational criteria for which human conduct was right and wrong and the criteria for what actions human beings can know merely by the light of nature they have sufficient grounds to perform is of overwhelming importance. In deliberating on their own personal lives, in choosing and living out a plan of life, human beings could judge differently for themselves and still hope that the outcomes of their judgements would not necessarily do grave harm merely because their judgements of what sort of life to live differed sharply from one another, because their tastes differed. But in politics such conflicts of judgement led more or less immediately to conflicts of

---

[18] Cf. Thomas Scanlon, 'Contractualism and Utilitarianism', in Amartya Sen and Bernard Williams (eds.), *Utilitarianism and Beyond* (Cambridge: Cambridge University Press, 1982), pp. 103–28; T. Nagel, *Equality and Impartiality* (Oxford: Oxford University Press, 1991).

[19] Locke, *A Letter concerning Toleration*, ed. J. Tully (Indianapolis: Hackett, 1983), p. 51; Dunn, 'Freedom of Conscience'.

will and hence to conflicts for power, to struggles over who was in the end to coerce whom.

If we ask exactly how Locke's conception of the Law of Nature articulates with his conception of politics, it is not hard to see the starkness of the theoretical dilemma that confronted him. On one horn of the dilemma, the practical implications of the Law of Nature are indeed precepts of terrestrial rationality: precepts which human beings have good reason to observe because of the given features of the world in which they live, and because of what they themselves are actually like. But on this assumption there is no occasion to ground the obligatory force of the Law of Nature on natural theology and divine power: on the premise that human beings, like all other aspects of the created order, are part of God's workmanship. Indeed there is no reason to regard the existence or will of a deity as of the slightest intrinsic relevance; and the laws of nature themselves, as Hobbes pointed out, are simply convenient articles of peace and not properly called laws at all. On the other horn of the dilemma, the horn which Locke himself in the end very plainly chose, the will and power of a concerned Divine Creator were indispensable to establishing both the obligatory force and substantial parts of the content of the Law of Nature; and neither of these could be validly inferred merely from what the world and human beings are naturally like.

This has sharp implications for an understanding of Locke's politics, which balances intense moral conviction with a high degree of strictly political scepticism and shores up the moral conviction in the end by the confident assurance that it will be vindicated and protected in the last instance by overwhelming power, which is not merely non-human but actually extra-terrestrial both in origin and incidence: not natural but supernatural.

The key question for the understanding of politics, in Locke's eyes, is the question of who is to be judge, wherever human purposes and actions come into conflict. In the state of nature, free and equal human beings, capable of guiding their actions by the Law of Nature, can and do come into sharp conflict with one another. Because they are all free and equal, and all subject to the Law of Nature, each has both the right and the power to judge when the others breach that Law, and to do their utmost to secure its just enforcement. Each, as Locke himself puts it, has the 'executive power' of the Law of Nature. They judge and punish each other as agents of the divine creator to whom they all belong. But they are, of course, fairly erratic agents of divine purpose, since they are so far from being impartial in their assessments of the rights and wrongs of conflicts between themselves and others. As human societies become richer and more densely populated, the occasions for conflict mutiply steadily, and the inconveniences of the state of nature which stem from human partiality and propensity to violence intensify sharply. Conflicts, in particular, over ownership and use of natural resources and over monetized wealth become increasingly acute. By the time that human history had reached late seventeenth-century England the inconveniences of the state of nature – a condition of unmediated potential conflict between the judgements of free, equal, intensely partial, and potentially lethal human beings – have become prohibitively high. What is imperatively required is an alternative to the state of nature; and that alternative is what Locke himself calls a 'civil society', or what we might call a legitimate political order, founded on the recognition of the rights of all its members. Please note what a civil society means for Locke, and the context in which the concept itself came to be invented. Civil society is the historical remedy for the inconveniences of the state of nature. What it provides is, in the first place, known standing laws (in place of the projective indeterminacy of a law of nature open to the promiscuous judgement and enforcement of all), in the second place, impartial judges (in place of the necessarily partial judgement of every adult human being), and, in the third place, at least in aspiration, effective powers of enforcement in place of the highly undependable coercive capacities of offended individuals and their friends and relations. A civil society can in principle be an effective remedy for the state of nature because its members alienate their own right and capacity to judge where the Law of Nature has been violated, and their own executive power of that law with which to enforce their judgements, to the legitimate political authority, which has a distinctly better chance of acting impartially and an altogether more drastic capacity to enforce its judgements on the recalcitrant. But although a true civil society can be an effective remedy for the inconveniences of the state of nature, no actual existing state is ever guaranteed to provide such a remedy in practice.

Locke's most important single conclusion about politics was that most existing human structures of power were very far from meeting the criteria for being a civil society: that most states simply were not legitimate political orders at all. Notably, the absolute monarchies of continental Europe, the French monarchy in particular, were very far from being legitimate political orders. In fact, he claimed, rather spectacularly, that these often proud and powerful political units were just a continuation of the state of nature itself. Now Locke himself had actually travelled in France for some four years before he wrote the *Two Treatises*, and it is worth asking how he can possibly have thought that this was true. How can he have supposed, for example, that France did not possess known standing laws, or that the ownership of property within it was not in most instances rather close in its degree of security to that prevailing at the time in England? No doubt, in fact, he imagined nothing of the kind. What he argued (and what in a sense the experience of the Huguenot population promptly confirmed in the years immediately following his writing of the *Two Treatises*), was not that there were no inconveniences of the state of nature for which the existing French state provided any kind of a remedy, but rather that there were some inconveniences of the state of nature which it drastically aggravated and reinforced: in particular the inconvenience of individual physical vulnerability in the face of massively concerted external violence.

In a state which was not a civil society, concentrated coercive power confronted individual subjects with an overwhelming danger. It did so, too, under conditions which gave them no effective means to restrain it or to hold it responsible. Furthermore, it did so with a degree of ideological condescension and even contempt which was profoundly humanly offensive (and which, Locke himself insisted, was even more offensive towards the deity to whom every human being truly belonged). In Locke's eyes the claim to absolute power was quite directly and frontally incompatible with the precepts of the Law of Nature. It denied human equality and freedom openly and in the first instance.

But what made Locke's political theory of enduring importance was not so much the fact that he denied the legitimacy of a wide range of human political authorities and endorsed the right of their subjects to take revolutionary action against them. It was also that he gave a particularly careful and searching account of why it was in principle so difficult to exclude either the need or the right to take such action even in the case of governments which have at some point in their history enjoyed a genuinely legitimate title to rule.

What made this so is in essence quite simple. A legitimate political authority can be an effective remedy for many of the inconveniences of the state of nature. But it cannot, of its very nature, hope to be a full and consistent remedy for all of them. It cannot hope to be so, fundamentally, because it cannot consistently and fully eliminate aspects of the state of nature from its own structures and procedures. Although it claims the title to judge many matters on its subjects' behalf, it consists simply of fallible human beings whose judgement is every bit as liable to error as that of the subjects over whom they exercise power and claim authority. Where that judgement is gravely abused, the claim to authority loses its validity; and where its subjects themselves judge it to have been gravely abused, they in turn no longer retain any clear grounds for respecting its interpretation of the law of nature and may, *in extremis*, even feel themselves entitled (and be wholly justified in so feeling) to resume their own alienated executive power of the Law of Nature and do their collective (and perhaps even their individual) best to punish their erring rulers.

The key premise of Locke's analysis of the right to revolution is the right of the people at large to judge when their rulers have broken their trust. This right of judgement, at some points in his text, is extended as a right (though it is certainly not recommended as a policy) even to single individual subjects. When the people do so judge and act upon their judgement, they make what Locke describes as an 'Appeal to Heaven'. And Heaven is, quite literally, the Tribunal which must in the last instance adjudicate what the Law of Nature demands of human agents, and punish and reward them accordingly. Locke took the idea of an avenging God with the utmost seriousness: 'the Hand of the Allmighty visibly held up and prepared to take Vengeance'.[20] It scarcely needs emphasizing that the political presence of the Law of Nature within the human world must be very much weaker if there is no Deity concerned to vindicate its demands and enforce them in the end with His overwhelming power.[21]

How does all this bear on the recent ideological history of civil society as a category?

When employed to demarcate benign from pathological political or social conditions today, civil society is usually interpreted to signify a reality which is not merely (a) analytically distinguishable from the state (a necessary condition for its employment for this purpose to make any sense at all), but also (b) referentially discrete from the state. Not infrequently, it is also used to signify a reality which (c) either is, or could and should be, causally independent from the state.

In my view, the last possibility, causal independence, whether normative or factual, is an absurd assumption, which has probably never been actualized anywhere where the category of the state has been actualized.

Even the second possibility, referential discreteness, is a pretty heroic presumption, which implies not merely that it is possible to tell, within the natural history of the universe, exactly where state starts and society or economy stop, but also that it is characteristically (or perhaps invariably) the case that each starts or stops at the same boundary lines: that they do not usually (or perhaps ever) overlap. I see no reason whatever to make this assumption.

---

[20] This structure of understanding comes out with particular clarity in Locke's discussion of the scope and limits of the right to toleration (Dunn, 'Freedom of Conscience') and of the claims of prerogative power (Dunn, *Political Thought*, ch. 11).

[21] Cf. John Dunn, 'The Dilemma of Humanitarian Intervention: The Executive Power of the Law of Nature after God', *Government and Opposition*, 29 (1994), 248–61.

If the category of civil society is only analytically distinguishable from the state, and not either causally independent of or referentially discrete from it, then it can be employed in a controlled manner to analyse features of the history of the universe only *ex-post facto* and not *ex-ante*. This feature makes it unsuitable in principle (that is, logically inapplicable) for purposes of causal explanation.

In the face of these points it is unhelpful to proceed by offering an analysis either of how the term civil society should be used or of how it most frequently is, since the history of its usage is by now so messy that neither is likely to prove illuminating. Even for purposes of normative political analysis, it is essential to establish a clear analytical distinction between the categories of state and civil society before employing the latter term to express criteria of political achievement which different territorial units, legal entities or assemblages of human beings satisfy differentially.

In normative political analysis at present (in my view, quite gratuitously) civil society is frequently employed to pick out a feature of the history of the universe which is presumptively good (or at least comparatively trustworthy) in contrast with a feature of its history (the state) which is tendentially or necessarily bad (or at least comparatively untrustworthy). This is not a contrast with which any competent political theorist could be content.[22]

The ideological purchase of the civil society/state couple is drastically different where civil society is thought of as consisting essentially in the economy or essentially in the society. Neither of these last two terms has any claim even in the loosest of senses to referential determinacy. But it is certainly helpful to be able to distinguish one analytically from the other. Where the ideological claim is essentially that civil society stands to state as good (or trustworthy) stands to bad (or untrustworthy), its political bearing is very different where the candidate proffered for trust is the economy from where it happens to be the society. The ideological source of the power of the claim is the presumption that the favoured candidate is an instance of free (and perhaps rational) choice, while the disfavoured is an instance of external (and non-rational) subjection.

It is possible to think about some features of either economy or society as consisting in free acts (in the former case, sales and purchases: in the latter, the beliefs and sentiments of human agents, and the acts which these lead them to carry out). But it is absurd in either case, whatever one's normative political views, to think of economy or society as simply consisting of freedom. Both in the economy and in society, chosen acts

---

[22] John Dunn, 'Political Obligation', in David Held (ed.), *Political Theory Today* (Cambridge: Polity Press, 1991), pp. 23–47.

are free only in a massively contextually dependent manner, pivoting, as Marxists insist, above all on the history of effectively secured control of the means of production. No one could interpret a pattern of ownership at time T as an instance of free choice, even if they might welcome the chance to misdescribe its causal antecedents exclusively in such terms. (Recollect Mr Mevs.) By the same token, not even the most aberrant of psychopaths can literally choose their sentiments or beliefs at time T, however skilful some of us may become at massaging them into a more user-friendly condition as the years go by.

It is also important to remember that the greatest single theorist of the state, Thomas Hobbes,[23] wrote out the fullest and most elegant version of his account of it as a defence of the view that, clearly understood, the legitimate monopolist under most circumstances of the means of coercion could be, should be, and rationally must be understood as a structure of free choice on the part of all its subjects. His argument is not wholly convincing.[24] But there is no reason to see it as on balance any less convincing than more recent defences of views that either economy or society can be felicitously understood as consisting at time T simply of free choice or agency.

To return belatedly to Locke, it is important firstly to register clearly that in his usage civil society does not refer to a political or social substance that can be set over against an existent state. What it refers to in modern terminology, if with a Hobbesian turn of phrase, is essentially the state liked: the non-pathological state.

Secondly, it is important to register that Locke's conception of politics was deeply hostile to the very idea of the state in its modern post-Hobbesian form[25] of a coercively effective monopoly claimant to the power to coerce legitimately, which is to be understood not as a set of particular human claimants to that power, nor as a given territory subjected to it, nor as a determinate set of subjects of that power (a populus or people), but as an integral structure of authority incorporating all three and, for as long as it lasts, analytically and normatively prior to each one of them.

These first two points are essentially just matters of linguistic hygiene – a reminder that the favourable overtones of the phrase civil society in the language we now happen to speak may be drastically at odds with the ways we now customarily use it – that the presumption (effectively now

---

[23] Quentin Skinner, 'The State', in Terence Ball, James Farr, and Russell Hanson (eds.), *Political Innovation and Conceptual Change* (Cambridge: Cambridge University Press, 1989), pp. 90–131.
[24] Dunn, 'Political Obligation'.
[25] Skinner, 'The State'.

within our very language) that civil society is itself a site of legitimate power may not be validly combinable with the presumption that it can in principle be empirically counterposed to a putatively empirical category of the state.

The third point is more constructive. In Locke's understanding of politics, civil society (the state liked) is a precarious conjunctural achievement, not ever a structural fact, and least of all a structural fact securely and permanently lodged in the order of nature itself. It is an achievement actualized in only a limited number of historical settings, if in some settings (England with its Ancient Constitution[26]) presumptively over a very long period of time. Where it has been actualized relatively protractedly, the prospects for resuscitating it when the conjuncture goes against it are relatively robust. Why? Well, essentially because the groupings of human beings set over against the state misliked (the pathological degeneration of civil society, the Stuart mimesis of continental absolutism) are in their existing solidarities, habits of practical co-operation, traditions of perception and sentiment, and in some measure even their residual institutional facilities, potentially still a single coherent political body, a single coherent political agent, a potential civil society in waiting. On Locke's understanding, it is logically true that any set of human beings could exhibit such a unitary political capacity – because all adult human beings are free individual agents. But it is emphatically not empirically the case that many of them are at all likely to do so. The Bosnians, the Serbs, and the Croats could all agree tomorrow to lay down their arms and smilingly recompose the Federal Republic of Yugoslavia. But actually, they won't. Where there is no recent and relatively solid history of unified political membership and institutionalized political co-operation, the presumption that any particular set of human beings will possess a unitary political capability was, in Locke's eyes, wholly gratuitous. This is important, I am afraid, because he happened to be right.

The fourth point is more important and quite a lot harder to understand. On Locke's view the central political implication of the Law of Nature issues from a very odd balance of faith and scepticism. The faith was a Christian faith, and the scepticism a political scepticism. It was the faith that picked out every adult human individual not just as a contingent site of potentially independent judgement (a view, after all, which had led Hobbes precisely to invent the concept of the state as its remedy), but also as a site of immense and ineliminable individual normative significance. Seen in terms of the political scepticism alone, this is no more encouraging

---

[26] J. G. A. Pocock, *The Ancient Constitution and the Feudal Law* (Cambridge: Cambridge University Press, 1957).

than Hobbes supposed it to be. It is precisely the irrepressible propensity of human beings to view themselves as of such individual normative significance that makes them, in Hobbes's eyes, such refractory material for what they all also want: namely, commodious living. But seen as Locke saw it, through both the faith and the scepticism simultaneously, it is at least still today of some imaginative use. How?

Civil society for Locke is the state liked. What does the state have to be to be deservedly likeable? (To be undeservedly likeable, as Bosnia – and perhaps other places closer to hand – serve to remind us, it may simply need to be zestfully murderous.) To deserve liking, it has to be as effectively purged of the state of nature as it can be. This is never very effectively purged. The fundamental character of politics for Locke, the problem of politics as such, is the juxtaposition of individual self-righteous and partial judgements about what is to be done. That is the state of nature; and it is still a state in which all men and women, and hence all groups, smaller or larger, of men or women, naturally find themselves. Civil society, in Locke's usage, is the optimal remedy for the state of nature. But it is a necessarily imperfect remedy: one which cannot in principle be made perfect. Historical escape from the state of nature can never be more than partial; and the putative political instruments for effecting that escape – call them, today, states, parties, political or even social movements – have such normative standing as they enjoy only in so far as they do genuinely provide such an escape: as they furnish for particular sets of human beings frameworks within which to live which enhance their security and their opportunities to resolve in a relatively impartial manner the endless conflict between their irretrievably partial personal judgements.

Locke's conceptualization of civil society is a powerful critical instrument for appraising the pretensions of modern state authority, not least because that was the purpose for which it was initially devised. But where it draws its power from is the analytically prior and altogether less anodyne category of the state of nature. If we want to think accurately and powerfully about political possibility, and about how to demarcate pathological from non-pathological social and political conditions, the category we shall need in the end is not Civil Society itself – however lexically specified. It is the conceptual foundation of the category as Locke uses it, the fulcrum of natural jurisprudential thinking, the State of Nature.[27]

27 John Dunn, 'Contrattualismo', *Enciclopedia delle scienze sociali* (Rome: Instituto dell'Enciclopedia Italiana, 1982), vol. II, pp. 404–17; and, for the general judgement, John Dunn, *The Cunning of Unreason: Making Sense of Politics* (London: Harper-Collins, 2000.)

4   Civil society in the Scottish Enlightenment

Fania Oz-Salzberger

I

The idea of civil society marks one of the faultlines running across the Scottish Enlightenment, at times in the open but more often underground. In the process of forming their political theories, eighteenth-century Scottish thinkers were able to combine several theoretical traditions and make new uses of established concepts. In the accessible, eclectic tenor of the Enlightenment, their application of terms previously used by theologians, philosophers, and jurists gave their writings fresh resonance. It was also burdened with new dissonances. This chapter deals with two major Scottish treatments of the concept of civil society, both of which based innovative arguments on traditional theories. David Hume and Adam Smith envisaged a civil society where economic and social transactions mattered as much as political institutions. Adam Ferguson insisted on the civic mainstays of modern civil society. The tensions ensuing from these theoretical differences between close friends and interlocutors suggest that the Scottish Enlightenment did not speak on civil society in one voice.

The Scottish reworking of the concept of civil society was inspired by seventeenth-century Continental theorists of natural law, notably Hugo Grotius and Samuel von Pufendorf, and by the innovative work of John Locke. Beyond these influences, it was stamped by the uniqueness of the Scottish condition. From a tool of legal theory and constitutional justification, the concepts of natural law were transformed into a science of political economy and a theory of the modern state.

The polity envisioned by Hume and by Smith was no longer a body politic accommodating a prince and his subjects, but a community of individuals pursuing multiple private interests. The core of this new

The analytical framework for my discussion was introduced in J. G. A. Pocock's seminal work, *The Machiavellian Moment: Florentine Political Thought and the Atlantic Republican Tradition* (Princeton, 1975), and further developed in Istvan Hont and Michael Ignatieff (eds.), *Wealth and Virtue: The Shaping of Political Economy in the Scottish Enlightenment* (Cambridge, 1983).

understanding of civil freedom was doubtless the legacy of Locke and the Glorious Revolution. Yet the Scottish thinkers were far more concerned than Locke about the role of manufacture and commerce, on the one hand, and polite sociability, on the other hand, in shaping the profile of modern society. Moreover, they were more inclined than the natural lawyers to regard the historical processes leading to polite, commercial modernity as the unintended outcomes of numerous human actions, often momentary and selfish, yet having the cumulative effect of promoting public welfare. This happy state of affairs could be accomplished by a system of governing institutions, ripe with age and wisdom, that administered justice and defence for a society of private manufacturers and traders. In Lockean terms, this was quite properly a *societas civilis*, yet with a new edge: things were happening outside the political sphere that deeply affected communal well-being and social mores. They also shed new light on political issues *par excellence*, notably the desirable extent of government expenditure, the significance of public debt, and the necessity for a standing army. In effect, discussion of civil society shifted from the conceptual world of the jurist to that of the political economist.

A different, at times even rival, Scottish concept of civil society evolved from the classical republican tradition. This Aristotelian and Ciceronian legacy, powerfully modernized by Niccolò Machiavelli and his English disciples, stressed the necessity of active virtuous citizenship. Instead of a society set in motion by natural or man-made laws, republican thought insisted on diligent self-government and self-defence by independent, moral, and vigorous men. Eighteenth-century Scots resorted to this tradition on several important occasions. Andrew Fletcher of Saltoun mobilized it to oppose the English–Scottish union. Half a century later, the republican concept of civil society was revived by proponents of a Scottish citizens' militia, and powerfully restated by Adam Ferguson. Significantly, both campaigns were doomed to failure.[1] It was the political economists' civil society, not the classical republicans' civil society, that prevailed.

Ferguson's *Essay on the History of Civil Society* (1767) is the only major Scottish work in which civil society plays a title role. This important book is central to our discussion, not only because of its deliberate attempt to redefine civil society in modern civic (that is, republican) terms, but also because Ferguson conducted a subtle and prolonged debate with the idea of civil society associated with Hume and

---

[1] See also J. G. A. Pocock's 'Cambridge Paradigms and Scotch Philosophers: A Study of the Relations between the Civic Humanist and the Civil Jurisprudential Interpretation of Eighteenth-Century Social Thought', and John Robertson, 'The Scottish Enlightenment at the Limits of the Civic Tradition', both in Hont and Ignatieff (eds.), *Wealth and Virtue*.

Smith. This debate is important in the Scottish context; yet, beyond Scotland the *Essay* was conducive to the re-emergence of 'civil society' as part of modern political discourse. The book's French readers, from Baron d'Holbach to Victor Cousin and August Comte, and its German admirers, from Gotthold Ephraim Lessing through Karl Marx to Werner Sombart, made its European significance a more interesting story than its British fame.[2] A generation later Ferguson's disciple Dugald Stewart effectively transmitted some of his ideas to several nineteenth-century thinkers, among them John Stuart Mill. Yet in Britain the *Essay* was soon all but forgotten, only to emerge in late nineteenth-century surveys as a quaint Scotch memento.[3] Not so in other European cultures. In Germany, France, and Italy Ferguson's name, his books, and his concept of civil society far outlived their British fame. Of all eighteenth-century Scottish thinkers Ferguson's ideas travelled best. His 'civil society' apparently inspired Friedrich Schiller and Benjamin Constant, and clearly affected Hegel and Marx.[4]

Neither Hume, nor Smith, nor Ferguson can be credited with a theory of civil society in the sense associated with Locke or Hegel. Hume and Smith did not make systematic use of the term, and mostly opted for 'state', 'nation', and 'community'. Ferguson offered no compact definition for the term, and often left the limits between civil and non-civil society uncharted. His lack of theoretical rigour is offset by abundant moral ardour. The *Essay* is not merely a history of civil society (or a universal history of mankind, which amounts to the same thing in his terms), but a forthright celebration of it. Ferguson, who spent his early adulthood as a military chaplain, wrote in a tone far more excited, with a far more outspoken sense of mission, than either Locke's or Hegel's prose would allow. 'It is in conducting the affairs of civil society,' a fairly typical sentence goes, 'that mankind find the exercise of their best talents, as well as the object of their best affections'.[5] What, then, was Ferguson celebrating, and what (or whom) was he up against?

---

[2] Among Ferguson's favourable British readers were James Boswell and Horace Walpole, Lord Shelburne and Lord Bute. See Hume to Ferguson, 10.3.1767 and Baron d'Holbach to Ferguson, 15.6.1767 both in *The Correspondence of Adam Ferguson*, ed. Vincenzo Merolle with an introduction by Jane Bush Fagg (London, 1995), vol. I, pp. 72–4, 77–8; see also Appendix D, ibid., vol. II, pp. 546–7.

[3] Cf. Leslie Stephen, *History of English Thought in the Eighteenth Century* (3rd edn, New York, 1949), vol. II, p. 182.

[4] See Laurence Dickey, *Hegel: Religion, Economics, and the Politics of Spirit 1770–1807* (Cambridge, 1987), Norbert Waszek, *The Scottish Enlightenment and Hegel's Account of Civil Society* (Dordrecht, Boston, and London, 1988), Fania Oz-Salzberger, *Translating the Enlightenment: Scottish Civic Discourse in Eighteenth-Century Germany* (Oxford, 1995).

[5] Adam Ferguson, *An Essay on the History of Civil Society* (originally published Edinburgh,

One key lies in David Hume's response to Ferguson's *Essay*. Hume, a generous friend who had previously secured Ferguson's professorship for him and gladly reported other readers' compliments, privately voiced a dislike of the *Essay*'s moralizing tone and spirit. A careful reading of the *Essay* can indeed reveal several direct assaults on Hume's philosophy, as well as that of Smith, but Hume's dissatisfaction probably went deeper than that. He may have felt that the tenor of Ferguson's book was leading away from his own project, retreating from the promises held by polite modernity for its private, economically interacting denizens. Hume's reaction, though private and restrained, was one of keen disappointment.[6] This ripple on the smooth surface of enlightened politeness points towards the hidden polemical import of Ferguson's *Essay on the History of Civil Society*.

If Ferguson's *Essay* can be read as a last-ditch attempt to preach antiquated moral community to a modern commercial society, it can also be read otherwise. It can be understood as a pioneering work where new things were done with old language. Ferguson set out to dig better foundations for the civic idea of the polity. He wished to make it acceptable to modern men, those who were at ease with commerce, material comfort, and political centralization. To this end he claimed for the republican language a concept which had so far served mainly in the language of natural jurisprudence. The term 'civil society' was a carefully chosen title-phrase for his book. He hoped to load it with fresh discursive energy and enlist it – perhaps for the first time in its history – in the service of a modern theory of active citizenship.

The very import of 'civil society' as a political concept was at stake. The disagreement between Hume, Smith, and Ferguson, which never took off as a fully-fledged debate, was partly about the relevance of this concept – in the sense that Ferguson gave it – to the modern polity. The aftermath is ironic, inasmuch as there is irony to be found in the history of ideas: Ferguson's 'civil society' travelled across linguistic and cultural borders, only to be transformed, in Germany, into something closer to the notions of his opponents at home. Its immediate future was *bürgerlich*, not civic.

1767), edited by Fania Oz-Salzberger (Cambridge, 1995), 149. Subsequent references are based on this recent edition. I should like, however, to acknowledge an editorial and scholarly debt to Duncan Forbes's valuable edition of Ferguson's *Essay* published by Edinburgh University Press in 1966.

6 Hume to Hugh Blaire, 11.2.1766, *The Letters of David Hume*, ed. J. Y. T. Grieg (Oxford, 1932), vol. II, pp. 11–12; cf. Richard B. Sher, *Church and Society in the Scottish Enlightenment: The Moderate Literati of Edinburgh* (Princeton and Edinburgh, 1985), pp. 195–8.

II

The eighteenth-century Scottish authors who made use of the term 'civil society' were able to draw on a variety of sources, not always semantically on par. Of great importance were Dutch and German theorists of natural law, particularly Samuel von Pufendorf, mediated by his French annotator Jean Barbeyrac. Their work was taken up by the Scottish jurist Gershom Carmichael and the Scottish-Irish philosopher Francis Hutcheson.[7] An almost total synonymy of *civitas* or *societas civilis* with the state is apparent in the writings of the German natural jurists. Pufendorf's early German translator clearly defined the 'oft-occurring' German term *bürgerliche Gesellschaft* as 'nothing but . . . the union of rulers and subjects which make a certain realm (*Reich*), republic and such like'.[8] A similar approach can be seen in Johann Heinrich Alsted, Gottfried Wilhelm Leibniz, and Heineccius.[9]

When focusing their attention on the foundation of civil or political society, and defining the profile of its founding members, the natural jurists resorted to the concepts of familial rule and property.[10] This was a crucial legacy to the Scottish legal and political thinking. Carmichael, who published an edition of Pufendorf's *De Officio Hominis et Civis* in 1724, described the historical and legal moment of the creation of government as an agreement or contract among heads of households. Having previously enjoyed domestic *imperium*, they promise to transfer it to a ruler or rulers embodying *imperium civile*.[11]

Francis Hutcheson, to whom we will return later, attempted to make the jurisprudential system of laws, rights, and duties reliant on a theory of individual moral sense, supporting a collective notion of the common good, safeguarded by the goodness of God. This proposal triggered a powerful rejection from David Hume, who found no divine guarantee of human goodness, and did not wish to make political society reliant on men's moral sense. As Hume famously argued in his *Treatise of Human Nature* (1739–40), pre-political society existed happily until the accumulation of property demanded institutional regulation of justice: 'The state

---

[7] Knud Haakonssen, *The Science of a Legislator: The Natural Jurisprudence of David Hume and Adam Smith* (Cambridge, 1981); James Moore and Michael Silverthorne, 'Gershom Carmichael and the Natural Jurisprudence Tradition in Eighteenth-Century Scotland', in Hont and Ignatieff (eds.), *Wealth and Virtue*, pp. 73–87.

[8] Manfred Riedel, 'Gesellschaft, bürgerliche', in *Geschichtliche Grundbegriffe*, ed. Brunner, Conze and Koselleck (Stuttgart, 1972), vol. I, p. 738. If alternative seventeenth-century denotations of *bürgerliche Gesellschaft* may be deduced from the translator's disclaimer, they did not leave their mark on jurisprudential discourse.

[9] Ibid.   [10] Ibid., p. 741.

[11] Moore and Silverthorne, 'Gershom Carmichael', p. 85.

of society without government is one of the most natural states of men, and may subsist with the conjunction of many families, and long after the first generation. Nothing but an encrease [*sic*] of riches and possessions cou'd oblige men to quit it.'[12] Even quarrels about property were more likely to erupt not within a particular society but between members of different societies: hence 'Camps are the true mothers of cities', and military authority precedes civil government.[13] The adjective 'civil' was thus opposed in Hume's *Treatise* not only to 'natural'[14] but also to 'military'. Perhaps to avoid confusion in this conceptual setting, Hume did not normally refer to governed society as 'civil society'. Nor did he use the term 'state'. In his *Enquiry concerning Human Understanding* (1747), he opted for the more clear-cut 'political society'.[15] Hume was later to use the term 'civil society' typically in the context of economic progress, as seen in *An Enquiry concerning the Principles of Morals* (1751):

For enjoyments are given us from the open and liberal hand of nature, but by art, labour and industry, we can extract them in great abundance. Hence the ideas of property become necessary in all civil society.[16]

The semantic emphasis was thus tilted, if only by way of association, towards the sphere of property and production. But this shift was not a uniform or unilinear process. The traditional jurisprudential sense was still hard at work in Thomas Reid's lectures on practical ethics. Civil society here is opposed to the state of nature, which is an 'unsocial State'. It is synonymous with 'political society', with 'civil government', with the state, indeed with 'human society' in general. It begins with a political compact among masters of families. It has an 'infancy', when human needs are simple and few. Then money is introduced, economic transactions grow in volume and complexity, and material wants multiply. Only in its advanced and polished state does society acquire the adjective 'civilized'; by then the natural human desire for distinction and preeminence is firmly focused on the pursuit of wealth. Civilized man is thus opposed to the 'savage', who is not the denizen of the state of nature but

---

12 David Hume, *A Treatise of Human Nature*, ed. L. A. Selby-Bigge, revised by P. H. Nidditch (Oxford, 1978), p. 541. For an analysis of the jurisprudential sources of Hume's political thought see Duncan Forbes, *Hume's Philosophical Politics* (Cambridge, 1975), pp. 27–32.
13 *Treatise*, pp. 539–41.
14 *Treatise*, p. 475, footnote 1. Hume says that he also opposes 'natural' to 'moral', depending on context.
15 David Hume, *An Enquiry concerning Human Understanding*, ed. L. A. Selby-Bigge, revised by P. H. Nidditch (Oxford, 1975), p. 205.
16 David Hume, *An Enquiry concerning the Principles of Morals*, ed. L. A. Selby-Bigge, revised by P. H. Nidditch (Oxford, 1975), p. 188.

of early civil society, and capable of social virtues sometimes exceeding those of his polished progeny. It is in civilized societies that the initial *raison d'être* of the body politic, defence by means of institutional justice, calls for utmost intellectual and political attention: this was the onus of Reid's legal philosophy, as well as Hume's and Smith's.[17]

To most of the Scottish thinkers, even those who found no use for 'civil society', the adjectives 'civil' and 'civilized' were of special importance. They belonged to the Scottish Enlightenment's explanation of modernity, which combined political economy and a theory of social cohesion. 'Civil' served in two roles: the jurisprudential role of explaining the sources, and hence the legitimacy, of political government; and (along with 'civility' and 'civilized') the ethical role of supplying moral groundwork for the new *homo economicus*. The first role involved the idiom of the natural jurists – the state as dispensing justice to defend and regulate individual men's claims to life and property. The second relied on an adjacent discourse, launched by Joseph Addison, which upheld politeness, polish, civility and refinement as mainstays of modern society. Politeness signalled the moral dimension of a modern world of economic transactions between benignly self-interested individuals.

Hume and Smith led the new Scottish belief in the civilizing powers of commerce, to use Nicholas Phillipson's apt phrase.[18] A plethora of self-interested actions could amount, in the sphere of production and trade, to collective well-being. But while individual interest was best served by individual acts, justice was best acted out as state monopoly. Hume considered Hutcheson's individual moral sense a potentially dangerous human tenet, favouring self and kin and kith at the expense of society at large.[19] Society was, at its best, a broad field of exchange among well-disposed but self-seeking individual agents. The currencies of exchange included money, language, and ideas. Justice was one of the cumulative products, and so were political institutions.[20] A good political system, once achieved, was not a playground for civic intervention or utopian revolution. Individual virtue is immaterial to it. The key to its upkeep is legislation; a job for informed professionals capable of scientific 'modelling' of government.[21]

Adam Ferguson opposed this move. His *Essay* can be read as an

[17] Thomas Reid, *Practical Ethics. Being Lectures and Papers on Natural Religion, Self-Government, Natural Jurisprudence, and the Law of Nations*, edited from the manuscripts with an introduction and a commentary by Knud Haakonssen (Princeton, 1990), pp. 132–5, 138–9, 160, 214, 233, 269, 285.

[18] Nicholas Phillipson, *Hume* (London, 1989), p. 32.

[19] Hume, *Treatise*, pp. 486–9; 534

[20] Hume, *Enquiry*, p. 306; *Treatise*, p. 490.

[21] 'That Politics may be reduced to a Science', *Essays, Moral Political and Literary* (Oxford,

argument against it. Ferguson aired and mobilized the term 'civil society' in order to halt the pillaging of civic terminology in favour of the new discourse of political economy.[22]

III

By the second half of the eighteenth century, 'civil society' may have become somewhat blurred with use: it is significant that Ferguson was the only British thinker in that period who deployed the term in the title of a major book. His bid to invest it with new rhetorical power, however, was supported by three near-contemporaries, Hutcheson, Montesquieu, and Rousseau. All three were read and quoted by Ferguson, the latter two with great relish. All three used 'civil society' in ways not openly divorced from its jurisprudential context, but nevertheless toyed with expanded or wayward meanings of the term.

The thinkers singled out here as probable direct sources for Ferguson's reworking of the term 'civil society' shared, broadly speaking, a common agenda. They all drew on the natural lawyers for their description of the incipient moment of government or political society, but they all wanted to say more about the moral nature of political membership.

Francis Hutcheson, whose effect on the Scottish Enlightenment can hardly be overestimated, offered a variation on the natural jurists' 'civil society'. He invested it with his path-breaking concept of the moral sense, a natural human faculty through which men reach their decisions about social and political arrangements. Hutcheson opposed the dichotomy of 'natural' and 'civil', arguing that man is 'fitted by nature to civil society', even if he did not always live in one. Civil society was founded when social groupings and the accumulation of property (itself also natural to man) called for government to prevent corruption. Hutcheson thus followed the main jurisprudential narrative, but with a new emphasis on the moral aspect of the foundation of civil society: 'not only dread of injuries, but eminent virtues and our natural high approbation of them, have engaged men at first to form civil societies'. Having submitted to civil power, men's sagacity is naturally subjected to the superior wisdom of the few who legislate and rule.[23]

Ferguson, who followed Hutcheson closely as far as the naturalness of

---

1969); Forbes, *Hume's Philosophical Politics*, pp. 229–30; Haakonssen, *Science of a Legislator*.

[22] Page numbers from the *Essay* (1995 edition) are given in brackets in the text.

[23] The quotations are from Hutcheson, *A Short Introduction to Moral Philosophy*, 2nd edn (Glasgow, 1753), pp. 266–7 and *passim*. Cf. Forbes, *Hume's Philosophical Politics*, pp. 32–8.

all social situations was concerned, abandoned him when it came to the divine guarantee of man's moral sense. Hume's removal of the theological prop had undermined Hutcheson's psychology. A new and persuasive analysis of human nature was required to provide an alternative explanation to men's capacity to exercise political virtue. This was one of Ferguson's main challenges.

Montesquieu, Ferguson's best-loved mentor, showed him the political framework for a viable civil society, without saying much about 'civil society' itself. In Book I of *The Spirit of the Laws* Montesquieu did make a passing distinction between the 'body politic' (*l'Etat Politique*), 'the united strength of all individuals', and the 'civil state' (*l'Etat Civil*), 'the conjunction of [the] wills' of those individuals. He credited these definitions to the Italian jurist Giovanni Vincenzo Gravina.[24] The distinction then echoes twice more in the same section, but not throughout the book. Montesquieu speaks of 'the political and civil laws of each nation', the former constituting its government and the latter supporting it. However, Montesquieu then tells us that his topic does not require a separation of 'the political from the civil institutions, as I do not pretend to treat of laws, but of their spirit'. While Gravina's distinction may be taken as an interesting predecessor of the later divorce of 'civil society' from the State,[25] there is no reason to suppose that either Montesquieu or his Scottish readers made significant use of it. What Ferguson did draw upon was Montesquieu's typology of governments and his clear advocating of those allowing political freedom: Montesquieu singled out to this end two forms of 'moderate' government, the mixed monarchy and the mixed republic. Ferguson was happy with either of these, but – despite outspoken tributes to Montesquieu (pp. 66–70) – his book was not essentially about the constitutional lineaments of political freedom, but about the historical conditions allowing an ever-active citizenry.

This brings us to the one thinker who may well have supplied the immediate trigger to the writing of Ferguson's book.[26] The whole first section of the *Essay*, and some of the book's other climaxes, were evidently conceived as a direct response to Rousseau's *Discourse on the Origins and Foundations of Inequality among Men* (1755). Like many

---

[24] Charles-Louis de Secondat, Baron de la Brède, Baron de Montesquieu, *De l'Esprit des Lois* (1748), book I, ch. 3. A different distinction between the usages of 'civil' and 'political' is that between 'civil slavery' and 'political servitude', book XV, ch. 1.

[25] Cf. Riedel, 'Gesellschaft, bürgerliche', p. 746.

[26] Rousseau's *Discours sur l'inégalité parmi les hommes* (1755) was cited twice in the *Essay* (pp. 11, 115–16), and paraphrased without acknowledgement at least once more (p. 119). Ferguson later returned to attack the *Discours* in his *Principles of Moral and Political Science: Being Chiefly a Retrospect of Lectures Delivered in the College of Edinburgh*, 2 vols. (London, 1792), vol. I, p. 55.

other readers of this work, Ferguson was as angry about it as he was impressed. Wherever Ferguson is at his most memorable, Rousseau is not far from the surface of the text.

Rousseau's piece famously depicted 'natural' human beings as solitary strollers. 'Civil society' began with the first claimant of a plot of land; we will shortly return to this seminal statement. In Rousseau's narrative, property bred conflict, law and government became requisite, and a political system was thus entered upon:

Such was, or may have been, the origin of civil society and laws, which gave new fetters to the poor, and new powers to the rich; which destroyed natural liberty for ever, fixed for all time the law of property and inequality, transformed shrewd usurpation into settled right, and to benefit a few ambitious persons, subjected the whole of the human race thenceforth to labour, servitude and wretchedness.[27]

To Ferguson, this conjectured state of nature was nonsensical. Empirically it was unfounded, and morally it was an affront: Rousseau's 'natural' man, lacking reason and language, is a mere brute. In the dashing opening of the *Essay* Ferguson made clear that 'Mankind are to be taken in groupes, as they have always subsisted' (p. 10) and that they were always 'a distinct and superior race' (p. 11). The animal lover in him, always ready to put in a word for dogs and horses, added elsewhere that such 'brutes' are in fact finer creatures than the human beings dreamed up by Rousseau, witless, unsociable and mute.[28]

Ferguson ought to have been made happier by Rousseau's modified view of civil society in *The Social Contract* (1762), where it is depicted in considerably kinder terms. There, 'although in civil society man surrenders some of the advantages that belong to the state of nature, he gains in return far greater ones', intellectual and moral growth and political and moral freedom.[29] Yet the fact remains that Ferguson did not refer to *The Social Contract* either in the *Essay* or in his later works. This may seem unfair to Rousseau, one more instance of the impatient hostility and selective reading practised by many of his contemporaries.

There is, however, another possibility. A careful reading of the *Essay* reveals that Rousseau's views in the *Discourse on Inequality*, and not those in *The Social Contract*, deeply affected Ferguson in a positive way, cropping up to support his best insights, and helping to blend the particular Fergusonian shade of his concept of civil society.

The first of these insights is Ferguson's idea of manly exertion.

---

[27] Rousseau, *Discours sur l'inégalité*, in *Oeuvres complètes*, Pléiade edition (Paris, 1959–65), vol. III, p. 178. The English translation of this passage is by Maurice Cranston.

[28] Ferguson, *Principles*, vol. I, p. 55. Jonathan Swift's Yahoos are summoned for support.

[29] Rousseau, *The Social Contract*, translated and introduced by Maurice Cranston (Harmondsworth, 1968), pp. 64–5.

Ferguson thought that only an active life, in the sense of physical effort as well as political participation, can do justice to man's nature. We achieve our greatest feats – Ferguson invariably referred solely to men – in adverse conditions:

'It is in the least favourable situations', says Mr Rousseau, 'that arts have flourished the most. I could show them in Egypt, as they spread with the overflowing of the Nile; and in Africa, as they mounted up to the clouds, from a rocky soil and from barren sands; while on the fertile banks of the Eurotas, they were not able to fasten their roots.'

This passage, freely adapted from Rousseau's *Discourse on Inequality*,[30] was a perfect motto for one of Ferguson's most seminal ideas. More than any other Scottish writer of his day Ferguson equated 'mankind' with 'men', and 'society' with active civic life. Polities owe their existence and well-being to the exercise of certain natural traits, which are essentially and exclusively masculine, such as play, pursuit and conflict. In 'rude' societies man is the hunter, gamester, warrior; in the ancient polities he was the soldier and statesman; in modern states he ought to maintain a rounded civic personality, a non-specialized political skill, and military prowess. Male nature and manly virtue form the crux of Ferguson's moral philosophy, defined as 'the study of what men ought to be, and of what they ought to wish, for themselves and for their country.'[31] His psychology focused on the 'disposition to action' and the love of adversity which 'every boy knows at his play'.[32] His idea of cognition and moral growth was political, and hence strictly limited to the strong sex ('The reason and the heart of man are best cultivated in the exercise of social duties, and in the conduct of public affairs'[33]). At the bottom of this great chain of masculine exertion are '[man's] associates, the dog and the horse', and other 'noble' animals who share his love of play and fight;[34] at the top are the loftiest human goals, political freedom and individual integrity, which must be supported by constant action and fruitful civic strife. 'The rivalship of separate communities, and the agitations of a free people, are the principles of political life, and the school of men', in the words of the *Essay*.[35] This endorsement of healthy conflict was not abandoned in the later, and politically somewhat mitigated, *Principles*: 'The trials of ability, which men mutually afford to

[30] Ferguson, *Essay*, pp. 115–16. 'Africa', alas, is Ferguson's misquote of Rousseau's 'Attica'.
[31] Ferguson, *Institutes of Moral Philosophy. For the Use of Students in the College of Edinburgh* (Edinburgh, 1769), p. 84.
[32] *Essay*, pp. 44–8.
[33] *Institutes*, p. 291.
[34] *Essay*, pp. 47–8; cf. *Principles*, vol. I, pp. 14–15.
[35] *Essay*, pp. 62–3.

one another in the collisions of free society, are the lessons of a school which Providence has opened for mankind.'[36] Competing boys, pugnacious savages and playful animals were all part of Ferguson's obstinate defence of the active role of individual citizens in a contingent, open-ended, and not necessarily progressive history of civil society.

Ferguson's second significant use of Rousseau comes in an unacknowledged paraphrase of the famous sentence opening the second part of the *Discourse on Inequality*. The original text, in English translation, reads:

The first man who, after fencing off a piece of land, took it upon himself to say 'this belongs to me' and found people simple-minded enough to believe him, was the true founder of civil society.[37]

Ferguson, in the chapter entitled 'The History of Subordination', echoes Rousseau thus:

He who first said, 'I will appropriate this field: I will leave it to my heirs;' did not perceive, that he was laying the foundation of civil laws and political establishments. He who first ranged himself under a leader, did not perceive, that he was setting the example of a permanent subordination, under the pretence of which, the rapacious were to seize his possessions, and the arrogant to lay claim to his service.

This paraphrase amounts to a subtle deconstruction of Rousseau's concept of civil society. By his own lights, Ferguson could not speak of the founding moment of civil society: as he had previously shown, civil society existed as far back as our knowledge can reach. The invention of property can thus only be credited with the foundation of 'civil laws and political establishments'. Society, in a non-institutional but still political sense, was there prior to property. However, Rousseau's resonant phrase serves Ferguson to work out his other great theme, the theory of unintended consequences in history. Immediately following the unacknowledged paraphrase of Rousseau, comes one of Ferguson's own most memorable passages:

Like the winds, that come we know not whence, and blow whithersoever they list, the forms of society are derived from an obscure and distant origin; they arise, long before the date of philosophy, from the instincts, not from the speculations, of men. The croud [*sic*] of mankind, are directed in their establishments and measures, by the circumstances in which they are placed; and seldom are turned from their way, to follow the plan of any single projector.

Every step and every movement of the multitude, even in what are termed enlightened ages, are made with equal blindness to the future; and nations

---

[36] *Principles*, vol. II, pp. 508–9.
[37] Rousseau, *Discours sur l'inégalité*, Pléiade edn, vol. III, p. 164. Translated by Maurice Cranston.

stumble upon establishments, which are indeed the result of human action, but not the execution of any human design. (p. 119)

Ferguson's civil society is the cumulative product of human actions that brought about complex, unintended, and unforeseen results. No writer since Bernard Mandeville's *Fable of the Bees* had phrased the idea so memorably. And no one, least of all Mandeville, made such an effort at accommodating the unintentional elements of human existence with active, conscious civic virtue.[38]

It thus turns out that Rousseau was the godfather-by-provocation of the two great themes underlying Ferguson's 'civil society': its dependence on men's active nature, and its gradual, unprojected, unforeseeable growth. Both these ideas clearly had other sources: the ethics of civic active life is as old as Aristotle and Cicero, and Mandeville's theory of unintended consequences was taken up by several thinkers of the Scottish Enlightenment. But the unique combination of these ideas and their application to civil society – in direct defiance of its immediate source of inspiration, Rousseau's use of the concept – was Ferguson's doing.

IV

Ferguson had no use for the term 'civil society' in the two compilations of his university lectures, the *Institutes of Moral Philosophy* and the *Principles of Moral and Political Science*. The *Essay*, however, was a different sort of book, intended for a more general public and written with rhetorical verve. Despite his decision to include 'civil society' in the book's title, Ferguson made no attempt at a compact definition of the term. He avoided any clear-cut distinction between 'society' and 'civil society', and declined to explain how or why the adjective 'civil', which he used often enough, was grafted onto 'society'. No moment in the discussion, and no moment in the history of mankind, were singled out to this end. And yet 'civil society' emerged from Ferguson's *Essay* endowed with a new coherence and energy, up and away from its stale jurispruden-tial context and its blurry civic connotation. The occurrences of 'civil society' in the text – eighteen in all, along with many more instances of 'civil' and its derivatives – repay attentive reading.

The *Essay* is a historical analysis of the merits of active political participation by a broad citizenry. It was almost the last in a series of attempts to bring Machiavelli's modern republicanism into British poli-

---

[38] Bernard Mandeville, *The Fable of the Bees, or Private Vices, Public Benefits* (1714), which argued that individual greed unintentionally enhanced public well-being. Ferguson attacked Mandeville's denial of 'the reality of moral distinctions' in the *Essay*, pp. 36–7.

tical thinking.[39] It also drew on Montesquieu's concepts of republican virtue and of moderate (or 'mixed') regimes in *The Spirit of the Laws*. Ferguson, however, treated the passage of time with more respect than either Machiavelli or Montesquieu: the *Essay* epitomizes an approach which Ferguson's pupil Dugald Stewart later called 'conjectural history', an account which involves a careful balancing of available evidence and philosophical conjecture. Ferguson was not averse to meta-historical speculation about progress and regress, but his history is pitched against the two extremes of unbreakable cycles and unilinear progressivism. The *Essay* teems with tension between these matrices, along with their fashionable eighteenth-century derivatives, and Ferguson's own case for voluntary human agency. The unintended dynamics of economic advance bang against the ever-present risk of moral decline, the virtues of the 'rude' nations confront the vices of the 'polite', the sweeping course of events is subtly channelled by wilful human intervention.

These distinctions were crucial to combat the facile reliance on the grand processes of modernity, which Ferguson spotted in Mandeville, Hume, and Smith. The *Essay*'s best moments are those where the language of fatalism is deconstructed in the service of individual political responsibility: 'Men of real fortitude, integrity, and ability, are well placed in every scene; . . . while they are destined to live, the states they compose are likewise doomed by the fates to survive, and to prosper' (p. 264). This was a fight about language, precisely because Ferguson engaged with recently published ideas. His polemics risked looking old-fashioned if it did not go on a linguistic offensive. Its two targets were the 'Addisonian' vocabulary of politeness, polish, civility, and refinement, as well as the jurisprudential language of laws, rights, civil liberty, and finally 'civil society' in the jurists' sense.

One way of dealing with these terms was an outright attack, ridiculing, say, 'the grimace of politeness' (p. 43). A second way was to expose a misuse, as in 'the boasted refinements . . . of a polished age' (p. 242). But Ferguson's main strategy was to claim (or reclaim) such terminology as part of his civic vocabulary:

The term *polished*, if we may judge from its etymology, originally referred to the state of nations in respect to their laws and government [and men civilized were men practiced in the duty of citizens]. In its later applications, it refers no less to their proficiency in the liberal and mechanical arts, in literature, and in commerce [and men civilized are scholars, men of fashion and traders].[40] (p. 195)

This was the crux of the matter: modern society has messed up several

---

[39] Cf. Pocock, *Machiavellian Moment*, pp. 499ff.
[40] The square brackets provide additions inserted into the text in the third (1768) edition.

basic concepts which merit etymological clarification, as a first step towards recollecting their ancient political significance. Not that Ferguson was eager to set back the clock of English or Scottish history so that professors, beaux, and bankers would vanish with a shriek: rather, he wished to remind his 'civilized' friends that they were, by original definition at least, citizens first and foremost.

The same bid to intercept and mobilize non-republican modern terminology was applied to 'civil society' itself. The term appears for the first time in the famous opening début of the *Essay*, where Ferguson demolishes, on a cue from Hutcheson, Rousseau's hypothetical state of nature where solitary creatures stroll. Yet Fergusonian sociability is from the start associated with war:

[Man] has one set of dispositions which refer to his animal preservation, and to the continuance of his race; another which lead to society, and by inlisting him on the side of one tribe or community, frequently engage him in war and contention with the rest of mankind . . . He is formed not only to know, but likewise to admire and to contemn; and these proceedings of his mind have a principal reference to his own character, and to that of his fellow-creatures, as being the subjects on which he is chiefly concerned to distinguish what is right from what is wrong. (p. 16)

Sociability is an 'instinctive propensity', Ferguson argues, even though man can analytically be seen 'either as an individual apart, or as a member of civil society' (p. 16). The dichotomy in this context is clear enough: Ferguson has no use for a 'social' state of nature, or for any alleged pre-political society. 'Civil society' is in this usage any society within which man's intellectual-moral faculty has context and, hence, relevance. And when he turns to discuss the ultimate goal of moral activity, happiness, 'civil society' and 'individual' are again poised in dichotomous (but not opposing) interplay: 'if the public good be the principal object with individuals, it is likewise true, that the happiness of individuals is the great end of civil society: for in what sense can a public enjoy any good, if its members, considered apart, be unhappy?' (p. 59).

Was there ever, for Ferguson, a society that is not 'civil'? Not, I think, in any political sense. There are of course societies such as the family, which did not interest Ferguson very much, and polite social intercourse, which he considered dangerous if divorced from citizenship. A defining adjective was therefore requisite. To begin with, 'civil' works in the text without reference to any process of civilization or any built-in notion of refinement. What we are left with is simply the 'nation', namely the state: rude or polished, free or corrupted. The alternative to civil society is simply universal violence (p. 17).

Even within this broadest of senses, civil society has some nuts and bolts: laws (p. 17), 'dignities', institutions, and 'offices', which, if not timeless, are at least very ancient (p. 79). There is even in some sense a 'formal convention' which represents a 'national concert'. Such convention stems from 'the necessity of a public defence', which 'has given rise to many departments of state' (p. 28).

Ferguson's point, however, was not to set up a contractual justification of the state, but rather to clear up one of the key assertions of the *Essay*: that rivalry between nations is conducive, indeed indispensable, for social bonding and civic well-being. Trade, he tells his economically minded friends, is not the hinge of civil society: it could be conducted even without national bonding and war. Yet civil society itself could not be maintained without the belligerency which brings about national cohesion (p. 28).

This context shows how emphatically non-juristic was Ferguson's use of the term 'civil society'. He was interested neither in a 'moment' of its emergence, nor in the state of nature as its legal opposite, but in the gradual appearance of its essential features, a range of political institutions and social transactions held together by the non-legal substance he called 'bonds' or 'bands'. Ferguson was certainly not concerned, at least in the *Essay*, with the legal basis of property: he constantly lamented the failure of modern societies to separate wealth from virtue and to establish social position on the latter alone. The fact that 'law has a principal reference to property' (p. 156) is but a sad reminder of human weakness. For Ferguson, modern laws 'secure the estate, and the person of the subject. We live in societies, where men must be rich, in order to be great' (pp. 161–2). But he admitted that the order was tall indeed: of all nations, Sparta alone managed to engineer a social scale independent of property ownership (pp. 158–60).

In Ferguson's usage 'civil' is no longer contrasted with 'natural', as in the natural law tradition and particularly in Hume. It is sometimes the rhetorical counterpart of 'rude', although 'rude nations' were not expelled from the history of 'civil society'. By making both 'civil' and 'rude' into morally ambiguous terms, Ferguson fully dispensed with the concept of civil society as a solution for a juristic problem. The polity becomes a natural phenomenon: it is as natural for the members of civil society to run their political affairs as it is natural for them, savages and modern Britons alike, to fight, hunt, or play.

The arts, too, are natural. So is the cumulative process of specialization in various crafts and professions: 'Knowledge is important in every department of civil society, and requisite to the practice of every art' (p. 168). Even poetry is subject to the beneficent effects of specialization. There was nothing wrong, for Ferguson, with the division of labour as long as it does not overrun into the political and military sphere. Public affairs, as opposed to private enterprises, must always be manually operated by keen amateurs: by large numbers, as large as possible, of alert citizens, who have retained the ancient skills of politics and fighting.

As the *Essay* rolls towards its climax, 'civil society' is gradually made more civic. It moves from signifying any social situation to signifying a state ruled by laws, and then on to signifying a polity of active citizens. The strategy of removing 'civil society' from its jurisprudential connotation is completed by imbedding it in Ferguson's civic language: almost all its occurrences are flanked by words which were highly significant in Ferguson's political idiom, a modern version of classical republicanism. Civil society is about 'spirit', 'excitement', 'business', and 'ardour' (p. 204). It is also about conflict and the joys of using force:

> Without the rivalship of nations, and the practice of war, civil society itself could scarcely have found an object, or a form . . . To overawe, or intimidate, or, when we cannot persuade with reason, to resist with fortitude, are the occupations which give its most animating exercise, and its greatest triumphs, to a vigorous mind; and he who has never struggled with his fellow-creatures, is a stranger to half the sentiments of mankind. (p. 28)

This was strong stuff by eighteenth-century standards. To Ferguson's contemporaries his insistence on rivalry was tasteless or quaint; to his posterity, such as the early central-European sociologists, it was fresh and pioneering.[41] Whatever else we can make of it, Ferguson's point is lucid enough: there is no civil society without internal and external strife.

Civil society began to acquire new features in zones where geography allowed free and spirited nations, facing one another with energizing rivalry, as in ancient Greece, to develop 'the genius of political wisdom and civil arts' (p. 106). Its institutions and laws were unplanned and developed gradually, since 'no constitution is followed by concert, no government copied from a plan' (p. 123). One crucial ingredient was the formation of 'habits', the acquisition of discipline, and the regulation of public affairs. Ferguson, a retired military chaplain who had seen combat and loved it, derived this insight from military reason. He regarded the timely acceptance of martial law as one of the strengths of civil society: 'he who has not learned to give an implicit obedience, where the state has given him a military leader, and to resign his personal freedom in the field, from the same magnanimity with which he maintains it in the political deliberations of his country, has yet to learn the most important lesson of civil society' (p. 143, cf. p. 93). War has a beauty of its very own,

---

[41] Ferguson's position as a founding father of sociology, primarily based on his treatment of group conflict, dates from Ludvik Gumplowicz, *Die socioligische Staatsidee* (Graz, 1892), pp. 67–70. See Oz-Salzberger, *Translating the Enlightenment*, p. 90.

not just as a corollary to civil society but as one of its finest arts. 'It is in being grafted on the advantages of civil society, that the art of war is brought to perfection; that the resources of armies, and the complicated springs to be touched in their conduct, are best understood. The most celebrated warriors were also citizens', those of Greece and Rome (p. 149). When no wars are fought, the military spirit must languish, and, by implication, the civic spirit is at risk (p. 202).

This, to a late twentieth-century gaze, is perhaps the remotest and darkest part of Ferguson's intellectual orbit. It must also be noted that the term 'civil society' appears more often in a military context than in any other environment in Ferguson's book. But leaving him there would be selling him short, for, 'happily for civil society', men's objects are not all belligerent. Had they been so, they would always have opted for monarchy. Yet in the political arena, as opposed to the military one, 'a national force is best formed, where numbers of men are inured to equality; and where the meanest citizen may consider himself, upon occasion, as destined to command as well as to obey' (p. 144). Liberty, posed by Ferguson in opposition to monarchical government, is about 'the communication of virtue itself to many; and such a distribution of functions in civil society, as gives to numbers the exercises and occupations which pertain to their nature' (p. 255). Civil society therefore ideally has a strong egalitarian and pluralist basis. Ferguson's republicanism was based on a large, and potentially growing, constituency of active participants.

By this stage 'civil society' is no longer simply the state, but the good state. There comes a point in the book where 'the history of civil society' leads us to concentrate exclusively on the 'happy nations', those kept in lively pursuit and strife by their climate, situation, and above all their stamina (pp. 117–18). Are moribund and slow-witted nations not civil societies? Although Ferguson never abandons the basic identification of state and civil society, his linguistic choices repeatedly suggest that 'civil society' refers mostly to polities with active citizenry, or at least to those with courageous remnants blowing on their republican embers, as in early imperial Rome. Ferguson employs the term for his highly idealized accounts of ancient republics, but also for his positive (if qualified) view of the modern Britons, a people represented in the government and able to 'avail themselves of the wealth they acquired, and of the sense of their personal importance', which in turn helped them to limit the monarchy and mix it with republican ingredients (p. 132).

While states or societies can become corrupted and bad, 'civil society' itself never appears in the text with a negative qualification, and rarely as a morally neutral term. 'Pure' monarchy is never referred to as civil society: it is in fact a type of corruption, though not the worst (pp. 250–1), and it is intended 'for a people not fit to govern themselves'.[42] Significantly, the single occurrence of 'civil society' in Ferguson's college textbook, the *Institutes of Moral Philosophy*, is in an egalitarian statement: 'Those are the most salutary laws which distribute the benefits and the burdens of civil society in the most equal manner to all its members.'[43] 'Civil society' is thus a misnomer for anything but a broad-based republic or a 'mixed' government with republican components.

A good form of government is, however, merely a necessary condition for the maintenance of a good 'spirit': Ferguson shared this conviction with his mentor, Montesquieu. Civil societies in the narrow sense are prosperous societies with 'a spirit of progress'. Yet progress, for Ferguson, was not merely a gradual advance in the 'civil and commercial arts', but also a political sphere kept alive by non-professionals and non-artists. The dichotomy between lively politics and tranquil subjection is linked to the early modern distinction between *negotium* and *otium*: good civil societies are constantly in business, unfailingly in a state of *negotium*. Decaying polities, ripe for a single ruler, fall into a state of *otium*. As Quentin Skinner has shown, in English and Scottish discourse of the sixteenth and seventeenth centuries the dichotomy of *otium* and *negotium* neatly fitted the political categories of monarchy, where the subject is peaceful and protected, and republic, where the citizen must actively defend the common weal.[44]

A striving for *otium*, for a state of immobile bliss, is the kind of mental mistake or bad omen which Ferguson might have called (had the term been available to him) a collective death wish. 'May the business of civil society be accomplished, and may the occasion of farther exertion be removed?', he asks (p. 204). Not, he responds, unless societies degenerate and die like individual men.

And do they? Ferguson himself argued that 'many of the boasted improvements of civil society, will be mere devices to lay the political spirit at rest, and will chain up the active virtues more than the restless disorders of men' (p. 210). Refinement, politeness, and commerce – those keynotes of civil society tuned to an Addisonian lethargy – can be its undoing. The *Essay*'s table of contents sums the story up: an 'advance-

---

[42] Ferguson, *Institutes*, p. 298.
[43] Ibid., p. 289. This is part of the chapter 'Of Political Law', where Ferguson's legalistic exposition of civil society often reveals his extra-legalistic ethics of political activism. Cf. the *Essay*, especially pp. 161–7, 263, 270.
[44] Quentin Skinner, 'Sir Thomas More's Utopia and the Language of Renaissance Humanism', in Anthony Pagden (ed.), *The Languages of Political Theory in Early Modern Europe* (Cambridge, 1987), pp. 123–57.

ment of civil and commercial arts' involves the 'separation of arts and professions', social 'subordination', and the emergence of complex 'manners of polished and commercial nations'. A strong causal thread leads from the heights of commercial modernity to the two concluding parts, 'Of the decline of nations' and 'Of corruption and political slavery'. Was the cycle, as in Aristotle or Polybius, viciously break-proof? If Ferguson thought so in his heart of hearts, he kept it to himself. He repeatedly dismissed the analogy between the history of nations and individual life cycles. Societies indeed decay and die, but their death – this is the *Essay*'s bottom line – may be indefinitely postponed if many men act as citizens should.

Civic wakefulness is thus the best option for the modern commercial state. There was no obscurantist retreat from the economists' modernity in Ferguson's thought, but neither did he suggest that we float blissfully into a society inhabited by private gain-seekers and run by professional politicians within a highly technical legal framework.

The closest Ferguson came to challenging his economist friends directly was in his appeal to those 'ablest writers' who deal with 'commerce and wealth . . . not to consider these articles as making the sum of national felicity, or the principal object of any state' (p. 140).[45] While complaining of a lack of public spirit, he continued (with his Scottish interlocutors clearly in mind), we provide the public with reasoning that is worse than having no political views at all:

[W]e would have nations, like a company of merchants, think of nothing but the increase of their stock; assemble to deliberate on profit and loss; and, like them too, intrust their protection to a force which they do not possess in themselves. (p. 140)

Here was Ferguson's case against Hume and Smith. To this end he had uprooted the judicial term 'civil society' and replanted it in republican soil:

During the existence of any free constitution . . . the members of every community were to one another objects of consideration and respect; every point to be carried in civil society, required the exercise of talents, of wisdom, persuasion, and vigour, as well as of power. But it is the highest refinement of a despotical government, to rule by simple commands, and to exclude every art but that of compulsion. (p. 260)

Such refined despotism lurks wherever the polished and polite lose sight of the *polis*, wherever the civil are no longer citizens (pp. 190, 195).

---

[45] A footnote added to the 1773 edition of Ferguson's *Essay* notified the readers of Adam Smith's forthcoming 'theory of national economy, equal to what has ever appeared on any subject of science whatever'.

Men who forget the etymology of the words they use will erase their deep moral logic, and eventually de-civilize their society.

V

Ferguson's civic use of the term 'civil society', and the other discursive battles I have attempted to map, made his republican stance almost untranslatable. This loss is especially noteworthy in the case of his German readers and admirers. Ferguson left several distinct fingerprints in German intellectual and literary texts written during his lifetime. The fundamental argument of his *Essay on the History of Civil Society*, the call for a modernized civic virtue, was not among them.

This is particularly striking, because Ferguson's *Essay* was instrumental in the renewed circulation of the term 'civil society' in later eighteenth-century Europe. The book was translated into several European languages. Its first translation, into German in 1769, proved the most significant. Gotthold Ephraim Lessing read him with great attention, Moses Mendelssohn paid tribute to him, and Friedrich Heinrich Jacobi brought him into one of his philosophical novels. Ferguson's writings enthralled the young Friedrich Schiller and comforted the grieving Novalis. Immanuel Kant made use of him, and so did Johann Georg Hamann and Johann Gottfried von Herder. Nor did Ferguson's reputation wane in the nineteenth century: Hegel praised him, and so did Marx. To this array of German readers Ferguson supplied a mixed bag of satisfactions. And, while his 'civil society' was demonstrably woven into a new German fabric of *bürgerliche Gesellschaft*, a great deal of its substance was lost on the way.

Ferguson, in his German recension, owed his fame not to the *Essay on the History of Civil Society*, but to his second volume, the university textbook *Institutes of Moral and Political Science*. As I have argued in detail elsewhere, it was the *Institutes* with its common-sense theory of knowledge and its gentle ethics of moral perfectibility, beautifully translated by Christian Garve, which spoke to the hearts of Hamann, Schiller, and Novalis. Yet readers with a taste for history and politics were drawn to the *Essay*. The new *Staatswissenschaftler* in Göttingen hailed his staunch historical empiricism, his rejection of a non-social state of nature. The Swiss historian Isaak Iselin admired his analysis of history from a republican vantage point. Ferguson's narrative of human history in terms of personal growth, his attempt to graft the process of moral development onto the history of material advance, provided a precious insight for the historical works of Lessing, Schiller, and Hegel. Schiller, in particular, may well have taken Ferguson's idea of play – the epitome of freedom in human interaction with society and with nature – and expanded it into the key concept of his *Aesthetic Education of Man* (1795).

Yet the German attempts at writing a universal history in the late eighteenth century, however much they were inspired by Ferguson's *Essay*, were far more teleological than his own work. They led to a perfect future, in terms of the human condition, which went against the grain of the Scottish analyses of modernity. Their work was in deep conflict with Ferguson's open-ended historiography, his acceptance of modern commercial society as a datum, and his refusal to escape to speculated Arcadias or states of future bliss. Significantly, the republican element in Ferguson's thought was all but lost in the German reception. His insistence on civic alertness and individual political participation were in most cases marginalized or flatly ignored.

Bürgerliche Gesellschaft became the standard rendering of *societas civilis* in the early eighteenth century. The translator of Pufendorf's *De jure naturae et gentium* into German felt obliged to clarify it, thus supplying us with a representative discussion of the concept:

This name expresses the author's Latin word *Civitas*. [T]he words *bürgerliche Gesellschaft* frequently occurring [in the translation] should not be understood to mean anything other than the authorities and subjects, bound together in obligation, which constitute a certain *Reich*, republic and the likes of them.[46]

It has been argued, especially by those considering the modern idea of civil society retrospectively from Hegel's use of the term, that the crucial feature of this 'classical' concept of civil society was a negative one, its alleged lack of distinction between the 'State' as an institution and 'Society' as a bond between citizens or subjects. According to this account, only when political economy redefined civil society as a sphere of free, self-interested individual economic agents, did 'society' become detached from the state, and, especially in German philosophy, even contrasted with it.[47] This is a contested analysis, not least because it tends to describe the absence of Hegel's future distinction as a conceptual flaw in earlier accounts of civil society, a reasoning that smacks of a fallacy.[48] More significant, in the present context, is the fact that pre-Hegelian

---

[46] Samuel von Pufendorf, *De jure naturae et gentium*, German translation, vol. II (Frankfurt am Main, 1711), quoted by Riedel, 'Gesellschaft, bürgerliche', p. 739.

[47] Riedel, ibid., p. 721.

[48] Ibid., p. 739. In 1807 Joachim Heinrich Campe's *Wörterbuch der Deutschen Sprache* (2 vols., Braunschweig, 1807–8), a dictionary sensitive to recent shifts of meanings, explained *bürgerliche Gesellschaft* as 'die Gesellschaft, welche den Staat bildet' (vol. I, p. 652). Elsewhere Campe equated it with *menschliche Gesellschaft*: vol. II, p. 338.

concepts of civil society were not made of one skin, not even where the Scottish Enlightenment was concerned.

German writers of the eighteenth century still normally understood *civitas*, or *bürgerliche Gesellschaft*, as denoting all political ties which form any kind of government, 'sive sit dynastia, sive baronia, sive comitatus, sive principatus', as Alsted put it in the early seventeenth century.[49] Gottfried Wilhelm Leibniz defined it as a 'natural community (*Gemeinschaft*)' whose members 'live together either in a city or in a country (*im Land*); their goal is temporal well-being'.[50] This definition could cover a monarchy as well as a feudal system of personal dependencies, as Thomasius indeed understood it.

The notion of *bürgerliche Gesellschaft* did not contain a strong space for the citizen, or, in his problematic German form, the *Bürger*. As late as 1807 Joachim Heinrich Campe's German dictionary still treated 'Bürger' first as 'a resident of a town', then as 'a member of the third estate', and only then, growing out of the second definition, 'also as a citizen of a state [*Staatsbürger*]'.[51] But *Staatsbürger* was a late eighteenth-century solution, and initially a very superficial one. Ferguson's term 'citizen' was translated as *Bürger*.[52] Neither the concept of *Bürger* nor that of *bürgerliche Gesellschaft* implied any participation of citizens as such in government, any channel of influence between the ruled and the rulers, or, indeed, any specific relation between rulers and ruled except for their being in the same political entity. In his *Philosophisches Lexicon* the Jena theologian Johann Georg Walch defined '*Bürger*', among other non-political meanings, as either a 'subject', or 'such person as is to be found in a *bürgerliche Gesellschaft*, and has subjected himself to an authority's power'. This contractarian definition proceeds, following Pufendorf's *De officio*, with a distinction between this state and the state of nature, or of sovereigns with respect to one another.[53] Thus the essential characteristic of *bürgerliche Gesellschaft* in Walch's definition was that its members were subjected to political authority. Furthermore, the total separation between subjects and rulers was especially underlined. Walch defined 'republic', this time following Pufendorf's *De jure*, as 'a civil society which [is] composed of rulers (*Regenten*) and subjects, who have united with one another for the preservation and promotion of the

---

[49] Quoted by Riedel, 'Gesellschaft, bürgerliche', p. 739.
[50] Quoted ibid.
[51] Campe, *Wörterbuch*, vol. I, p. 652 (in the definition for *bürgerlich*).
[52] For example, in Christian Friedrich Jünger's translation of Ferguson's *Essay*, *Versuch über die Geschichte der bürgerlichen Gesellschaft* (Leipzig, 1768), 90, and in Adam Ferguson, 'Von Staatsgesetzen', *Hannoverisches Magazin* (November, 1771), 1498.
[53] Johann Georg Walch, *Philosophisches Lexicon* (Leipzig, 'improved edition', 1733), p. 333.

common well-being (*gemeine Wohlfahrt*).' The definition readily included 'princes'.[54]

Kant brought this sharp separation between rulers and ruled to its logical conclusion. 'The Civil Union', he wrote in his *Philosophy of Law*, 'cannot, in the strict sense, be called a *Society*; for there is no sociality in common between the Ruler and the Subject under a Civil Constitution. They are not co-ordinated as Associates in a Society with each other, but the one is *subordinated* to the other.'[55] This distinction, and Kant's further distinction between 'active' and 'passive' citizens, would not be possible in Ferguson's view of civil society.[56]

Kant, however, did not altogether dispose of the concept of civil society. He stipulated its future perfection by means of his concept of Right. It is 'the greatest problem for mankind', he wrote, to accomplish 'a civil society administrating justice universally' ('eine allgemeine das Recht verwaltende bürgerliche Gesellschaft').[57] Justice, not civic participation; perfection and harmony, not civic interaction and turbulence: there was nothing Fergusonian about Kant's conceptualization of the term.

The German use of the concept of civil society can thus be seen as a reworking of it within the early modern jurisprudential paradigm, and not within its eighteenth-century republican paradigm. But something novel was happening: State and Society were decisively moving apart in late eighteenth-century German discourse. Campe's dictionary, often sensitive to recent shifts of meaning, defined *bürgerliche Gesellschaft* in 1807 as 'the society which composes the state'.[58] By that time Hegel had engaged with the sphere of individual economic transactions which was to become his 'civil society', distinct from the state by the very essence of the human intercourse taking place within it. Hegel's Scottish mentors are of crucial importance here: Ferguson may have furnished Hume with an acute sense of the distance between the classical polity and the modern commercial society. But it was Hume and Smith, with their analysis of the private sphere of exchange, who worked their way more easily into the new *bürgerliche Gesellschaft*. All that was needed was to ignore the civic aspects of Hume's political essays, and the irreducible element of

---

[54] Ibid., p. 2156.
[55] Immanuel Kant, *Grundlegung der Metaphysik der Sitten* (1791), translated by W. Hastie as *The Philosophy of Law* (Edinburgh, 1887), vol. I, iii, p. 41. Kant continues: 'Those who may be co-ordinated with one another must consider themselves as mutually equal, in so far as they stand under common Laws. The Civil Union may therefore be regarded not so much as *being*, but rather as *making* a Society.'
[56] Ibid., vol. I, ii, p. 44.
[57] *Idee zu einer allgemeinen Geschichte in weltbürgerlicher Absicht* (1784), Fifth clause.
[58] Campe, *Wörterbuch*, vol. I, p. 652.

civil responsibility spelled out in the fifth book of Smith's *Wealth of Nations*.[59]

The German rejection of the Scottish republican understanding of civil society was a complex process. No intelligent reader of Ferguson's *Essay* in Jünger's translation could fail to see that the *Bürger* described by Ferguson was no mere *Untertan*, that he was an active participant in political life. The translator himself, at one point, intelligently corrects Ferguson's text when the author, somewhat surprisingly, fails to make the obvious distinction between the two terms. Ferguson writes 'the subjects of monarchy, like those of republics . . .', and Jünger, with untypical boldness, renders it into '*die Unterthanen einer Monarchie, gleich den Bürgern freyer Staaten . . .*'[60] There was no crude mistranslation or misunderstanding here. Rather, the original civic, activist, meaning inherent in the English terms 'civil society' and 'citizen' were lost in the translation, thus removing some crucial connotations available to British readers. The result was that the jurisprudential vocabulary took over the key concept of 'civil society' and precluded a full view of its republican application.

German thinkers who did come to terms with the republican challenge often did so with a civilized sneer or with an elegiac resignation. Reviewers blamed Ferguson for embellishing the barbarisms of ancient Sparta and Rome. They dismissed him as a quaint British Aristotelian. The sophisticated Christian Garve, who translated Aristotle and Cicero as well as Ferguson, shrewdly commented that it was impossible to translate the English term 'public spirit' into German: 'No virtue, no characteristic, is in fact rarer among us.'[61] In the writings of Herder, Christoph Martin Wieland, and Georg Schlosser, the civic tradition was seen as a thing of the past, a long-lost element of classical or Germanic antiquity.

As some of his German readers recognized, Ferguson's 'civil society' was British through and through. Hume and Smith might argue against the viability of full-fledged classical republicanism in the modern state, but they would not consider it moribund or irrelevant. They might regard the active citizen-soldier as an anachronism, but they would not dismiss him as an academic invention or a romantic forgery. Quite different was the situation of their German contemporaries. In their political culture

---

[59] For detailed discussions, and alternative interpretations, of Hegel and his Scottish mentors see Waszek, *The Scottish Enlightenment*, and Laurence Dickey, *Hegel: Religion, Economics, and the Politics of Spirit 1770–1807* (Cambridge, 1987).

[60] *Essay*, p. 71; *Versuch*, p. 105.

[61] C. Garve, 'Anmerkungen', in his translation of Ferguson's *Institutes: Adam Fergusons Gründsätze der Moralphilosophie* (Leipzig, 1772), p. 331.

there were no embers to blow upon, no rhetoric to fuel and no vocabulary to snatch from the natural lawyers' texts. The bid to reclaim politics from politeness, and citizenship from civility, would have been a useless exercise even had it survived the challenge of translation.

This was best understood by Friedrich Heinrich Jacobi, who examined the Scottish ideas of civil society in his *Sturm und Drang* novel *Woldemar* (begun as a fragment in 1779). As his young protagonists, modern German men and women, stroll in the garden and discuss Ferguson's idea of a civil society, one of them remarks that civic virtue was long dead in the Holy Roman Empire. Citizenship, he says with great emotion, is extinct. Armies are made up of forced recruits:

Thus, lacking feelings of fatherland and freedom, lacking all interests of the heart, lacking courage and lacking love, employing prisoners for our guard and protection the thousand-year Reich is upon us, and we proclaim it with a new kind of enthusiasm, with the strange enthusiasm of materialism, with the rapture of cold blood.[62]

Jacobi did not live to see it, but a future did lie ahead. It came with German national revival during the war of liberation, and with its nineteenth-century experiments with liberalism, nationalism and unification. And it rested on a theory of civil society that reworked the private and the public, the meaning of civil freedom, the role of history and the scope for ultimate perfection, in a way profoundly different from the Scottish ideas so avidly read by Jacobi's young idealists.

[62] F. H. Jacobi, *Werke*, ed. F. Roth and F. Köppen, vol. V (Leipzig, 1823), pp. 166–7.

5 Enlightenment and the institution of society: notes for a conceptual history

Keith Michael Baker

'Je dis *social*, et je me sers d'un mot dangereux dans la discussion, par la multiplicité des idées vagues qu'on s'est formées à son occasion.' So warned Mirabeau in the *Essai sur le despotisme*.[1] And rightly so. Few words can have been more generously invoked in the course of the eighteenth century; none seem now more difficult for the historian to pin down. Yet, by the same token, none was more central to the philosophy of the Enlightenment. 'Progress', 'civilization', 'toleration', 'utility': such keywords of enlightened philosophy are unthinkable without 'society' as their implied referent; they all assume its logical priority and moral value as the essential frame of collective human existence. 'Society' and 'Enlightenment' belong together. The *Encyclopédie* of Diderot and d'Alembert suggested as much when it declared 'social' to be a 'mot nouvellement introduit dans la langue, pour désigner les qualités qui rendent un homme utile dans la société, propre au commerce des hommes'.[2] It made the point even more explicit when it announced, in its definition of the 'philosophe', that 'la société civile est, pour ainsi dire, une divinité pour lui sur la terre'.[3] The Enlightenment invented society as the symbolic representation of collective human existence and instituted it as the essential domain of human practice.

This chapter (first published in William Melding and Wyger Velema (eds.), *Main Trends in Cultural History* (Rodopi, 1994); reprinted with permission) draws on research for an article on '*société*' in the *Handbuch politisch-sozialer Grundbegriffe in Frankreich, 1680–1820*, edited by Rolf Reichardt and Hans-Jürgen Lüsebrink. I wish to thank Rolf Reichardt for providing research materials relating to the project. I have also learned much about this topic from discussion and shared research with Daniel Gordon, whose help I am most grateful to acknowledge here. Finally I would like to thank François Furet, Mona Ozouf and the participants in their seminar at the Ecole des Hautes Etudes en Sciences Sociales, as well as the participants in the 1991 summer school of the Dutch Graduate School for Cultural History, and my colleagues Carolyn Lougee, Paul Robinson and James Sheehan, for their generous critical responses to earlier versions of this chapter.

[1] Honoré-Gabriel de Riqueti, comte de Mirabeau, *Essai sur le despotisme* (London, 1775), p. 57.
[2] Denis Diderot and Jean le Rond d'Alembert (eds.), *Encyclopédie ou Dictionnaire raisonné des sciences, des arts et des métiers, par une société des gens de lettres*, 17 vols. (Paris, 1751–61), vol. XV, p. 251.
[3] *Encyclopédie*, vol. XII, p. 510.

If we can map the semantic field of *société* and its cognates in eighteenth-century discourse, then, we can reasonably hope to learn something about the Enlightenment in the process. And not only about the Enlightenment. For us, too, 'social' has the kind of multiplicity of vague connotations to which Mirabeau referred. For us, too, civil society is, as it were, a divinity on earth. Society is our God, the ontological frame of our human existence. The social (as anyone who presumes to question its priority is reminded) is our name for the 'really real'. It secures the existential ground beneath our feet, presenting a bedrock of reality beneath the shifting sands of discourse.

Such a map seems far from realization and would certainly be impossible to draw in the space of the few pages that follow. I aim only to prompt discussion by offering some preliminary notes on an investigation in progress.

The evidence of the dictionaries

To claim, as the *Encyclopédie* did, that the term *social* was newly introduced in the middle of the eighteenth century was, strictly speaking, erroneous. But it is indisputable that, with its sister terms, it assumed a new centrality in French discourse during this period. The INLF/ARTFL database of French language texts suggests a surge of occurrences of *société* and its cognates in the last decades of the seventeenth century, particularly the 1670s and 1680s, followed by a steady increase in usage of the terms in the course of the eighteenth century.[4] French writers were

---

[4] Searching the ARTFL database for occurrences of *société(s)*, *social(e)(es)-(-aux)*, *sociable(s)*, and *sociabilité* during the seventeenth and eighteenth centuries, Daniel Gordon has arrived at the following calculations. I wish to thank him for allowing me to use here a table now published in his *Citizens without Sovereignty. Equality and Sociability in French Thought, 1670–1789* (Princeton, N.J., 1994).

The table presents the number of occurrences of any of these four words per decade and the frequency of these occurrences per thousand words in the database.

Date	No.	Per 1,000	Date	No.	Per 1,000
1601–10	40	0.0189	1701–10	74	0.0880
1611–20	27	0.0385	1711–20	87	0.0750
1621–30	12	0.0043	1721–30	105	0.1156
1631–40	13	0.0156	1731–40	553	0.1246
1641–50	12	0.0126	1741–50	357	0.1735
1651–60	93	0.0527	1751–60	1102	0.2450
1661–70	16	0.0297	1761–70	1746	0.3728
1671–80	136	0.0669	1771–80	1811	0.4528
1681–90	197	0.1164	1781–90	1047	0.2445
1691–1700	98	0.0530	1791–1800	1396	0.6265

The database (now much larger) then contained approximately 300 works from the

talking more frequently about *société*. No less important, they were talking about it in new ways.

At the beginning of the seventeenth century, *société* carried a range of essentially voluntaristic meanings, clustered around two poles: association or partnership for a common purpose, on the one hand; friendship, comradeship, companionability, on the other. Thus one finds *société* defined by Robert Estienne's *Dictionnaire françois–latin* (1549) as *societas* (partnership or association for a common purpose), *consortium* (a community of life or possessions), or *contubernium* (literally, the comradeship implied in the sharing of a tent; hence a fellowship, band or brotherhood; cohabitation or concubinage). Estienne's definitions are followed exactly by Henri Hornkens's *Receuil de dictionaires francoys, espaignolz et latins* (1599) and Jean Nicot's *Thresor de la langue francoyse* (1606), and closely by Randle Cotgrave's *Dictionarie of the French and English Tongues* (1611), which defines *société* as 'societie, fellowship, consort, companie'. (Cotgrave also gives *sociable* in the sense of 'sociable, companiable, familiar, courteous, gentle, friendlie'.)

The voluntaristic connotations of the term are made even clearer in Pierre Richelet's *Dictionnaire françois*, published in 1680. There *société* is defined in its strictest sense as a 'contrat de bonne foi par lequel on met en commun quelque chose pour en profiter honnêtment' (examples: 'Entrer en société avec quelqu'un'; 'Rompre le contrat de société qu'on avoit fait avec une personne'), while its more figural sense is given as 'amitié' or 'liaison' (examples: 'Ils sont dans une *étroite société*'; 'Faire société avec quelqu'un'). Richelet seems to align *sociable* clearly with the latter meaning of *société* as friendship or companionship, since 'ce mot se dit des personnes & veut dire avec qui on peut faire société, qu'on peut fréquenter, qui n'est point d'humeur farouche'. *Société civile*, which now makes what seems to be its first dictionary appearance in French, seems, on the other hand, to be more ambiguous. Its definition as 'commerce civil du monde' is supported by the example: 'il faut retrancher les méchans de la société civile'. But this leaves quite unclear whether *société* is *civile* in this usage because it is characterized by *civilité*, or because it is shared by the members of a single *civitas* (the common polity of a single city, state, or country).

Richelet's treatment of the term *société* seems confirmed and amplified

seventeenth century and 500 from the eighteenth century. It should be emphasized, however, that this is not, in any strict statistical sense, a representative sample of French works published during the period. ARTFL, the Project for American and French Research on the Treasury of the French Language, University of Chicago, is a joint project of the Institut National de la Langue Française (Centre National de la Recherche Scientifique, Paris) and the University of Chicago.

in Rochefort's *Dictionnaire général et curieux contenant les principaux mots et les plus usitez en la langue françoise*, published in 1685. For Rochefort, 'ce mot signifie communement un Contrat, par lequel deux, ou plusieurs mettent quelque chose en commun'. But that usage of the term is not his essential concern: 'icy ce mot, *société*, est pris pour une conversation civile'.[5] Rochefort, then, is interested in *société* above all as a sphere of conversation, communication, and fellowship. But he introduces a different note by situating that exchange within a quintessentially human domain of mutual dependence. God, he insists, is sufficient unto himself; the animals lack language and communication. Both are accordingly 'hors des liens de toute société & communauté'. Only man is neither perfect enough to be independent nor so imperfect as to be incapable of conversation. This is why 'en qualité d'animal sociable & civil, il est nécessaire qu'il ait beaucoup de choses communes avec tous les individus de son espèce, & encore plus avec ceux de son païs & bien plus encore avec ceux de sa maison'.[6] Alongside *société* as contract, and under the sign of *société* as companionability, Rochefort introduces into his dictionary the notion of *société* as human interdependence.

This is the meaning of *société* that suddenly becomes primary, five years later, in Antoine Furetière's *Dictionnaire universel* (1690). Furetière does not abandon the more voluntaristic definitions characteristic of earlier dictionaries. But he prefaces them with another:

SOCIETE. s.f. Assemblée de plusieurs hommes en un lieu pour s'entrecourir dans les besoins. Les sauvages vivent avec peu de *société*. Les hommes se sont mis en *société* pour vivre plus commodément & plus poliment; ils ont fait des loix sévères contre ceux qui troublent la *société* civile.[7]

Since this definition, or variations upon it, recurs frequently throughout the eighteenth century, it is worth pausing here to identify its principal components.

First, society belongs in the order of needs, to which human beings respond through common action and mutual support. The notion that such a form of association is natural to human beings is not explicitly stated here, but it is made clear enough in the accompanying definition of *sociable* as 'd'un naturel doux & disposé à vivre en compagnie', with the remark that 'l'homme est le seul animal naturellement *sociable*, qui peut faire liaison, amitié avec un autre, pour s'entrecourir'. The same theme

[5] César de Rochefort, *Dictionnaire général et curieux contenant les principaux mots et les plus usitez en la langue françoise* (Lyons, 1685), p. 691.
[6] Ibid., p. 692.
[7] Antoine Furetière, *Dictionnaire universel, contenant généralement tous les mots françois tant vieux que modernes et les termes de toutes les sciences et des arts*, 3 vols. (The Hague and Rotterdam, 1690), vol. III: *s.v.* 'Société'.

was sounded in the *Dictionnaire de l'Académie françoise* in 1694, where *société* is defined as 'fréquentation, commerce, que les hommes aiment naturellement à avoir les uns avec les autres', with '*la société est une chose naturelle aux hommes, les hommes se deffendent, se maintiennent par la société . . .*' given as examples.

Second, this gathering of men is a fact of human institution; in Furetière's language, men have 'placed themselves' in society to live more comfortably and politely. Society is at once natural to human beings and instituted by them. As the *Dictionnaire de l'Académie françoise* put it in 1762, it is an 'assemblage d'hommes qui sont unis par la nature ou par des lois, commerce que les hommes ont naturellement les uns avec les autres'. But what is the function of laws within such a gathering? Clearly, one of their principal functions is to defend civil society. As Furetière remarks with an example, men 'ont fait des loix sévères contre ceux qui troublent la sociéte civile'.

Hence a third, recurring theme in the eighteenth-century dictionaries: the theme of society as potentially endangered or troubled. In 1694, for example, the *Dictionnaire de l'Académie françoise* offers '*cet homme étoit ennemy de la société*' as an example; in 1762, it adds '*troubler la société. Il mérite d'être banni de la société civile*'. Society is an order of peace and stability that must not be disturbed. The bonds of society must be preserved from those who threaten them. And it is worth emphasizing, in this context, the close lexical relationship between *société* and *liens*. 'Les liens de la société' becomes a recurring phrase in the course of the eighteenth century. Society is *bonds*; society is human order, an order whose tranquillity must not be threatened. 'Society' is the name for the interplay of individual human wills; it is also the name for that which constrains and orders those wills, preventing them from producing anarchy. Hence the force of the topos of 'troubling' society: the enemy of society, as the *Dictionnaire de l'Académie françoise* remarks, deserves to be banished from it.

Each of these themes resonates in the treatment of *société* in the *Encyclopédie* of Diderot and d'Alembert, which contains two principal articles on the subject. That largely devoted to the jurisprudential meaning of the term offers the broadest possible definition of *société* as 'une union de plusieurs personnes pour quelque objet qui les rassemble'.[8] Possible societies may thus include *sociétés générales* (those generic to the human species) and *sociétés particulières* (those occurring within a particular state, town, or other location). General societies include marriage ('la plus ancienne de toutes . . . qui est d'institution divine'); the

---

[8] *Encyclopédie*, vol. XV, pp. 258–9 (*s.v.* 'Société [*Jurisprud*.]').

family ('une société naturelle dont le père est le chef'); the *société civile ou politique* formed by the union of several families in a single city, town, or village (whose members 'sont liés entre eux par leurs besoins mutuels & par les rapports qu'ils ont les uns aux autres'); and, finally, the *société universelle* composed of all men 'd'un même pays, d'une même nation & même du monde entier'. Particular societies, in their turn, may include those formed for purposes of religion ('communautés & congrégations, ordres religieux'), for temporal affairs ('communautés d'habitans, les corps de ville'), for the administration of justice ('les compagnies établies pour rendre la justice'), for the arts and sciences (universities, colleges, academies, and other literary societies), for the conferral of honours ('ordres royaux & militaires'), or for financial, commercial and other undertakings. In this last context, indeed, *société* is little more than a synonym for 'contract'.

Les *sociétés* qui se contractent entre marchands, ou entre particuliers, sont une convention entre deux ou plusieurs personnes, par laquelle ils mettent en commun, entre eux, tous leurs biens, ou une partie, en quelque commerce, ouvrage, ou autre affaire, pour en partager les profits, ou en supporter la perte en commun, chacun selon ses fonds, ou suivant ce qui est réglé par le traité de société.[9]

Clearly, then, *société* is a capacious term. Clearly, too, the term has a capacity to efface understandings of collective existence traditional to the Old Regime. It is remarkable, for example, that this discussion reserves no particular privilege to the monarchical state, whose ghost appears to hover somewhat uncertainly over the border between *société civile ou politique* and *société universelle*. It is remarkable, too, that town governments, *corps* of magistrates, colleges, and universities can be placed unproblematically under the same rubric as financial and commercial undertakings. No distinction is found to be necessary between collectivities instituted by divine or royal authority and those deriving from a contract among individuals, between those bodies exercising public power and those subject to it. Virtually all human activities are caught within the frame of this definition, and they appear, above all, as common *human* activities. The barest possible reference to the divine institution of marriage seems merely to point up the secular force of the term *société* in its general attribution to forms of association natural to humankind, or instituted for conscious human purposes.

[9] *Encyclopédie*, vol. XV, p. 258. The expanded version of this article in the *Encyclopédie méthodique* was even more direct. Its formulation of this sentence read: 'Nous entendons ici particulièrement par le mot *société*, une convention par laquelle deux ou plusieurs personnes mettent en commun, entre eux, tous leurs biens, ou une partie, . . . etc.', *Encyclopédie méthodique. Jurisprudence*, 10 vols. (Paris, 1782–91), vol. VII, p. 609.

The second, more substantial article on *société* published in the *Encyclopédie* treats it as a term of ethics. It would be interesting to be able to identify all the sources of this text. But we can at least recognize two substantial ones: Jean-Jacques Burlamaqui's *Principes du droit naturel* (1747) and Claude Buffier's *Traité de la société civile* (1726), excerpts from which are liberally folded into the text.[10] Burlamaqui's appearance here is perhaps predictable: one would hardly expect the major *Encyclopédie* article on the subject of society to be untouched by the natural law tradition of which he was an influential expositor in the middle of the eighteenth century. But Buffier – the Jesuit best known for his role in the popularization of Lockean philosophy in France – is a more intriguing source, not least because his *Traité de la société civile* represented a sustained attempt to elaborate the principles of a rational and secular social ethic, and to explain the rules and rewards of social civility, within an ultimately religious framework.

Perhaps the most striking feature of this *Encyclopédie* article is the abandon with which it multiplies the reasons that society is at once natural and necessary to humankind – almost as if the spectre of anarchy and disorder is so strong that it must be exorcized with as many arguments as possible. 'Les hommes sont faits pour vivre en *société*', the argument begins. This is so because God wished that 'les liens du sang & de la naissance commençassent à former entre les hommes cette union plus étendue qu'il vouloit établir entr'eux . . . Telle est en effet la nature & la constitution de l'homme, que hors de la *société*, il ne sauroit ni conserver sa vie, ni développer & perfectionner ses facultés & ses talents, ni se procurer un vrai & solide bonheur.'[11] In this reasoning, men's natural needs make them interdependent; the diversity of their talents fits them to help one another. Moreover they have been endowed by their Creator with sociability, 'cette inclination liante & sociable' which guarantees their preservation and happiness. 'Ainsi, tout nous invite à l'état de *société*; le besoin nous en fait une nécessité, le penchant nous en fait un plaisir, & les dispositions que nous y apportons naturellement, nous montrent que c'est en effet l'intention de notre créateur.'

After these arguments, drawn principally from Burlamaqui, come the principles of social ethics drawn from Buffier. These ultimately derive from a simple proposition: 'je veux être heureux; mais je vis avec des hommes qui, comme moi, veulent être heureux également chacun de leur

---

[10] *Encyclopédie*, vol. XV, pp. 252–8 (*s.v.* 'Société [*Morale*]'). Lacretelle added even more excerpts from these two authors when he expanded the article for the *Encyclopédie méthodique*. See Pierre-Louis Lacretelle (ed.), *Encyclopédie méthodique. Logique, métaphysique et morale*, 4 vols. (Paris, 1786–91), vol. IV, pp. 137–49.

[11] *Encyclopédie*, vol. XV, p. 252.

côté: cherchons le moyen de procurer notre bonheur, en procurant le leur, ou du moins sans y jamais nuire'.[12] The utilitarian and egalitarian assumptions of this formulation are remarkable. But they are soon limited in their implications. If (still following Buffier) 'l'égalité de nature entre les hommes, est un principe que nous ne devons jamais perdre de vue,' this principle is quickly shown to be compatible with the subordination that is 'le lien de la *société*'. Relations of superiority and inferiority exist for the happiness of society: if arbitrary use of superior power would be destructive to social order on the one hand, so would refusal to accept the bonds of subordination on the other. By this argument, the social contract is transformed into a contract of inequality.

Tel est le contrat formel ou tacite passé entre tous les hommes, les uns sont au-dessus, les autres au-dessous pour la différence des conditions; pour rendre leur *société* aussi heureuse qu'elle le puisse être; si tous étoient rois, tous voudroient commander, & nul n'obéiroit; si tous étoient sujets, tous devroient obéir, & aucun ne le voudroit faire plus qu'un autre: ce qui rempliroit la *société* de confusion, de trouble, de dissension; au lieu de l'ordre & de l'arrangement qui en fait le secours, la tranquillité, & la douceur.[13]

Similarly, the utilitarian implications of the initial formulation are rapidly reabsorbed into the glutinous principle of sociability, with its attendant sentiments of justice and compassion, beneficence and generosity. These, it turns out, are 'les seuls & les vrais liens qui attachent les hommes les uns aux autres, & qui peuvent rendre la *société* stable, tranquille, & florissante'.[14] They are also sentiments that must be regarded as engraved in human hearts by their creator.

This reasoning has one purpose: to demonstrate that no matter how rational and useful to society the principles of ethics may be, there would be nothing fixed or unbreakable in them without religion to sustain them. 'Otez une fois la religion, vous ébranlez tout l'édifice des vertus morales: il ne repose sur rien.'[15] The conclusion is all the more true, the article asserts, to the extent that the establishment of societies has produced new needs and new desires, thus substituting cupidity, venality, and avarice for the spirit of hospitality and generosity. All the more need, then, for a force that has enough influence on human minds to 'maintenir la *société*, & l'empêcher de retomber dans la confusion & le désordre';[16] all the more reason to conclude that the authority of religion is absolutely necessary.

Which is not to say that the authority of religion is necessarily absolute. Quite the contrary. For the article now takes a Lockean turn. If religion is demonstrably necessary to civil society, the argument now runs, the

---

[12] Ibid., vol. XV, p. 252.   [13] Ibid., vol. XV, p. 254.
[14] Ibid., vol. XV, p. 254.   [15] Ibid., vol. XV, p. 255.
[16] Ibid., vol. XV, p. 256.

resources of religion must be used in the manner most advantageous to society. In instituting civil society, men have renounced their natural liberty and subjected themselves to the rule of a sovereign power for the specific purpose of mutual protection; salvation is neither its cause nor its goal. For that reason, the goals and interests of religion must be strictly distinguished from those of civil society. Sin must be distinguished from crime; the rights of religion separated from those of society. Erastianism (taken to its extreme by Hobbes) and ultramontanism must both be resisted; both, it suddenly appears, 'ont trouvé une barrière insurmontable dans la noble & digne résistance de l'Eglise gallicane, également fidèle à son Dieu & son roi'.[17]

This abrupt intrusion of gallican sentiment simply points up the obvious fact that this text is less a sustained argument than an entire repertory of themes, cobbled together from a variety of sources. Society appears here as a fact of human interdependence and the effect of a contract; it is the consequence of needs and the outcome of benevolence; it is the postulate of equality and the reality of subordination; it is the bonds of sociability, the hope for peace and tranquillity, the fear of anarchy and disorder. Above all, it is one side of a conceptual pair. This article reveals quite clearly the centrality of the Enlightenment engagement between society and religion. Neither could be thought without reference to the other: the institution of society as the conceptual frame of human collective existence required (indeed, it found its ultimate logic in) the displacement and reworking of the prior claims of the divine.

Nowhere is this made more evident than in the article on *société* subsequently added to the section of the *Encyclopédie méthodique* on *Théologie*, published in 1790. This article does not mince words. In essence, it is a blast against the monstrous idea of the social contract. Society, the author insists, is natural to humankind:

L'on convient assez que l'homme est destiné par la nature à vivre en société avec ses semblables, que réduit à une solitude absolue il seroit le plus malheureux de tous les animaux. Ceux d'entre nos Philosophes modernes qui se sont avisés de soutenir le contraire n'ont persuadé personne.[18]

In this account, society derives from human needs, which have also been the essential spur to the development of civilization. But to allow that society is grounded in human needs is far from admitting that it owes its existence to a contract among individuals in pursuit of their common utility. For the author of this article, those modern philosophers who

---

[17] Ibid., vol. XV, p. 258.
[18] Nicolas-Sylvestre Bergier, ed., *Encyclopédie méthodique. Théologie*, 3 vols. (Paris, 1788–90), vol. III, p. 510.

have claimed as much contradict themselves by denying on the one hand the existence of obligations among men prior to human convention ('c'est l'Athéisme pur') while assuming on the other that such a convention would be binding (an impossibility in the absence of some prior obligation to keep agreements made). Moreover, they can show no logical reason why a contract of society could ever bind the successors of those first individuals who had made it. It follows from this argumentation that 'le prétendu *pacte social* est une absurdité'. God, in giving mankind the need to live in society, has also imposed upon it the obligations of social life. 'C'est donc l'intention & la volonté du Créateur qui est le principe des lois de la société; le besoin en est le signe, mais il n'en est pas le fondement.'[19]

Behind the necessity of society there lies, in this account, the necessity of religion. God, it turns out, is the ultimate founder of society. 'Sans consulter les hommes', the divine author of human inclinations and needs established 'la société naturelle & domestique' by sanctifying the indissoluble bond of marriage. When families became numerous enough to join together in a nation, God founded 'la société nationale & civile' by holding out to all humankind the example of the Jews. When the time came that all the peoples of the earth were capable of fraternity, 'Dieu a envoyé son Fils unique pour fonder entre eux une *société religieuse universelle*':[20] a society in which there would be neither Jew nor Greek; a society in which natural and civil law were confirmed and more fully explained by a gospel appropriate to the needs and circumstances of the humanity to which Jesus appeared. Nothing could be less true, therefore, than the claim that religion rendered men *insociables*, cruel in their fanaticism and disordered in their zeal. Patriotism, after all, the author was careful to point out, while it was a sentiment approved by God when not pushed to excess, could also become 'ambitieux, conquérant, dévastateur & oppresseur.'[21] Religion, to the contrary, inculcated respect for social order as the work of God himself; how, then, could it be dangerous to *l'esprit social*?

We should not forget that by the time this article appeared the Civil Constitution of the Clergy was already under discussion. The coincidence merely serves to emphasize the extent to which this defence of religion is already cast in social terms. The necessity of society here becomes the essential argument for the indispensability of religion. Christianity assumes the form of a social gospel, a stage in the progressive advance of

---

[19] Ibid., vol. III, p. 511.
[20] *Encyclopédie méthodique*, vol. III, p. 511.
[21] *Encyclopédie méthodique*, vol. III, p. 512.

human civilization towards universal fraternity. Religion emerges as the guarantee of social order; but in the process the discourse of religion has been subordinated to the discourse of society. Religion is ultimately justified in the name of society, not vice versa.

This article was not, however, to be the last word under the rubric of *société* offered by the *Encyclopédie méthodique*. For in addition to its expanded version of the original *Encyclopédie* article on this topic, the section on *Logique, métaphysique & morale* added another to the lengthy *Supplément au dictionnaire de morale* with which it concluded in 1791. This article begins as follows: 'Je veux chercher si dans l'ordre civil il peut y avoir quelque règle d'administration légitime & sûre, en prenant les hommes tels qu'ils sont, & les loix telles qu'elles peuvent être . . . . L'homme est né libre, & par-tout il est dans les fers . . . .' The source scarcely requires identification, for the article proceeds by drawing verbatim and at great length on those chapters of Rousseau's *Du contrat social* treating the origins of society, the form of the social contract, the nature of sovereignty and the general will, the action of the Legislator and the identity of the people. There is more interest to be found in speculating on the reasons for this last-minute resort to Rousseau. It would be satisfying indeed to be able to conclude that the editor of the section on *Logique, métaphysique & morale* had turned to Rousseau's text explicitly to counter the arguments against the social contract theory in the article on *société* in the section on *Théologie*. But the placement of the new article makes it seem more likely that it served the more mundane needs of an editor rushing for copy to fill out the last of his volumes!

Nonetheless, Rousseau's belated appearance does endow with a certain logic the entire sequence of articles on *société* to be found in the *Encyclopédie* and the *Encyclopédie méthodique*. Within this sequence, we move from the jurisprudential notion of 'society' as a specific contract, formed by particular persons for their particular purposes, to the philosophical generalization of 'contract' as the essence of human association. We shift between the theological repudiation of the idea of the social contract and its philosophical affirmation; between an insistence on the divine institution of society and an emphasis on the institution of the divine as a political instrument for the creation of a people. We are taken from a notion of society as a necessity deriving from human needs and sustained by human sociability to a notion of society as the free invention of human will. Contract or bonds? Nature or artifice? Religion or society? This is the conceptual grid within which the discussion of the social in the two editions of the *Encyclopédie* seems to operate.

It seems clear from the dictionaries, then, that a critical shift in the meaning of *société* occurs at the end of the seventeenth century. The earlier, voluntaristic associations of the term with partnership, companionability, and civility do not disappear; but they are joined by a more general meaning of society as the basic form of collective human existence, at once natural to human beings and instituted by them, a corollary of human needs and a human response to those needs. Henceforth, the semantic charge of *société* oscillates between the twin poles of freedom and necessity, between the voluntarism of free contract, on the one hand, and the constraints of collective human existence on the other. Chronologically, the transparence of society as free contract and open companionability thickens into the complex necessities of human interdependence. Philosophically, society as contract is opposed to society as bonds. Metaphysically, society replaces religion. The eighteenth century resounds with the debate between those who favour one side of these oppositions or the other. How then might we explain the origin and dynamics of this configuration?

Contract or bonds?

We might begin with the point made by Otto von Gierke in his study of *Natural Law and the Theory of Society*. Gierke's analysis revolves around a fundamental distinction (found in Roman law) between *societas* and *universitas*. A *societas* is a collective body formed by partnership or free association (*consocatio*), in which the individual members remain distinct; a *universitas*, in contrast, is a corporate body existing in and of itself. In other words, a *societas* derives its collective identity from its individual members, while a *universitas* endows them with its corporate identity. The historical thrust of modern natural law theory, Gierke argued, was precisely to collapse *universitas* into *societas*, dissolving all corporate existence into an association of individuals. *Societas* was the sign under which the traditional logic of the organic whole was subverted by the modern logic of individualism.[22]

Gierke's analysis became a starting point for Louis Dumont when the latter began his study of the genesis of individualism in modern Western society in 1965.[23] Eventually, Dumont substituted his own distinction between 'holism' and 'individualism' for Gierke's terminology – but not first without a nostalgic lament regarding the impossibility of reinstating

---

[22] Otto von Gierke, *Natural Law and the Theory of Society, 1500–1800*, trans. Ernest Barker (Boston, 1957), *passim*, but esp. pp. 44–79.

[23] Louis Dumont, 'The Modern Conception of the Individual. Notes on its Genesis and that of Concomitant Institutions', *Contributions to Indian Sociology*, 6 (1965), pp. 13–61.

universitas in the place of *societas* as the appropriate term to designate the social whole.

> The word by which the old scholastics designated society, or corporations in general, *universitas*, 'whole', would much better fit the alternative view [to methodological individualism], which is our own, that society with its institutions, values, concepts, language, is sociologically prior to its particular members, the latter becoming human beings only through education into and modelling by a given society. It is unfortunate that, instead of *universitas*, we have to use *societas* or 'society' to designate the social whole; but the fact shows the legacy of modern Natural Law and its progeny.[24]

Dumont argues that all traditional societies have been holistic in the sense that they have seen the social totality as ontologically prior to individual persons, in consequence privileging hierarchy over equality. Individualism, by contrast, appears as the distinctive feature of modern Western society. Only there, Dumont suggests, was holism repudiated and ontological primacy given to the individual as an 'independent, autonomous, and thus (essentially) non-social *moral* being';[25] only there could social existence be seen as ultimately reducible to the actions of free and equal individuals. In his initial account of the genesis of modern individualism, Dumont emphasized the significance of the differentiation of politics from the all-embracing realm of religion, a process resulting in the decomposition of an organic, hierarchical, divinely instituted social order into secular states composed of individual citizens. His more developed analysis goes further in emphasizing the critical importance of the appearance of an autonomous economic sphere, in which interaction among human beings was structured by the relationship of individuals to things rather than their relations to one another as parts of a social whole. 'The primacy of the relations [of men] to things over the relations between men . . . This was the decisive shift that distinguishes the modern civilization.'[26]

The basic shift in ideology occurred, in Dumont's analysis, with Locke and Mandeville. Filmer still represented a holistic conception of a universe structured by hierarchy and subordination. Opposing him, Locke presented a view of the world cast in terms of equality and property. Human beings, he argued, are the property of God, who has furnished the rest of nature to their use. Collectively lords and possessors of nature, they are equal in the property they have in their persons; subordination among them thus becomes an empirical fact (or political

---

[24] Dumont, 'Modern Conception of the Individual', pp. 30–1.
[25] Louis Dumont, *From Mandeville to Marx: The Genesis and Triumph of Economic Ideology* (Chicago, 1977), p. 8.
[26] Ibid., p. 81.

contrivance) rather than an ontological principle. 'In the guise of possession of property . . .', Dumont concludes, 'individualism raises its head, knocks down any remnant of social submission and ideal hierarchy in society, and installs itself on the throne thus made vacant'.[27] This does not mean, however, that Locke allows for no constraints upon individualism. In Dumont's analysis of his theory, subordination is replaced as a principle of order by the moral obligations men owe one another as rational creatures and members of a common human species.

But this residual constraint upon individual action – or, at least, on individual economic action – was to be eliminated in its turn by Mandeville's equation of private vices with public virtues. *The Fable of the Bees* freed the marketplace from the constraints of general morality, claiming for it instead a special morality that produced the general good through the interplay of selfish individual interests. Reconceptualized according to the logic of this economic model, Dumont argues, society ceased to be the actualization of a rational, moral blueprint for general benevolence laid out for all humanity by its Creator; it became instead the indirect and unintended outcome of individual selfishness. The mechanism by which individual interests are harmonized is 'not something willed or thought by men, but something that exists independently of them. Society is thus of the same nature as the world of natural objects, a nonhuman thing or, at the most, a thing that is human only insofar as human beings are part of the natural world.' In other words, society is 'demoted from a fact of consciousness to a fact of physical nature. Everything points to the supremacy of the Individual having been bought at the price of degrading relations between men to the status of brute natural facts.'[28] In Dumont's account, then, Mandeville's conception of market society marked the definitive destruction of holism by the principle of individualism. The eventual triumph of this model was irreversible. Ultimately, it left the modern world no alternative to the logic of acquisition but the contradictory, pathological, violent – and necessarily futile – effort of totalitarianism to reinstate subordination within an individualistic universe.

The modern conception of society as the mechanism harmonizing individual interests thus appears, in Dumont's history, as the flimsiest of possible veils for the triumph of an individualism justifying its liberation from traditional constraints by a feigned dependence on nature. This characterization, however, became the target of one of the most interesting and suggestive critical responses to the appearance of Dumont's

[27] Ibid., p. 54.   [28] Ibid., p. 54.

work, a review published in *Annales* by Marcel Gauchet in 1979.[29]
Gauchet endorsed the general terms of Dumont's definition of the
essential historical problem: that of explaining the unprecedented and
unparalleled shift, in the modern Western world, from a religious holism
to a secular individualism, 'l'illusion d'indépendance et d'autosuffisance
d'un sujet censé ontologiquement pré-exister à la société alors qu'il en est,
et notamment dans cette croyance une *création*'.[30] He accepted, too, that
there was a necessary relation between individualism and the emergence
of the modern conception of society. But Gauchet reversed the logic of
that relationship. In his analysis, individualism was not simply a
symptom of the dissolution of the primacy of the social whole as that had
been understood in traditional religious terms. It was also a necessary
condition for what he once again called (following Karl Polanyi) the
'discovery of society' – its discovery in strictly sociological terms, disengaged from the religious representations in which it had hitherto
expressed its own existence. Not until the ideological primacy of individual interests was postulated, he argued, could constraints upon those
interests be discovered in the operation of an autonomous social order
subject to its own laws. Only with the emergence of the individual could
society appear as that objective domain beyond the will of individuals.

C'est dans la société où chacun n'a en vue que lui-même (ses 'intérêts') et se pense
indépendamment du tout social qu'une entreprise d'elucidation de ce qui lie
'objectivement' les individus entre eux, sans qu'ils le sachent, devient possible,
qu'un travail de dévoilement par exemple de ce que ces individus emancipés
doivent à la culture dans laquelle ils baignent commence à prendre sens. Avec la
séparation de l'individu, se révèle un au-delà des individus: tel est le paradoxe à
prendre en compte s'agissant de cette mutation cruciale des représentations et des
valeurs.[31]

These analyses are helpful in clarifying important aspects of the
conceptual matrix of *société*, as we have seen it emerge in the eighteenth-
century French dictionaries. With Gierke, we can see that *société* takes its
modern meaning not in opposition to individualism, but as its essential
expression. Society and the individual are not, in historical terms,
fundamentally opposed. Instead, they appear together. To speak of
collective human existence as *société* is to speak of it as an *association* of
individuals. In this sense, the term is essentially voluntaristic.

---

[29] Marcel Gauchet, 'De l'avènement de l'individu à la découverte de la société', *Annales,
E.S.C.* 34 (1979), pp. 451–63. Gauchet elaborated upon the arguments of this review
considerably in his far more general subsequent study, *Le désenchantement du monde: une
histoire politique de la religion* (Paris, 1985).
[30] Gauchet, 'De l'avènement de l'individu', p. 454.
[31] Ibid., p. 460.

With Dumont and Gauchet, too, we can grasp the force of the secular connotations of the term *société* in its opposition to a religious representation of the world as the emanation of a divine will. *Société* replaces religion as the ultimate ground of order, the ontological frame of human existence.[32] In the course of the eighteenth century, Christian apologetics is increasingly cast in social terms. The necessity of society becomes the essential argument for the necessity of religion; religion is defended as the guarantee of social order. But in the process the discourse of religion is subordinated to the discourse of society. At the end of the century, Raynal simply drew the logical consequence from this development. Among the Chinese, that model of Enlightenment, he reported, 'tout ce qui lie et civilise les hommes est religion, et la religion elle-même n'est que la pratique des vertus sociales'. The preservation and improvement of human society had become the yardstick for all religions.[33]

With Gauchet, too, we can grasp the logic of the relationship between what might be called 'thin' and 'thick' conceptions of society – between society as the expression of human choice and society as the constraints upon such choice; between society as 'contract' (the transparent effect of individual wills) and society as 'bonds' (the obscure, unintended effects of the interplay of those wills).

But there are significant limits to these interpretations, at least as I see them. First, their emphasis falls too exclusively on the problem of the emergence of an economic model of society. Without denying the evident historical significance of the concept of commercial society, I think it is important to remember that this was not the only form of the concept of society, nor necessarily the first to appear. (The idea of society as a domain of civility was certainly earlier and no less important in France.)[34]

Second, we should perhaps be wary of speaking (with Gauchet, following Polanyi) of the 'discovery of society', as if it were a positivity whose true reality was simply waiting to be revealed by the eclipse of religion. Society is not the solid reality seen by human eyes as soon as they were disenchanted with religion – this, of course, is a version of the Enlightenment myth. Society is an invention not a discovery. It is a representation of the world instituted in practice, not simply a brute

---

[32] On this theme, see especially Gauchet, *Le désenchantement du monde*, pp. 233–91 and Brian C. Singer, *Society, Theory and the French Revolution: Studies in the Revolutionary Imaginary* (London, 1986).

[33] Guillaume-Thomas-François Raynal, *Histoire philosophique et politique des . . . deux Indes*, 7 vols. (The Hague, 1776), vol. I, p. 150.

[34] This notion is fully discussed in Daniel Gordon, 'The Idea of Sociability in Pre-Revolutionary France' (PhD dissertation, University of Chicago, 1990), and *Citizens without Sovereignty*.

objective fact. This is not to deny, of course, that there is interdependence in human relations. It is simply to point out that there are many possible ways in which this interdependence might be construed. *Society* is the conceptual construction of that interdependence we still owe to the Enlightenment.

Finally, neither Dumont's nor Gauchet's analysis seems historical enough, at least for my taste. They deal with a great transformation, a mutation in human understanding of the world. But neither asks why or how this transformation might have occurred, or to what problems it might have been a response.

The institution of society: a hypothesis

What problems, then, did the invention of society solve? In what historical context, and why, did it so suddenly emerge as the ontological ground of human existence? It goes without saying that I can only touch superficially on these questions in this brief chapter. But I wish to suggest the hypothesis that the Enlightenment conception of society was instituted in response to a set of related problems in several domains: the epistemological, the ethical, the religious, and the political.

The epistemological problem can be most simply stated as the problem of scepticism revived in the sixteenth century as pyrrhonist arguments were rediscovered and mobilized in the context of the Reformation struggle over competing religious claims. The spectre of pyrrhonism, as Richard Popkin has clearly shown, haunted European philosophy from the Reformation to the Enlightenment.[35] It was the spectre that Descartes sought to exorcise definitively by wresting a new criterion of certainty from the very experience of doubt. But it was also the spectre conjured up once more in the philosophical debates over Newtonian philosophy. For Newton offered a mathematical description of the effects of gravity while refusing to offer a rational explanation of its cause. In the eyes of his critics, his theory therefore fell far short of the new criterion for scientific certainty established against the sceptics, the criterion of science defined as rationally demonstrable knowledge grounded on the nature of things.

Newton's defenders responded to these attacks by turning the limits of Newtonianism into its greatest virtue. Claiming that his great success was achieved precisely by his refusal to feign rational explanations, they found in his discoveries a remarkable confirmation of Locke's insistence

---

[35] Richard Popkin, *The History of Scepticism from Erasmus to Spinoza* (Berkeley and Los Angeles, 1979).

that reason was a reliable instrument, provided only that human beings refrained from using it to plumb the vast 'Ocean of Being', turned their backs upon questions of final causes that they could never answer, and accepted the necessity of living in the 'twilight' of probability when they could not attain to the full light of rationally demonstrable certainty.[36] But how could one accept limited, probable knowledge without opening the way to sceptical despair? What warrant could there be for mere truths of fact lacking the logic of demonstration? The answer was suggested by one of Newton's most influential expositors, the Dutch physicist 's-Gravesande. *'We must look upon as true, whatever being deny'd would destroy civil Society, and deprive us of the Means of living'*, 's-Gravesande explained in his *Mathematical Elements of Natural Philosophy*.[37] In this argument, not rationally demonstrable certainty but the necessity of society and the needs of common human existence became the existential guarantee of imperfect human knowledge. For how could it be otherwise, demanded 's-Gravesande: 'who could live a Minute's time in Tranquillity, if a Man was to doubt the Truth of what passes for certain, whatever Experiments have been made about it; and if he did not depend upon seeing like Effects produced by the same Cause?'[38]

Variations on 's-Gravesande's answer to the sceptics echoed throughout the century of Enlightenment as philosophers not only dared to know (in Kant's phrase), but also dared *not* to know. 'Il ne faudrait point détourner l'homme de chercher ce qui lui est utile, par cette considération qu'il ne peut tout connaître', Voltaire insisted against Pascal. 'Nous connaissons beaucoup de vérités; nous avons trouvé beaucoup d'inventions utiles. Consolons-nous de ne pas savoir les rapports qui peuvent être entre une araignée et l'anneau de Saturne, et continuons à examiner ce qui est à notre portée.'[39] *Consolons-nous*: in this manner, human society – its needs, its pleasures, its progress – became the principal compensation for an acceptance of the limitations on the human mind that Pascal found so terrifying.

The point found expression in many ways. But its most thoroughgoing exposition came from David Hume, whose response to the sceptics was an avowedly naturalistic and sociological one. In his most sceptical moments, Hume imagined himself 'some strange uncouth monster, who

[36] I have discussed this development more fully in my *Condorcet. From Natural Philosophy to Social Mathematics* (Chicago, 1975), pp. 87–95 and 129–38.

[37] Willem Jacob 's-Gravesande, *Mathematical Elements of Natural Philosophy, Confirmed by Experiments: or, An Introduction to Sir Isaac Newton's Philosophy*, trans. J. T. Desaguliers, 6th edn, 2 vols. (London, 1747), vol. I, p. 7. Italics in original.

[38] 's-Gravesande, *Mathematical Elements of Natural Philosophy*, vol. I, p. 7.

[39] [François-Marie Arouet] Voltaire, *Lettres philosophiques*, ed. Raymond Naves (Paris, 1951), p. 173.

not being able to mingle and unite in society, has been expell'd all human commerce'.[40] Abstract reason could not cure this sceptical disease; but nature could, and did. Even the sceptic continues to reason and believe, Hume insists in a famous passage of his *Treatise of Human Nature*. 'Nature has not left this to his choice, and has doubtless esteem'd it an affair of too great importance to be trusted to our uncertain reasonings and speculations.'[41] It is nature, he argues, that ultimately sustains in each human being '*a degree of belief, which is sufficient for our purpose, either in philosophy or common life*'.[42] It is nature that makes each absolutely and necessarily 'determin'd to live, and talk, and act like other people in the common affairs of life'.[43] And it is nature, finally, that offers the cure for the sceptical affliction in the pleasures of human society. 'I dine. I play a game of back-gammon, I converse, and am merry with my friends':[44] these acts of sociability become Hume's ultimate answer to the sceptics. Locke's 'twilight' of human knowledge has been transformed into the intimate glow of the dining room, the salon and the coffee-house. An epistemological middle-ground has been constructed between absolute certainty and absolute doubt: a liveable, human middle-ground, experientially sustained by the natural 'commerce and society of men'.

But scepticism was not simply an epistemological problem. It was also a moral one. Recent work by Richard Tuck and Istvan Hont has emphasized the extent to which the modern theory of natural law was also an effort to counter the radical new challenge of pyrrhonism in the domain of morality.[45] They point out that Grotius responded to the sceptic's denial of the existence of rational and universal principles of justice by deriving such laws from the one undeniable fact of human nature upon which the sceptic insisted: 'that love, whose primary force and action are directed to self-interest'. From this fact, he derived his natural laws regarding the right to self-preservation and the obligation to avoid injury to others. These laws, Grotius now argued, were to be understood as principles of an 'intermediate' kind of justice 'character-istic of human-kind'; principles without which the very fact of human society was inconceivable; principles that would be valid 'though we should grant, what without the greatest Wickedness cannot be granted,

---

40 David Hume, *A Treatise of Human Nature*, ed. L. A. Selby-Bigge (Oxford, 1888), p. 264.
41 Hume, *Treatise*, p. 187.   42 Hume, *Treatise*, p. 185.
43 Hume, *Treatise*, p. 269.   44 Hume, *Treatise*, p. 269.
45 Richard Tuck, 'Grotius, Carneades and Hobbes', *Grotiana*, n.s. 4 (1983), pp. 43–62; 'The "Modern" Theory of Natural Law', in *The Languages of Political Theory in Early-Modern Europe*, ed. Anthony Pagden (Cambridge, 1987), pp. 99–119; Istvan Hont, 'The Language of Sociability and Commerce: Samuel Pufendorf and the Theoretical Foundations of the "Four-Stages Theory",' in ibid., pp. 253–76.

that there is no God, or that he takes no Care of human Affairs'.[46] In elaborating a theoretical basis for society as grounded in common human needs, Grotius and his successors thus sought to construct a post-sceptical, specifically human morality that would remain binding on human beings even in the absence of a God concerned with humankind.

It has been argued, in response to Tuck, that Grotius's hypothetical admission of the possibility of God's non-existence or lack of concern was no more than a restatement of a late-medieval argument.[47] But the hypothesis was given a powerful new force by the resurgence of Augustinianism in the religious sensibility of the seventeenth century. Augustinianism was the nightmare of the individual radically separated from God, the problem against which Luther struggled so mightily – and which he inflicted upon an entire age. It was the intimation that the Fall had severed humanity and nature so radically from God that humankind could neither strive for grace nor approach by human means the spiritual reality informing the universe. It was the despair of the sinner cut off from a now-hidden God, and hence from true communion with his fellows. How might it be possible to live in a world from which God had withdrawn? No one confronted this question more directly than the French Jansenists at the end of the seventeenth century. It was Nicole, for example, who first analysed the logic of society as a merely (and irremediably) human order in which individual sinners acting out of self-love might produce (without their knowledge of intent) the same effects as if they had acted out of charity.[48] (Mandeville simply took up this argument and revalorized it.[49]) It was La Rochefoucauld who found in the devices of civility and the sociability practised by the *honnête homme* a substitute for the true morality of Christian love.[50] (The *Encyclopédie* article defining the 'Philosophe' stands as evidence of the subsequent transmutation of this *honnête homme* into the *philosophe*.[51]) It was Jean Domat, drawing at once upon the reasonings of the Jansenists and the natural law school, who found in self-love all the disorders of society

[46] Grotius [Hugo de Groot], *The Right of War and Peace*, ed. J. Barbeyrac (London, 1738), xix (Prolegomena XI); Tuck, 'Grotius, Carneades and Hobbes', pp. 53–5.
[47] Leonard Besselink, 'The Impious Hypothesis Revisited', *Grotiana*, n.s. 9 (1988), pp. 3–63.
[48] Pierre Nicole, 'De la charité, et de l'amour propre', in *Essais de morale . . . . Nouvelle édition, revue et corrigée*, 4 vols. (Paris, 1672–88), vol. III, pp. 118–70.
[49] Laurence Dickey, 'Pride, Hypocrisy and Civility in Mandeville's Social and Historical Theory', *Critical Review* (Summer 1990), pp. 387–431.
[50] François duc de la Rochefoucauld, 'De la société', in *Réflexions diverses. Oeuvres complètes*, ed. L. Martin-Chauffier, rev. Jean Marchand (Paris, 1964), pp. 504–7. Jean Starobinski, 'La Rochefoucauld et les morales substitutives', *Nouvelle revue française*, nos. 163–4 (1966), pp. 16–34 and 211–29.
[51] Herbert Dieckmann, *Le Philosophe, Texts and Interpretation* (St. Louis, 1948).

after the Fall – and the very means that God had chosen to remedy them![52] (Domat's analysis of the spirit of the laws, in turn, posed many of the questions taken up by Montesquieu.) In these analyses, society could appear as an essentially human order, an order in which choices of sinful, self-regarding individuals might nevertheless reproduce the bonds of a common humanity. For the Jansenists, this was no more than a feeble logic of the liveable. But it was a logic the Enlightenment accepted and revalorized. It was a logic that allowed the *philosophe* to consecrate civil society as the new divinity on earth.

In religious terms, then, it seems that *société* emerged, in response to the problem of Augustinianism, as a bearable middle-ground between grace and despair. But Augustinianism had political as well as social implications. A world from which God was hidden was a world in which authority was delegitimized and political order dissolved. It was a world condemned to civil strife and religious wars. It was a world ultimately offering only the terror of the choice that seemed so starkly presented by Hobbes: the choice between brutal anarchy and absolute, even arbitrary power. But the Enlightenment evaded that choice; and it did so by recourse to a notion of society as an autonomous ground of human existence, a domain whose stability did not require the imposition of order from above, and whose free action did not necessarily degenerate into anarchy and disorder below. In England, this self-regulating human domain of order and stability was called up most famously by Locke; in France, no one explored its conditions of possibility more profoundly than Montesquieu.

The Enlightenment conception of society, we might then conclude, was a creative response to the epistemological, moral, religious, and political dimensions of the generalized seventeenth-century crisis of values I have here called Augustinianism. It could be objected, of course, that this Augustinianism was no more than individualism in its Christian guise: the individualism of the sinner separated from God, denied the communion of his fellows, limited in his reason, flawed in his morality. In that case, however, the Enlightenment conception of society was neither the shabby veil for individualism suggested by Dumont, nor the abrupt discovery of the order constraining individualism suggested by Gauchet. It was rather the invention of a human middle-ground between certainty and doubt, religion and relativism, grace and despair, absolute power and anarchy. It was the institution of a bearable, imperfect – but possibly ameliorable – human world.

---

[52] Jean Domat, *Traité des lois*, in Joseph Rémy, ed., *Oeuvres complètes de J. Domat*, 4 vols. (Paris, 1828–30), vol. I, p. 26.

6   Hegel and the economics of civil society

Gareth Stedman Jones

Systematic interest in Hegel's conception of 'civil society' began in the 1930s and at least until the 1970s remained deeply intertwined with the crisis-torn course of twentieth-century European politics. A catastrophic sequence of events and conflicts – the Nazi seizure of power, the triumph of Stalinism, the decay and collapse of the Third Republic in France, the Second World War, and the division of Europe – imposed a strangely distorted shape upon the understanding of Hegel's political philosophy. By his admirers he was presented as a prophet, an analyst of the contradictions of capitalism, a critic of liberalism, a clear-sighted realist. By his enemies, he was seen as a champion of totalitarianism, a glorifier of an all-powerful bureaucracy, the mouthpiece of an authoritarian state, a blithe apologist of history's juggernaut path, no matter how many victims were crushed beneath its wheels.

During the last thirty years the quality of writing on Hegel has improved. Gradually and unevenly, the balance has shifted from polemic to scholarship. Furthermore, with the discovery and publication of earlier versions of *The Philosophy of Right* in the early 1980s, the nature of the problem has changed. It has become easier to document, and to some extent situate, changes Hegel made between 1817 and 1821 in the presentation of his political thought, including the first introduction of his new conception of 'civil society'. But how significant these changes were and why they were made is still a matter of debate.

In the twentieth century, Hegel's distinction between civil society and the state was primarily of interest to Marxists, sociologists, and critical theorists. In their eyes Hegel's analysis was prophetic. In one way or another, it was seen to prefigure modernity, whether in the form of industrialisation, imperialism, the welfare state or the depoliticized bureaucratic state of modern capitalism. Here in contrast, it will be suggested that Hegel's distinction was addressed to an ethical ideal rather

This article forms part of a larger essay on Hegel and Civil Society which will be published in my forthcoming book.

than a sociological reality, that it formed part of his depiction of the *rational* state and this state itself cannot be understood except as the expression of a new stage of religious enlightenment.

Methodologically, Hegel's 'rational state' was the product of an attempt to reconcile two fundamental and in some senses conflicting insights thrown up by the debate within the *Aufklärung* in the final decades of the eighteenth century and borne out by the course of the French Revolution and the Napoleonic Wars.

The first insight was that no belief or institution should or would survive unless it could be justified by reason.[1] This had been demonstrated by the whole trajectory of world history between 1789 and 1815. It was the implicit premise of Protestant Christianity and the explicit presumption of Kant's *Religion within the Limits of Reason Alone*. As a criterion, it entailed a radical rejection of the remnants of feudalism, civil inequalities and unjustified political or economic privilege. It also implied the free use of judgement and thus freedom of opinion, religious toleration and the separation of church and state. It clearly set Hegel apart from the conservative thought of the Restoration period.

The second insight appeared to undercut the force of the first. It was that reason could not be treated as if it existed beyond the constraints of time and place. Reason was embodied in language and culture. Languages and cultures changed over time and differed across space. Thus reason should be considered the highest expression of the spirit of a people. This had been the main criticism levelled at Kant's philosophy by Hamann and Herder and it implied the need for a new conception of history if reason's claim to universality were to be sustained. This insight had also been borne out by the course of the French Revolution. For, basing themselves upon mechanical, atomistic, and ahistorical conceptions of universality, the French had failed to discover principles which might underpin a viable constitution. In important ways, they had simply replicated the defects of eighteenth-century absolutism. In place, therefore, of what Herder and later Schiller had called the 'machine-state' which could only treat men as 'cogs', the constitution of a true state should be considered a living organism, an evolving expression of the development of the spirit of the people.[2]

---

[1] As Hegel wrote in the case of Wurttemburg in 1816, 'in a political constitution nothing should be recognised as valid unless its recognition accorded with the right of Reason . . . One must regard the start of the French Revolution as the struggle of rational constitutional law against the mass of positive law and privileges by which it had been stifled', *Hegel's Political Writings*, ed. T. M. Knox and Z. A. Pelczynski (Oxford, 1964), pp. 281, 282.

[2] See anonymous (G. W. F. Hegel), 'The Oldest Systematic Programme of German Idealism', in *The Early Political Writings of the German Romantics*, ed. F. C. Beiser

The period of constitution-making which followed the fall of Napoleon in 1815 provided Hegel with an unexpected opportunity to round out his constitutional conceptions, first in Wurttemberg and then in Prussia. Hegel was convinced that the notions of the rational and of the organic went together, that it was 'only by virtue of its rational form that the state is an organism' and that 'the constitutional monarchy' was the only viable embodiment of this rational organic form.[3] An organic conception of the state would preserve liberal freedoms while dispensing with a contractual basis for political obligation. By borrowing a quasi-biological notion of how an organism incorporated its 'inorganic' environment, Hegel believed he had found the means by which the free pursuit of individual interest, the central feature of 'commercial society', could be encompassed within a new vision of political community. The distinction between the constitution or political state and 'civil society' thus formed the main component of an 'organic' alternative to the 'the external state', 'the state of necessity', the contractual state as it had been conceived by the modern tradition of natural law.[4]

Hegel's theory was initially stimulated by questions directed at the French Revolution by Schiller and soon after reformulated in the light of a new philosophy of nature pioneered by Hegel's friend, Schelling. It was designed to resolve problems with which he had wrestled since the 1790s, problems relating to religious and political regeneration in the light of the results of the *Aufklärung* and the French Revolution. By the same token, however, it was not particularly well designed to anticipate the new social and political conflicts of the nineteenth century and this helps to explain why almost from the beginning it was so misunderstood.

The essay will examine the limitations of the successive attempts to portray Hegel as the prophet of modern social theory. The removal of misleading constructions which have been placed upon Hegel's intentions and his achievement should counter any lingering temptation to demonize Hegel's social thought. But, by the same token, it will also underline the difficulty of applying his insights and solutions in the present.

I

The term *bürgerliche Gesellschaft* (civil society) had already acquired contentious political connotations by the time Hegel began to write.

(Cambridge, 1966), p. 4; G. W. F. Hegel, 'The German Constitution', in *G. W. F. Hegel Political Writings*, ed. Lawrence Dickey and H. B. Nisbet, trans. H. B. Nisbet (Cambridge: Cambridge University Press, 1999), pp. 162–3; G. W. F. Hegel, *Elements of the Philosophy of Right*, ed. A. Wood, trans. H. B. Nisbet (Cambridge, 1991, henceforward *Phil. R.*), §§259, 269, 276, 286.
3 Hegel, *Phil. R.*, §308, p. 347.   4 Ibid., §183, p. 221.

Originally the German rendering of the classical term *societas civilis sive res publica* (civil or political society in contrast to the state of nature or to domestic society and the household), *bürgerliche Gesellschaft* from the time of the French Revolution became associated with the progress of the third estate. Thus the major conservative theorist of the Restoration period, Carl Ludwig von Haller, denounced as 'the mother and source of all the errors of the revolutionary epoch' 'the wretched idea of a romish civil society which has now been extended to all other forms of social relationship'. Haller believed it was possible in place of 'civil society' to return to the idea of 'natural society', in effect a restoration of feudal relations.[5] It was not therefore surprising that Hegel's use of the term in *The Philosophy of Right* was treated not so much as an analysis as an endorsement of the new associations of the term. Therefore, just as it had initially been attacked from the right, so within a few years, it became an object of attack from the left. Not long after Hegel's death in 1831, the radical Young-Hegelian, Arnold Ruge, began to distinguish between the *bürgerliche Gesellschaft* of today and the *menschliche Gesellschaft* of tomorrow, while Marx denounced the theory as a justification of private right. In *The German Ideology* Marx and Engels labelled Hegel's construction a *Bourgeoisie Gesellschaft*.[6]

But if radicals of the Vormärz period had begun to chastise Hegel for his acceptance of the 'bourgeois' and 'egoistic' character of *bürgerliche Gesellschaft*, in the disenchantment which followed the defeats of 1848, more serious doubts began to be raised about the authenticity of his liberalism. It was in these years that the legend of Hegel as political sycophant took root. According to the relentlessly hostile biographical study of Rudolf Haym, after first praising the prince of 'the wren kingdom' of Wurttemberg 'with asiatic panegyrics', Hegel went on to provide 'the scientific domestication of the spirit of the Prussian Restoration'.[7] Even the supposedly liberal idea of civil society did not escape suspicion. Haym accused Hegel of having realized that granting 'the semblance of recognition' to progressive moments of modern political reality would be the best way of making the liberalism of these designations 'dull or innocuous'.[8]

But even among those still prepared to defend Hegel's philosophical legacy, the intellectual distinctiveness of Hegel's treatment of civil society

---

[5] See M. Riedel, 'Gesellschaft, bürgerliche', in *Geschichtliche Grundbegriffe*, vol. II, ed. O. Brunner, W. Conze, and R. Koselleck (Stuttgart, 1975), p. 773.

[6] Ibid. pp. 782, 784.

[7] R. Haym, *Hegel und seine Zeit* (Berlin, 1857), pp. 353, 359.

[8] Ibid., p. 380, and see also R. P. Horstmann, 'Uber die Rolle der bürgerlichen Gesellschaft in Hegels Philosophie', *Hegel Studien*, 9 (1974), pp. 220–40.

and his purpose in distinguishing it from the 'political state' provoked little comment. Set in relation to an increasing tendency to redefine 'civil society' simply as 'society' (*Gesellschaft*) understood to mean social organization and social behaviour apart from, or prior to, government, it may be that the peculiar features of Hegel's treatment escaped attention, especially in the epoch after 1848, when, as Marx put it, Hegel became a 'dead dog'.[9] For this reason, Hegel's reading of political economy, which was to attract so much attention in the twentieth century, occasioned only cursory discussion.

Characteristic was the treatment found in the earliest major biography of Hegel, that of Karl Rosenkranz in 1844. According to Rosenkranz, Hegel wrote a detailed commentary on Sir James Steuart's *Principles of Political Oeconomy* over a period of three months in 1799. Rosenkranz wrote of its 'many fine observations' and its struggle 'to save the heart (*Gemüth*) of man amidst the competition and mechanical interaction of labour and commerce'.[10] Nevertheless he did not see fit to include this evidence of Hegel's first systematic encounter with political economy among the appendices to his book and thereafter the manuscript was lost.

Marx, of course, was the one great exception to this general neglect of the social and economic dimensions of Hegel's thought. It is not, therefore, surprising that the current interest in Hegel's picture of civil society originated in the investigation of the connection between Hegel and Marx. But the story of Marx's engagement with the *Philosophy of Right* or with the *Phenomenology* really belongs to the twentieth rather than the nineteenth century. For beyond some brief recollections by Engels and a few condensed paragraphs from the Preface to Marx's *Critique of Political Economy* of 1859 or from the 'Postface' to his second edition of *Capital*, the nineteenth-century reader had no access to the part played by Hegel's depiction of civil society in the formation of Marx's 'materialist conception of history'.[11] The extent of that engagement only began to become clear with the publication of Marx's unfinished 1843 critique of *The Philosophy of Right* in 1927 and of his so-called *Economic*

---

[9] Riedel, 'Gesellschaft, bürgerliche', pp. 788–91; K. Marx, *Capital*, vol. I (Harmondsworth, 1976), pp. 102–3.

[10] See K. Rosenkranz, *G. W. F. Hegels Leben* (Berlin, 1844), p. 86, and the discussion in H. S. Harris, *Hegel's Development: Towards the Sunlight 1770–1801* (Oxford, 1972), pp. 434–6. I have cited Harris's translation (p. 435); on the significance of the term *Gemüth* see N. Waszek, *The Scottish Enlightenment and Hegel's Account of Civil Society* (Dordrecht, 1988), pp. 114–15. In this passage the word implies 'wholeness', and probably refers to its use as a middle term between 'sensation' and 'thought' in Schiller's *On the Aesthetic Education of Man*, a formative influence on Hegel's stance towards political economy.

[11] See F. Engels, 'Ludwig Feuerbach and the End of Classical German Philosophy', in *Karl Marx and Frederick Engels. Selected Writings* (New York, 1968).

and Philosophic Manuscripts of 1844 in 1932. The significance of these discoveries had already been partially anticipated with the publication of George Lukács's *History and Class Consciousness* in 1923. Relying at that stage upon published writings, Lukács stressed the continuity of 'dialectical' thinking which united Marx and Hegel. According to Lukács, it was this conception of the dialectic which represented the revolutionary core of Marxism in contrast to the bland and reformist positivism of the Second International.[12]

Even if Lukács later disowned *History and Class Consciousness* for reasons of Communist orthodoxy, the great strength of the book was to point out the undeniable – the dependence of Marx upon Hegel and the continuities between Marx's early preoccupations and those of his later thought. More problematic, though undoubtedly still an important contribution to scholarship, was Lukács's attempt in the following decade to tone down his earlier heterodoxy by highlighting hitherto neglected 'economic' themes in Hegel's youthful writings and to present his outlook as a kind of *marxisme avant la lettre*. This study, *The Young Hegel*, written in Moscow during the 1930s, was first published in 1948, but only became well known after the publication of the second edition in 1954.[13] It contained a detailed analysis of Hegel's writings before the *Phenomenology* of 1807, virtually all of which had first been published between 1907 and 1936. In Lukács's account, the young Hegel, almost alone among his contemporaries, already perceived the crisis-ridden character of modern capitalist production and the alienated character of factory work. Behind the author of *The Philosophy of Right*, the staid conservative theorist of the modern state, Lukács revealed a youthful and precocious critic of capitalism, only prevented from anticipating the full scope of the Marxian position by the immaturity of the proletariat at the time.

Lukács's work was valuable because it was the first to scrutinize Hegel's awareness of Adam Smith and the other economists during his time at Berne (1793–6), Frankfurt (1797–1800), and Jena (1801–6) and to draw attention to the depictions of the world derived from modern political economy found in his early lecture courses. But by treating the young Hegel as a prefiguration of Marx, Lukács both exaggerated the

---

[12] See G. Lukács, *History and Class Consciousness*, trans. R. Livingstone (London, 1971), esp. chapter 1.

[13] Lukács wished to situate Hegel in a 'progressive German tradition', which ran from Leibniz to Feuerbach, and which he wished to counterpose to the 'irrationalist tradition', pre-eminently represented by Schelling. See Lukács's preface to the second edition of G. Lukács, *The Young Hegel. Studies in the Relations between Dialectics and Economics*, trans. R. Livingstone (London, 1975), pp. xi–xiii.

originality of Hegel's preoccupation with political economy and seriously distorted the character of his interest. In particular, by focusing so completely upon Hegel's concern with the economy while dismissing as a reactionary 'legend' the self-evident preoccupation with the reform of Christianity that was its accompaniment, Lukács appeared to miss the point of these writings.[14] He failed to perceive that Hegel's ambition was not to transcend the exchange relations of the modern economy, but to incorporate them within a new vision of an integrated moral and political community or what he was later to call 'ethical life' (*Sittlichkeit*).[15] Arguably, this ambition still preoccupied him fifteen years later in the published version of *The Philosophy of Right*.

As more recent research has revealed, Hegel was not the first German thinker to take seriously the findings of political economy.[16] Questions about the cultural, political, and religious implications of commercial society were salient among the concerns of the German intelligentsia in the second half of the eighteenth century, particularly from the 1770s onwards. The works of Ferguson, Steuart, and Smith on political economy and commercial society were all rapidly translated into German in the 1760s and 1770s and were quickly seen to pose problems, whether to the theorist of art, to the civic and religious moralist, or to the cameralist statesman.[17] Ferguson's sombre picture of the disintegration of ancient virtue and poetry formed the basis of Schiller's famous lament in the *Aesthetic Education of Man*:

That polypoid character of the Greek States, in which every individual enjoyed an independent existence but could, when need arose, grow into the whole organism, now made way for an ingenious clock-work, in which, out of the piecing together of innumerable but lifeless parts, a mechanical kind of collective life ensued. Church and State, law and customs, were now torn asunder; enjoyment was divorced from labour, the means from the end, the effort from the

---

[14] Lukács, *The Young Hegel*, p. 16.

[15] The German word *Sitte* means both custom, and ethical norm. *Sittlichkeit* refers to the ethical norms, customs and institutions of a particular society. It was initially inspired by the ideal state described in Plato's *Republic* and was set against the individualist morality of modern times (*Moralität*) which Hegel associated primarily with Kant. In his 1802 *Essay on Natural Law* Hegel associated *Sittlichkeit* exclusively with the ancient *polis*. But from the end of his time at Jena Hegel came to believe that notions of *Sittlichkeit* could not only be associated with the modern political commuity, but all the more strongly since this community could now encompass within it subjectivity, individual moral judgement and the pursuit of particular ends which characterized Civil Society. See G. W. F. Hegel, *Elements of the Philosophy of Right* (Cambridge, 1991), §260, pp. 282–3.

[16] See Waszek, *The Scottish Enlightenment*, chapter 2; L. Dickey, *Hegel: Religion, Economics and the Politics of Spirit, 1770–1807* (Cambridge, 1987), pp. 192–204; K. Tribe, *Governing Economy. The Reformation of German Economic Discourse, 1750–1840* (Cambridge, 1988), chapters 6–8.

[17] Waszek, *The Scottish Enlightenment*, pp. 56–71; Dickey, *Hegel*, pp. 187–91.

reward. Everlastingly chained to a single little fragment of the Whole, man himself develops into nothing but a fragment; everlastingly in his ear the monotonous sound of the wheel that he turns, he never develops the harmony of his being, and instead of putting the stamp of humanity upon his own nature, he becomes nothing more than the imprint of his occupation or of his specialised knowledge.[18]

It was also from the writings of Ferguson, Schiller, and Montesquieu that in his essay on 'The positivity of the Christian Religion' the young Hegel drew his contrast between ancient and modern religion. The 'imaginative religion' of Greece and Rome was 'a religion for free peoples only', who 'obeyed laws laid down by themselves', 'obeyed men whom they had themselves appointed to office, waged wars on which they themselves decided . . . and sacrificed their lives by thousands for an end which was their own'. By contrast, 'the positive religion' of Christianity emerged in a world in which 'the picture of the state as a product of his own energies disappears from the citizen's soul'.[19] The ancient *polis* had been replaced by a Christianity which had itself become lifeless because based upon mindless obedience to external authority. This was the religious analogue of the devitalization of political and social life in eighteenth-century Germany. The Revolution in France had transformed it into an urgent political problem.

Few have gone as far as Lukács in associating Hegel with a secularized reading of religion in the 1790s. But it has not been uncommon to interpret the Hellenism of the young Hegel and his contemporaries as an anti-Christian position.[20] This reading again, however, appears mis-judged. The criticism was of Lutheran orthodoxy rather than of the Christian religion as such and it is best seen as an attempt to continue and extend the reformulation of Christian ethics and theology following the critique of orthodox Christianity initiated in the 1780s and 1790s by

---

[18] F. Schiller, *On the Aesthetic Education of Man in a Series of Letters*, ed. and trans. E. M. Wilkinson and L. A. Willoughby (Oxford, 1967), p. 35. On Ferguson's contrast between ancient and modern poetry see A. Ferguson, *An Essay on the History of Civil Society (1767)*, ed. D. Forbes (Edinburgh, 1966), p. 77. On the character of the modern division of labour, Ferguson wrote 'manufacturers . . . prosper most, where the mind is least consulted, and where the workshop may, without any great effort of imagination, be considered as an engine, the parts of which are men', ibid., p. 183.

[19] G. W. F. Hegel, *Early Theological Writings*, trans. T. M. Knox (Chicago, 1948), pp. 154, 156.

[20] See W. Kaufmann, 'The Young Hegel and Religion', in *Hegel*, ed. A. MacIntyre (New York, 1972), pp. 61–100; R. Plant, *Hegel* (London, 1973), p. 36. Charles Taylor adopts a somewhat equivocal position; he insists that Hegel never abandoned Christianity during the 1790s, but at the same time that he judged Christianity 'a failed religion' as against the harmonious 'expressivism' achieved by the religion of ancient Greece, C. Taylor, *Hegel* (Cambridge, 1975), pp. 51–64.

Lessing and Kant.[21] As Lawrence Dickey has recently argued, the civic dimensions of this reformulation can be seen as a new version of the hope of a re-collectivized Christian commonwealth espoused by pietist and radical undercurrents of the Lutheran tradition as 'the Second Reformation' or the third age of the spirit.[22]

Conjoined with this theological context of the 1790s was the impact of Schiller. For Schiller provided a way of coming to terms with the failure of the French Revolution and the promise of an alternative route by which its ideals might be realized. Thus, once the political expectations raised by the Revolution had subsided, hope focused upon the ultimate regeneration of ethics by means of an aesthetic education of the people. By aesthetic means, it was hoped, the moral insight of Kant's categorical imperative and the ethical redirection proposed in his *Religion within the Limits of Reason Alone* might be introduced into the lived realities of everyday existence.[23] What was envisaged was not political or economic revolution, but reform as the result of a change of sensibility, of a process of regeneration through a programme of *Bildung*.[24]

After 1798 Hegel increasingly distanced himself from this programme in its original form. His hopes of a *Volksreligion* based upon a Kantian notion of autonomy, yet at the same time intended to recapture the oneness of religion, politics and culture supposedly characteristic of the ancient world, came to seem increasingly unreal. First, by 1798 it had become clear that the abstract rationalistic moralism of this programme was incompatible with the possibility of substantive political community. Secondly, by 1803 or soon after, it had also become clear that any attempt to revive the political 'substantiality' of the ancient *polis* could only be achieved at the expense of the liberal freedoms which accompa-

---

[21] See in particular Lessing's distinction between 'the Christian religion' and 'the religion of Christ' and the historical progressive view of revelation in *Lessing's Theological Writings*, ed. H. Chadwick (London, 1956), pp. 82–99, 106. For Kant see I. Kant, *Religion within the Limits of Reason Alone*, ed. T. M. Greene and H. H. Hudson (New York, 1960).

[22] The notion of the three ages, that of the Father, of the Son, and of the Holy Ghost, went back to the twelfth-century prophecies of Joachim of Fiore. These were revived and given an *aufklärische* interpretation by Lessing in the 1770s and 1780s, with an announcement of the imminence of the third reign (*Reich*) in which virtuous behaviour would no longer be intermixed with hope of reward or fear of punishment in an afterlife. This conception played an important role in Kant's reformulation of ethics in *The Critique of Practical Reason*. The notion of a 'second Reformation' or *Lebensreformation* went back to the position adopted by radicals at the time of the Luthern Reformation. It was taken up by German pietists in the seventeenth and eighteenth centuries. The relationship between Wurttemberg pietism and Hegel's cultural and religious formation is traced in Dickey, *Hegel*, parts I and II.

[23] See anonymous (Hegel), 'The Oldest Systematic Programme of German Idealism', pp. 3–5.

[24] On the various meanings attached to *Bildung* during this period see R. Geuss, 'Kultur, Bildung, Geist', *History and Theory* 35 (1996), pp. 151–65.

nied modern life. If, therefore, a modern version of *Sittlichkeit* were to be possible, both strands of the original programme would have to be reconceived.

On the one hand, Hegel criticized Kantian moralism as the basis for political community not simply because of its asceticism, but also because of its attempt – in common with the rest of the modern tradition of natural law – to found the modern state upon the provisional and individualistic basis of contract. This provided the starting point of Hegel's criticism of modern theories of natural right, which he began to formulate from 1802.[25] On the other hand, after an attempt to theorize a modern version of the ancient *polis* at the beginning of his time in Jena, Hegel abandoned any idea of a return to the supposedly *immediate* unity between man and sensuous nature, citizen and *polis* of the ancients. As he wrote in the *Phenomenology*: 'reason *must* withdraw from this happy state; for the life of a free people is only in principle or immediately the *reality* of an ethical order'.[26] The higher condition, unknown to the Greeks, of subjective spiritual development required a separation and estrangement from the natural condition. The immediate oneness of man and community, expressed in the ancient world by art, was replaced in the modern world by a higher and mediated unity based upon the mutual recognition of subjectivities, implicit in civil society, manifest in the state, and articulated in philosophy.

What therefore needs stressing against the Lukácsian approach is that at no point was the object of Hegel's criticism the exchange economy itself. In his earliest writings in the 1790s, economic problems were effectively ignored. When they did become a focus of concern during his time in Frankfurt and Jena, it was as a reaction against the naiveté of his earlier moral asceticism. His attempt now was to devise a theory of political and moral community which both acknowledged the centrality of exchange as the basis of the collective interdependence of modern society and yet transcended its individualistic concerns and its apparent lack of moral content. Hegel's ambition was to construct a modern version of *Sittlichkeit*, not at variance with commercial society, but building upon it. This meant furnishing civil society with institutions which would diminish the impact of the instabilities of the economy and incline its members towards participation in the communal structures of collective political life. The project did not look to a society *beyond* exchange. If anything, its spirit was optimistically reformist.

[25] See G. W. F. Hegel, *Natural Law: The Scientific Ways of Treating Natural Law, its Place in Moral Philosophy, and its Relation to the Positive Sciences of Law*, trans. T. M. Knox (Philadelphia, Pa., 1975).

[26] G. W. F. Hegel, *Phenomenology of the Spirit*, trans. A. V. Miller (Oxford, 1977), p. 214.

II

Lukács's book was followed by a general revival of interest in Hegel's social and political thought and in the 1960s the grotesque polarities of Hegel interpretation began to soften. Hegel was no longer simply the lonely ancestor of Marx in the Communist world or the great if dissembling atheist, the prophet of existentialism and phenomenology in France. Nor conversely was he still so uniformly condemned as the cynical apologist of the Prussian *Machtstaat*, the champion of *Staatsrason* and forerunner of Treitschke.[27] Even in the English-speaking world he now began to be re-admitted to contemporary debate after a lengthy period of philosophical excommunication provoked by the rise of analytical philosophy, two world wars and the baleful influence of Karl Popper.[28]

But if the treatment of Hegel was now kinder, the conception of history which accompanied it too often remained stylized and schematic. The new picture of Hegel which took shape in the 1960s and 1970s was above all that of a *realist*. No longer the proto-Marxist critic of estrangement and exchange relations, he now became the prescient observer of the emergence of a modern economy and a shrewd analyst of its social problems and policy dilemmas. Little interest was taken in the political or philosophical considerations which might have prompted Hegel to distinguish between civil society and the state. Instead, the distinction tended to be taken for granted and Hegel's account saluted for its hard-headed attention to the trajectory of modern industrial society with its attendant problems of industrialization, commercial fluctuation, proletarianization and colonial expansion.

In some versions of this approach, that of Raymond Plant for example, Hegel was presented not only as a probing and prophetic critic of economic liberalism, but also as a pioneer of communitarian solutions to economic problems or even – with a suitable translation of terminology to fit modern conditions – a prophet of the twentieth-century welfare state.[29] Others, starting from similar assumptions, praised Hegel

---

[27] The association of Hegel with an apology for the authoritarianism of the Prussian state goes back to R. Haym, *Hegel und seine Zeit* (Berlin, 1857).

[28] The arraignment of Hegel with Plato and Marx as architects of totalitarianism occurs in K. Popper, *The Open Society and its Enemies* (London, 1945), chapter 12. For a clear and balanced acount of the revival of interest in Hegel among philosophers in the English-speaking world see S. B. Smith, *Hegel's Critique of Liberalism: Rights in Context* (Chicago, 1988), chapter 1 and *passim*.

[29] See in particular R. Plant, 'Hegel on Identity and Legitimation', in *The State and Civil Society. Studies in Hegel's Political Philosophy*, ed. Z. A. Pelczynski (Cambridge, 1984), pp. 227–44.

for precisely the opposite reason, namely his supposed acknowledgement of the intractability of the problems of civil society and his refusal to pretend that real solutions existed. According to Shlomo Avineri, for example, Hegel's discussion encompassed analyses of pauperization, social polarization, economic imperialism, and colonization. It enabled him to grasp, like few others, the predicaments of modern industrial society and the future course of nineteenth-century European history.[30]

Such approaches tended to be characterized by two weaknesses. The first was a tendency to overstate the novelty or modernity of Hegel's position by incorporating anachronistic presuppositions into his argument. The second, the result of a mistaken idea of Hegel as realist or sociological prophet, was a tendency to miss or misunderstand the normative components in Hegel's account of civil society.

On the first point, just as it has already been pointed out that Hegel was not the first German to read Steuart or Smith, so it ought to be emphasized just how dependent upon Steuart and Smith Hegel's economic discussion remained. There is little to suggest that he engaged in any systematic reading of political economy after Smith.[31] Most of his later examples could easily have been drawn from a diligent reading of the newspaper. Similarly, when placed in the context of the German discussion of economic and social issues in the 1780s and 1810s, it does not seem that there was anything especially original about the particular practical measures proposed in *The Philosophy of Right*. Hegel's depiction of the instability and fashion-prone character of capitalist markets added little to what had been written by Steuart and were considerably less detailed than those of his contemporary, the romantic reactionary Adam Müller.[32] Similarly, his remedies for commercial fluctuation and pauperization were considerably less original, certainly less drastic than those proposed by Fichte in his *Geschlossene Handelstaat* of 1805.[33]

Hegel was sympathetic to Steuart's belief that the commercial economy was not self-regulating, that it needed steering by 'the statesman'.[34] He also believed, although this is less explicitly stated in the published version of *The Philosophy of Right*, that civil society possessed an

---

[30] S. Avineri, *Hegel's Theory of the Modern State* (Cambridge, 1972), pp. 153–4.

[31] Hegel mentions Ricardo and Say in his account of the 'system of needs' but there is no evidence that he had read their works, see *Phil. R*, §189, p. 227.

[32] See A. H. Müller, 'Uber einem philosophischen Entwurf von Herrn Fichte, betitelt der geschlossene Handelsstaat', in *Adam Müllers vermischte Schriften über Staat, Philosophie und Kunst* (Vienna, 1812), vol. I, pp. 324–46; and 'Adam Smith' (1808), in *Adam Müller ausgewählte Abhandlungen*, ed. J. Baxa (Jena, 1931), pp. 76–81. See also T. Harada, *Politische Okonomie des Idealismus und der Romantik* (Berlin, 1989).

[33] See J. G. Fichte, 'Der geschlossene Handelsstaat: ein philosophischer Entwurf' (1800), in J. G. Fichte, *Sammtliche Werke* (Berlin, 1845), vol. I, pp. 387–513.

[34] *Phil. R*, §236, pp. 261–3.

obligation to provide work for all its members.[35] He connected this obligation with the impossibility of anticipating sudden changes in the character of distant markets.[36] But, as Rosenkranz originally noted, Hegel's acceptance of Steuart was qualified by his desire to combat 'what was dead' in 'the mercantile system'.[37] According to Waszek, Steuart, Smith and Hegel were broadly agreed that different forms of state intervention were legitimate in the case of market failure. The difference was that, while Smith believed that state intervention had usually proved counter-productive and should be avoided except in cases of acute distress, Steuart considered market failure an endemic feature of an exchange economy. He therefore argued for virtually constant state supervision and a high level of planning which ranged from price controls to a population policy aimed at maintaining full employment.[38]

Faced with these alternatives, Hegel stayed close to Smith. His overall concern was both to avoid *laissez-faire* as one doctrinaire extreme and at the same time to keep away from the constant petty surveillance of everyday life which he associated with Fichte's state.[39] As he remarked in *The Philosophy of Right*:

The individual must certainly have a right to earn his living in this way or that, but on the other hand, the public also has a right to expect that necessary tasks

---

[35] Understanding of Hegel's *Philosophy of Right*, indeed of his political philosophy as a whole, has been transformed since the 1960s by the publication of the lecture notes of students who attended Hegel's lecture courses on the Philosophy of Right. In 1973–4 K.-H. Ilting published *Vorlesungen über Rechtsphilosophie 1818–1831* in four volumes (henceforward *VRP*). The most important of these sets of lecture-notes, published for the first time, are found in volumes III and IV. Volume III contains the transcription by H. G. Hotho of the lecture course 'Philosophie des Rechts' as delivered by Hegel in Berlin in the winter of 1822–3. Volume IV contains the transcription by K. G. Griesheim of the course delivered in the winter of 1824–5. These notes reveal that Hegel elaborated considerably upon the main text of the published lectures. As they make clear he was less politically guarded and more straightforwardly liberal in the lecture-hall than he was in the published version of the course, more detailed in his analysis of the economic and social problems of civil society, more explicit in his policy recommendations, and more prepared to illustrate his argument with extensive and topical empirical examples. The suggestion that members of civil society possessed a right to work occurs in the Hotho transcription of 1822–3: 'the individual must have the right to earn his livelihood in this way or that and this must be arranged according to the needs of consumers', *VRP*, vol. III, pp. 695–6.

[36] 'But the main reason why some universal provision and direction are necessary is that large branches of industry are dependent on external circumstances and remote combinations whose full implications cannot be grasped by the individuals who are tied to these spheres by their occupations', *Phil.R*, §236, p. 262.

[37] Rosenkranz, *Hegels Leben*, p. 86.

[38] Waszek, *The Scottish Enlightenment*, pp. 186–8.

[39] See Hegel's attack on Fichte's suggestions for passport regulations, *Phil.R*, 'Preface', p. 21 and see also *VRP*, vol. IV, p. 617, where Hegel complains that 'Fichte's whole state is police'.

will be performed in the proper manner. Both viewpoints must be satisfied, and the freedom of trade should not be such as to prejudice the general good.[40]

Pragmatic criteria were to be applied in relation to state intervention and the solutions envisaged ranged from public works programmes and progressive taxation to reform of the Poor Law and colonization.[41] In sum, however, these were remedies which did not differ radically from the spectrum of proposals practised or advocated within the policy-making circles of the better-run German states in the first two decades of the nineteenth century.[42]

In his broader picture of the social and cultural problems created by the modern economy, again Hegel relied heavily on Smith. Like Smith, in his description of the effects of the divisions of labour upon the condition of the labourer, Hegel highlighted the stupefying effect (*Verstumpfen*) of the specialized, mechanical, and repetitive tasks found in modern manufacture. Work became duller and more one-sided, making the operative ever more dependent on one narrow occupation.[43] But in this instance Hegel was more sanguine than Smith since he believed that with further mechanization the problem would resolve itself. In *The Philosophy of Right* he simply noted that, 'the abstraction of production makes work increasingly *mechanical*, so that the human being is eventually able to step aside and let a *machine* take his place'.[44] But in the 1822–3 version of the lectures, referring to England where machines had been destroyed by 'breadless workers' (presumably the Luddites) he commented, 'men can be occupied in something better than work which machines are capable of performing'.[45] Earlier in Heidelberg in 1817, his optimism had been explicit: 'but once factory work has reached a certain degree of perfection, of simplification, mechanical human labour can be replaced by the

[40] *Phil. R*, §236, pp. 262–3.
[41] One should be wary about the implication that Hegel's discussion of 'systematic colonisation' (*Phil. R*, §248, p. 269) looks forward to post-1870 conceptions of imperialism. The terms of Hegel's argument in favour of colonies mainly look back to Steuart (see Waszek, *The Scottish Enlightenment*, p. 203), but they are off-set by the observation that 'the liberation of colonies itself proves to be the greatest advantage to the mother state', *Phil. R*, §248, p. 269. This view was based on the often-noted development of British industry and trade *after* American independence, and by 1820 it had become the political and economic commonplace.
[42] For a general discussion see Tribe, *Governing Economy*. Raymond Plant elsewhere has noted how far Steuart was influenced by the cameralist tradition, epecially Justi. See R. Plant, 'Hegel and Political Economy', *New Left Review*, 103 (1977), p. 85.
[43] See *VRP*, vol. IV, pp. 502–3. Hegel associated this work especially with factories. By this he meant large manufactories similar to the 'pin factory' described by Adam Smith. He is not referring to the steam-powered factories of the later nineteenth century. But he was not unaware of the direction of later develoment; he says 'the spiritual result is that man allows machines, weaponry, steam, furnaces etc. to step into his place and simply superintends them', ibid., p. 503.
[44] *Phil. R*, §198, p. 233.   [45] *VRP*, vol. III, p. 613.

work of machines, and this is what usually comes about in factories. In this way, through the consummation of this mechanical progress, human freedom is restored.'[46] As for the recurrent threat of unemployment accompanying industrial progress, Hegel in most of his comments does not appear to have regarded this as an intractable problem. His standpoint was that of matter-of-fact prudence: 'the workers, particularly the factory workers, who are deprived of their subsistence by machines, quickly become discontented and new positions must be opened to them'.[47]

It is particularly among those who have treated Hegel's 'civil society' as if it were simply the description of a newly emerging socio-economic reality that there has been a tendency to conjoin discussion of these problems of commercial society with that of the creation of 'the rabble' (*das Pöbel*), as if the 'rabble' were no more than an archaic term for the 'proletariat' and were the inevitable product of the system of needs.[48] Much of the bleakness and hopelessness attributed to Hegel's picture of civil society by modern commentary is the result of running these two accounts together. This line of interpretation began with the pioneering study of Joachim Ritter at the end of the 1950s and it set the tone of much subsequent commentary.

In Ritter's interpretation, the appearance of 'the rabble' was seen as a synonym for the process of proletarianization and treated as part of a single transformation in which 'industrial, civil, class society' became 'a world society'. In this scenario, society was seen as identical with 'the system of needs' and the division of labour became 'the sole constitutive principle of society'. This division of labour allegedly produced a separation of the means of labour from labouring individuals and thus led to the formation of a class society and a polarization between increasing wealth and increasing poverty. As a result, large numbers fell beneath a certain level of subsistence and formed a rabble, which confronted the propertied class 'without mediation'. Further on, impelled by 'the law of rising production' and in a vain attempt to avert this process, civil society was forced to seek new consumers for the 'goods it has overproduced'. It embarked upon the road to colonization and so became global.[49]

---

[46] G. W. F. Hegel, *Lectures on Natural Right and Political Science: The First Philosophy of Right (Heidelberg 1817–1818)*, trans. J. M. Stewart and P. C. Hodgson (Berkeley, Calif., 1995 (henceforward *Phil.R* (Heidelberg)), p. 177.

[47] *VRP*, vol. IV, p. 503.

[48] Hegel's discussion of the 'rabble' as found in *Phil.R*, §243–5, pp. 266–7.

[49] See J. Ritter, *Hegel and the French Revolution*, trans. R. D. Winfield (Boston Mass., 1984), p. 71.

Was this really what Hegel believed? The lack of any specific geo-graphic referent in his discussion of the expansion of population and industry in paragraph 243 of *The Philosophy of Right* and in his initial statements in paragraphs 244–6 form the basis of such an interpretation. What this reading neglects, however, is the conditional clause which inaugurates the discussion: 'if (*wenn*) the activity of civil society is unrest-ricted . . .'.[50] Furthermore, the examples given in the additional para-graphs (*Zusätze*), the pauper populations in England and Scotland and the *lazzaroni* of Naples, hardly suggest that what Hegel is offering in paragraphs 243–8 is an analysis of what Karl-Heinz Ilting entitles 'the dialectic of modern industrial society'.[51] A major weakness of this 'modern-industrial-society' approach is that it does not distinguish between questions of structure and questions of ethos and that it incorporates the latter within the former as its supposed ideological reflection. Thus the creation of the 'rabble' becomes the unavoidable cost of satisfying the needs of *homo economicus*.

Such a resolutely modernist reading also highlights the second major weakness of this form of interpretation. For what is obscured by the rendering of these passages in quasi-Weberian or neo-Marxian terms is the normative intention behind Hegel's treatment of civil society. The connection between the analysis of 'the system of needs' in the first section of the chapter and the proposals put forward in the second and third sections – on 'The Administration of Justice' and on 'The Police and the Corporation' – become difficult to follow. Yet these connections are crucial. For the continuous process of exchange depicted in the first section is made possible by a legal framework which protects property and person in the second section, and now in the modern world has to be supplemented by the forms of welfare and security outlined in the third section. As Hegel put it, it was not enough that 'the *undisturbed security* of *persons* and *property* should be guaranteed', it was also necessary that 'the livelihood and welfare of individuals should be *secured* – i.e. that *particular welfare* should be *treated as a right* and duly *actualised*'.[52] Hegel was arguing that, just as a legal system had helped to stabilize – and civilize – the relationship between state and household in antiquity, so now in civil society new laws and institutions must provide an ethical framework within which the creative energies of free individuals would be cultivated and their destructive effects diminished.

In the ancient world, according to Hegel, 'the proper beginning and original foundation of states' had rightly been equated with 'the intro-

---

[50] *Phil. R*, §243, p. 266.
[51] *VRP*, vol. IV, p. 607.   [52] *Phil. R*, §230, p. 260.

duction of *agriculture* and of *marriage*. Agriculture meant the end of savagery and the nomadic life, the introduction of 'exclusive private property' and civil law. The institution of the marriage bond meant that need came to mean *care for the family* and possession of *family property*; henceforth, the family was 'the primary basis of the state'.[53] But the institutions of antiquity were no longer sufficient to contain the pressures of the modern world. Since the end of antiquity, the spread of Christianity, the development of law, and the elaboration of 'the system of needs' had each in different ways nurtured the growth of what Hegel called 'subjective particularity': the unmediated relationship of the individual to God, freedom of individual judgement, subjectivity, the self-interested pursuit of particular goals, individualism. This was a principle to which the ancient *polis* could assign no legitimate place.

Conversely, it was the ability of the modern state to incorporate subjective freedom within a political community which in Hegel's view constituted its great strength.[54] The theorization of this new reality produced two conceptual innovations within Hegel's political philosophy. Firstly, the higher spheres of art, religion, and philosophy, 'absolute spirit', were seen to transcend the boundaries of the state, of 'objective spirit' and could no longer be discussed within its confines. Secondly, within the sphere of 'objective spirit', Hegel introduced the idea of civil society as a new space which had opened up between the family and the formal constitution of the state. This was the sphere in which subjective freedom could flourish. 'The concrete person who, as a *particular* person, as a totality of needs and a mixture of natural necessity and arbitrariness, is his end, is one *principle* of civil society.'[55]

In civil society, unlike Plato's *Republic* or the contemporary Orient, individuals could no longer be ascribed occupations according to lineage or political fiat. The positions occupied by individuals were now the result of chance and subjective choice and they were unavoidably accompanied by a degree of inequality, which Hegel considered inseparable from the new-found freedoms and opportunities which civil society offered. As he put it in the Griesheim version of the lectures:

here man must show what he is, he is upon a stage where he must produce everything, in part through imitation, in part forced by need to exert all the strengths that are in him. Man as man, therefore as particular individual must come into existence and must become actual; this belongs by right to subjective freedom, a freedom which we value very highly especially in modern times, where each can still make himself into that which he feels to be his vocation.[56]

---

53 Ibid., §§201, 203, pp. 234–5.   54 Ibid., §260, p. 282.
55 Ibid., §182, p. 220.   56 *VRP*, vol. IV, p. 509.

How then was this new space of subjective freedom and the pursuit of individual ends to be reconciled with the supra-individual values which, according to Hegel, informed both the family and the political community as a whole? Hegel's answer was that civil society itself presupposed institutions which went beyond individual goals. These institutions, however, must be reinforced and accorded legal existence if civil society were to be governed by appropriate ethical norms and its divisive tendencies averted. Firstly, as Hegel stressed, for all the supposed arbitrariness of the desire of self-oriented individuals to satisfy an infinite variety of particular needs, civil society was not as atomistic as it first seemed. Its activities presupposed a system of reciprocal interdependence whose pattern had been discerned by political economists.[57]

Indeed, unconscious and unintended though it may have been, this pattern also possessed a real, if perverse ethical significance, already dramatized by Mandeville in his notorious coupling of private vice and public virtue in *The Fable of the Bees*. In his chapter on civil society, Hegel treated this fable as the first stage of a journey starting from the naked particularity of individual goals within 'the system of needs' and ending at the point at which 'the *ethical returns* to civil society as an immanent principle' in the form of 'the corporation'. The moral of this story was that 'in the very act of developing itself independently to totality, the principle of particularity passes over into universality, and only in the latter does it have its truth and its right to positive actuality'.[58] Or put more concretely:

in civil society, each individual is his own end, and all else means nothing to him. But he cannot accomplish the full extent of his ends without reference to others; these others are therefore means to the end of the particular (person). But through its reference to others, the particular end takes on the form of universality, and gains satisfaction by simultaneously satisfying the welfare of others.[59]

Provision for 'the welfare of others' was ensured by the administration of justice, the police, and the corporation. As in antiquity, what mattered was the presence of an appropriate legal-institutional framework, insuring the transfer or reallocation of resources when the need arose. In the ancient world, private property and marriage had refined and enlarged the notion of 'need'. Welfare, therefore, like all forms of labouring and domestic activity (that which was the preserve of the *oikos*) had become the preserve of the family. In the modern world, however, the family was ceasing to perform these functions. It was no longer in a position to

---

[57] *Phil. R*, §189, pp. 227–8.
[58] Ibid., §186, p. 223.   [59] Ibid., §182, p. 220.

provide the capital and skill which could secure the livelihood of the individual or supply the requisite resources in the case of incapacity; it was now 'subordinate'. Conversely, civil society had become 'the immense power which draws people to itself and requires them, to owe everything to it, and to do everything by its means'. Not only did it tear 'the individual away from family ties', but 'it substitutes its own soil for the external inorganic nature and paternal soil from which the individual gained his livelihood and subjects the existence of the whole family itself to dependence on civil society and to contingency'. Such was the extent to which functions had been transferred that the individual had now become 'a son of civil society'.[60]

This idea of civil society as a new 'universal family' in place of the former household organization of welfare, was not merely a metaphor. It meant 'that if a human being is to be a member of civil society, he has rights and claims in relation to it, just as he had in relation to his family' and conversely that 'the individual owes a duty to the rights of civil society'. In practice, this now empowered the state to take over the education of children when parents failed in this duty and to protect the individual 'against himself' in cases of penury.[61] Similarly, the elaboration of this quasi-familial approach was of particular importance in the way in which civil society dealt with poverty and impoverishment.

If the poor in modern times possessed a right to relief, it was not only because in general 'individuals have a right to the earth' because 'they have a right to live'. It was also because they lacked further access to the possession of landed property. As Hegel stated in the original Heidelberg version of the lectures, 'for individuals the general resources belonging to society constitute the aspect of inorganic nature, which has to present itself to them in such a way that they can take possession of it. For the whole earth is occupied, and they have in consequence to rely on civil society.'[62] Furthermore this claim was strongly reinforced by the more volatile conditions of civil society and the arbitrary changes it wrought in the fortunes of individuals. Such persons, reduced to poverty by contingency, now lacked the 'natural' means of acquiring property and were at the same time increasingly deprived of a material claim upon their kin. Therefore, for the poor it was essential that 'the universal authority' take over the role of the family.[63]

These welfare functions of civil society at large were discharged by 'the police', who were responsible for 'the actualisation and preservation of the universal which is contained within the particularity of civil society'.

---

[60] Ibid., §238, p. 263.   [61] Ibid., §239, 240, p. 264.
[62] *Phil. R* (Heidelberg), §118, p. 209.   [63] *Phil. R*, §241, p. 265.

But the role played by the police in preserving this universal was more residual than ideal. The guidance the police provided was that of an *'external order and arrangement'*. The true mode by which *the ethical* returned to civil society as an 'immanent principle' was that of the 'corporation'.[64]

The weakness of a descriptive-realist interpretation of Hegel's account of civil society is highlighted by the seminal role assigned to 'corporations' in the modern world. For Hegel, 'the corporation' would act as a basic civic unit knitting together the multifarious concerns of civil society and binding them through representation in an estates' assembly to the deliberative and executive functions of the state. Formed from every trade and profession, these corporations would remain under 'the higher supervision of the state'. They would act as legally recognized professional associations with powers to determine the recruitment of new entrants, to enforce standards of work, and to organize the welfare of their members.[65] Unlike the familial role of 'civil society in general', which, as Hegel conceded, remained 'more indeterminate' and 'more remote from individuals and their particular requirements', the corporation truly possessed 'the right to assume the role of a *second* family for its members'.[66] Indeed, Hegel claimed that 'as a guarantor of resources, the institution of the corporation corresponds to the introduction of agriculture and private property' in antiquity, with comparable ethical effect. For just as then, 'need' and 'possession' had been incorporated within the sphere of the family, so now the role of intermediate institutions within civil society would be to replace the destructive association of prestige with the unending accumulation of individual wealth by more civic and social forms of recognition and self-fulfilment.

Outside the membership of 'a legally recognized corporation', according to Hegel, isolation would reduce the individual to 'the selfish aspect of his trade'; his 'livelihood and satisfaction' would lack *'stability'*; 'he will accordingly try to gain *recognition* through the external manifestations of success in his trade, and these are without limit, because it is impossible for him to live in a way appropriate to his estate, if his estate does not exist'. Conversely, within the corporation, livelihood and capability would be 'recognized', the individual would be 'somebody' and would have *'his honour in his estate'*. Within the corporation, impoverishment would also be easier to bear: 'the help which poverty receives loses its contingent and unjustly humiliating character, and wealth, in fulfilling the duty it owes to its association, loses the ability to provoke arrogance

[64] Ibid., §249, pp. 269–70.   [65] Ibid., §255, p. 273.
[66] Ibid., §252, p. 271.

in its possessor and envy in others'.[67] Thus for Hegel, if *'family'* was the first *ethical* root of the state, 'the *corporation'* was the second. 'The sanctity of marriage and the honour attaching to the corporation' were 'the two moments round which the disorganisation of civil society revolves'.[68]

The strangeness of this account of the corporation passes unremarked in all those commentaries which wish to stress Hegel's awareness of 'the nature of modern society'. For the fact was the 'corporations', as Hegel described them, did not even compose an inchoate part of an emerging system of modern social and political forms. They neither existed, nor were they to come into existence. They could not even be accorded some form of ideal-typical existence as a concentrate of what empirically was only to be found in a fragmented or amorphous state. The recent historical record gave no support to such a construct. The abolition of guilds and professional associations by the Chapelier law of 1792 was thought by many to be at the core of the French Revolution, just as it had been at the heart of the pre-revolutionary programme of reform championed by Turgot and Condorcet, and it was reiterated under the Directorate. Similarly in Britain, Adam Smith's condemnation of guilds and state-maintained apprenticeship regulation in *The Wealth of Nations* had been unambiguous. Smith's advocacy of universal education had been in part a replacement for an officially sanctioned apprenticeship system which, as well as constricting the mental horizons of operatives, trapped them all too effectively within the confines of the existing division of labour.[69] On the other side of the argument were various areas of the German confederation in which local guild monopolies still held sway. But there was nothing either in the short or medium term to suggest that the beleaguered associations of *Handwerker* of Vormärz Germany were likely to accept, let alone encourage the transformation of their organizations into liberal professional bodies. It is true that some of the liberal Prussian reformers, notably Von Humboldt and Chancellor Hardenberg, also promoted a revamped social and political role for 'corporations' in schemes of national representation in the 1810s. But such proposals never got beyond the drawing board. However it is to be explained, Hegel's argument about corporations must be seen not only as removed from the future, but also as substantially out of step with contemporary historical reality, and, even worse from a Hegelian standpoint, guilty of proposing in its place an 'abstract' and insubstantial 'ought'.

---

[67] Ibid., §253, p. 272.   [68] Ibid., §255, pp. 272–3.
[69] See A. Smith (ed.), *The Wealth of Nations*, (Oxford, 1976), vol. I, vii, 28; vol. I, x, 5, 16, 17, 42; and E. Rothschild, 'Adam Smith, Apprenticeship and Insecurity', Centre for History and Economics Discussion Paper, July 1994, pp. 1–48.

Finally, when examined more closely, it can be seen that Hegel's discussion of the creation of a 'rabble' (*das Pöbel*), far from pointing forward to the emerging contours of 'industrial society', forms part of the same normative construction of the transition from 'civil society' to 'the state'. Unlike the later Marxian proletariat whose formation was the inescapable outcome of capitalist development, there was nothing inevitable about the appearance of 'the rabble'. Indeed much of the discussion of the issue in *The Philosophy of Right* concerned 'the need to prevent a rabble from emerging'.[70] Furthermore, although 'the increasingly mechanical nature of work' figured among the causes of its appearance, what preoccupied Hegel was its 'ethical basis'. One major test of the rightness and effectiveness of the quasi-familial role assigned to corporations and the police in Hegel's vision of civil society would be their capacity to prevent the rabble's emergence. Hegel was clear that 'poverty in itself does not reduce people to a rabble'. The 'ethical basis' of such a creation was the polarization between wealth and poverty which occurred in societies without corporations and estates. Such circumstances produced 'a disposition', 'an inward rebellion against the rich, against society, the government etc.'.[71] It was in countries where the absence of corporations meant that the potentially endless pursuit of individual gain was unchecked by 'the honour of belonging to an estate' that complaints were heard 'about that luxury and love of extravagance' of the business (*gewerbetreibenden*) classes, which is associated with the 'creation of a rabble'.[72]

Above all, this was an argument about England. Hegel found it necessary to counter the English-based claims that 'with freedom of enterprise, business-life flourishes'[73] or more specifically that 'industry flourished better after the removal of corporations'. 'Experience tells us the contrary', Hegel insisted. The example of England should not be used since 'unlike every other people, England has the whole world as its market'. Equally, however, it possessed 'the most monstrous poverty and rabbledom (*Pöbelhaftigkeit*) and a large part of this sickness is to be attributed to the removal of the corporations'.[74] While people complained about the way in which the old guilds abused the monopoly position, both in England and in France freedom of enterprise had

[70] *Phil.R*, §240, p. 264.   [71] Ibid., §244, p. 266.

[72] Ibid., §253, pp. 271–2. Here I have dissented from H. B. Nisbet's otherwise excellent translation. The rendering of '*gewerbetreibenden*' as 'professional' seems to me misleading; I prefer Knox's rendering as 'the business classes', see *G. W. F. Hegel The Philosophy of Right*, ed. and trans. T. M. Knox (Oxford: The Clarendon Press, 1952), p. 153.

[73] *VRP*, vol. IV, p. 625.   [74] Ibid., III, p. 711.

produced a worse situation.[75] 'In England large capitalists so oppress the others' that whole branches of industry came into the hands of a few, who possessed no authorized monopoly, only that bestowed by their large capital 'and this is the worst of all monopolies'.[76]

The consequence of this polarization in England between the rich few and the impoverished many was the growth of a poor-rate amounting annually to nine or ten million pounds, 'far more than the whole state revenue of Prussia'. The creation of this rabble was frightening: it was 'the diseased part of an England, which is otherwise so flourishing'.[77] In particular, those receiving relief were supported without having to work in return, a fact contrary 'to the principle of civil society and the feeling of self-sufficiency and honour among its individual members'. But the alternative of making them work would only exacerbate the problem of overproduction and unemployment, which had led to the demand for relief in the first place. These, then, were 'the results achieved by poor-rates, boundless donations, and equally limitless charity, and above all by the abolition (*Aufhebung*) of the corporations'.[78]

Hegel's anxiety about the *Pöbel*, therefore, is not easily transformed into a prescience about industrialization and an emergent 'proletariat' as a universal phenomenon represented by England. But nor, on the other hand, does it appear that Hegel was basing himself upon empirical observation of the conditions of the Germanic Confederation of his day. There are no first-hand references to the situation in Wurttemburg, the Palatinate, or Prussia. Nor is there a general discussion of the economic problems of post-war Central Europe. Social historians have argued that in the German-speaking lands from the end of the eighteenth century, those traditionally referred to as the *Pöbel* – the mockingly entitled *ordo plebeius* or social stratum beneath the small-holding peasantry in the countryside and the artisanate in the towns – began to grow disproportionately in numbers and broke out from their traditional confines and restrictions.[79] It was anxiety about the growth of this impoverished population beneath estate society that led the more conservative German

---

[75] On France Hegel reported in 1822–3: 'some years ago the French Ministry for the progress of industry conducted an enquiry. The Chambers of Commerce answered that trade flourished to a greater extent since the abolition of corporations. But trade has an ulterior motive and does better the more miserable the working class is and therefore the cheaper it works so that the merchant can purchase more cheaply. But forms of work in enterprises since the abolition of corporations had become worse', *VRP*, vol. III, p. 712.

[76] Ibid., vol. IV, pp. 626–7.

[77] Ibid., vol. III, p. 704.   [78] *Phil.R*, §245, p. 267.

[79] See W. Conze, 'Vom "Pöbel" zum "Proletariat". Sozialgeschichtliche Voraussetzungen für das Sozialismus in Deutschland', in *Moderne deutsche Sozialgeschichte*, ed. H. U. Wehler (Cologne, 1973), pp. 111–37, at pp. 113–14.

states to impose restrictions upon marriage and immigration in the first decades of the nineteenth century.

Hegel was certainly aware of these developments, but he made no specific reference to those symptoms of the expansion of the *Pöbel* – rising population, peasant emancipation or pressure on employment among *Handwerker* – which would be vigorously discussed in the debate about 'pauperism' in the 1830s and 1840s.[80] Instead, all the examples which Hegel chose to illustrate the problems of the *Pöbel* appeared to have been drawn from abroad. In particular, he dwelt upon two sources: first, the debate about the reform of the Poor Law in England and Scotland; secondly, reports of the frightening contrast between luxury and squalor in great cities, above all London.[81]

In effect, Hegel's *Pöbel* was introduced, not as the victim of economic and social change, but rather as the penalty for the dismantling of the moral and juridical framework necessary to civil society. Indeed, in both instances, the case Hegel attempted to argue was ethical rather than economic. On pauperism, Hegel was concerned to demonstrate the loss of integrity that accompanied the provision of relief without work. On the moral dangers of the great city, London could be used as the most powerful symbol of those myriad juxtapositions of luxury, corruption, and misery which so preoccupied European observers of metropolitan life in the first half of the nineteenth century.

'In this infinitely rich town', he wrote, 'the poverty is so horribly vast that we can scarcely have any conception of it'.[82] This was a continuation of what he had argued in the first version of these lectures ten years before in Heidelberg in 1817. There it had been argued that the possibility of earning a living among a numerous and wealthy population drew many people into the capital city – once again, the example was London – 'but for the individual this possibility is a matter of chance, and the rabble increases with leaps and bounds along with poverty'.[83] Thus, if Hegel's picture of the *Pöbel* looks forward at all, it is not to the Manchester of Frederick Engels's *Condition of the Working Class in*

---

[80] See S. Mayer, 'Die Anfänge des politischen Radikalismus im vormärzlichen Preussen', in S. Mayer, *Radikalismus, Sozialismus und bürgerliche Demokratie* (Frankfurt, 1969), pp. 7–108; R. Bocj, *Grenzenloses Wachstum? Das rheinische Wirtschaftsbürgertum und seine Industrialisierungsdebatte 1814–1857* (Göttingen, 1990).

[81] On Hegel's reading of English sources see M. J. Petry, 'Hegel and the *Morning Chronicle*', *Hegel-Studien*, 11 (1976), pp. 11–80; M. J. Petry, 'Propaganda and Analysis. The Background to Hegel's Article on the English Reform Bill', in *State and Civil Society*, ed. Pelczynski, pp. 137–59; *Hegel's Political Writings*, ed. Knox and Pelczynski, pp. 295–330; N. Waszek, 'Hegels Exzerpte aus der *Edinburgh Review*', *Hegel-Studien*, 20 (1985), pp. 79–111; N. Waszek, 'Hegels Exzerpte aux der *Quarterly Review*', *Hegel-Studien*, 21 (1986), pp. 9–25.

[82] *VRP*, vol. IV, p. 494.   [83] *Phil. R* (Heidelberg), §118, p. 211.

England nor to the 'Coketown' of Charles Dickens's *Hard Times* but rather to Eugene Sue's *Mysteries of Paris* or Henry Mayhew's *London Labour and the London Poor*.

Hegel was an anxious and generally well-informed follower of the postwar debate about the Poor Law both because it highlighted the dangers of accepting the ethos of *laissez faire* and because it could be employed as a negative example to set beside his own emphasis upon a political system built upon corporations and estates. But neither his depiction of 'the rabble', nor his suggestions for handling the problem of poverty demonstrate a discernible awareness of the magnitude of the difficulty that the *Unterschichten* would soon pose for his political philosophy. That difficulty was not so much the economic problem of novel and destabilizing forms of poverty, but the political problem posed by the exclusion of a growing segment of the population from participation in the structures and institutions of political life. It is characteristic of Hegel's cautious and conservative approach in this area that he did not seek to consider how this 'rabble' might be included within corporations. Yet corporations, as has been seen, were to be *both* the surrogate in the modern economic and social domain for the functions once played by the family *and* the means by which members of civil society would be politically represented.[84]

The first serious attempts to confront the problem of 'the proletariat' from a Hegelian perspective unsurprisingly discarded Hegel's own discussion of 'the social question' as unusably archaic. Only a year after his death, Hegel's colleague Edouard Gans in 1832–3 spoke of the necessary organization of 'civil society' according to the mechanism of laws of political economy, which created the division between the wealthy and those whose unsecured existence consigned them to the 'rabble'. The validity of the idea of 'civil society' depended upon the overcoming of this 'fact'.[85] Gans also wholly eliminated the corporations' role in political representation. A decade later, the most ambitious quasi-Hegelian discussion of 'the social question' apart from Marx, that of Lorenz von Stein, involved serious consideration of universal male suffrage, a solution which in Hegel's eyes was unthinkable.[86] Hegel's theory simply

---

[84] *Phil.R*, §252, p. 271.
[85] Riedel, 'Gesellschaft, bürgerliche', p. 782.
[86] See L. von Stein, *Der Sozialismus und Communismus des heutigen Frankreichs*, 2 vols. (Leipzig, 1848), vol. I, pp. 34–5, 151–4, 180–1. Stein shared none of Hegel's optimism about the role of corporations. In his view, once birth was replaced by property as the main qualification for political participation – as consequence of the principle of civil equality established by the French Revolution – a struggle between the propertied and the propertyless for the possession of the state became unavoidable. His main solution to the 'social question' was the existence of monarchy as the embodiment of the state above the struggles between classes in society, ibid., pp. 50–63.

did not anticipate what contemporaries would call 'the social question'. It is clear from his apparent exclusion of mere day labourers from corporations that the institutions which Hegel devised to mediate the otherwise depersonalized relationship between the individual and the state still presupposed a stable social and occupational geography of professional associations and artisanal guilds connected to the state through a renovated system of estates. This was a system in which the emergent 'proletariat' could have no place.

7 Civil society and the Marxist tradition

Joseph Femia

If the idea of civil society generates confusion, the Marxist tradition must bear part of the blame. To put this observation in context, it would be helpful to look briefly at how the idea evolved. Civil society (from the Latin *societas civilis*) entered European discourse in the fifteenth century. Contrary to modern use, it did not denote a natural, or pre-state, type of society. Indeed, it was counterposed to such natural groupings as the conjugal and the paternal. Rather, it referred to the condition of living in a civilized political community sufficiently advanced to include urban life, formal legal codes, and other cultural refinements. In its original form, then, civil society was not identified with social or economic arrangements and practices *apart from* the state; on the contrary, it was synonymous with political society – understood as an artificial contrivance of free individuals.

Crucial to the development of the concept was the onset of modernity. Customary models of authority were progressively undermined by the commercialization of land, labour, and capital; by the growth of the market economy; by great scientific discoveries, such as the Copernican system; and by the Protestant Reformation, which destroyed the corporate unity of the Catholic *ecumene*. The break with past traditions and customs, as the binding forces of society, engendered the search for new principles of moral unity. Because of the detachment of individual human beings from their defining social matrix, from the primordial givens of existence – kith, kin, membership in the Universal Church – there emerged a tendency to conceive people in terms of their humanity alone. In Hegel's words, 'the ego comes to be apprehended as a universal person in which all are identical'.[1] On the level of political theory, this focus on equal and autonomous individuals manifested itself in the idea of the 'contract' as the basis of political authority. Listen to Locke:

Where-ever . . . any number of Men are so united into one Society, as to quit

---

[1] G. W. F. Hegel, *The Philosophy of Right* (1821), ed. and trans. T. M. Knox (Oxford: The Clarendon Press, 1952), para. 209, p. 134.

every one his Executive Power of the Law of Nature, and to resign it to the publick, there and there only is a *Political, or Civil* Society. And this is done where-ever any number of Men, in the state of Nature, enter into Society to make one People, one Body Politik under one Supreme Government.[2]

Civil society is the realm of political association instituted among men when they take leave of the 'state of nature' and enter into a commonwealth. Civil society is therefore coterminous with political society; there does not yet exist that differentiation of civil society from the state which we find in later usage. The relevant antithesis was still 'nature/civilization'. But unlike Hobbes, who also posited the transformation of *status naturalis* into a civilized order, Locke claimed that the natural state was not an asocial state, i.e. a condition of perpetual war, but an embryonic form of the social state, where human relations were governed by natural laws, and where an exchange economy rooted in property rights managed to function, if imperfectly. Men leave the state of nature because of its 'inconveniences' rather than its savageries.[3] Thus Locke's 'state of nature' closely resembles what we, in modern parlance, call 'civil society': the totality of private and particular interests and relationships. Still, terminology matters: it was Hegel who introduced the distinction between 'state' and 'civil society', and it is to him that we now turn.

Civil society in Hegel

The core of his political philosophy is to be found in *The Philosophy of Right*, published in 1821. There Hegel explains how 'man' can attain freedom ('the worthiest and holiest thing in man')[4] through the 'transition from an ethical substantiality which is immediate and natural to the one which is intellectual and so both infinitely subjective and lofty enough to have attained universality of form'.[5] The highest stage of this mediation is 'ethical life', which is divided into three moments, whose combination encompasses the multi-faceted nature of human institutions. They are the family (ethical life 'in its natural or immediate phase'),[6] civil society (ethical life 'in its division and appearance'),[7] and the state ('freedom universal and objective').[8] Each of these is a network of human relationships organized according to a different principle, and it is the dialectical interaction among the three moments which enables us to

---

[2] J. Locke, *Two Treatises of Government* (New York: Mentor, 1965), citation from *Second Treatise*, p. 368.

[3] Ibid., p. 316.

[4] *The Philosophy of Right*, addition to para. 215, p. 273.

[5] Ibid., para. 187, p. 125.   [6] Ibid., para. 157, p. 110.

[7] Ibid., para. 33, p. 36.   [8] Ibid.

realize the freedom implicit in the human spirit. In other words, we do, and should, relate to each other in all three of the following modes: (a) particular altruism (b) universal egoism, and (c) universal altruism.

How, then, does Hegel define 'civil society', the sphere of universal egoism? It is, in brief, the specific arena of economic activity, based on property exchange, where – in Hegelian terms – particular individuals develop their self-consciousness and set forth their claims for want-satisfaction and personal autonomy. To Hegel, the creation of civil society, by fostering self-subsistent individuality, is a great 'achievement of the modern world'.[9] In ancient times, by contrast, 'subjective particularity was not incorporated into the organisation of society as a whole'.[10] While individuals pursued their self-interest, their activities were circumscribed by a suffocating system of religious and political constraints. Yet Hegel is anxious to distance himself from the free-market assumptions of the classical economists. For in civil society freedom 'is lost in particularity'. Rather than breeding a natural order, which must be freed from the restrictions and distortions of political interference, civil society 'affords a spectacle of extravagance and want as well as of the physical and ethical degeneration common to them both'.[11] Hegel, however, is not entirely dismissive of Adam Smith's 'invisible hand', integrating it into his philosophical system as yet another form of dialectical reason working 'behind the backs' of human agents. Self-interest and self-assertion are the *motives* of activity in civil society, but these can be realized by the individual only through reciprocal action with others. Self-seeking thus becomes a contribution to the satisfaction of the needs of everyone else:

by a dialectical advance, subjective self-seeking turns into the mediation of the particular through the universal, with the result that each man in earning, producing and enjoying on his own account is *eo ipso* producing and earning for the enjoyment of everyone else.[12]

But, as we have seen, 'this mutual interlocking of particulars' is far from perfect.[13] In Smith's model, poverty is always marginal – the result of deviation from free-market principles. In Hegel, pauperization and alienation are endemic to the capitalist system. If civil society is in 'a state of unimpeded activity', if the 'amassing of wealth is intensified', the 'dependence and distress' of the labouring class is guaranteed.[14] Poverty

[9] Ibid., addition to para. 182, p. 266.
[10] Ibid., para. 206, p. 133.
[11] Ibid., paras. 229, 185; pp. 145, 123.
[12] Ibid., para. 199, pp. 129–30.
[13] Ibid., addition to para. 189, p. 268.
[14] Ibid., para. 243, pp. 149–50.

grows in proportion to the growth of wealth; they are two aspects of a zero-sum game: 'When luxury is at its height, distress and depravity are equally extreme . . .'.[15] Hegel's whole analysis of civil society turns on the overcoming of this inherent contradiction, this clash of warring interests between rich and poor. For him, the realization of ethical life through its embodiment in a universal framework begins but does not end in civil society. Intimations of universality are provided, first, by the system of interlocking needs, wherein the livelihood and happiness of one man is interwoven with the livelihood and happiness of all. In this sense, civil society is a 'universal family', albeit one full of conflict.[16] Second, civil society is naturally divided into different branches, or 'corporations', which organize and promote particular interests and needs. Through corporations, individuals recognize the value of membership in a group and recover something like the sense of belonging that characterizes the nuclear family. Third, civil society includes (and here Hegel differs from the present-day linguistic convention) the administration of justice, the judicial machinery, whose purpose is to protect property and the physical integrity of the person. In carrying out such functions, civil society achieves 'the unity of the implicit universal with the subjective particular', though the universality in question is merely that of abstract, or individual, right.[17]

In fact, Hegel's model of civil society – the free market plus the administration of justice – roughly corresponds to the ideal society of the classical liberals, like Locke and Smith. But Hegel, while recognizing the similarity, points out that, for them, the state is nothing but a convenient 'partnership' to achieve personal goals and satisfy certain basic *physical* needs. The authority of the state is therefore 'external' and contingent; it is not an expression of our deep inner need to identify with the social whole.[18] Hegel, for his part, refuses to see self-interest as the *ultima ratio* of social organization: civil society does not embody the final end of human life. To his mind, the state should not safeguard self-interest but *transcend* it. Political life is a mode of relating to other human beings not out of prudential calculation but out of solidarity, out of the will to live in a community. Hegel, as a defender of private property, did not think it possible to *eliminate* the tension between the general interest and the conflicting private interests, but such tension could, he thought, be substantially lessened through state regulation and public debate. Hegel, it might be said, expressed the ideology of the Prussian bureaucracy: the

---

[15] Ibid., addition to para. 195, p. 269.
[16] Ibid., para. 239, p. 148.
[17] Ibid., para. 229, p. 145.
[18] Ibid., para. 157 and addition to para. 182, pp. 110, 266.

good of the state was independent of private interests and did not derive from them, yet the state could fulfil its role as the expression of man's self-consciousness only by containing within itself a differentiated civil society. His attitude towards civil society was ambiguous. On the one hand, it was an essential requirement of freedom, part of the dialectical progression of man towards self-recognition. On the other, any society that allowed the forces of civil society to rule unimpeded would destroy itself.

Civil society in Marx

Marx's view of bourgeois economic life was much more straightforward. Although he agreed with Hegel that modern society was defined by a split between 'man as citizen' and 'man as private individual', Marx did not believe that the cleavage between universal and particular could be resolved within the existing regime of private property. His analysis of civil society either dismissed or ignored the incipient signs of communal mutuality to which Hegel attached so much importance; Marx's civil society was a Hobbesian nightmare of isolated and aggressive individuals, bound together precariously by the cash nexus. The process of atomization began with the demise of feudalism, a type of social order where:

the elements of civil life such as property, the family, the mode and manner of work, for example, were raised into elements of political life in the form of landlordism, estates, and corporations. In this form they determined the relation of the particular individual to the *state as a whole*.

Because the participative actors in the public sphere were the direct expression of economic roles, the 'vital functions and conditions of civil society always remained political'.[19] But bourgeois 'emancipation', which reached its apotheosis in the French revolution, destroyed the estates, corporations, and guilds, along with their privileges and obligations, and 'thereby *abolished the political character of civil society*'. The economic realm was now liberated from political interference, and civil society – once composed of collective units – was shattered into its constituent elements: individuals. The political spirit, which had been fragmented 'in the various cul-de-sacs of feudal society', was now gathered up, so to speak, freed from its entanglement with civil life, and turned into an ideal communal sphere, where deracinated 'man' participates by virtue of his humanity alone and not because of any social functions he might perform.[20] However, the fulfilment of political idealism amounted to the

---

[19] 'On the Jewish Question', in *Writings of the Young Marx on Philosophy and Society*, ed. and trans. by L. D. Easton and K. H. Guddat (New York: Doubleday, 1967), pp. 238–9.
[20] Ibid., p. 239.

fulfilment of the crass materialism of civil society: 'The throwing off of the political yoke was at the same time the throwing off of the bond that had fettered the egoistic spirit of civil society.'[21] Political life takes on an abstract, illusory quality, remote from everyday concerns. In it, man is 'an imaginary member of an imagined sovereignty, divested of his actual individual life and endowed with an unactual universality'. Man thus leads a double life, a 'heavenly and an earthly life'. In the heaven of political life, he regards himself as a communal being, full of public spirit and mindful of the general interest. In the 'earthly' existence of civil society, however, he acts as a *private* individual, treating other human beings as means to his own ends, and even reducing himself to a means, the plaything of 'alien', market forces.[22] The spirit of civil society is the spirit of pure egoism, of the *bellum omnium contra omnes*. Civil society becomes the chief source of human alienation, 'an expression of the *separation* of man from his *community*, from himself and from other men'.[23]

And yet, according to the theorists of bourgeois freedom, 'man as a member of civil society' is '*authentic* man'. The purpose of citizenship is essentially to preserve the interests and 'rights' that are part and parcel of the capitalist economy. The liberal revolution 'regards civil society – the realm of needs, labor, private interests, and private right – as the *basis of its existence*, as a *presupposition* needing no ground, and thus as its *natural basis*'.[24] For Marx, the subordination of politics to economics is not a hidden reality to be exposed; it is an obvious fact, openly proclaimed by the defenders of bourgeois liberty themselves. But Marx, needless to say, expresses this agreed perception in much more negative terms than they do:

the unsocial nature of civil life, of private property, trade, industry, and the mutual plundering of different civil groups . . . this debasement, this *slavery of civil society* is the natural foundation on which the *modern* state rests.[25]

He also inflates the explanatory primacy of economic life into a universal historical truth. Civil society, he informs us, 'is the true focus and scene of all history'. Accordingly, he pours scorn on 'the old conception of history which neglects real relationships and restricts itself to high-sounding dramas of princes and states'.[26]

Hegel, in believing that the dramatic activities of 'princes and states' actually made a difference, could take a much more relaxed attitude

---

[21] Ibid.   [22] Ibid., pp. 225–6.   [23] Ibid., p. 227.   [24] Ibid., p. 240.
[25] 'Critical Notes on "The King of Prussia and Social Reform"' (1844), in *Writings of the Young Marx on Philosophy and Society*, p. 349.
[26] 'The German Ideology', in *Writings of the Young Marx on Philosophy and Society*, p. 428.

towards the intrinsic conflict of civil society. Although he rejected the classical liberal notion of a 'natural' harmony among the diverse interests thrown up by bourgeois economic relations, he nevertheless thought that the institutionalization of class relationships within the political structure need not prevent the unification of the community in a comprehensive totality. Because of his faith in the integrative role of the state, he could celebrate differentiation and mediation, however divisive they might appear on the surface. Marx could not. For him, the 'real relationships' of civil society penetrate every crevice and corner of the state, thus negating its claim to express the universal interest. *Pace* Hegel, the only way to end human alienation is to dissolve civil society as we know it. The point is not, as it was for Hegel, to *combine* the universal and the particular in a dialectical synthesis; rather we must universalize the particular – 'socialize' the organization of labour and industry by subjecting it to public ownership and democratic accountability. Moreover, the dissolution of civil society is also the dissolution of the abstract political state:

> By making its *political existence* actual as its *true* existence, civil society also makes its civil existence *unessential* in contrast to its political existence. And with the one thing separated, the other, its opposite, falls.[27]

No longer will civil society be a mass of conflicting egoisms; no longer will the state be an abstract, unreal community. The public/private distinction will be transcended in a form of communal self-government where economic life is guided by democratic procedures and political life is given substantive or (as Marx would say) 'real' content. In this way, man absorbs his own species nature and 'merges' his personality and interests with those of his fellow human beings. To quote Marx:

> Only when the actual, individual man has taken back into himself the abstract citizen and in his everyday life, his individual work, and his individual relationships has become a *species-being*, only when he has recognized and organized his own powers as *social* powers so that social force is no longer separated from him as *political* power, only then is human emancipation complete.[28]

Marx was right to be suspicious of the role of citizenship in a capitalist market economy. The popular idea that we will periodically set aside our mundane, egoistic interests and vote (or otherwise behave) as public-spirited citizens is, at best, an idealistic abstraction. At worst, it is a deceitful cover for the substantial identity between the interests pursued

---

[27] 'Critique of Hegel's Philosophy of the State', in *Writings of the Young Marx on Philosophy and Society*, p. 202.
[28] 'On the Jewish Question', in *Writings of the Young Marx on Philosophy and Society*, p. 241.

in each sphere. Also, when one examines the institutional principles of the liberal state, it is not hard to make the case that they are instrumental to bourgeois class dominance. For example, the freedom enjoyed by all individuals to dispose of their own resources does suit a mode of production that requires labour power to be sold for wages through individual employment contracts. Similarly, the equality of all individuals before the law means that law enforcement will, as a matter of course, favour the interests of the propertied groups: everyone's property is equally protected, but some have a lot more of it than others. Yet it is simplistic to attribute the state/society split to the needs of capitalism. As Gianfranco Poggi argues:

> It had earlier found fundamental expression in the slow but inexorable disen-tanglement of the Western state from the Church[es] and Christianity through the tortuous story that leads from *cuius regio eius religio* through religious tolerance and freedom of conscience to the 'secular state'. In this story, it would seem, not economic interests but *raison d'état* and a momentous, autonomous development in religious awareness and in moral consciousness played a critical role. Matters of creed and cult, not of property and contract, had been the first to be claimed as 'private' with respect to the state.[29]

Of course, Marx simply assumed that 'matters of creed and cult' were subservient to those of 'property and contract'. His view of history was partial – predetermined by his theoretical angle. The 'emancipation' of the state from its entanglement with all aspects of life was actually a complex historical process, impelled by ideas as much as by economic necessity.

Marx's economic reductionism also prevented him from grasping the *moral* foundations of modern capitalism. To the ideologists and practi-tioners of the new economic order, civil society was not simply a 'neutral' space of market exchange. It was primarily an ethical realm of solidarity held together by the force of moral sentiments and natural affections.[30] The Protestant Reformation, by redefining grace – once an other-worldly attribute – as a function of life in the world, and by conceiving individuals as autonomous moral subjects, partaking in a transcendental majesty, endowed entrepreneurial activity and methodical labour with a profound spiritual dignity. As Weber noted, for the pioneers of capitalism, there was something much greater at stake than the bottom line or the cash nexus. It was nothing less than the salvation of souls. Economic conduct was to be guided by a strict ethical code, enjoining rights and obligations in equal measure. To the Marxist determinist, however, this code was

---

[29] G. Poggi, *The Development of the Modern State* (London: Hutchinson, 1978), p. 120.
[30] See A. Seligman, *The Idea of Civil Society* (New York: The Free Press, 1992), chapter 2.

little more than cynical window-dressing, designed to hoodwink the masses.

Civil society in Gramsci

Economic reductionism is not a charge that could be levelled against Antonio Gramsci, who – alone amongst Marx's eminent disciples – tried to develop the concept of civil society. By and large, the classical Marxist tradition was content to accept Marx's identification of civil society with 'commercial and industrial life',[31] which, in the capitalist market economy, reduces human beings to acquisitive and predatory egotists who relate to one another in purely contractual or instrumental terms. As someone whose Marxism was shaped by an early adherence to idealist philosophy, Gramsci was not entirely satisfied with this analysis. He agreed, as all Marxists must, that power was of its very nature asymmetrical and exercised by superordinate over subordinate classes. But he did not see capitalism as an ethics-free zone, a Hobbesian state of nature where the strong dominate the weak through threats and violence. On the contrary, exploitative exchange relationships are, in Gramsci's view, underpinned by a complex of moral injunctions that make these relationships seem right and proper to all parties in the exchange. Capitalism does not turn us into rational calculators, pursuing our objective interests in an ethical vacuum. For we necessarily define our interests in terms of our ideals and values – the evaluative categories that enable us to find meaning in an otherwise meaningless world. These ideals and values may be 'false', or class-biased; they may mystify us and cloud our judgement; but we can never detach ourselves from some moral perspective or other.

These heterodox ideas form the basis of the concept of hegemony, Gramsci's main contribution to political theory. Writing in the early 1930s, Gramsci posed the question of why capitalism survived when, as he and other Marxists believed, the objective conditions existed for a transition to Communism. The answer, for Gramsci, lay in the super-structure, which he divided into two levels:

one that can be called 'civil society', that is the ensemble of organisms commonly called 'private', and that of 'political society' or 'the state'. These two levels correspond on the one hand to the function of 'hegemony' which the dominant group exercises throughout society and on the other hand to that of 'direct domination' or command exercised through the State and 'juridical' government.[32]

---

[31] 'The German Ideology', in *Writings of the Young Marx on Philosophy and Society*, p. 469.
[32] A. Gramsci, *Selections from the Prison Notebooks*, ed. and trans. by Q. Hoare and G. Nowell Smith (London: Lawrence and Wishart, 1971), p. 12.

The first set of institutions (churches, parties, trade unions, universities, the press, publishing houses, voluntary associations of all kinds) disseminate the ideology of the dominant class, thus ensuring its cultural and spiritual supremacy over the subordinate classes, who consent to their own subordination. Conversely, the 'apparatus of state coercive power' enforces discipline in those cases where 'spontaneous consent has failed'.[33] While this seems clear enough, Gramsci's usage is not entirely consistent. In a number of passages, including the one quoted above, civil society is *outside* the state,[34] but elsewhere he refers to a 'general notion' of the state, comprising *both* political society *and* civil society.[35] The former usage occurs whenever he wants to use 'civil society' as an analytic tool for explaining the difference between East (Russia) and West (including his native Italy). In Russia, prior to the revolutionary events of 1917, social order was maintained primarily by force, since 'the State was everything, civil society was primordial and gelatinous'. In the West, however, 'there was a proper relation between State and civil society'. Exhibiting his curious fondness for military metaphors, he tells us that the state was 'only an outer ditch, behind which there stood a powerful system of fortresses and earthworks: more or less numerous from one State to the next'.[36] In another quotation, Gramsci prefers simile to metaphor, though the basic point remains the same. The organs of civil society, we learn,

are like the trench systems of modern warfare. In war it would sometimes happen that a fierce artillery attack seemed to have destroyed the enemy's entire defensive system, whereas in fact it had only destroyed the outer perimeter; and at the moment of their advance and attack the assailants would find themselves confronted by a line of defence which was still effective. The same thing happens in politics.[37]

The 'fortresses and earthworks' (or is it 'trench-systems') of civil society form capitalism's second line of defence against revolution. In countries where social order rests essentially on consent and ideological integration, the strategy for revolution cannot simply replicate the paramilitary strategy of the Bolsheviks, who were able to seize power through a kind of *coup d'état*. In the West, Marxists must engage in protracted cultural struggle to subvert the bourgeois consensus. Only when the battle for 'hearts and minds' has been won can the revolution succeed.

The reader will by now have noticed an oddity in Gramsci's terminology. For the classical Marxist tradition, civil society refers to the infrastructure, the totality of material conditions and relationships. But

---

[33] Ibid.   [34] Ibid., pp. 235, 238.   [35] Ibid., pp. 244, 261, 263.
[36] Ibid., p. 238.   [37] Ibid., p. 235.

civil society in Gramsci's writings belongs to the superstructure, since it comprises ideological/cultural relations. This rather baffling terminological innovation has provoked some controversy among students of Gramsci. Bobbio identified the main issue with exemplary clarity:

Now, if it is true that civil society is, as Marx says, 'the focal point, the theatre of all history', does not this shift in the meaning of civil society in Gramsci induce us to ask the question if, by any chance, he has not located 'the focal point, the theatre of all history' elsewhere?[38]

Bobbio's answer is that Gramsci's linguistic deviance is indicative of idealist proclivities, the fruit of his Hegelian upbringing. It is indeed intriguing that Gramsci claims to derive his definition of civil society from Hegel, not Marx. In a passage from the *Notebooks*, Gramsci speaks of civil society 'as Hegel understands it, and the way in which it is often used in these notes . . . as the ethical content of the State'.[39] Here, as in other parts of his *Notebooks*, we might infer that Gramsci was either confused or perversely intent on confounding the reader. For Marx, too, invoked Hegel (and rightly so) when he equated civil society with the economic structure. Recall, however, that, in *The Philosophy of Right*, civil society includes not only the sphere of material relations, but also voluntary forms of organization, such as professional and trade associations, which Hegel describes as the 'ethical root of the state'.[40]

Bobbio concludes that Gramsci's transposition of civil society from the base to the superstructure 'necessarily has a decisive bearing on the Gramscian conception of the relations between base and superstructure'. The intention must be to reverse what Marx took to be the direction of causation. Whereas he saw the base as primary and the superstructure as secondary, in Gramsci 'it is exactly the opposite'.[41] Bobbio's interpretation has been challenged by Jacques Texier, who cites many passages from the *Notebooks* which suggest a standard Marxist theory of the relation between structure and superstructure.[42] To be sure, Gramsci could hardly have been more orthodox when he asserted, for example, that the '*ensemble* of the superstructures is the reflection of the *ensemble* of the social relations of production', or that hegemony 'must necessarily

[38] 'Gramsci and the Conception of Civil Society', in N. Bobbio, *Which Socialism?*, ed. R. Bellamy and trans. R. Griffin (Cambridge: Polity Press, 1988), p. 149. The essay was first published in 1968.
[39] A. Gramsci, *Quaderni del Carcere*, ed. V. Gerratana, 4 vols. (Turin: Einaudi, 1975), vol. II, p. 703.
[40] *The Philosophy of Right*, para. 255, p. 154,
[41] 'Gramsci and the Conception of Civil Society', pp. 150–1.
[42] J. Texier, 'Gramsci, Theoretician of the Superstructures. On the Concept of Civil Society', in *Gramsci and Marxist Theory*, ed. C. Mouffe (London: Routledge & Kegan Paul, 1979). First published in 1968 (in French).

be based on the decisive function exercised by the leading group in the decisive nucleus of economic activity'.[43] The argument advanced by Bobbio is based more on logical inference than on textual evidence, as he is unable to point to a single passage where Gramsci affirms the causal primacy of the superstructure(s). But Bobbio's logic is faulty: the proposition that Gramsci's unorthodox use of terminology *necessarily* has profound theoretical significance is certainly a *non sequitur*. Perhaps, however, we should refrain from dismissing Bobbio's argument altogether. While Gramsci never denied the primacy of economics, he always rejected economic *determinism*. Cultural and political phenomena could not simply be 'read off' from, or reduced to, objective material circumstances. Herein lies Gramsci's main criticism of orthodox Marxism – and it is plausible to assume that his redefinition of civil society was his way of alerting other Marxists to the importance of ideas in social life.

Gramsci's identification of civil society with the 'ensemble' of voluntary associations also enabled him to suggest a novel way of conceiving the 'withering away of the state':

It is possible to imagine the coercive element of the state withering away by degrees, as ever-more conspicuous elements of regulated society (or ethical State or civil society) make their appearance. The expressions 'ethical state' or 'civil society' would thus mean that this 'image' of a State without a State was present to the greatest political and legal thinkers, in so far as they placed themselves on the terrain of pure science (pure utopia, since based on the premise that all men are really equal and hence equally rational and moral, i.e. capable of accepting the law spontaneously, freely, and not through coercion, as imposed by another class, as something external to consciousness) . . . In the doctrine of the state becoming regulated society, between a phase in which 'State' will be equal to 'government', and one in which 'State' will be identified with 'civil society', we will have to pass through a phase of the night-watchman State; that is, a coercive organization which will safeguard the development of the continuously growing elements of regulated society, and which will therefore gradually reduce its authoritarian and coercive interventions.[44]

The 'withering away of the state' is thus equivalent to the progressive absorption of state functions by the voluntary transactions and organizations of civil society. But the quotation raises a fundamental question: does Gramsci really believe that a 'State without a State', or a 'regulated society', devoid of 'authoritarian and coercive interventions', is actually possible? Apparently not, since he describes it as 'pure utopia', based on a dubious egalitarian assumption. And yet, the final sentence in the quotation implies that the 'night-watchman' or minimal state is only a

---

[43] *Selections from the Prison Notebooks*, pp. 366, 161.
[44] Ibid., p. 263. I have amended the translation. (For the Italian text, see *Quaderni del Carcere*, vol. II, p. 764.)

transitional stage in a natural progression towards the 'regulated society'. The puzzle can be resolved if we realize that Gramsci did not use 'utopian' in a pejorative way. Consider his interpretation of Marxism (or, in Gramsci's prison code, 'the philosophy of praxis') as a form of historicism:

That the philosophy of praxis thinks of itself in a historicist manner, that is, as a transitory phase of philosophical thought, is not only implicit in its entire system, but is made quite explicit in the well-known thesis that historical development will at a certain point be characterised by the passage from the reign of necessity to the reign of freedom. All hitherto existing philosophies (philosophical systems) have been manifestations of the intimate contradictions by which society is lacerated . . . But even the philosophy of praxis is an expression of historical contradictions . . . ; this means that it too is tied to 'necessity' and not to a 'freedom' which does not exist and, historically, cannot yet exist . . . At the present time the philosopher – the philosopher of praxis – . . . cannot escape from the present field of contradictions, he cannot affirm, other than generically, a world without contradictions, without immediately creating a utopia.

This is not to say that utopia cannot have a philosophical value, for it has political value and every politics is implicitly a philosophy, even if disconnected and crudely sketched.[45]

In other words, the Marxist theorist living in the kingdom of necessity cannot, by definition, predict what will happen in the kingdom of freedom. To attempt to do so is to abandon applied science and to indulge in utopian day-dreaming – but this is not necessarily a bad thing if it inspires people to constructive action. Moreover, what is 'utopian during the reign of necessity could become "truth" [reality] after the passage' to freedom.[46] Gramsci, it seems, is being agnostic (or realistic) about the possibility of achieving a fully 'regulated society'. While it is something he favours, and while he can imagine the steps that might bring it about, the historicist nature of his Marxism precludes him from forecasting its realization, or even whether such realization is possible.

Post-Marxism

Subsequent decades have confirmed the wisdom of Gramsci's pragmatic perspective. Communism (the 'State without a State') remains a Platonic essence with no prospect of material existence. Since Marx wrote, many socialists have followed Gramsci in doubting the practicality of this stateless paradise, though these same critics usually affirm its splendid-

[45] Ibid., pp. 404–5.
[46] Ibid., p. 407.

ness as an ideal. In recent 'post-Marxist' discourse,[47] however, writers who are generally sympathetic to the Marxist and socialist tradition have argued that the coalescence of civil and political society is not just utopian but downright dangerous.

This conclusion, previously associated with Marxism's liberal detractors, is drawn with particular incisiveness by André Gorz. He concedes the point, made repeatedly by Marx's army of critics, that a socially controlled economy requires growth, rather than diminution, of the state apparatus:

Since it advocates social integration not through the random play of multiple initiatives and conflicts, but through consciously willed planning or programming of the activity of society, socialist political theory implicitly gives society precedence over the individual and assumes their common subordination to the state.[48]

But, according to him, the state is more than a functional necessity; it is also a precondition of freedom. Where the necessary constraints and obligations of social life are codified in the form of objective laws, the duty of obedience is circumscribed and there remains scope for autonomous activity. Where, on the other hand, 'love' or 'reason' become the governing principles of social action, people would come under tremendous pressure to 'conform' in all spheres of life. For, in the absence of *external* constraints, the cohesion of the community would depend solely upon *internalized* constraints, common to each and every individual and (inevitably) endowed with a quasi-sacred status. As Gorz says, there is no law so tyrannical as the duty to love or care for one's fellow citizens.[49] 'The existence of a state separate from civil society', he concludes, 'is thus the essential prerequisite to the autonomy of civil society', to the existence of a 'space' for self-organization, voluntary exchange, and alternative thought.[50] He wants civil society to embrace a plurality of movements and aspirations – a plurality 'understood not simply as a plurality of parties and trade unions but as the coexistence of various ways of working, producing and living, various and distinct cultural areas and levels of social existence'.[51]

'Post-Marxists' obviously seek to marry the insights of Marxist analysis with those of liberalism. But are the parties to the marriage contract

---

[47] For a useful discussion of 'post-Marxism', see C. Pierson, *Marxist Theory and Democratic Politics* (Cambridge: Polity Press, 1986), chapter 6.
[48] A. Gorz, *Farewell to the Working Class: An Essay on Post-Industrial Socialism*, trans. M. Sonenscher (London: Pluto Press, 1982), p. 77.
[49] Ibid., pp. 109–11.
[50] Ibid., pp. 112, 118.
[51] Ibid., p. 79.

truly compatible? Gorz himself admits that 'classical socialist doctrine' (not just Marxism) 'finds it difficult to come to terms with political and social pluralism'.[52] Let us examine why this is so. Civil society as we know it, as a realm of free activities unencumbered by political interference, found its theoretical justification in early liberal philosophy, which saw individuals as essentially autonomous entities, secure in their individuality beyond communal ties and referents. Moreover, the universal value previously bestowed upon the social whole was, in liberal thought, transferred to these bearers of private interests and goals. Adam Seligman has persuasively argued that both 'the transcendental status of the individual' and 'the division of individual identity into universal/moral and private/egoistic components' were 'critical for the idea of civil society'.[53] Rather than the collectivity, it was the individual himself who served as the fundamental unit of political life: society was no longer a universal but existed only as a derivative of the individual. There is a neat theoretical fit between this ontological framework and the core assumption of civil society: that acts of conscience and expressions of personal conviction stand inviolable over against the State as the exercise of a higher right. Conversely, it is hard to square this assumption with a doctrine like socialism, which – in Gorz's own words – 'implicitly gives society precedence over the individual and assumes their common subordination to the state'.[54] Notwithstanding Gorz's best dialectical efforts to distinguish them, there may be a logical connection between the central planning of production and distribution, on the one hand, and the 'repressive, inquisitorial, normalising, and conformist quality' of socialist morality, on the other.[55] Both stem from the same vision of 'man' and society, and there are no historical examples of one existing without the other.

Another difficulty in 'post-Marxist' treatments of civil society is one that should trouble *all* 'pluralists', whether socialist or liberal. Can civil society really be a glittering display of 'various ways of working, producing and living, various and distinct cultural areas'?[56] Seligman puts the case that for pluralism to work, it must be a 'pluralism of motives and interests', not a pluralism of 'affective ideological universes'.[57] For the minimal functioning of society depends on the universalization of trust, which in turn depends upon shared perceptions and evaluations. The fashionable identification of civil society with 'new

[52] Ibid.
[53] *The Idea of Civil Society*, p. 79.
[54] *Farewell to the Working Class*, p. 77.
[55] Ibid., p. 91.   [56] Ibid., p. 79.
[57] *The Idea of Civil Society*, p. 179.

social movements'[58] begs the question whether these 'movements' are compatible with each other or with older 'movements' or – indeed – with the central value system of the community. It is hard to disagree with Seligman's pessimistic conclusion: 'when these associations are ethically construed as different "metaphysical" or normative universes, . . . they represent not the realization but the destruction of civil life'.[59] The resultant instability might be attractive to radicals, but they should not pretend that the conflictual interaction of 'autonomous movements, aspirations, struggles, desires and oppositions' makes for a viable model of social order.[60]

Concluding remarks

The role of civil society in Marxist thought is less than consistent. Is it substructural (Marx) or superstructural (Gramsci)? Is it a purely descriptive and explanatory concept (Marx) or an ethical ideal as well (Gramsci)? Must we transcend it (Marx) or expand it (Gramsci)? With respect to its future development, should we be optimistic (Marx) or sceptical (Gramsci)? Such contradictions reflect Gramsci's status as a 'revisionist' Marxist, paving the way for later 'post-Marxists', like Gorz, who tried to rescue Marxism's rational kernel (society's precedence over the individual) from its more absurd dogmas (economic reductionism, 'the withering away of the state') by developing a normative conception of civil society that could easily appeal to liberals. But we are left with two questions – and each of them probably requires a negative answer. First, can socialist 'holism' safely underpin an ideal rooted in liberal individualism? The second question, which should exercise liberals as well as 'post-Marxists', is this: can a pluralistic vision of civil society happily embrace 'movements, aspirations, struggles, desires and oppositions' that are openly hostile to liberal values? In arguing that the modern idea of civil society is intrinsically linked to a specific way of life and a specific way of thinking, Marx perhaps displayed more insight than his recent, 'flexible' disciples.

[58] See J. Cohen, 'Strategy or Identity?: New Theoretical Paradigms and Contemporary Social Movements', *Social Research*, 52, no. 4 (1985), pp. 663–716.
[59] *The Idea of Civil Society*, p. 197.
[60] Gorz, *Farewell to the Working Class*, p. 118.

Arguments in the South

8   Civil society in an extra-European perspective

J. R. Goody

'Civil society', does it exist? As a concept developed in the West, certainly. It arose first in Ancient Greece, and was elaborated in the Enlightenment, to characterize in a favourable light one's own institutions (or society) in contrast to those of others. The 'other' varied, but included both barbarians and despots. In the eighteenth and nineteenth centuries these 'uncivil' societies embraced past autocrats and present orientals whose societies were thought to have been unable to develop in the manner of Western Europe. After a period of neglect, the term has recently been called back into use in political discourse.

In the present period of post-Cold War adjustment, 'civil society' carries, as earlier, a heavily normative burden. It is what we in the West have and wish to see developed not only in Eastern Europe but in the East more generally. Like the associated notions of democracy and representation, of law and freedom, especially as they apply to the market, its absence in the East is seen as having impeded the earlier process of modernization, and even now as restricting the exercise of human rights. We can recognize its contemporary role as a battle-cry. But does it carry any serious weight in the comparative analysis of political systems as distinct from representing a theme in Western political thought?

I want to discuss briefly the concept of civil society in relation not so much to political philosophy as to sociology, anthropology, and history. Then I consider whether, despite its use to denigrate the other, it can serve any useful purpose to analyse the West, the earlier or the later East, or even, in view of the very different conditions that obtained, Africa. But first let me attempt some elucidation.

The Aristotelian conception of the unity of society and the state, or of civil and political society, has been contrasted with the disaggregation of civil society and the state in the early modern period.[1] Aristotle saw civil

---

[1] J. Cohen and A. Arato, in A. Honneth *et al.*, *Cultural–Political Interventions in the Unfinished Project of the Enlightenment* (Cambridge, Mass.: MIT Press, 1992), p. 122.

society as 'a domination-free association of peers who communicatively and publicly establish their goals and norms of action and who regulate their interaction through principles of justice'. Every phrase in this description calls for an extended commentary, which is why it is difficult to align with any social data. Suffice to say that it adds up to a highly idealistic ideal-type of democratic control.

The early modern conception has been seen as taking the form either of stressing pluralistic normative integration or of postulating individualistic, utilitarian forms of action. Durkheim and others followed the first course, neo-conservatives the second. In both we are faced with the problem of timing similar to that found in the case of national law. Many see this as a doctrine originating in the seventeenth century; Leo Strauss and others find it already present in Aristotle, though it was fully harmonized with 'civil society' by Aquinas. That is the background of the phrase from the standpoint of 'conceptual history'. We should add an alternative starting point that has been developed among those intellectuals connected with contemporary 'social movements' such as Solidarity in Poland. 'Civil society', like human rights, is what authoritarian regimes lack by definition. It is what the Greeks, the Enlightenment and we today have; it is what despotic governments, whether in the past or the present, the here or the elsewhere, do not have.

In its early modern aspect, the notion of civil society has been seen as linked to the European society of that period. Habermas outlines the emergence during the eighteenth century of a new sphere between private life and public authority under the old name of civil society (*Zivil Societät*) or simply society. That represented a new type of 'publicity' (*Öffentlichkeit*) based in principle on the autonomous voluntary association and reasoned communication of free and equal individuals'.[2] That activity was located at the level of the social, a public sphere which penetrated the state through the parliamentary principle, dissolving the absolutist's *arcana imperii*. It also formed the subject of Locke's enquiries into the development of new political forms. In other words 'civility' enters into social and political life through the intervention first of voluntary associations and reasoned discussion, then through the modification of the monolithic powers of the state by the medium of Parliament. The notion is associated with a long-term 'civilizing' of political and indeed societal relations which is seen as resulting from pressures from 'non-government organizations' on the one hand and from public opinion on the other.

It is superfluous to note that these discussions are deeply embedded in

[2] Ibid., p. 129.

Western political theory, Western philosophy, and Western social theory. They embody concepts developed in the course of Western intellectual history, often as political instruments. But let us turn to questions that bear not so much on the intellectual history of the concept but on its possible use as an analytical tool for comparative purposes. I begin with a general remark which relates to the separation of society and polity implied in the usage itself. In the Parsonian model, the polity is neither distinct from nor coincidental with society; it is part of a wider whole in the sense of the social system. The alternative assumption results from the looser usage of specialists. Economists, for example, call 'social' and 'cultural' anything that is incapable of being analysed within their particular framework; 'society' somewhat arbitrarily denotes 'the rest' or 'the other', as in the phrases 'economy and society', religion and society, or 'family and society'. The polity is a sub-system of the social system, though one which often displays a certain dominance in social life because of the state's role in territorial relationships, in the control of physical force, and in law-making and government more generally. But not all societies possess centralized institutions or state organizations of this kind. In these other cases, to suggest that the polity is the state of society would clearly be nonsense.

The Western orientation embedded in the notion of 'civil society' is not of course necessarily an impediment to its use. Natural science has thrived upon its Western base. However, in the case of the social sciences and the humanities problems do arise with such ethnocentric terms. I have referred to two main usages of the concept of civil society, for short, the Greek and the early modern. For Habermas the decisive break came with the Enlightenment, that is, with the further development not only of democracy ('communication between free and equal individuals') but also of rationality, since that communication has to be 'reasoned'. In other words, we cannot divorce this argument from the claim that a new form of rationality was developed in the West, a form that Weber called the 'rationality of world mastery'. Others see this development not as an altogether new form of rationality but as the more thoroughgoing application of an already existing variety, inherited from Aristotle, elaborated to the limits by Descartes with his famous formula: 'I think, therefore I am.'[3] But in either case that rationality is considered to result in the Enlightenment and the development of modern knowledge systems, especially in the natural sciences, though it also took an economic form intrinsic to the development of capitalism, industrialization, modernization.

[3] E.g. Ernest Gellner, *The Conditions of Liberty* (London: Hamish Hamilton, 1992).

I do not reject the Enlightenment idea of a long-term progression (even 'progress') towards 'civility', the kind of progression that Elias has discussed in Western Europe at the level of spitting and other bodily functions. But such a development of restraint and 'manners' is not limited to Western Europe, is more diversified than that scheme suggests, and is less deeply rooted in the psyche and the society than the word itself implies. 'Civilized' is more appropriate as a technical archaeological concept than as a moral one. It does not require much ransacking of the memory to recall the acts perpetrated some fifty years ago by those who claim Goethe and Beethoven as their cultural ancestors, and who pride themselves on their civility. Or the more recent horrors done in the name of the great Khmer civilization of Angkor Wat. Or the contemporary atrocities committed by inhabitants of that centre of Balkan civility, Sarajevo. The history of all civil and civilized societies, especially imperial, colonial, and immigrant ones, is blood-stained in similar ways. There is no straightforward unilineal shedding of the 'uncivil'.

It is obvious that the past three hundred years have seen major developments in the West in the importance of parliamentary government (and of electoral systems of choosing representatives) as well as in secularized knowledge and in the economy. However, there is a problem in describing these events as well as in explaining them if they are dealt with at the level of the birth of democracy, or of rationality, or of civil society. That is the case whether we are dealing with Athens or with the Enlightenment. Take democracy. Contrary to much received opinion, representation of a kind has existed in many other forms of government, possibly in all, in ships of eighteenth-century pirates as well as in tribal chiefdoms. What we have experienced more recently is its extension and elaboration in the nation-state, first, in the West (though not in its colonies), then elsewhere. There are of course many differences in the forms of representation and in their efficacy; compliance with authority, clearly a variable, has been reduced in significant ways in the modern West, but the difference is a matter of degree; representation of people's interests did not begin with the Enlightenment, though it was certainly extended.

The same can be said of the application of rationality to economic and 'cultural' activities, as seen in the development of the economy and of knowledge systems. As far as economic development is concerned, Indian and Chinese participation in the ancient trading systems of the eastern oceans certainly required the application of 'rational' techniques. Regarding knowledge systems, parallel techniques were as clearly utilized to create the Encyclopaedias of Sung China as the summae of medieval Europe. Neither the abilities nor the capacities (I see the first as biological, the second as cultural) to carry out 'rational' actions were absent in the East and it is Western myopia that looks upon the world in such a paternalistic light, or rather in the absence of light, as the Unenlightened, those whom the Enlightenment never reached. That myopia also applies to the concept of civil society, for here too is an institution that the West claims to have invented at a certain (disputed) moment in time and which others did not or could not develop. Once again, the idea has taken root by selecting a specific historical situation in the West, important in terms of world history, and attributing to it some very general qualities. Indeed there is a kind of moral evaluation attached to the very concepts of civility, rationality, and enlightenment, qualities that are seen as contributing to the so-called European miracle and that are necessarily unique to the West. That approach makes for an ethnocentric and suspect social science which does little to clarify the analysis of the undoubted achievements that took place at that time, but which must be seen in the light not only of those of ancient Greece, but of those of earlier Mesopotamia, of the Arab Middle East and of Tang and Sung China. In each of these periods, achievements have to be accounted for not in terms of the attribution of general qualities (e.g. mentalities) which others are held not to possess, since the achievements represent at best a temporary advantage which is about to be lost or overtaken, but on a more specific basis. Not in other words by 'rationality' as a unique possession but possibly by 'rationalizing', by specific techniques of logical operation that are more contextually dependent.

Whereas, in Western thought, whether rationality had its birth either in Ancient Greece or in the post-Renaissance West, it is by definition a European product which is then offered to the rest of the world. For Weber, Western rationality was 'the rationality of world mastery', just as for Habermas and many others the emergence of this feature at the time of the Enlightenment has an explanatory value in accounting for contemporary Western achievement, in contrast not only to its earlier past but to the non-European societies which failed to make the break at all.

The third use of the notion of civil society as emerging in 'social movements' carries a similar moral evaluation that places it equally on the side of the angels. There it can be seen as one of the main 'weapons of the weak', allowing individuals and groups to battle with 'the state'. That possibility is almost universally welcomed, whatever the government (except of course by the government, for whom political action of this kind may be 'counter-revolutionary' or just disturbing, that is, seen as creating a disturbance). Civil society then becomes attached to the notion of civil liberties, of human rights, embodied in formulae such as 'liberté, égalité, fraternité', which revolutionary social movements embrace and which the state, even the revolutionary state, tends to reject or at least to compromise. But in this way, the notion of civil society again becomes a Western attribute, since the 'despotic' societies of the East were not thought to allow such opposition to develop.

The use of these concepts is clearly linked to nineteenth-century (and earlier) discussions about those 'other' societies which displayed 'traditional' types of authority and had absolutist regimes, even Asiatic forms of dominance where no interference was brooked with the decisions of the ruler. This kind of Alice in Wonderland, 'off with their heads', view of Asian regimes lay at the back of the many references to static, stagnant, despotic, autocratic, absolutist governments. Nor was the idea confined to Marx and Weber. In the earlier eighteenth century, Europeans had sometimes used the East to promote utopian notions. Tacitus had done this with the Germans, so the Jesuits did the same with China and the British the village community in India. However, the rapid growth of knowledge and the onset of industrialization created a gap between West and East, leading to a radical devaluation of the latter. It was no longer purely ethnocentrism or xenophobia that was involved; there was an evident superiority in knowledge systems and in the economy that called for an explanation.

Enshrined in many European discussions of the Indian polity was the notion of the obstructive, indeed destructive, role of the supreme power of the ruler. In the middle of the eighteenth century the British author and administrator, Robert Orme, wrote of this autocratic power, especially in the legal domain. He called the government 'despotic' partly because of the misunderstanding about land tenure. 'All the lands in the kingdom belong to the King', he declared. In fact this arrangement was little different from the claims made on behalf of European monarchs and referred to certain over-riding political rights possessed by the ruler, which were closely related to his claim to collect taxes and extract services. Others attributed the failure of India to develop a capitalist system to the power wielded by the monarch and to the consequent insecurity and status of merchants whose property might be confiscated any time and who therefore preferred to keep their wealth in jewels rather than to invest in production; in fact many Jains, an important merchant group, would not put money into agricultural land in India for the religious reason that farming involved the taking of life. Royal interference in production and exchange played its part but that was not unknown in Europe; for instance, in 1505 the King of Portugal declared a royal monopoly over the spice trade. It is true that Eastern governments tended to be more centralized than the feudal ones of the West, which were more locally centred after the decline of the Roman Empire. But these arguments of Western scholars were partly dependent on the idea that 'law' did not exist in Asian societies; despotism was arbitrary and inimical to the predictability of law. Without law there was a Hobbesian state of nature in which commerce and industry could not flourish and which was diametrically opposed to the order of a 'civil society', though it should be added that for other writers, such as Locke and Rousseau, the state of nature was not violent but pacific. Moreover the rapacity and the despotism of Eastern rulers has often been exaggerated while that of the West has been underplayed. Extensive trade did develop in India and merchant groups flourished from an early date as we see in their strong support of Buddhism and Jainism from the sixth century BCE.

Of the legal situation in India Orme wrote that 'a government depending upon no other principle than the will of one, cannot be supposed to admit any absolute laws into its constitution; for these would often interfere with that will'.[4] The notion of 'absolute laws' is connected with their universal application to all citizens. But it is also linked to the idea that civil society and perhaps natural law itself, like the rights of man (human rights), are applicable to all societies. Such extreme universalism runs into conflict not only with extreme cultural relativism, which regards legal and social systems as essentially incomparable, but also with a more convergent, less divergent view that would see different types of legal or jural arrangement as being appropriate to certain regions, levels of development, or categories of society. That view would allow for greater flexibility than, say, the idea that representative government or even democracy must necessarily take one of the forms developed in the West to warrant the name. The contrary was recently argued by the former prime minister of Singapore when he complained that because of the trade surplus that Asians had with the United States, they were subject to pressure, especially from human rights groups, when, for example, Singapore decides to hang drug smugglers or cane a miscreant. These protests he described as 'a little bit of one-upmanship – We are a superior civilisation, come up to our standards.' But he insisted there is 'nothing universal about human rights. We will change in time but so too will Western norms, for they are not universal.'[5] While laws are not infinitely variable, neither are they absolute in this sense of being universally applicable.

The idea that Eastern societies were not just different but different in basic ways that prevented them from 'modernizing' were crystallized in Marx's concept of oriental government which was associated with the

---

[4] R. Orme, *Historical Fragments of the Mogul Emprire, of the Morattoes and of the English concerns in Indostan, from the year MDCLIX* (London, 1805 [1792]), p. 403.
[5] *The Straits Times*, 29 November 1993.

static, oriental mode of production, a theory developed by Wittfogel in a well-known study, entitled *Oriental Despotism* (1957). Weber saw these societies as characterized by 'traditional' authority and as lacking the legal rationality of Western bureaucratic systems. The details of their arguments need not concern us here. What is clear is that they took over notions of the East that dwelt upon the autocratic nature of authority, whether of the King or of the family head, contrasted with the 'democratic' systems of the West, characterized by pluralism, by checks and balances, by countervailing institutions, by parliamentary assemblies, and by juries in which the populace were represented. In fact at an earlier period, between *c.* 600 and 321 BCE, India had had a series of 'republican' institutions in addition to the orthodox monarchies. These republics are said to have originated either in 'tribes' (presumably acephalous peoples) or in refugees from the kingdoms themselves. As so often, the kingdoms rose in the rich Ganges plain while the republics (or 'tribes') were found in the hill areas. There they had elected leaders, voting procedures (copied by the Buddhists), and assemblies; it was these latter areas that gave birth to the heterodox religious movements of Jainism and Buddhism that broke away from Hinduism and the caste system.[6]

Even the states were not as despotic as the West thought. If we look back at Orme's account we will see that he is struck by a contradiction. For 'if the subjects of a despotic power are everywhere miserable, the miseries of the people of Indostan are multiplied by the incapacity of the power to control the vast extent of its dominion'.[7] So the limitations of the mode of communications constrains the practice of despotism. As a consequence, there was a significant area of freeplay, of plurality, between the private and public worlds.

That was the same in China. We hear much from modern social scientists about 'the reach of state', 'the emperor in the village'. Undoubtedly the impress of the state made itself felt to a greater extent and over a greater area than in India, which was politically more fragmented. The penetration of a written corpus was everywhere profound, from the political as well as the general 'cultural' point of view. In China the polity deliberately took control of the religious system and encouraged a tradition of secular written work, whereas in India religion and polity, the Brahmin and the Kshatriya, were more directly opposed, especially for Hindus under the long period of Muslim rule. Nevertheless,

---

[6] Romila Thapar, *A History of India* (Harmondsworth: Penguin Books, 1966), p. 53.

[7] Orme, *Historical Fragments*, 400. Other accounts took a more sympathetic line, including the seventeenth- and eighteenth-century ones of China influenced by the reports of later Jesuits, but this was the one pursued by later Western social theory.

state power had its limits in China as in India. One indication is the fact that from the end of the fourteenth century to 1893 there existed an imperial ban on emigration and overseas travel. Nevertheless, during this period millions of Chinese established themselves beyond the edge of the southern coasts.[8] 'Despotic' rule did not stop them settling in Nanyang, in the regions around the Southern Seas.

Earlier notions about Eastern despotism have been modified not only for the mechanical reason that the reach of the state could never remain absolute over long periods. Recent work by historians and other social scientists has brought out the civil aspects of that society. These studies are well known to specialists but have made little impact on Western social theory. The latter clings to Weberian notions of traditional patrimonial authority, which fit neatly with ethnocentric folk models about the Uniqueness of the West. The newer data challenge such assumptions. For example, Scott's work on 'weapons of the weak', on resistance to authority, as a general feature of advanced agricultural societies was carried out in Southeast Asia and later generalized from there. In many parts of Asia, historians have studied collective movements against authority, for that certainly did not go unchallenged. Here I want to focus not on acts of rebellion but on the positive sense of plurality and civility that one gains from reading, for example, accounts of Edo in seventeenth-century Japan, or of the coastal Chinese city of Hangzhou at the time of Marco Polo in the late thirteenth century, which one recent commentator described in the following terms:

The city was noted for its charitable institutions as for its pleasures. There were public hospitals, nurseries, old people's homes, free cemeteries, help for the poor, and state institutions from which the officials benefited more often than the poor. The poor were sometimes the object of private charity on the part of the rich merchants who wanted to make a name for themselves by doing good works.[9]

Charity and its accompanying institutions were not a prerogative of the West; once again they were features of the socio-economic stratification of urban social life.

At this time Hangzhou was the southern capital of China with a population of between 1,000,000 and 1,500,000. The city of Hankow (or Wuhan) developed much later but it too raises the question of civil society. Discussions of modernization in the West recognize the critical role played by the city in this process. This special form of urban life is seen as providing the necessary conditions for the emergence of the idea

---

[8] Wang Gungwu, *Introduction to Chin-Keong Ng, Trade and Society: The Amoy network on the China Coast 1683–1735* (Singapore, 1983).

[9] E. Balazs, 'The Birth of Capitalism in China', in E. Balazs (ed.), *Chinese Civilization and Bureaucracy: Variations on a Theme* (New Haven: Yale University Press, 1964), p. 99.

of freedom and the equality of individuals before the law, as well as of the free alienation of property. In Europe these developments were held to have hastened the passing of feudalism with fundamental results both politically and intellectually.

Politically, it left a heritage of democracy . . . as well as the concept of a corporate political body with a clearly demarcated public sector in terms both of budgetary accounting and professional civil service. Intellectually, it fostered the primacy of rationality, both in legal procedure and in an economic focus on calculability of returns on investment – in Weber's words, the medieval urbanite was well 'on the way to becoming an economic man (*homo oeconomicus*)', . . . laying the groundwork for early capitalism.[10]

Western social theorists saw the type of city that promoted this development as first emerging in medieval Europe, beginning with the relatively independent commune that appeared in northern Italy during the course of the eleventh century. From there the institution soon spread to France, Germany, and the Low Countries. That was the thesis of Henri Pirenne in his work on *Medieval Cities* (1925) and it formed the basis of Max Weber's essay on *The City* (*Die Stadt*). A commune of this kind was more than an urban settlement; according to Weber it was marked by the dominance of trade – commercial relations, a court with at least partially autonomous law, and a government with some room for independent action. Its inhabitants required some liberty.

For Weber Eastern towns, and specifically those in China, failed to meet these criteria; nor did European towns before the eleventh century. Neither had succeeded in making the passage from traditional to rational. On the political level he saw the heavy central administration as allowing little autonomy; the town's role as a garrison or 'princely city' was more important than as a market. It was a centre of 'rational administration' rather than of commerce, where the inhabitants continued to identify with their native places and with their families rather than with the town itself. In the town they were sojourners, temporary visitors. 'All communal action there remained engulfed and conditioned by purely personal, above all by kinship relations.' So these settlements, vast as they were (and in the second half of the nineteenth century Hankow was among the largest in the world, just as Hangzhou had been in the thirteenth) lacked a notion of citizenship and any way of enforcing 'contractual autonomy'. The existence of clans and guilds served only a segment of the population, pointing to the absence of either a 'polis' or a 'commune', or, if one extends the notions, of a polity or a community.

[10] W. T. Rowe, *Hankow: Commerce and Society in a Chinese City, 1796–1889* (Stanford: Stanford University Press, 1984), p. 3. My account is derived from this excellent study of Hankow in the nineteenth century.

The ideas of Weber were not accepted only by Europeanists. For example, the notion of the particularistic character of Chinese economic behaviour was taken up by Levy and Feuerwerker; that of the failure of urban development by Balazs and Eberhard. The latter saw the possibility of industrial development in the Sung as inhibited by the structure of the town, while the former characterized the government as despotic while the town was overly dependent on the countryside.

Conclusions of this kind have been radically altered by more recent work on China, especially on its urban life. Skinner has called attention to the hierarchy of commercial central places, which was distinct in various respects from the hierarchy of administrative ones.[11] Elvin has pointed to the non-administrative structures of social and political power within large urban centres like Shanghai.[12] Rowe's detailed study of Hankow shows that contractual guarantees were provided by the administration and that Chinese firms used 'principles of rational capital accounting' in 'a rational, orderly market'. The importance of guilds as 'proto-capitalist corporations' and the existence of other voluntary associations helped Hankow to escape 'heavy-handed bureaucratic domination'.[13] In other words Chinese cities were not as monolithic as had been supposed, leaving room for the development of trading and commercial relations as well as providing an opening for the adoption of Western industrialization and Western knowledge.

The erroneous view of the Eastern city has also been challenged for India, at least for Ahmedabad, one of whose historians, Gillion, has written:

The traditional cities of India are most often viewed through the eyes of Bernier and other European travellers who visited the Mughal court, and in the light of Weberian and Marxist analysis. They are contrasted with the self-governing towns of medieval Europe with their charters, esprit-de-corps, united bourgeoisie, and independent military power. They appear to be disunited, often ephemeral conglomerations of subjects, dependent on the court and the military official elite, and prevented from free association by caste rivalries and other religious constraints. But Ahmedabad was, to some extent, an exception. Here was a city with a corporate tradition and spirit, an hereditary bourgeois elite, and a history of financial, commercial, and industrial activity.[14]

Its wealth came from trade, industry, and handicrafts which were independent of the patronage of a single court; its merchants and

---

[11] William G. Skinner, *The City in Late Imperial China* (Stanford, Calif.: Stanford University Press, 1977).
[12] Mark Elvin, *The Pattern of the Chinese Past* (London: Eyre Methuen, 1973).
[13] Ibid., p. 10.
[14] K. L. Gillion, *Ahmedabad: A Study in Indian Urban History* (Berkeley: University of California Press, 1968), p. 5.

financiers made up a distinct social stratum, wielding considerable power through the institutions of the city head (*Nagarseth*) and the *mahajans* or guilds. If it did not enjoy urban autonomy on the European model, 'the government of the city was responsive to their wishes'. The later history of Ahmedabad represents 'the transformation of an important traditional centre of trade and industry into a modern industrial city, under the leadership of an indigenous financial and mercantile elite'.

Changes in the view of at least some Eastern cities have led to a revaluation of East–West differences. Rather than treating the East and the West as following totally different trajectories in the medieval period, the feudal road on one hand and that of 'Asiatic exceptionalism' on the other, recent accounts suggest that we should think of two varieties of a single configuration, the tributary state.[15] Such an approach has the advantage of recognizing the common roots of both East and West in the Bronze Age, with its Urban Revolution (as Childe called it) and bringing political science closer to the findings of prehistory.

In this perspective we should find similar but not identical regimes developing in both parts of Eurasia, so there is no longer any call for the radical distinctions found in the writings of Weber, Marx, and many other thinkers. A similar criticism applies to 'world systems theory', where 'the other' is always peripheral to the European centre. But this was hardly the situation in the early medieval period when the major region for manufacturers, trade, and knowledge centred on China and India, nor yet in the thirteenth century when the Muslim Middle East achieved a dominant position in the commercial networks.[16] The same criticism applies to the 'critical theory' of Jürgen Habermas, which places so great an emphasis on the role of the European Enlightenment in the development of systems of knowledge, and of 'civil' (and 'civilized') society, to the neglect of the major achievements of earlier China and elsewhere. This is an area where critical theory has not been critical enough, largely because it has not taken a sufficiently global point of view.

In the pages that follow I want to suggest that most Western analysts have not only got it wrong about the East (and hence necessarily about the West, since one is seen in opposition to the other), but also about a wide range of other political systems. For whether or not we find an explicit discussion on the Western model of law, of representation, of a 'civil' way of life, in these other societies, something of these features can nevertheless be discerned even in those African societies that have

[15] E.g. E. R. Wolf, *Europe and the Peoples Without History* (Berkeley: University of California Press, 1982).
[16] J. Abu-Lughod, *Before European Hegemony: The World System, A.D. 1250–1350* (Oxford: Oxford University Press, 1989).

minimal forms of government ('tribes without rulers'). At the same time the 'states' that possess centralized institutions are far less 'despotic' and far more 'civil' than is often allowed.

The civil society in pre-colonial Africa?

In Africa we find polities of two main kinds. Let us consider West Africa. One kind was characterized by an ordered hierarchy of chiefs, at the top of which stood a paramount, with varying degrees of 'power'; the other was characterized by masters of the Earth, Earth priests, or custodians of the Earth shrine as they are variously called. The former (centralized) also had their priests, and their chiefs had magico-religious powers, while the latter (non-centralized) had clan elders and even some embryonic or absorbed chiefs who exercised a very limited authority. Nevertheless, the distinction between these different forms of polity was clear enough to the participants. It was also a distinction that was central to the analysis of African political systems offered by Fortes and Evans-Pritchard in their seminal collection bearing that title;[17] they called the former, Type A, 'states' (or 'primitive states' in Kabery's subsequent study), and the latter, Type B, acephalous (headless) or segmentary peoples; I myself often refer to the latter as 'tribes' for convenience. Now in Africa these two types of polity, states and tribes, existed in tandem; they were not simply evolutionary stages that replaced one another (though over the longer term that did happen) but were present side-by-side and articulated in the one regional framework. Between the states lay acephalous structures, which were not simply remnants of earlier social formations but often stood in opposition as well as in juxtaposition to their neighbours. In areas that were difficult of access, like the Bandiagara scarp in Mali inhabited by the Dogon on whom so many earlier French anthropologists cut their teeth, or like the Scottish Highlands, the Albanian hills, or similar regions in India and China, these peoples often deliberately avoided state power. Some communities escaped from its clutches as the result of self-imposed exile following a failed attempt to take over a kingdom, others through the gradual decay of central power, or yet others perhaps as the result of an active search for an alternative life-style. In any case they often prized what we would call their 'freedom', a liberty not guaranteed by law in the formal sense but by customary sanctions; the law of the law-court is only one of several possibilities, and one that is inevitably associated with states.

---

[17] M. Fortes and E. E. Evans-Pritchard, *African Political Systems* (Oxford: Oxford University Press, 1940).

It was not only true in Africa but elsewhere too that some peoples appear deliberately to have chosen a non-state existence. The Yao are described as a minority people, living in Guangxi, Guangdong, and other provinces in South and Southwest China. This name was given by the dominant Han to peoples living in mountainous areas, and hence difficult to control, absorb or educate.[18] They speak not one but a variety of languages belonging to the Sino-Tibetan group, and know themselves by a number of different names. They appear to be indigenous, hill-dwelling agriculturalists and no doubt some amongst them are just that. But recent research suggests that some of their ancestors were settled in the plains around Lake Dongthing in the middle basin of the Yangzi River. They took to the hills in order to avoid having to give corvée services to 'reactionary rulers, and preferred instead to enter the primitive forests of the deep mountains and build their homes with their own hands, to protect their life of freedom'.[19]

The kind of acephalous polity that is classically represented by the pastoral Nuer of the southern Sudan has been described as leaderless, lawless, feuding, in short, anarchic. It lacked the very criteria of sovereignty as understood by generations of political philosophers in the West. And not only in the West; it has been the view of states and their members everywhere, in China, India, in the Near East, that such peoples represent disorder.

The major contribution of Fortes and Evans-Pritchard was to bring about a re-assessment of this view. Some earlier anthropologists had been concerned with the problem of 'law', in the broadest sense, with the way that order or a substantial measure of order was maintained in these societies. It is true that in a number of conflict situations, they would resort to self-help. But feuding was not pure violence; it was regulatory in an important sense, although it did not appear as such to states whose first claim was to a monopoly on the use of force, at least beyond a domestic level. Such polities were, as Evans-Pritchard and others have insisted, highly structured and norm-orientated. Nor was self-help their only form of sanction on behaviour; an array of others placed checks on deviant behaviour. Indeed, it is clear that all human societies have to face 'the problem of order', as Parsons called it, thinking back to Spencer and to Durkheim's *Division of Labour in Society*. And order could be achieved without the external instrument of sovereigns, kings, rulers, or chiefs. As Evans-Pritchard once again showed, a very important mechanism was

---

[18] Fei Xiaotong, 'Fifty years investigation in the Yao mountains', in Fei Xiaotong, *The Yao of South China: Recent International Studies*, ed. J. Lemoire and Chiao Chien (Paris, 1991).

[19] Ibid., 17–18.

the segmentary (as distinct from the centralized) arrangement of families, villages, and clans, or indeed of other kinds of social group, who acted together in some context and were opposed in others.

Segmentary processes involve conflict as well as co-operation, hence the importance of the feud. In African states, disputes were regularly taken to the chief who represented the community to the outside (as *dux*) as well as giving judgements within (as *rex*). Their presence penetrated right down to the family level, for while revenue was rarely raised by regular taxation, subjects had obligations to work on his farm and he also collected contributions from each litigant in court, as well as from travellers passing through the kingdom. His presence made itself felt in many ways, though the extent of what has been called 'the reach of the state' differed as between kingdoms, partly as a function of the distance of the periphery from the centre, partly through variations in the ability to command force, partly for a number of other reasons.

How did civil society manifest itself in these different regimes, firstly in the rule of law and indeed of 'justice', of human rights, secondly in the existence of plural sources of power? Acephalous polities are inevitably pluralistic, with decision-making resulting more from discussion rather than from command. A limited authority rests with a number of institutions, secret societies, age sets, local groups. It is also true that the lineage or clan is frequently dominant at a local level. As a result it is difficult to escape from specific decisions or from customary agreements, for these are sustained not simply by a minority of elders but by the community in depth. Law in the most general meaning of that word, 'lawful behaviour', is therefore widely observed and respected.

Such societies lack not only formal law but a formal polity in the original, restricted, sense of that word. There is not a lack of governance but a lack of government in the sense of a governing body of a centralized kind. In other words there is little or nothing to which 'civil society' could be opposed.

However, the states of Africa do possess a central government that is organized around a ruler. Despite the prevalent image of autocratic chiefs extracting unquestioned obedience from their peoples, this kind of Austinian situation is rare. In the kingdom of Asante in West Africa the paramount was described as 'he who speaks lasts'. In Gonja, to the North, the paramount was even more remote and I have called that polity 'an overkingdom' on the ancient Irish model. Quite apart from the shadowy nature of the rulers, even at the divisional level, power of an important kind lay in the hands not only of subordinate chiefs, responsible to their subjects, of organizations of 'young men' who were specifically not chiefs, and of a multitude of religious functionaries whose appeal was to forces outside the polity itself, but there was a very important 'estate' of Muslims who followed a different set of rules, legitimized by the Prophet and the Holy Book, and who carried on wide-ranging commercial activities. These involved trading with merchants outside the kingdom, so that they had a different set of social relationships, as well as religious, spatial, and temporal ones, from the ruling estate. It is true that they married frequently with members of that estate and from many points of view the kingdom as a whole was culturally homogeneous. But they possessed a certain degree of 'independence' because of these outside links, both with Allah and with other groups of Muslims, through whom they might exercise their influence with external powers to intervene in the affairs of the kingdom.

In conclusion, among the acephalous peoples of Africa, as in the hills of China, we find evidence of populations who prefer to place themselves as far as they can from the power of the state. Some may be said to choose a measure of political freedom, but their existence betrays little of the anarchy and disorder often attributed to them by outsiders. Even in the simple states of Africa, there is some space for manoeuvre between the personal and the public. Public protest was more difficult than in Asia, and often took the form of 'exit' rather than 'voice', as it frequently did in Europe. Nevertheless 'commoner resistance' did exist and acted as some kind of restraint on oppression.

The case of Africa is very different from that of the major societies of the Eurasian continent. In the latter, they had all benefited from the agricultural developments of the Bronze Age which were accompanied by the development of urban communities, based on advanced agriculture, with a high degree of specialization and the use of writing. It was under those conditions that 'civilization' first developed. While the Greeks clearly elaborated the notion of 'civil society' in the most literal sense, both its uniqueness and the particular virtues of the European commune, especially in preparing the way for economic advance, have been greatly exaggerated. That is also the case with the idea that the Enlightenment established a special form of rationality that lies behind Western achievements. Achievements there were, but they need to be looked at from a global perspective, not one resting on the thoughts of Western scholars alone.

9   On civil and political society in postcolonial democracies

Partha Chatterjee

I

Bankimchandra Chattopadhyay, the most renowned modernist literary figure in nineteenth-century Bengal, died on 8 April 1894. Three weeks after his death, a memorial meeting, organized by the Chaitanya Library and the Beadon Square Literary Club, was held at the Star Theatre in Calcutta.[1] It was decided that the speakers would be Rajanikanta Gupta, the historian, Haraprasad Sastri, the famous scholar of Buddhism and early Bengali literature, and Rabindranath Tagore, then a young but already much acclaimed poet. Nabinchandra Sen, one of the most respected senior figures on Bengal's literary scene and a younger contemporary of Bankim in the civil service, was asked to preside. To the surprise of the organizers, Nabinchandra refused. In his place, Gurudas Banerjee, judge of the Calcutta High Court, presided over the meeting. The address on Bankim delivered by Rabindranath that day later went on to become something of a landmark essay in Bengali literary criticism. Memorized by generations of schoolchildren, it has been for more than a century a staple of the formation and transmission of aesthetic canons in Bengal's new high culture.

What will concern us here is not the assessment of Bankim's literary output or of his historical role, on which much has been written.[2] Instead, our concern will be the reasons for Nabinchandra Sen's refusal to come to Bankim's memorial meeting. The poet Nabinchandra was

Earlier versions of this paper were presented and discussed at academic meetings in Calcutta, Hyderabad, New York, Philadelphia, and Tashkent. I am grateful to all of those who discussed the paper with me. I am especially grateful to Sudipta Kaviraj for his thoughtful comments which led to the present version of the paper.
[1] All three institutions survive today, more than a hundred years later, although performances at the Star Theatre were stopped after a fire destroyed part of the building a few years ago.
[2] Most recently, and brilliantly, by Sudipta Kaviraj: *The Unhappy Consciousness: Bankimchandra Chattopadhyay and the Formation of Nationalist Discourse in India* (Delhi: Oxford University Press, 1995).

known to have been close to Bankim and, although he did not often share what he thought were the latter's excessively Westernized literary tastes, he clearly deferred to his superior erudition, intellect, and public standing. The reasons for Nabinchandra's refusal had nothing to do with Bankim. Nabinchandra objected to the very idea of a public condolence meeting.

'Imitating the English, we have now begun organizing "condolence meetings",' Nabinchandra wrote. 'As a Hindu, I do not understand how one can call a public meeting to express one's grief. A meeting to express grief, think of it!' 'How many buckets have you arranged for the public's tears?', he is said to have remarked to one of the organizers. 'Our' grief, he claimed, was 'sacred'; it drove one into seclusion. 'We do not mourn by wearing black badges round our sleeves.' A meeting in a public auditorium could only create, he thought, the atmosphere of a public entertainment; this was not 'our way of mourning for the dead'.[3]

Soon after the memorial meeting, Rabindranath Tagore wrote an essay in the journal *Sādhanā*.[4] Entitled 'The Condolence Meeting', the essay began by mentioning the objection that had been raised to the public condolence of Bankim's death. It was true, he said, that the practice was hitherto unknown in the country and that it was an imitation of European customs. But, like it or not, because of our European contacts, both external conditions and subjective feelings were undergoing a change. New social needs were arising, and new ways would have to be found to fulfil them. Because of their unfamiliarity, these might seem artificial and unpleasant at first. But merely because they were European in origin was not a good reason for rejecting them outright.

The main point of objection to the idea of a public condolence meeting seems to have been its *kṛtrimatā*, artificiality. That which is *kṛtrim* is a product of human action: it is an artifice – fabricated, unnatural. Sometimes it indicated a 'mere' form, empty within; sometimes it could even describe behaviour that is insincere, false. This is what Nabinchandra would have meant when he referred to the showing of grief by wearing a black armband. The *kṛtrim* form of a public meeting was inappropriate, he must have said, for expressing an emotion as intense and intimate as grief at the death of a loved one.

In his essay, Rabindranath straightaway took up the question of artificial social forms. A certain *kṛtrimata* was unavoidable if social

---

[3] Nabinchandra Sen, *Āmār jīban*, vol. V (1913) in *Nabīncandra racanābalī*, vol. II, eds. Santikumar Dasgupta and Haribandhu Mukhati (Calcutta: Dattachaudhuri, 1976), p. 253.

[4] Rabindranath Thakur, 'Śoksabha' (May–June 1894) in *Rabīndra-racanābalī*, vol. X (Calcutta: Government of West Bengal, 1989), pp. 291–9.

norms were to be followed, he said. Surely, not everything could be left to individual taste and feeling. Artificiality could be said to be a defect in matters which were strictly internal to the self, where individual feelings reigned supreme. But society being a complex entity, it was not always easy to determine the boundary between the domain of the individual and that of society. In matters pertaining to society, certain universally recognized rules had to be followed if social relations were not to degenerate into anarchy. For example, Rabindranath pointed out, grief at the death of one's father, or – another example – the feelings of a devotee towards god, could be said to involve some of the most intimate and intense emotions in human life. Yet society claims to lay down the procedures of funerary and other associated rites to be followed on the occasion of a father's death, or, in the other case, the procedures of worship to be followed by all devotees, irrespective of individual preference or taste. This is so because society deems it necessary to regulate and order these aspects of life in a way that is beneficial for all of society.

Having made this general point about the necessary 'artificiality' of all social regulations, Rabindranath then goes on to argue that Indian society was for a long time largely a 'domestic society' or a 'society of households' (*gārhasthyapradhān samāj*), a society in which the strongest social bonds rested on the authority of parents and other elders within the family. The specific forms of social regulation in India reflect this domestic character of traditional society. But this was now changing.

Recently there have been some changes in this society of households. A new flood has swept into its domain. Its name is the public.

It is a new thing with a new name. It is impossible to translate it into Bengali. The word 'public' and its opposite 'private' have now come into use in Bengali . . .

Now that our society consists not only of households but also of an emergent public, the growth of new public responsibilities has become inevitable.[5]

One such new public responsibility was the public mourning of the death of those who had devoted their lives not just to the good of their own households but to the good of the public. The form of mourning was 'artificial' as before, but it was now a form in which not just the members of the household but members of the public were required to participate.

What is interesting about this part of Rabindranath's argument is the explicit identification of a new domain of social activity involving 'the public' and of new social regulations ordering these public practices. But he then goes on to make some observations about this emergent public domain that are still more interesting.

[5] 'Śoksabhā', p. 293.

I do not deny the fact that the public in our country is not appropriately grief-stricken by the death of great men. Our public is still young; its behaviour bears the mark of adolescence. It does not recognize its benefactors, does not realize the true value of the benefits it receives, easily forgets its friends and thinks it will only receive what is given to it but will not incur any obligations in return.

I say such a public needs to be educated, and discussions in public meetings are a principal means of such education.[6]

What we have here is a public which is not *yet* a proper public and a group of social leaders who think of their role as one of guiding this public to maturity. Rabindranath, as we can now recognize easily, is only restating here the fundamental problematic of the nationalist project of modernity under colonial conditions. The driving force of colonial modernity is a pedagogical mission.

What a 'proper' public must look like is also, needless to say, given by world history. Rabindranath has no doubt about this. The examples that come to his mind in the context of Bankim's death are from the literary world of Europe and the relationship there between eminent literary figures and the public:

we do not have a literary society in our country and in society itself there is no cultivation of literature. Social practices in Europe make it possible for eminent persons to appear on numerous occasions at numerous public meetings. Their circle of acquaintances is not restricted to their family and friends; they are at all times present before the public. To their compatriots, they are close at hand and visible. Which is why at their death, a shadow of grief falls over the whole country.[7]

By contrast, great men in India, despite their greatness, are not similarly visible in public. 'Especially since women have no place in our outer society, our social life itself is seriously incomplete.' The kind of intimate knowledge of a great person's life, habits, and thoughts that can evoke love and gratitude among ordinary people is completely lacking in our society. Instead of loving and respecting our great men, we turn them into gods to be worshipped from afar. The condolence meeting, argued Rabindranath, was precisely the occasion at which those who were close to a great person could tell the public what he was like as a human being, with faults and idiosyncracies. They could make the great man as a private person visible to the public.

It is easy to recognize the sort of public sphere Rabindranath was wishing for. It was a public sphere consisting of not only books and journals and newspapers but also active literary societies, literary gatherings, an involvement of the public with things literary and cultural, an interest of ordinary people in greatness not as a superhuman gift but as a human achievement. Following Habermas, we can even sense here a hint

[6] Ibid.   [7] Ibid., p. 294.

of that new conception of personhood where the private and the intimate are, as it were, always oriented towards a public. Rabindranath, we can see, was imagining for his own country a world of literary activity embedded in a public sphere constituted by a variety of civil social institutions, the sort of world he himself had seen at first hand when, some fifteen years ago, he had lived in England for more than a year as a student.

Was Nabinchandra not appreciative of a public sphere of this kind? What was the older poet objecting to? Many years after this incident, when writing his autobiography, Nabinchandra Sen returned to the subject. He was, as can be expected, strongly derisive of literary societies and literary gatherings, dismissing them as places where people met for idle talk, or rather idle listening. His idea of commemorating great literary figures was a very different one.

If instead of these utterly wasteful meetings and speeches, the organizers were to preserve the birthplaces of the ancient and [modern] poets of Bengal and hold a sort of religious festival (*debpujār mata utsab*) every year at those places, then we can pay our respects to our great writers, hold a community gathering and at the same time bring credit to the cause of Bengali literature. Mendicant *bairagis* and itinerant singers have in this way turned the birthplaces of the Vaisnava poets Jayadeva, Chandidas and Vidyapati into places of pilgrimage where they hold annual festivals. But we, instead of following this sacred and 'indigenous' (*svadeśī*) path, thanks to English civilization and education, spend our time organizing these laughable condolence and memorial meetings devoid of all true compassion.[8]

He indeed suggested that like the Vaisnava poets of old, the birthplaces of modern writers like Madhusudan, Dinabandhu, and Bankim should be turned into places of pilgrimage where devotees would gather once every year.

Nabinchandra also gave in his autobiography a particularly caustic description of Bankim's condolence meeting.

The condolence meeting was held. When Rabi Babu finished his long, meandering lament, wiped the tears from his eyes and sat down, the audience – so I was told – started shouting from all sides, 'Rabi Thakur! Give us a song!' The eminent Gurudas Babu, who was chairing the meeting, was much annoyed by this and said that Rabi Babu had a bad throat and would not be able to sing today . . . They say in English that people go to church not to worship but to listen to the music. Perhaps it is truer to say that they go there to display their clothes. Similarly in our condolence meetings, people walk in chewing *pan*, humming a tune from Amrita Babu's latest farce, asking for a song in Rabi Thakur's effeminate voice and generally expecting a good evening's entertainment.[9]

---

[8] *Āmār jīban*, p. 208.
[9] Nabinchandra's description of this incident, though coloured by his prejudices, is not

Nabinchandra seems clearly unwilling to accept that a public condolence meeting, like many other formal occasions in modern European social life (including going to church), has any significance apart from mere show. Indeed, he is unprepared even to accept that humanization of greatness which is part of the celebration of ordinary life which lies, as Charles Taylor has pointed out, at the heart of the transformation in social consciousness brought about by Western modernity.[10] Nabinchandra would rather have the great deified after their death, their birthplaces turned into places of pilgrimage, their statues 'worshipped with flowers and sandalpaste'. This, he would say, was 'our' way of collectively expressing our gratitude to the great.

We have here the seeds of a serious disagreement. Does modernity require the universal adoption of Western forms of civil society? If those specific forms have in fact been built around a secularized version of Western Christianity, then must they be imitated in a modernized non-Christian world? Are the normative principles on which civil social institutions in the modern West are based so culturally particular that they can be abandoned in a non-Western version of modernity? These questions have been raised often enough in recent discussions. I wish to discuss here only a particular aspect of the matter.

II

I have not brought up this incident at the beginning of this chapter merely to present one more curiosity from the history of colonial modernity in nineteenth-century Bengal. I think this largely forgotten disagreement can be shown to have an interesting significance for us today, one that was not clear to any of the antagonists a hundred years ago. In order to bring this out, let me first state that the question of condolence meetings is not, as far as I can see, a matter of debate today. Their form is largely the same as in the West, with the laying of wreaths, observing a minute's silence and memorial speeches. These practices of a secularized Western Christianity are rarely recognized as such in India today: they have been quite thoroughly domesticated in the secular public life of the country's civil institutions. Of course, it is not unusual to find a few indigenous touches added on, such as the garlanding of portraits or the burning of incense sticks. Music can be part of such a secular function: in West Bengal as well as in Bangladesh, by far the most

entirely far from the truth. Tagore's most recent biographer quotes another source which gives a similar account. Prasantakumar Pal, *Rabijībanī*, vol. IV (Calcutta: Ananda, 1988), p. 3.

[10] Charles Taylor, *Sources of the Self* (Cambridge, Mass.: Harvard University Press, 1990).

likely music on such an occasion would be something composed by Rabindranath Tagore himself. However, the atmosphere would not be one of a public entertainment: Nabinchandra's fears on this count have proved to be unfounded. Rabindranath's hopes of grooming a public into maturity seem to have been borne out.

This, of course, only concerns public institutions of civic life whose formal practices are recognized as being secular. In other collective institutional contexts, which it would be grossly misleading to call 'private', there is, needless to say, on an occasion such as the death of a prominent person or of someone closely connected with the institution, the continued observance of practices that are clearly recognized as religious. In the domain of the state itself, however, the political pressure to be scrupulously 'secular' requires state authorities to assemble, para-doxically enough, a representative collection of practices from a variety of religions. Each of these – recitations, prayers, discourses, music – is presented in a state mourning ceremony as representing a religion; what makes it a part of a 'secular' state function is the simultaneous presence in one event of all of these representative religions of the country. We will return to this difference between secular public practices in civil institu-tions and state institutions when we talk about the relation today between civil society and political society.

III

Let us now turn to the family, civil society, political society, and the state. These are classical concepts of political theory, but used, we know, in a wide variety of senses and often with much inconsistency. I must clarify here the sense in which I find it useful to employ these concepts in talking about contemporary India.

Hegel's synthesis in the *Philosophy of Right* of these elements of what he called 'ethical life' spoke of family, civil society, and the state, but had no place for a distinct sphere of political society.[11] However, in under-standing the structure and dynamics of mass political formations in twentieth-century nation-states, it seems to me useful to think of a domain of mediating institutions between civil society and the state. The sharpness of the nineteenth-century distinction between state and civil society, developed along the tradition of European anti-absolutist think-ing, has the analytical disadvantage today of either regarding the domain of the civil as a depoliticized domain in contrast with the political domain

[11] G. W. F. Hegel, *The Philosophy of Right*, ed. and trans. T. M. Knox (Oxford: The Clarendon Press, 1952).

of the state, or of blurring the distinction altogether by claiming that all civil institutions are political. Neither emphasis is helpful in understanding the complexities of political phenomena in large parts of the contemporary world.

I find it useful to keep the term 'civil society' for those characteristic institutions of modern associational life originating in Western societies which are based on equality, autonomy, freedom of entry and exit, contract, deliberative procedures of decision-making, recognized rights and duties of members, and other such principles. Obviously, this is not to deny that the history of modernity in non-Western countries contains numerous examples of the emergence of what could well be called civil–social institutions which nevertheless do not always conform to these principles. Rather, it is precisely to identify these marks of difference, to understand their significance, to appreciate how by the continued invocation of a 'pure' model of origin – the institutions of modernity as they were meant to be – a normative discourse can still continue to energize and shape the evolving forms of social institutions in the non-Western world, that I would prefer to retain the more classical sense of the term civil society rather than adopt any of its recent revised versions.[12] Indeed, for theoretical purposes, I even find it useful to hold on to the sense of civil society used in Hegel and Marx as bourgeois society (*bürgerliche Gesellschaft*).

An important consideration in thinking about the relation between civil society and the state in the modern history of countries such as India is the fact that whereas the legal-bureaucratic apparatus of the state has been able, by the late colonial and certainly in the post-colonial period, to reach as the target of many of its activities virtually all of the population that inhabits its territory, the domain of civil social institutions as conceived above is still restricted to a fairly small section of 'citizens'. This hiatus is extremely significant because it is the mark of non-Western modernity as an always incomplete project of 'modernization' and of the role of an enlightened elite engaged in a pedagogical mission in relation to the rest of society.

But then, how are we to conceptualize the rest of society that lies outside the domain of modern civil society? The most common approach has been to use a traditional/modern dichotomy. One difficulty with this is the trap, not at all easy to avoid, of dehistoricizing and essentializing 'tradition'. The related difficulty is one of denying the possibility that this other domain, relegated to the zone of the traditional, could find ways of

---

[12] An account of some of these versions is given in Jean L. Cohen and Andrew Arato, *Civil Society and Political Theory* (Cambridge, Mass.: MIT Press, 1994).

coping with the modern that might not conform to the (Western bourgeois, secularized Christian) principles of modern civil society. I think a notion of political society lying between civil society and the state could help us see some of these historical possibilities.

By political society, I mean a domain of institutions and activities where several mediations are carried out. In the classical theory, the family is the elementary unit of social organization: by the nineteenth century, this is widely assumed to mean the nuclear family of modern bourgeois patriarchy. (Hegel, we know, strongly resisted the idea that the family was based on contract, but by the late nineteenth century the contractually formed family becomes the normative model of most social theorizing in the West as well as of reformed laws of marriage, property, inheritance, and personal taxation. Indeed, the family becomes a product of contractual arragements between individuals who are the primary units of society.) In countries such as India, it would be completely unrealistic to assume this definition of the family as obtaining universally. In fact, what is significant is that in formulating its policies and laws that must reach the greater part of the population, even the state does not make this assumption.

The conceptual move that seems to have been made very widely, even if somewhat imperceptibly, is from the idea of society as constituted by the elementary units of homogeneous families to that of a *population*, differentiated but classifiable, describable, and enumerable. Michel Foucault has been more perceptive than other social philosophers of recent times in noticing the crucial importance of the new concept of population for the emergence of modern governmental technologies.[13] Perhaps we should also note the contribution here of colonial anthropology and colonial administrative theories.

Population, then, constitutes the material of society. Unlike the family in classical theory, the concept of population is descriptive and empirical, not normative. Indeed, population is assumed to contain large elements of 'naturalness' and 'primordiality'; the internal principles of the constitution of particular population groups is not expected to be rationally explicable since they are not the products of rational contractual association but are, as it were, pre-rational. What the concept of population does, however, is make available for governmental functions (economic policy, bureaucratic administration, law and political mobilization) a set of rationally manipulable instruments for reaching large sections of the inhabitants of a country as the targets of 'policy'.

---

[13] See especially Michel Foucault, *The History of Sexuality* (Harmondsworth: Viking, 1985).

Civil social institutions, on the other hand, if they are to conform to the normative model presented by Western modernity, must necessarily exclude from its scope the vast mass of the population. Unlike many radical theorists, I do not think that this 'defect' of the classical concept needs to be rectified by revising the definition of civil society in order to include within it social institutions based on other principles. Rather, I think retaining the older idea of civil society actually helps us capture some of the conflicting desires of modernity that animate contemporary political and cultural debates in countries such as India.

Civil society in such countries is best used to describe those institutions of modern associational life set up by nationalist elites in the era of colonial modernity, though often as part of their anti-colonial struggle. These institutions embody the desire of this elite to replicate in its own society the forms as well as the substance of Western modernity. We can see this desire working quite clearly in the arguments of Rabindranath Tagore quoted at the beginning of this chapter. It is indeed a desire for a new ethical life in society, one that is in conformity with the virtues of the Enlightenment and of bourgeois freedom and whose known cultural forms are those of secularized Western Christianity. All of these are apparent in Rabindranath's argument for new secularized public rituals. It is well recognized in that argument that the new domain of civil society will long remain an exclusive domain of the elite, that the actual 'public' will not match up to the standards required by civil society and that the function of civil social institutions in relation to the public at large will be one of pedagogy rather than of free association.

Countries with relatively long histories of colonial modernization and nationalist movements often have quite an extensive and impressive network of civil social institutions of this kind. In India, most of them survive to this day, not as quaint remnants of colonial modernity but often as serious protagonists of a project of cultural modernization still to be completed. However, in more recent times, they seem to have come under siege.

To understand this, we will need to historicize more carefully the concepts of civil society, political society, and the state in colonial and post-colonial conditions.

IV

The explicit form of the post-colonial state in India is that of a modern liberal democracy. It is often said, not unjustifiably, that the reason why liberal democratic institutions have performed more creditably in India than in many other parts of the formerly colonial world is the strength of its civil social institutions which are relatively independent of the political domain of the state. But one needs to be more careful about the precise relationships involved here.

Before the rise of mass nationalist movements in the early twentieth century, nationalist politics in India was largely confined to the same circle of elites which was then busy setting up the new institutions of 'national' civil society. These elites were thoroughly wedded to the normative principles of modern associational public life and criticized the colonial state precisely for not living up to the standards of a liberal constitutional state. In talking about this part of the history of nationalist modernity, we do not need to bring in the notion of a political society mediating between civil society and the state.

However, entwined with this process of the formation of modern civil social institutions, something else was also happening. I have explained elsewhere how the various cultural forms of Western modernity were put through a nationalist sieve and only selectively adopted, and then combined with the reconstituted elements of what was claimed to be indigenous tradition.[14] Dichotomies such as spiritual/material, inner/outer, alien/indigenous, etc., were applied to justify and legitimize these choices from the standpoint of a nationalist cultural politics. We would have noticed in the debate between the two poets cited above a clear example of this politics. What I wish to point out here in particular is that even as the associational principles of secular bourgeois civil institutions were adopted in the new civil society of the nationalist elite, the possibility of a different mediation between the population and the state was already being imagined, one that would not ground itself on a modernized civil society.

The impetus here was directly political. It had to do with the fact that the governmental technologies of the colonial state were already seeking to bring within its reach large sections of the population as the targets of its policies. Nationalist politics had to find an adequate strategic response if it were not to remain immobilized within the confines of the 'properly constituted' civil society of the urban elites. The cultural politics of nationalism supplied this answer, by which it could mediate politically between the population and the nation-state of the future. In the debate between the two poets, Nabinchandra's arguments anticipated this strategic answer. It would, of course, be explicated most dramatically and effectively in what I have elsewhere described as the Gandhian moment of manoeuvre.[15]

[14] *The Nation and Its Fragments: Colonial and Postcolonial Histories* (Princeton: Princeton University Press, 1994).
[15] *Nationalist Thought and the Colonial World* (London: Zed Books, 1986).

This mediation between the population and the state takes place on the site of a new political society. It is built around the framework of modern political associations such as political parties. But, as researches on nationalist political mobilizations in the Gandhian era have shown repeatedly, elite and popular anti-colonial politics, even as they came together within a formally organized arena such as that of the Indian National Congress, diverged at specific moments and spilled over the limits laid down by the organization.[16] This arena of nationalist politics, in other words, became a site of strategic manoeuvres, resistance, and appropriation by different groups and classes, many of those negotiations remaining unresolved even in the present phase of the post-colonial state. The point is that the practices that activate the forms and methods of mobilization and participation in political society are not always consistent with the principles of association in civil society.

What then are the principles that govern political society? The question has been addressed in many ways in the literature on mass mobilizations, electoral politics, ethnic politics, etc. In the light of the conceptual distinctions I have made above between population, civil society, political society, and the state, we need to focus more clearly on the mediations between population on the one hand and political society and the state on the other. The major instrumental form here in the post-colonial period is that of the developmental state which seeks to relate to different sections of the population through the governmental function of welfare. Correspondingly, if we have to give a name to the major form of mobilization by which political society (parties, movements, non-party political formations) tries to channel and order popular demands on the developmental state, we should call it democracy. The institutional forms of this emergent political society are still unclear. Just as there is a continuing attempt to order these institutions in the prescribed forms of liberal civil society, there is probably an even stronger tendency to strive for what are perceived to be democratic rights and entitlements by violating those institutional norms. I have suggested elsewhere that the uncertain institutionalization of this domain of political society can be traced to the absence of a sufficiently differentiated and flexible notion of community in the theoretical conception of the modern state. In any case, there is much churning in political society in the countries of the post-colonial world, not all of which are worthy of approval, which neverthe-less can be seen as an attempt to find new democratic forms of the

[16] One set of studies of Indian nationalist politics which explicitly addresses this 'split in the domain of politics' is contained in the volumes of *Subaltern Studies* published in India by Oxford University Press, and in several monographs written by historians contributing to that series.

modern state that were not thought out by the post-Enlightenment social consensus of the secularized Christian world.

There are at least four features of political society in post-colonial democracies which need to be noted. First, many of the mobilizations in political society which make demands on the state are founded on a violation of the law. They may be associations of squatters, encroachers on public property, ticketless travellers on public transport, habitual defaulters of civic taxes, unauthorized users of electricity, water, or other public utilities, and other such violators of civic regulations. It is not that they are associations of citizens who merely happen to have violated the law; the very collective form in which they appear before the state authorities implies that they are not proper citizens but rather population groups who survive by sidestepping the law. Second, even as they appear before the state as violators of the law, they demand governmental welfare as a matter of 'right'. There is a clear transformation that has occurred here from 'traditional' notions of the paternalistic function of rulers. Even as we may look for specific genealogies of the 'pastoral function' in non-Western societies, the rhetoric of rights is without doubt a very recent mass phenomenon in these countries and can only be regarded as the effect of a process of globalization of modern governmental technologies along with the language of democratization. Third, even as welfare functions are demanded as a right, these rights are seen to be collective rights. They are demanded on behalf not of individual citizens (since this position is, in any case, unavailable to violators of the law) but of a 'community', even if this community is only the product of a recent coming together through the illegal occupation of a particular piece of public land or the collective illegal consumption of a public utility. Individual rights have no standing when the individuals are known violators of the law; collective rights can mean something when an older ethic of subsistence is married to a new rhetoric of democratization. Finally, the agencies of the state and of non-governmental organizations deal with these people not as bodies of citizens belonging to a lawfully constituted civil society, but as population groups deserving welfare. The degree to which they will be so recognized depends entirely on the pressure they are able to exert on those state and non-state agencies through their strategic manoeuvres in political society – by making connections with other marginal groups, with more dominant groups, with political parties and leaders, etc. The effect of these strategic moves within political society is only conjunctural, and may increase or decrease or even vanish entirely if the strategic configuration of (usually) local political forces change. But that is the ground on which these relations between population groups and governmental agencies will operate within political society. This is very different from the well-structured, principled and constitutionally sanctioned relations between the state and individual members of civil society.[17]

In conclusion, I wish to suggest three theses that might be pursued further. These arise from the historical study of modernity in non-Western societies:

1. The most significant site of transformations in the colonial period is that of civil society; the most significant transformations occurring in the post-colonial period are in political society.
2. The question that frames the debate over social transformation in the colonial period is that of modernity. In political society of the post-colonial period, the framing question is that of democracy.
3. In the context of the latest phase of the globalization of capital, we may well be witnessing an emerging opposition between modernity and democracy, i.e. between civil society and political society.

Before ending, I should make a final remark on my story about the two poets and death. Rabindranath Tagore won the Nobel Prize for literature in 1913 and went on to become by far the most eminent literary figure in Bengal. In his long and active career, he steadfastly held on to his early commitment to an ethical life of public virtue, guided by reason, rationality, and a commitment to a modernist spirit of humanism. Since his death in 1941, however, he of all modern literary figures has been the one to be deified. On the day he died, when his body was taken through the streets of Calcutta, there was a huge stampede when people fought with one another in an attempt to collect relics from the body. Since then, his birthplace has been turned into a place of pilgrimage where annual congregations are held every year – not religious festivals in their specific ceremonial practices, and yet not dissimilar in spirit. We could easily imagine the older poet Nabinchandra Sen chuckling with delight at the predicament of his more illustrious junior. The disagreement over 'our' way of mourning for the dead has not, it would appear, been resolved as yet.

---

[17] I have discussed these points at greater length in 'Community in the East', *Economic and Political Weekly* (Bombay), 32, 6 (7 February 1998); 'L'Etat et la communauté en Orient', *Critique Internationale* (Paris), 2 (Winter 1999), pp. 75–90.

10 Civil society and the fate of the modern republics of Latin America

Luis Castro Leiva and Anthony Pagden

I

'Civil society' is a notoriously elusive term. Nowhere, perhaps is this more obviously so than in contemporary Latin-American political thought.[1] In the past two decades or so the phrase has been used to describe a bewildering range of political and social projects for a future solution to the continent's multiple difficulties. As with other uses of the term in the so-called developing world, civil society is seen as an alternative to conventional politics, expressed as a *social process* governed by the activities of actors and agencies, all of which are located outside the scope of the state. In its most extreme form, it has also become a narrative in which society is set *against* the state.

In view of such diffuse political expectations, it seems appropriate to begin by stating the main thrust of our argument: that far from having no significant history, as most of its advocates have supposed, the concept of civil society as it is used in Latin America can only be understood as the outcome of a very distinctive historical experience: namely the attempt to enact a republican constitution as the only true form of government.[2] No understanding of the place of civil society in Latin America today is possible without a perception of the role republicanism has had to play as the moral basis for all forms of political life. But any attempt to account for the resonance which the concept 'republicanism' has for the citizens of most modern Latin-American republics must begin with one historical and conceptual question – what was meant by a 'true republic'? – and end

---

[1] The literature on the subject is neither as rich nor as extensive as one might wish. See, however, Nikolaus Wertz, *Pensamiento sociopolítico en América latina* (Caracas: Nueva Sociedad, 1995). For a recent analysis of the concept in the context of the revolutionary left see Jorge Castañeda, *La utopía desarmada* (Mexico: Planeta, 1993), pp. 215–18.

[2] Thomas Paine's vision of representative republican government as a universal moral and political good, underpinned as it was by the existence of the United States, was shared by most Latin Americans. Paine was widely read in Spanish. See *La Independencia de la costa firme justificada por Thomas Paine treinta años ha*, translated by Manuel García de Sena (Caracas, 1987. First edn 1811), see especially pp. 88f.

with another – what was meant by a 'true *democratic* republic'? Predictably, the answer to these questions will depend upon an understanding of the ways in which a number of different political languages – classical republicanism, the natural law, the *derecho indiano* (the law governing the former Spanish-American colonies), and the *ius comune* (civil law based upon custom and statute and conceived as a form of *ratio scripta*, 'written reason')[3] – have combined over the centuries since the Spanish conquest. For it is the fusion of these idioms with the more familiar concepts of liberalism and natural rights which have been responsible for the creation of the dense notions of both civil society and republicanism as they are employed today.

Once this is understood, we shall be in a better position to grasp the irony of the current confusion of the multiple meanings of the term. For the normative grounds for a state of *civility* (what Cicero had understood by the term *societas civilis*) were the creation of a society based upon the notion of a common good – or *res publica*. This would be brought into being by a civilist legal tradition deduced from the ideal of the *ius comune*, an ideal which in turn was grounded on the wider notion of natural law and embodied in the doctrine of political representation. Yet it is, of course, precisely these features of the modern republic which the rambling modern use of the term 'civil society' has discarded in its present struggle against the state.

A contradiction between society and the state was, however, built into Spanish-American republicanism from the beginning.[4] The lawyer, Francisco Javier Yañez, one of those responsible for drafting the first Venezuelan constitution, characterized the difficulties involved when he construed 'modern' representative government in this way.

From what has been said, we know that society and government differ essentially with respect to their origins and their object. Society grew out of men's needs, government was the offspring of their vices. Society is always directed towards the good; government is intended to reprieve the bad. Society came first. It is independent and free in its origins. Government was created by society and for society, the former being the instrument of the latter. Society rules; government serves. Society has created force and government, which has received this force

---

[3] On this see Francesco Galasso, *Introduzione al diritto comune* (Milano: A. Giuffre, 1951), and on the place of the *ius comune* – or *derecho comun* – in the New World see Alfonso García Gayo, 'El Derecho común ante el nuevo mundo', *Estudios de historia de derecho indiano. II Congreso del instituto internacional de historia del derecho indiano* (Madrid: Instituto nacional de estudios jurídicos, 1972), pp. 147–66, esp. pp. 158–9.

[4] The term 'Spanish America' precedes 'Latin America'. For convenience we have used the former to designate the colonies of the Spanish monarchy, and the latter to describe the modern republics. The distinctions, however, have far greater significance for the cultural, ethical and political identity of the continent. See A. Ardao, *Estudios latinoamericanos de historia de las ideas* (Caracas: Monte Avila, 1978).

from society, ought to be devoted entirely to the service of society. Society is essentially good. Government can be, and indeed in many parts of the world is, bad.[5]

Republicanism, however, in both its ancient and its modern forms had always sought not a conflict between government and society but the conflation of one with the other. For if the object of the commonwealth was public happiness, then clearly whatever was most likely to procure that happiness was in the best interests of all its citizens. This would be true whether those citizens were, as they had been in the city states of the ancient world, wholly subsumed within the larger community and given over, like Montesquieu's Romans, to military pursuits, or, as in the modern republic, dedicated to a life of largely private and predominantly commercial activities.[6]

The flaw in the conception of republicanism in Latin America, which made it possible for a republican like Yañez to speak of a conflict between society and government, may be found in a dispute over the grounds on which to establish political obligation. From the very beginning an attempt had been made to fuse republicanism with liberalism. What Simón Bolívar – to whom we shall return – called 'la republica liberal' has, since Independence, been perceived as the objective of all the states created out of the former Spanish Empire. The problem was that liberalism and republicanism, far from being initially complementary, instead offered distinct and contrasting sets of moral and political alternatives. Furthermore republicanism was itself divided not merely into the now familiar distinction between ancient and modern, but also over the scope, method, and content of the relationship between political identity and political obligation. Could a true republic possess universal and epistemically conceived practices, or historically and culturally conditioned ones? Should, that is, the political obligation within a republic derive, as Montesquieu had argued, from the nature of things as determined by the particularities of each culture or, should they, as Rousseau and the ancients had claimed, be a reflection of a supposedly unchanging human nature inscribed in the consciousness of the natural law?

The founding fathers of the new Latin-American republics were thus faced with a number of conflicting moral and political dilemmas. Should they adopt the North-American invention of representation, or insist

---

[5] *El manual político del venezolano* (Caracas: Academia nacional de la historia, 1969. First edn 1824), p. 29.

[6] For an account of this ancient model, see Wilfried Nippel, 'Ancient and modern republicanism: "mixed constitution" and "ephors"', in Biancamaria Fontana (ed.), *The Invention of the Modern Republic* (Cambridge: Cambridge University Press, 1994), pp. 6–26.

upon the direct participation of all citizens, as in the ancient republics? Should the Latin-American republics, again like the United States, attempt to be wholly secular or deist, or should they, in recognition of their cultural history, look for inspiration within the Catholic world? Or should they attempt to combine all of these things at once?[7]

The all-embracing, and seemingly transcendental, properties often ascribed to the concept of civil society should be seen in the context of the contending strategies which emerged during the initial formation of the Spanish American political experience, which sought by turns to be both republican and liberal, both particular and universal, ancient and modern. This was further exacerbated by the tension which existed, and still exists, between the communitarian longings which underpin most forms of republicanism and the social logic which sustains the individualist, 'societal' inclinations of the contractualist, liberal elements within modern Spanish-American republicanism.[8]

In order to understand how these confusions arose, and why they continue to exert a directing influence over any possible political future in Latin America, it will be necessary to condense, somewhat fitfully it is true, 185 years of the history of republicanism.

II

This history can be divided into two periods. The first runs from the declarations of Independence in the first decade of the nineteenth century and the subsequent adoption of republicanism as the dominant political form by all of the new states, to the discovery of Latin-America by the Comintern in the 1920s.[9] The second goes from this date until the present day. This trajectory, as we shall see, precisely reverses the history of Spanish-American republicanism. At the very beginning of the history of the new Latin American republics, the politics of freedom was intended to secure a *res publica* in order to create a civil society, which would be capable of delivering public happiness for all its members. It was the state which was seen as the only instrument capable of generating civility within a polity which, until independence, had been wholly devoid of any autonomous political culture. It was the state which became the essential

---

[7] See Juan Germán Roscío, *El Triunfo de la libertad sobre el despotismo* (Caracas: Monte Avila, 1983. First edn 1817). This is perhaps the first complete work on politics ever written in Latin America.

[8] 'Individualism' is used here in its modern legal and political sense. See Louis Dumont, *Essai sur l'individualisme* (Paris: Editions du Seuil, 1983), p. 96 and M. Villey, *La Formation de la pensée juridique moderne* (Paris: Montcrestien, 1963).

[9] See Manuel Caballero, *Latin America and the Comintern 1919–1943* (Cambridge: Cambridge University Press, 1986).

moral force behind the *res publica*, and thus the chosen subject of history and the leading agency of any possible social change or individual identity. Today the role of politics has been inverted. Now it is the role of society to eliminate, as far as possible, the state.

Both historical periods are witness to two distinct kinds of political failures. The first marks the doomed attempt at the creation of a flourishing republic, and the slow suffocation by notions of 'patriotism' and civic obligation of the modern liberal conception of liberty.[10] It is the history of the misfortunes of the notion of 'public happiness', as the basis for a new political order in Latin America. Ultimately it marks the death of liberalism at the hands of republicanism. For although they have all attempted to achieve their social well-being as polities, no Latin-American republic has yet succeeded in being either a 'liberal republic' or a 'true republic' – as Rousseau would have understood the term – let alone a modern commercial republic such as the United States.

The second phase of our history marks the rise and fall of another philosophy of history, namely the appropriation by socialism of the republican experience, and its bid to re-describe the absorption of the state by society as the outcome of a world revolution. In this form it marks an entirely different kind of political and moral failure, the failure to secure a socialist, as opposed to a civil, republic, something of which the national histories of Chile, Nicaragua, and Cuba have all been tragic examples.

III

The character of the first stage of our brief history is best captured in the writings of the most significant of the early theorists of the Independence movements in Spanish America: Simón Bolívar, 'the Liberator' of what is now Venezuela and Colombia. For the models which provided the inspiration for Bolívar's ill-fated union of Colombia la Grande were to be great *respublicae* of the Ancient World: Athens, Sparta, Thebes, and Rome. It was the history of these states, he told the Congress of Angostura in 1819, convened to draft a constitution for the new republic, which would 'serve us as a guide in this course', not anything drawn from the history of the Spanish Empire, still less from the indigenous polities of the New World.[11]

---

[10] Luis Castro Leiva, 'The Dictatorship of Virtue or the Opulence of Commerce', *Jahrbuch für Geschichte von Staat, Wirtschaft und Gesellschaft Latinamerikas*, 29 (1992), pp. 195–240.

[11] Simón Bolívar, *Obras completas*, ed. Vicente Lecuña (La Habana, 1950), 3 vols., vol. III, pp. 684–5. For a more extended account of Bolívar's historical borrowings see Anthony Pagden, *Spanish Imperialism and the Political Imagination* (London and New Haven: Yale University Press, 1990).

Isolated in this way from any compelling historical legacy, Bolívar, and those who reasoned like him, were compelled to create nations *ex nihilo*. But imagined states are always, as one anonymous and hostile observer noted in 1820, in danger of becoming 'a world which is, in some way fantastic, that can be made to justify the past and authorize the hopes of the future'.[12] Bolívar was, and was conscious of being, in the full Machiavellian sense of the phrase, a 'New Prince', and he remained throughout his career committed to the vision of a new kind of society, what he termed 'the liberal nation' (*nación liberal*), which was to be composed of a new kind of man: 'the good citizen'.

Bolívar's 'liberal nation' was to be a community of free men guaranteed equality before the law which would be responsive to, if not dictated directly by, public opinion; a community, furthermore which would be directed towards the happiness of its members and would be free from 'factions and parties'. In this generalized account, at least, Bolívar was echoing contemporary European liberal views, those of the French pamphleteer Dufour De Pradt, 'the sublime philosopher', who played Aristotle to his Alexander, of Jeremy Bentham, who offered his services as the ideal legislator for the new state, and of Benjamin Constant, who, unperceptively perhaps, thought of Bolívar as little more than a potential Napoleon.[13] Where Bolívar differed radically from European liberals – and, indeed, from Jefferson and Washington – was in his insistence that the *nación liberal* could only be achieved in the shape (or something very close to it) of the virtuous republic of Rousseau's *Contrat social*. As Luis Castro has observed elsewhere, Bolívar's entire political project can be viewed as a flawed, and ultimately impossible, attempt to transform Book III of the *Contrat social* into a constitution.[14] His concept of liberty, that is, was far closer to the concept of the liberty enjoyed within the ancient republics of Athens and Rome than it was to what Constant famously described as 'modern liberty', and which was, *mutatis mutandis,* exemplified in the United States, that 'society of saints' – as Bolívar, not without irony, called it on more than one occasion. This disjuncture between ancient and modern liberty was to have far-reaching, and ultimately disastrous, consequences for Latin America.

The liberty provided by the *modern* republic, and subsequently by liberal democratic society, created what, in Rousseau's terms, comes

---

[12] *Reflexiones sobre el estado actual de la América, o cartas al Abate de Pradt* (Madrid, 1820), p. iv. The author is anonymous.

[13] On the Constant/De Pradt controversy see *Bolívar y Europa en las crónicas, el pensamiento político y la historigrafía,* ed. Alberto Filippi, vol. I, no. XIX (Caracas: Ediciones de la presidencia de la república, Comité ejecutivo del bicentenario de Simón Bolívar), pp. 288–347.

[14] *La Gran Colombia, una ilusión ilustrada* (Caracas: Monte Avila, 1985).

close to being a contradiction, the 'private citizen'. Men, that is, may be men *and* citizens.[15] They have access, if only as voters, to a political life, which they had been denied under the monarchies of the *ancien régime*; but they are not wholly subject to it. The liberal state, in other words, provided its citizens not merely with *political* liberty, but also with civil liberty. And, as Constant's own distinction between civil and political liberty suggests, it was the liberal republic – unlike its classical, or Rousseauian predecessor – which was responsible for the creation of a visible, if still sometimes indistinct, collective domain which lies beyond the household and is therefore subject to laws of conduct – what in the eighteenth century went under the heading of *moeurs* – but not directly to any external or coercive power, although it forms the basis of that power.

As we all know, the concept of such an autonomous civil society was first made explicit and given theoretical definition by Hegel. As Norberto Bobbio has conveniently described it: 'A wholly different history begins with Hegel, for whom, for the first time, "civil society" does not describe the State in its totality, but represents only a moment in the process of the formation of the State.'[16] Bobbio's history, perhaps, makes too much of the Hegelian moment. But it is clear in the writers of the eighteenth century – and in particular for our purposes Montesquieu – that the Ciceronian *societas civilis* is both anterior in historical time to the formation of the political, and a necessary condition of its creation. The discussion in Book 19 chapter 14 of the *Esprit des lois* makes this abundantly clear. Laws 'regulate the actions of citizens – *moeurs* regulate those of men'. Sometimes, however, 'these things are confused'. One example Montesquieu gives of a state in which this has happened is China, a society, as he explains elsewhere, whose famous 'immobility', and despotic state, could be explained precisely by the ability of the Tartars to collapse the civil into the political. Liberty, therefore, depends for its existence, and survival, upon a mutually if also tacitly agreed set of culturally enforced conventions. It depends, furthermore, as both Montesquieu and Constant realized, but Bolívar perhaps did not, upon the existence of a compelling *image* of a community, in which each private individual would wish to place his or her trust.

Bolívar's conception of the ideal republic is problematic, and ultimately muddled. In a number of crucial respects, it is far closer to the account to be found in Montesquieu than it is to that of Rousseau. He recognized that any republic created in the first half of the nineteenth century could not ignore the existence in all modern societies of the civil.

---

[15] See in general, Judith Shklar, *Men and Citizens. A Study of Rousseau's Social Theory* (Cambridge: Cambridge University Press, 1969).

[16] *Stato, governo, società. Per una teoria generale della politica* (Turin: Einaudi, 1985), p. 32.

He even went so far as to tell the *Congreso constituyente de Bolivia*, in 1826, that personal security and civil liberty guaranteed by a just administration was all that was required of a liberal state. 'The political organization matters little', he concluded, 'so long as the civil is perfect.'[17] But despite his recognition of the need for some of the features of modernism, Bolívar's republic was predominantly ancient. The republic alone could 'regenerate the character and customs which tyranny and war have bequeathed to us' and the republic alone was able to create in the rain forests 'a Moral Power, taken from the depths of antiquity and from those forgotten laws which, at one time sustained virtue among the ancient Greeks and the Romans'. 'We shall', he told the legislators at Angostura in a passage which, at least as far as the sentiments it expresses, could have been taken directly from the *Contrat social*,

take from Athens the Areopagus and the guardians of customs and the Laws; from Rome take the censors and the domestic tribunals, and by making a holy union of all these moral institutions, we will revive in the world the idea of a people which is not content to be only free and strong, but also wishes to be virtuous. We will take from Sparta its austere establishments and by creating out of these three streams a fountain of virtue, we will give to our Republic a fourth force whose strength will be the childhood and the hearts of men, the public spirit, good customs and Republican morality.[18]

This vision, he assured his listeners, was no mere 'candid delirium' but 'a thought which, perfected by experience and enlightenment, is capable of becoming very effective'.[19] To many, Sparta itself may have seemed little more than 'a chimerical invention', but instead Lycurgus had produced 'real effects', effects which had sustained 'Glory, Virtue, Morality, and, in consequence, natural happiness'.[20] (It is not insignificant that, as Bolívar well knew, Montesquieu had put Sparta in the same category as China, as a society in which the state had collapsed the distinction between 'laws' and 'customs'.)

Bolívar's understanding of the identity of the true republic was broadly characteristic of, although conceptually and rhetorically more powerful than, that held by most of the founders of the new Latin-American states. The most enduring consequence of this vision was to heighten the significance of such concepts as moral rationality, the supremacy of the general will, and the pursuit of 'public happiness'. The science of legislation and the role of the legislator were thus entrusted with the 'sublime' task of nation building. Eventually these essentially enlightened views on the role of legislation become characteristic of what has come to be called Latin-American *constitutionalism*. It was as if the science of

---

[17] *Obras completas*, vol. III, p. 769.   [18] Ibid., vol. III, p. 692.
[19] Ibid., pp. 693–4.   [20] Ibid., pp. 683–4.

Rousseau's legislator had been fused with the powers of the 'New Prince' so as to will the construction of citizens out of men.[21]

In the end, however, Bolívar's image of the virtuous republic of Venezuela turned out to be all too chimerical an invention. In his final years Bolívar himself became as despairing of the future of the continent as any of the North American, and British, observers had been. America, he famously said, was ungovernable. It was bound to fall into mob rule and if devolution were at all possible in human history, then America was soon destined to recreate the original state of chaos.[22]

The virtuous republic that was to have been Colombia la Grande had been based on the assumption that such a society *could* be created out of a world which was racially heterogeneous, economically divided and which, with the exception of the criollo elite, had no previous sense of itself as a community of any kind. At one level Bolívar's failure can be described as a failure to acknowledge fully his own tacit and faltering recognition that no modern state could adequately be founded upon the principles of ancient liberty. At another it might be characterized as an inability to see that, for the would-be creator of new states, the legacies of his two favoured authors, Montesquieu and Rousseau, led to two very different conclusions. Montesquieu also possessed a vision of republican liberty which was as 'ancient' as Rousseau's, in that it, too, was of a society 'moved' by the virtue of its citizens. But Montesquieu had also recognized that even the most virtuous of societies depends for its creation and survival upon its prior cultural constitution, upon precisely the degree to which it possessed a sustainable civil society. Republics, furthermore, were exceptionally fragile in this respect because they depended, far more than monarchies did, 'on the customs, habits and attitudes of the citizens far more than on explicit legislation'. Without a powerful structure of such customs, habits, and attitudes – without, that is, a civil society – already in place it would prove impossible to create a new republic.

Bolívar had learned from Montesquieu that, as he warned the legislators at Angostura, any law code must be in accord 'with the religion of its inhabitants, its inclinations, its riches, its size and its commerce, its customs and its habits' and he chided those who thought that 'the

[21] For a contemporary analysis of a not dissimilar European view of the power of legislation see Benjamin Constant's critique of Gravina, Montesquieu, and Filangieri in *Commentaire sur l'ouvrage de Filangieri* in *Oeuvres de Gaetano Filangieri* (Paris, 1822), vol. VI, p. 40.
[22] See 'Carta al General J. J. Flores', 9 November 1830 in Simón Bolívar, *Doctrina del Libertador* (Caracas: Biblioteca Ayacucho, 1976), p. 99.

blessings from which [the North Americans] benefit are due exclusively to the form of their government and not to the character and the customs of the citizens'.[23] He knew that the state of nature was a real place, all too often directly encountered by the banks of the Orinoco, and that the men in it were not natural. Most of those with whom he was acquainted, in particular after three hundred years of Spanish rule, had been 'perverted by illusions of error and by noxious incentives'. Before such creatures could be made into citizens, the legislators at Angostura had first to – as he phrased it – 'constitute men' out of the former vassals of the Spanish Monarchy. But he failed to recognize the full extent of the hold which the accumulated legacy of those 'illusions of error and noxious incentives',[24] real or fictive, had over men's minds, that the heterogeneous social groupings of the disintegrating Spanish Empire were hardly likely to respond undirected to the call of the General Will. What they required, in addition to the satisfaction of their own immediate interests, was precisely some sense of belonging to a civil community, rather than an artificial nation-state. And this neither Bolívar's rhetoric nor Bolívar's belief in constitutional restraints could provide.

The abstractions which Bolívar urged upon the various representative bodies he advised – liberty, public opinion, virtue, moral power – had no imaginative force, outside a powerfully constituted community. In absence of a civil society it was only the military who could prevent a return, to use Bolívar's language, to the state of nature, because in the end it was only the military for whom the ancient republic – which had, of course, been itself little more than an armed camp – had any lasting imaginative power.

The legacy of Latin America's 'New Prince' was to prove fateful on several counts. In the first place it pre-empted any possibility of rede-scribing – as the Spanish liberals of 1812 were to do – the present and the future of the new states in terms of a political consensus based upon a liberal-Whiggish tradition which could trace its origins back to the supposed 'Ancient Constitution' of Castile. Secondly, in nations which had been cut adrift by revolution from their previous communal histories, it filled the space which should have been occupied by a civil conscious-ness with a form of political romanticism.[25] Thirdly, it inspired an enduring commitment to a utopian conception of the 'true' republic as an organic entity lying outside time yet based upon a precise historical vision, a paradox which meant that, in Latin America, the best way to be

---

[23] *Obras completas*, vol. III, p. 681.
[24] Ibid., vol. II, p. 678.
[25] The term is, of course, Carl Schmitt's, *Political Romanticism* [*Politische Romantik*], trans. G. Oakes (Cambridge, Mass.: MIT Press, 1986).

a conservative was to be a revolutionary. (It is this which underpins the otherwise oxymoronic title of Mexico's former ruling political party: the 'Institutional Revolutionary Party'.)

As a consequence, the wars of independence, and the ideologies which had brought them about, became for all the Latin-American republics the Archimedean point, on which all politics were henceforth made to turn, both historically and morally. Both contractualism and something akin to Bolívar's own brand of political romanticism were thus conceived as the means of making the transition from the natural to the civil state, from slavery under the Spanish monarchy to freedom in the new states, and even, in time, from this to the related, but quite different condition of 'true democracy'.

As things stood at the turn of the nineteenth century, only very few of the nascent Latin American republics could achieve the standards of civility set by such abstract political ambitions. The league-table of civilized nations drawn up by the Victorian pundit Viscount James Bryce made this clear:

> Whether better or worse, however, and by whatever name the government of these States may be called, none of them is a democracy. But it is one of the oddest instances of the power of a word that the less educated persons and even many of the more educated among the free nations have continued, especially in the United States, to believe them to be, because called 'Republics', entitled to a confidence and sympathy which could not be given to a military tyranny under any other name. Chile, Argentina, Uruguay, and Brazil belong to a different category. They are true Republics, if not all of them democracies.[26]

Bryce's judgement was roughly similar to Bolívar's own views on the likely fate of both republicanism and democracy, and it was shared at the time by many Latin-American intellectuals.[27] Since then, however, things have changed in a number of significant respects. The continent has witnessed the reversal of Bryce's league table. Chile, Argentina, Brazil, and Uruguay, once 'true republics', have all degenerated at crucial periods in their histories into brutal military tyrannies. Venezuela, Colombia, and Mexico, by contrast, have developed into more or less structured, if not totally coherent, political communities and somewhat awkward, and occasionally unstable, democracies. The insular republics of Cuba and Haiti, continue to defy classification. They are certainly not democracies and Cuba is still, possibly, the last remaining tribute to

---

[26] *Modern Democracies* (London: Macmillan and Co., 1921), 2 vols., vol. I, pp. 216–17.
[27] See Leopoldo Zea, 'Aurora de un nuevo mundo, parte II: La filosofía como conciencia de lo americano', in *La Filosofía como compromiso de liberación*, preface by Arturo Ardao, chronological selection and bibliography by Liliana Weinberg de Magis and Mario Magallón (Caracas: Ediciones Biblioteca Ayacucho, 1991), vol. 160, especially p. 107.

Rousseau's republicanism in this, or any other, continent. Haiti, after a head-start in the last century, is desperately trying to begin its republican and democratic experiment all over again. Both states have revealed the weakness of their political experience at a time when socialism has been defeated in Nicaragua.

Today, most of the 'true republics' are trying to organize peace, justice, and concord, through universal suffrage and a commitment to the language of rights. And all have undergone dramatic changes to their economic structures. (Witness, for instance, the modernization programme implemented within the last decade in Chile, Argentina, Brazil, Mexico, Peru, and Bolivia.) Finally, there has also been a marked change of attitude north of the Pecos. The vocabulary, and the experience, of Bryce's 'less educated person, especially in the United States', have been transformed in the second half of this century. North America has become the leading empire of the world, and there, contrary to Maine's predictions, the word 'republic' has been replaced by the much more expansive 'democracy'. Whereas in Latin America 'the forms of action' of republicanism, to adopt F. W. Maitland's vocabulary, might indeed have been buried, its ethical and political idioms still 'rule us from their graves'.[28]

The widely accepted association between a 'true republic' and a 'true democracy' is, at best, questionable. But the idea which lies behind both Bryce and Bolívar's views, and which can be traced back to Montesquieu, is still politically compelling. Namely, that in order for there to be democracy within republicanism, and therefore something which might be called a 'true popular republic', there must exist some moral and political expertise in the art of self-government at either a local or national level, in which all the citizens of the republic can participate directly.[29] The paradox for the Bolivarian *respublica* is that it was precisely such a shared political experience, as an expression of the *civil* disposition of the citizen body, which was lacking in the ancient, and Rousseauian, conception of the republic.[30]

Civil society, furthermore, clearly depends for its continuing survival upon the effectiveness of a working constitution. But any such constitution requires a past sense of civility, which its turn relies upon pre-

---

[28] F. W. Maitland, *The Forms of Action at the Common Law* (Cambridge: Cambridge University Press, 1971. First edn 1909), p. 1.

[29] This had become fully entrenched in Latin America by the end of the nineteenth century. See Natallo R. Botana, *La libertad política y su historia* (Buenos Aires: Editorial Sudamericana, 1991), pp. 66 ff.

[30] For a recent appraisal of this thesis and its interpretation as a consequence of a political conception of modernity, see François Xavier Guerra, *Modernidad e independencia* (Madrid: Colecciones Mafré, 1992).

existent civic customs, a collective purpose, and the willingness on the part of the members of the political community to trust one another. Clearly, as Bolívar learnt to his cost, no constitution can be made to yield the civility on which it has itself to rely if it is to have any effective purchase upon its citizens' loyalty. Conversely, the lack of social and political maturity has traditionally in Latin America called not for the creation of such customs but for the persistent expression of unrestrained civic enthusiasm and republican patriotism in the romantic quest for a 'true republic'. The outcome of this conflict has generally been dire, and since it has inevitably resulted in the insistence upon legislation as the cure for all social ills, it has become emblematic of a particularly Latin American form of constitutionalism.[31] 'There was', as Bryce noted,

in fact no basis whatever for common political action, so the brand new constitutions which a few of the best-educated colonial leaders had drafted on the model of the United States . . . did not correspond to anything real in the circumstances of the new so-called republican states.[32]

None of the new states in Latin America acquired constitutions anything like that of the United States, if only because, as Bolívar himself had seen, no former colony of the Spanish monarchy possessed the political experience which the peoples of the Thirteen Colonies had traditionally enjoyed.[33] In so far as the modern republics have tried to conceive their collective lives according to a constitutional form of republicanism, awkwardly wishing to be both 'liberal' and 'virtuous' at the same time, they have failed both to acquire the kind of political consciousness necessary for those who wish to lead their lives as autonomous individuals, and to secure the kind of virtuous *respublica* based upon the logic of patriotic self-denial which Bolívar and those like him had so hoped for. Since in Spanish America each of these political options has been socially perceived as dependent upon the success of the other, and since classical republicanism is closely associated with militarism, this has posed a constant threat to the liberal and democratic aspirations of these republics. It is at this point, the point where Bolívar's dream for a virtuous republic which could be both virtuous *and* liberal would seem to have run into the sand with ultimately disastrous consequences for the future of most of the new states in the region, that the second phase of our history begins.

---

[31] The contrast is between the concept of *rational*, *normative*, and *sociological* constitutions. On this see Manuel García Pelayo, *Derecho constitucional comparado* (1950), in *Obras Completas* (Madrid: Centro de Estudios Constitucionales, 1994), vol. I, pp. 259–69.

[32] Ibid., p. 211.

[33] See Pagden, *Spanish Imperialism*, pp. 147–8.

IV

In his observations on grammar in the *Prison Notebooks*, Antonio Gramsci distinguished between what he called 'immanent' grammar and 'normative' grammar, and attempted to explain the relationship of these two forms to the development of world history and to the rise of nationalism.[34] Questions such as 'What do you mean?', 'Explain yourself better', or 'What does that mean?' are, he claimed, the terms which constitute a society's control over its language and language users. Gramsci offers a point of entry into the difficulties which faced Latin-American political theory after the advent of Marxism.[35] For the normative use of the concept of civil society in Latin-American politics can be seen as an instance of this interplay between the desire to fix and control the language of politics and the wider culture's persistent demand for clarification, modification, and change. It shows, too, we suggest, the various ways in which Marxism still maintains, an – albeit muted – control over the cultural and practical purchase of the concept of civil society in contemporary politics.

For Gramsci every 'normative grammar' is an instance of an 'historical grammar' and since no 'historical grammar' can be confined within national boundaries, every such grammar must be seen as forming part of world history. Today these claims have taken on massive economic and sociological significance, particularly in the light of what Gramsci had to say about culture and of the place of 'peripheral' societies in the history of the 'world'. Terms such as 'democracy', 'the market', and 'civil society' itself, and the semantic structures in which they can be made to have some imaginative force, are all taken to apply indiscriminately to the 'world'. In Latin America the supposedly universal applicability of civil society followed closely upon the collapse of the universal language – Marxism – to which Gramsci was himself referring. Civil society might perhaps be thought of as the antithesis to Marxism, but it also shares with Marxism an appeal to what is believed in some sense to belong to human nature independently of culture.[36]

This late entry of the concept of civil society into the political discourse

---

[34] *Quaderni del carcere*, ed. Valentino Gerratana (Turin: Einaudi, 1975), 4 vols., vol. III, pp. 2346–51.

[35] On the presence of Gramsci in Latin American political thought, see José Arico, *La cola del diablo: intinerario de Gramsci en América Latina* (Caracas: Editorial Nueva Sociedad, 1988).

[36] In this respect, too, John Dunn (this volume) is probably right to insist that if we want a fully coherent description of civil society, we have to begin with an account of the law of nature, even if such an account is hardly likely to be widely available in the modern world and it is difficult to see in what it would now be grounded.

of most Latin American republics follows, furthermore, the late entry of Marxism itself into the political cultures of the southern hemisphere. The former history shadows the latter as the latter shadows the history of the evolution of republicanism as we have attempted to describe it.

The story begins precisely with the Comintern's refusal to acknowledge the cultural and political significance of the republican and liberal ideas of civility when dealing with the Latin-American states. This refusal originated with the semi-colonial status conferred upon the Latin-American countries during the Sixth World Congress in 1928 by the strategists of a world revolution directed from Moscow. Latin-American Marxists reacted strongly to what they saw as little more than a revised version of the older relationship between colony and metropolis. Their response took the form of an appeal to the value attached to their status as independent nations, their legal capacity to act within the League of Nations, and their recognized capacity to lead an active diplomatic existence within the international arena. 'Indignantly', in the words of one of their number, they took up the cause of the cultural values, of 'civility' as an integral part of the ethical and political understanding of what it meant to be an independent republic, a sovereign state endowed with a civil law. They saw their identities not, as the Soviet Marxists had done, as transcending all existing cultural values, but as the *outcome* of such values, and in particular as the product of the relationship between republicanism and the civil values of public international law, which they regarded as a central feature of organized and *civilized* nations. This, of course, had no place in the Marxist theory of revolution at all, except as features of the bourgeois state the revolution is destined to replace.

Gradually the nature of the Latin-American republics became the subject of a very complex theoretical discourse concerned with their identity as societies. This attempted to find an answer to a number of questions: namely, could these republics be described as 'dependencies' rather than 'colonies'? Were they feudal or agrarian, just how industrialized were they, and how far, if at all, had they travelled towards the condition of the 'bourgeois state' (*bürgerliche Recht*) system which is the necessary condition of the proletarian revolution? Most troubling of all was the question of who was to be the 'subject' of the revolution, and was that revolution, which would henceforth guide world history, in any way connected to the individual history of such 'dependencies'?[37] Eventually these sterile and for most Latin Americans – no matter how persuaded

---

[37] See, for instance, V. R. Haya de la Torre, *El Antiimperialismo y el APRA* (Lima: Ediciones culturales marfil. Seventh edn, 1982).

they were of the truth of Marxist historicism – offensive debates, were to have far-reaching consequences for the development of Marxism in Latin America.

The response of Latin-American Communists was an attempt to fuse Marxism with notions of 'civility' and 'republicanism' in an ideology which combined nationalism with Marxist universalism and which insisted upon what has subsequently come to be called the politics of identity. (Similar fusions would appear slightly later in other areas of the South, although none would have their origin in the attempt to combat what was seen as a form of Soviet-centred cultural imperialism.) For most Latin Americans, however, their resistance to the Comintern's narrative of world history was by no means the mere assertion of a competing national historical narrative. It demanded instead a re-evaluation of the origins and nature of their form of republicanism and of its relationship to ideas of civility, democracy, and popular government in the context of the Communist world revolution. Eventually this developed into the alternative Communist or socialist conceptions of politics to be found in the works of José Carlos Mariátegui and Victor R. Haya de la Torre in Peru or Romulo Betancourt in Venezuela. Mariátegui, in particular, who has frequently been described as a Latin American forerunner of Gramsci, provided the most powerful refutation of the Comintern's semi-colonial history. By stressing the role played by race and indigenous cultural life, and by refusing to use the word 'Communist' even of the party itself, he reclaimed the values of local historical and cultural narratives at the expense of the universalist claims of Marxist world history.[38]

In the absence of a bourgeoisie, or indeed of a recognizable proletariat, the issue of civility within a republican society re-surfaced as the basis for a new mode of socialism. What was called 'Aprismo' (after APRA, the Alianza Popular Revolucionario Americana founded by Victor R. Haya de la Torre) in Peru and 'Betancourismo' (after Rómulo Betancourt[39]) in Venezuela followed this conceptual lead. By insisting upon the need for a nationalist revolutionary struggle based upon a political class (*policlasista*), rather than one based on the Party's vision of the transformation of the state into a Soviet satellite (as for instance, Cuba was eventually to become), the concept of political nationalism fused with republican civility widened still further the gap between those who envisaged a

---

[38] See, for example, 'El problema de Indio' in *Siete ensayos de la realidad peruana*, preface by de Anibal Quijano (Caracas: Ediciones Biblioteca Ayacucho, 1979), vol. 69, pp. 20–1.

[39] On Betancourt see Arturo Sosa Abascal and Eloi Lengrand, *Del Garibaldismo estudiantil a la izquierda criolla: los orígenes marxistas del proyecto de A.D. (1928–1935)* (Caracas: Editorial Centauro, 1981) pp. 295ff.

revolution within the earlier local republican tradition, and those who adhered to the view that *the* Revolution could only take place on the world-historical stage. More significantly still, these versions of national Marxism confronted the Comintern by stressing the substantive moral character of civility and its relation to the liberal conception of universal suffrage as part of a revolutionary struggle, and not merely a component of the process of bourgeois reform. In this way the idea of democracy, as a form of political and social life, was assimilated to the earlier republican ideals associated with Jacobinism.

These nationalist versions of Marxism have had, however, a damaging effect on the historical understanding of the role which the concept of republican civility has played in Latin America. For they conflated two previously distinct historical accounts: that of the civic virtues of republicanism and liberalism, on the one hand, and that of the rise of the bourgeois liberal state within the dependent, or semi-colonial, societies of Latin America on the other. This conflation of the 'liberal' and the republican moments in the history of state formation was as much the product of a Marxist world history written *for* Latin America, as it was the outcome of a retreat from world history as written *by* Latin-American nationalists.

One outcome of this debate was an increasing confusion in the political languages employed by groups on both the left and the right over the distinction between the idea of civility within a modern representative republic and that within an essentially Roman agrarian and military *civitas*. It also helped to reinforce the earlier Enlightenment conflicts over the optimal political state which, as we have seen, similarly failed to distinguish between civility as an exchange between private citizens and civility as, in Bolívar's characterization, the basis of a *poder moral* within a 'virtuous' and ancient *respublica*.

More recent Marxist political practices have only deepened these tensions. The political failure of Cuba and Nicaragua has, in different ways, served to reinforce the view that civility, as embodied in the republican concept of the rule of law (*estado de derecho*), was merely an ideological illusion.[40] Neither of these societies was able, in practice, to sustain a non-partisan structure of civil law. In this they may have been – and Castro's Cuba certainly is – closer to the realities of the ancient Roman republic, but they came nowhere near to fulfilling their initial promise as the socialist embodiment of the modern republic. At the same

---

[40] This view is stated most clearly by E. B. Pashukanis, 'The Marxist Theory of State and Law', in *Selected Writings on Marxism and Law*, ed. P. Berne and R. Sharlet (New York: Academic Press, 1980), p. 278.

time the more obviously liberal elements associated with the political experience of these republics, the autonomy of the citizen and the self-reflexiveness of civic consciousness, were subjected to similar ideological distortion.

The German construction of 'civil' as *bürgerliche*[41] and the subsequent Marxist interpretation of state formation effectively detached the term 'civil society' from its historical origins in the classical ideal of an independent republic with a popular government. The identification of the 'civil' with a particular class (the bourgeoisie) had the effect of establishing the concept as something which was irredeemably associated with the *ancien régime*, and at the same time of projecting this limited bourgeois conception of the civil into the future in the form of – from the Marxist perspective – a wholly undesirable social individualism. If, that is, civil society were to survive anywhere at all in the world, it could do so only as the expression of the dialectical forces of late capitalism.[42] Latin American Marxism thus had the effect of sustaining the force of Maine's observation, that all societies evolve from an idea of civility as status to one of civility as contract,[43] and that the history of societies such as those which had arisen in Latin America should be seen as one of unplanned transition from a form of corporate empire to a liberal bourgeois state. And since democracy and popular government was the final outcome of the struggle for universal suffrage, the *bürgerliche* conception of civility turned the state into the focus, and the chosen political arena, for the revolutionary struggles of the various Latin-American Communist Parties.

Three later developments in the theory and practice of Marxism, however, substantially altered this vision: the collapse of the Cuban model, the effects of the invasion of Czechoslovakia,[44] the break with the orthodox Communist Parties and with the Soviet Union and, at another level, the Althusserian revolution within orthodox Marxism itself. Each of these, in its different way, helped to bring back the cultural significance

---

[41] For a more extensive account of the Marxist uses of the term see Manfred Reidel, 'Bürger, Staatsbürger, Bürgertum', in Otto Brunner, Werner Conze, and Reinhart Koselleck, eds., *Geschichtliche Grundbegriffe: historisches Lexikon zur politisch-sozialen sprache in Deutschland* (Stuttgart: Ernst Klett, 1972), vol. I, pp. 716–22.

[42] See, for instance, Carlos Rangel, *Del buen salvaje al buen revolucionario* (Caracas: Monte Avila, 1976) and Plinio Apuleyo Mendoza, Carlos Alberto Montaner, and Alvaro Vargas Llosa, *Manual del perfecto idiota latino-americano* (Barcelona: Plaza Janes, 1996).

[43] *Primitive Society and the Ancient Law* (Boston: Beacon Press, 1963. First edn 1861), pp. 165, 168.

[44] An important account of the Latin American response to these events is to be found in Teodoro Petkoff, *Checoslovaquia. El socialismo como problema* (Caracas: Colección perpectiva actual, Monte Avila 1990).

of politics and to re-awaken interest in the concept of civility within an independent liberal republic.

The evident failure of Castroism advanced social democratic alliances as the best way to secure and legitimate popular government. It now became clear that universal suffrage and the rule of law brought liberty in civilized nations, not the gun. Similarly, structural and social change came to be seen as the strengthening, rather than the replacement, of the values of the bourgeois liberal state. The invasion of Czechoslovakia signalled the break with the orthodox Communist Parties in Europe and with Havana. It was also responsible for the emergence of new forms of political agency, in particular the idea of social movements, of widespread political and social change in a variety of different social arenas, and a new more generous conception of the party. Finally Althusserianism (diffused throughout Latin America by Althusser's Chilean pupil Marta Harneker) and Nicos Poulantzas's conception of political autonomy, lent some epistemological complexity, if not legitimacy, to the old semi-colonial status conferred upon the Latin-American Communist Parties.[45] Furthermore, the spectacular failure of Communist regimes across the world forced upon the intellectual elite on the left a new uncertainty, and with it the recognition of the need for greater complexity. They therefore pounced upon the apparent certainty offered by the Althusserians in an attempt to retrieve in theory what they could no longer find in the practice of their beliefs.

The cultural and ethical transformation of politics which these events brought about, and the subsequent liberation from the confines of ideological reductionism, shaped the nature of all subsequent political discourse, in particular in its relation to the concept of civil society. It introduced into the language of Marxism the belief that the concept of civil society, rather than the state, was the arena from which new social movements would emerge and, as such, was the proper forum for the officially anointed spokesperson of the revolution: the intellectual. From the translation of this newly discovered belief into cultural practice there emerged two major, and related, political commonplaces: the 'deepening of democracy' and 'state reform'.

State reform was, in a sense, a way of revisiting the modernizing agendas of the past. What seemed new in either its Gramscian or structuralist garb was precisely the emergence of a new form of political agency and the arrival of the intellectuals as the principal cultural directors of the reformist project. Located now within the machinery of

---

[45] See Nicos Poulantzas, *Poder político y clases sociales en el estado capitalista*, translated by Florentino M. Torner (Mexico: Siglo veintiuno, 1973), especially pp. 331–41.

government, rather than – as they had once been – in opposition to it, the intellectuals attempted to legitimate in social terms the complete trans- formation of the state both practically and conceptually. The general effect of this was to offer to the cultural imagination of the ordinary citizen the vision of a contrast between a state which, in its unreformed condition, was unable or unwilling to govern, and a society which, while it desired state reform, was seemingly incapable of achieving it.

The quest for a 'deeper' democracy had similar results. The traditional Marxist view of the formal character of democracy was revised. Universal suffrage which had been a key liberal argument in the defence of 'nationalism' against radical revolutions – Betancourt's Venezuela against Castro's Cuba, for instance, or Chamorro's Nicaragua against the Sandinistas – and an equally important component in the liberal defence of Chile's socialist experiment, was now shown to be dependent upon an inefficient state apparatus (predominantly, of course, a welfare one) and closely linked to an unrepresentative and sometimes corrupt party system. The state lost its appeal and by so doing threatened the legitimacy of democracy as it had traditionally been understood. State reform, that is, carried with it an institutional logic which called for an overall reform of the ways in which the whole idea of political representa- tion had been conceived. It implied a revision of the role of suffrage and of the place both played in the construction of what was now emerging as a new *liberal* democracy.

The drive towards greater political participation, as an essential moral ingredient in this process, focused attention on the restricted access to government which prevailed in all Latin American states. Party politics, political parties, and the operation of interest groups, all came under attack. The idea of a liberal understanding of civility and its related republican, civic conception of citizenship were now no longer regarded as purely ideological objectives or the instances of mere historical curiosity. A new substantive conception of democracy came to replace the older more formal understanding of what was involved in citizenship and the practice of representation. Thus the problem of political 'con- stituency' as a problem of agency and identity became the object of a significant cultural dispute. Local government, municipalities, neighbour- hood associations, and cooperatives, once colonized by party politics or dismissed as the corporate or communal remains of the *ancien régime*, were now being summoned to rescue society from the grip of the established political system.

The combination of these events helps to explain the rediscovery of the concept of civil society as a result of the demise of Marxism. By expanding the concept of politics beyond the limits of the formal process of government, and by conceiving of the state itself as the embodiment of social practices, the state, culturally and intellectually, if not yet in practice, withered away. Thus, we would suggest, Latin-American Marxism has handed over to Latin-American political culture a new kind of political consciousness, endowed with a new object of concern: society. It is now society which has become the subject, as well as the object, of its political thinking.

V

In the light of this history we may now be in a better position to understand the role which the concept of civil society has come to play in the politics of contemporary Latin America. Broadly speaking, the concept operates at three levels. In the first place it offers a critique of party-political reason; in the second, it supposedly embodies a move from abstract political representation to concrete social representation; and in the third it provides a general critique of the state in its role as the subject of social and economic change.

In its first sense it has been welcomed almost everywhere as a true alternative to the old party system. It has been presented as a challenge to the power of the party as the subject of history and as the chief mediating agency between the state and society. In contrast to party reason, which represented the professional enclosure of politics and their dependency upon militancy and discipline, civil society stands for the aggregation of interests within the open spaces offered by self-directed social and economic exchanges. These, furthermore, are said to be determined only by those who have a legitimate interest in them, a claim which allows for greater social interaction and expansion in arenas where the state no longer operates as effectively as it once did – and in many cases no longer operates at all. Furthermore since Latin-American Marxism conceived the party as universal in nature, its supposedly cognitive control over human history was granted quasi-religious attributes. The abandonment of this universalism and the dwindling of the emotional appeal of centralism – both conceptual and institutional – which necessarily accompanied it, has resulted in the creation of diffuse imaginative spaces which civil society has increasingly come to fill.

As a move away from abstract political representation and towards concrete social representation, or the aggregation of group interests, civil society constitutes the most powerful attack as yet launched against the prevailing political systems and institutional practices of political participation in Latin America. The member groups or even single individuals that have been created by the practical efficacy of the concept have come to regard their particular interests and their particular social milieux as the transparent expression of their social practices.[46] Given the social creativity and individual flair of the informal economy in many Latin American states, this is hardly surprising. In Peru, for instance, it has been established that in the 1980s 48 per cent of the economically active members of the population worked in the informal sector and contributed 38.9 per cent of the nation's GNP.[47] In the context of a true *civil society*, it is now the citizen's power to act in his or her own separate interests which constitutes his or her political identity, not, as had previously been the case, the degree of his or her commitment to a political party, whether of the left or the right.[48]

The logic of this cultural shift – which in public opinion has been massive – has operated in several different ways, not all of them convergent.[49] It has moved from a centralized conception of government agency to decentralized ones; from the predominance of an abstract, and largely Romanized, understanding of public law to the attempted reconstruction of ancient regional public authorities, the *Cabildos* or *Municipios* which had governed the towns under the Spanish Empire in accordance with Castilian civic traditions. In this context it has moved, too, from a formal and normative jurisprudence to one based upon neighbourhood consent and communal enforcement, one in which votes are now looked upon not as civic duties but also, and increasingly so, as market transactions.

As a critique of the nation-state, the notion of civil society has had a number of contradictory results. In general, it has accelerated a tendency towards anarchy, which had been a constant feature of most Latin-American republics since independence. By exposing the state's inability to provide its citizens with most of the public goods which the reform programmes of successive Latin American governments had promised to deliver, 'civil society' seems to be detaching the citizen body from all forms of political allegiance or political representation. The result is a clash of collective and divergent modes of political representation with respect to all of the prevailing forms of social control. Law, social

---

[46] See Vera Da Silva Telles, 'Sociedades civiles e a contrucão de espacos publicos' in Evalina Dagnino (ed.), *Os anos 90. Politica e sociedade no Brasil* (São Paolo: Editora brasiliense, 1994), pp. 91–104, and Hernando de Soto, Enrique Ghersi, and Mario Ghibellini, *El otro sendero* (Lima: Instituto libertad y democracia, 1986).

[47] Fernando Iwasaki Cauti, *Nación peruana: entelequía o utopía, trayectoria de una falácia* (Lima: Centro nacional de estudios socio-económicos, 1989), p. 131.

[48] For a useful comment on this, and some revealing comparisons with southern Italy see Robert Putnam, *Making Democracy Work* (Princeton: Princeton University Press, 1993).

[49] See, for instance, the observations in the report of the 'Comision presidencial para la reforma del estado', *La descentralización del estado: una oportunidad para la democracia* (Caracas: Comision presidencial para la reforma del estado, Editorial arte, vol. 4, 1989).

conventions, and even religion, are being challenged at a time when new forms of civility are still neither powerful enough nor extensive enough to transform what they promise into established practice. As these recent versions of modernization stretch the old belief systems to their limit, there is an increasing scope for lawlessness and even a return to revolution, as recent events in Mexico, Venezuela, Argentina, and Colombia have shown. The concept of civil society is thus caught between a flight from conceptions of the state into anarchy, and a ubiquitous programme of economic modernization claiming to be the expression of universal democracy. As the search for some kind of equilibrium within each society continues so the gap between the possible solutions widens. And over the whole process hovers the ever-present threat of authoritarianism, particularly in those areas, such as defence and security, where the anarchic tendencies of civil society make it particularly vulnerable to state action.[50]

In conclusion, in Latin America, as in other 'developing' regions, but perhaps more markedly than in most, the idea of civil society as a critique of the state on behalf of what amounts to a virtually stateless society, appears to have defeated the idea that economic and social development should be a state-governed political enterprise. This has meant the retrieval of the social at the expense of the state, and the redirection of politics into the social and cultural. It has resulted in the awareness of the need to re-draw the ordinary boundaries of the political in such a way that the state is no longer the natural centre of all political activity.

As a consequence, the term civil society has foisted upon the political imagination of most Latin-American societies the illusion not only that the civil is now the only true source of agency and productivity, but that it is also the only source of a meaningful social identity and therefore of all transparent political relationships, both personal and collective. Because it is these things, civil society has also come to be seen as the only domain in which true political experience and hence real solidarity is possible. Culturally, however, these illusions can be seen to be pulling in two contrary directions. On the one hand, the concept of civil society derives much of its imaginative force from a communal social logic whose roots, as we have seen, are firmly located in the republican experience shared by all modern Latin-American states. On the other, both the concept, and its current uses, owes much to predominantly North American conceptions of libertarian political and economic individualism and their strongly competitive understanding of the civil.

---

[50] See Alain Rouqie, *L'Etat militaire en Amérique latine* (Paris: Editions du Seuil, 1982), pp. 57–93.

Such illusions of the possible power of the concept serve indeed to enforce a paradox and a deep historical irony. With hindsight, the general shape of the paradox seems clear enough. If Latin-American Marxism could be said to have brought about the withering of the bourgeois state, this was by revolutionary default, not by revolutionary means. For what emerged was not a classless and state-less society but rather a reactionary devolution to a previous state in the hemisphere's history. The quest of this new order was precisely to recover the initial political objective of the Latin-American republics as the moral and substantive enactment of a popular representative democracy. The inflation of the language of Marxism and its subsequent demise drove the political intelligentsia into more-or-less doomed attempts to restore communal and corporate intimations of a not-so-bourgeois conception of civil society. This could only be found in the patriotic remnants of classical republicanism, as the only possible challenge to rising economic liberalism. Republicanism conceived of as the basis for one conception of civil society now finds itself opposed to another which claims a universalism reminiscent of the older Marxism but proclaimed now in the name of commercial society and the world economy.

VI

We have argued that the history of republicanism provides a key to the understanding of the confusing state of the concept of civil society in Latin-American politics today. From the beginning the Latin-American republics have developed two distinct political strategies. They have attempted to reconstruct the Ciceronian virtuous *respublica*, yet at the same time they have persistently worked against this vision in the interests of modern commercial republicanism. So as the *societas civilis* is made to evoke echoes of Rousseau and attempts to relive the socialist longings of the Jacobins, its cultural appeal will always run counter to the liberal dimension of the republican ideal. As Geoffrey Hawthorn has pointed out, it is by no means the case, as the champions of the concept in the North have so persistently claimed, that 'civil society' is necessarily both democratic in its political expression and liberal in its economic implications.[51] As the case of China has shown, the very opposite may be the case. And in most of the modern republics of Latin America it has been precisely the tension between the possible outcomes of a concept of 'civil society' and the ideology of republicanism which, as Bolívar's own

---

[51] This volume, pp. 269–86.

claims revealed, has been the ultimate source of the continent's general failure to secure any lasting basis for a flourishing popular government.

Ever since Independence the republics of Latin America have hovered in this way between modern and ancient republicanism. And since the terms 'society' and 'civility' have different and sometimes antithetical connotations within these two contending political languages, they pose equally conflictual aspirations to political identity. The idea that civil society can constitute a new subject for world history is, at least in its Latin-American setting, at best a pious delusion, at worst the source of potentially disastrous political confusion. It is, as Geoffrey Hawthorn has stressed, at best unrealistic to hope that the kind of alternatives to the state which are now of so much interest to political theorists, can actually come to *replace* the state.[52] They are, at best *ad hoc* solutions, interim and unstable. In the presence of this confusion it is doubtful that there can be a pragmatic settlement which will combine the conception of civility with that of private citizenship. But if there is to be such a settlement, it can only lie in the hope that what goes under the name of civil society can finally transform the conception of citizenship within the *respublica*, and finally transform the order of the state itself.

[51] Ibid.

11   The Western concept of civil society in the context of Chinese history

Thomas A. Metzger

Introductory remarks

To what extent has China ever had a civil society? What role has the Western ideal of the civil society played in modern Chinese thought? To what extent has this role converged with the Western ideal or been shaped by the indigenous intellectual tradition? To what extent have Chinese demands for the strengthening of the civil society been politically rational or prudent? To what extent is it epistemologically proper to use a Western category like 'civil society' to analyse the lives of people whose own ways of conceptualizing their lives traditionally lacked this category?

It is convenient to deal first with the epistemological question. Etically imposing a Western category on Chinese facts would be obviously justified if one believed that global history follows laws that Westerners happened to discover, or that ideals like 'civil society' are based on universal human rights, or that such categories at least are part of a universally homologous terminology which one can properly use to analyse the facts of human life even when this terminology is unknown to the people one is studying. In the Chinese intellectual world, therefore, where none of these three beliefs has been seriously challenged, there is no epistemic obstacle to using 'civil society' as a category with which to analyse Chinese history. In much of the Western academic world, these three beliefs have been seriously challenged, whether by Karl Popper's denial that there are laws of history, Alasdair MacIntyre's catalogue of philosophical objections to the notion of objective, impersonal norms, or Richard J. Bernstein's discussion of objections to any kind of 'objectivism' in the pursuit of knowledge.[1] Yet even in the West, many currently

Some of this chapter overlaps with Thomas A. Metzger, 'Modern Chinese Utopianism and the Western Concept of the Civil Society', in San-ching Chen, ed., *Kuo T'ing-i hsien-sheng chiu-chih tan-ch'en chi-nien lun-wen-chi* (Papers Commemorating the Ninetieth Birthday of Professor Kuo Ting-yee; 2 vols.; Taipei: Institute of Modern History, Academia Sinica, 1995), vol. II, pp. 273–312.

[1] Karl Popper, *The Poverty of Historicism* (London: Routledge and Kegan Paul, 1957); Alasdair MacIntyre, *After Virtue* (Notre Dame: University of Notre Dame Press, 1981);

prominent trends refer to universal human nature (whether in medical, psychological, ethical or epistemological contexts), to universal cognitive modes such as 'rational choice', to universal sociological or economic functions, to global patterns of social evolution, and to the 'convergence' of only partly 'diverging' industrial societies.[2]

Moreover, a purely emic understanding of historical activity is probably unattainable, not to mention undesirable, since explaining the past requires putting it into a frame of reference understandable to people in the present, whether foreigners or natives. Still more, as cultures change, natives frequently feel it proper to analyse their own culture by borrowing foreign ideas, as illustrated by contemporary Chinese discussions of Chinese history using the Western idea of the civil society. If foreign ideas cannot be properly used to analyse a culture, a native using them would have to be regarded as having emigrated out of her own culture even as she felt she was just trying to interpret it. Thus the very scholars seeking to avoid etic frameworks would end up imposing one on her own understanding of her life. Such an absurdity can be avoided only by realizing that cultures are not clearly bounded systems. To the extent that they consist not of almost unexplainable customs, such as setting off firecrackers to celebrate a wedding, but of 'because' statements, they entail a reflexive discourse or 'argument' that is carried on by people often crossing social or ethnic boundaries, such as Chinese serving as American professors and vice versa.[3] If one accepts Bernstein's 'hermeneutic' solution to the problem of obtaining knowledge, any category of historical analysis may be used which can be defended by those who use it as in accordance with the rules of successful thinking they regard as veridical.[4] In other words, people inevitably will use categories that way; there is no logical way of showing that they should not, and, obviously, if

---

Richard J. Bernstein, *Beyond Objectivism and Relativism* (Philadelphia: University of Philadelphia Press, 1983). Anthropologists use 'etic' to describe a conceptual framework for analysing a human group when that framework differs from the ideas which the members of that group are accustomed to use when discussing their own lives; 'emic' describes the latter ideas.

[2] Obvious examples are the writings of Talcott Parsons, Lawrence Kohlberg, Alex Inkeles, and Karl Marx. A concept of universal human nature is also basic to John Dunn's political theory. See e.g. John Dunn, *Western Political Theory in the Face of the Future* (Cambridge: Cambridge University Press, 1993), pp. 97, 102, 105, 109, 115.

[3] The increasing tendency to see culture as an 'argument' is illustrated by Robert N. Bellah, Richard Madsen, William M. Sullivan, Ann Swidler, and Steven M. Tipton, *Habits of the Heart* (Berkeley: University of California Press, 1985), pp. 301–3. In my *Escape from Predicament* (New York: Columbia University Press, 1977), p. 14, I suggested that 'Nothing tells us more about a set of shared orientations than the way it defined the issues of controversy.'

[4] This argument is made in my 'Hayek's Political Theory: Notes on His *Law, Legislation and Liberty*' (unpublished).

there were, it would be useless. The idea of bypassing etic categories is a chimera. Refining them is the only feasible methodology.

Western definitions of 'civil society'

Even though the meanings attached to 'civil society' in the West have been so various, an attempt to sum up the Western definitions of this term is needed in order to figure out whether any Chinese definitions diverged from the Western and whether China ever had a 'civil society'. First, David Held offers what I would call a sociological definition when he says that 'civil society retains a distinctive character to the extent that it is made up of areas of social life – the domestic world, the economic sphere, cultural activities and political interaction – which are organized by private or voluntary arrangements between individuals and groups outside the direct control of the state'.[5] Some would add that, to amount to a civil society, such political interaction cannot be fragmented and excessively particularistic: it has to constitute what Jürgen Habermas called 'the public sphere'.[6] Second, there is a normative, political definition often overlapping this descriptive, sociological one: the idea that this public sphere *should* be strengthened at the expense of the state. This view can be expressed conservatively (the emphasis on legality, private property, markets, and interest groups) or in more leftist ways (the emphasis on empowering groups prevented by allegedly prejudiced or selfish elites from interacting on the basis of equality with their fellow citizens).

The third definition is the classical one. St Augustine, for instance, quoting 'Cicero with approval . . . defines civil society or the commonwealth as "an assemblage (of men) associated by a common acknowledgment of right and by a community of interests" '.[7] As is made clear by a number of chapters in this volume, this concept of civility as a common ground shared by the state with the rest of society was traditionally grounded in a philosophical way, notably in some concept of universal, rational human nature. In more recent times, however, especially as the philosophical derivation came under fire, this idea of civility has been used in a more simply empirical or anthropological way to describe the political culture allegedly needed by the normative modern society, often

---

[5] David Held, *Models of Democracy* (Stanford: Stanford University Press, 1987), p. 281.
[6] Frederic Wakeman, Jr., 'The Civil Society and Public Sphere Debate: Limited Western Reflections on Chinese Political Culture', prepared for the Berkeley Conference on Culture, Religion, and Chinese Economic Development, 26–28 February 1992.
[7] Leo Strauss and Joseph Cropsey (eds.), *History of Political Philosophy* (Chicago: The University Chicago Press, 1987), p. 181. Cicero's concept was rooted in Greek philosophy. See e.g. Aristotle's views in ibid., pp. 128–9. I am grateful to Robert J. Myers for bringing this superb collection of essays to my attention.

viewed as combining the structure of the modern national state, economic modernization, great interconnectedness with other societies (as illustrated by the global economy), free enterprise, and what John Dunn calls 'the modern constitutional representative democratic republic'.[8]

The idea that such a modern democratic state requires a certain kind of political culture or certain 'personality' traits has been suggested by scholars as various as Sunil Khilnani, Samuel P. Huntington, Alex Inkeles, and Friedrich A. Hayek, though not always by using the term 'political culture'.[9] I have elsewhere tried to enter this evolving discussion about the kinds of orientations or other conditions hypothetically needed to produce the 'civility' a modern society seems to require, listing: (1) considerable cultural homogeneity; (2) cordial, trustful relations between fellow citizens who are strangers to each other, a condition not fully met in Chinese societies, as scholars agree; (3) some political consciousness, such as a sense of nationalism; and (4) the assumption that the realization of moral–sacred values at least partly depends on the moral performance of the political centre, as illustrated by the basic Confucian ideal of *nei-sheng wai-wang* (within, a sage, without, a true king). Also, (5), politics cannot just revolve around a shared saga of past glory, suffering, struggle, and present ambitions, what Robert N. Bellah calls 'a community of memory'. It must be based also on the intention to follow an abstract, unifying principle, such as the Greek idea of justice or the Confucian idea of *jen* (compassionately equating the needs of others with one's own). Political disagreement can then consist of arguments about who is being hypocritical instead of murderous struggles between groups who merely feel victimized by each other. Moreover, (6), this concept of principle has to be linked to the idea of the ruler's accountability to the people, an idea common to all axial civilizations, as S. N. Eisenstadt has noted; (7), accountability has to be linked to the kind of emphasis on legality Quentin Skinner saw arising some five centuries ago in the West; and (8), civility entails what Sunil Khilnani called the legitimization of politics as 'a terrain upon which competing claims may be advanced and

---

[8] Dunn, *Western Political Theory*, p. 128.

[9] As argued in my 'Hayek's Political Theory', he viewed the proper social order as resting on the interrelations between markets, the state, and society's 'ethos'. See e.g. Friedrich A. Hayek, *Law, Legislation and Liberty* (3 vols. Chicago: The University of Chicago Press, 1983, 1976, and 1979), vol. III, pp. 156–66. For Samuel P. Huntington's view that certain orientations are 'the foundation of democratic stability' (namely 'disillusionment and the lowered expectations it produces'), see his *The Third Wave* (Norman: University of Oklahoma Press, 1991), p. 263. Overlapping the idea of a political culture facilitating democracy is that of the psychological characteristics of the 'democratic personality', basically seen as opposite to those of the 'authoritarian personality'. See Alex Inkeles, 'National Character and Modern Political Systems', in Francis L. K. Hsu, ed., *Psychological Anthropology* (Cambridge: Schenkman Books, Inc., 1972), pp. 202–40.

justified', a political marketplace complemented by an open intellectual marketplace and the free economic marketplace.[10] This eighth condition seems inseparable from the seventh, the idea of a differentiation between competing, substantive demands and procedural, formal, morally neutral 'rules of the game'.

As I have argued elsewhere, the main ideological trends in twentieth-century China have strongly resisted legitimization of the three market-places, aiming for a kind of *Gemeinschaft* comfortably guided by universally recognized standards of 'reason' and 'morality' rather than dependent on the frighteningly unpredictable interplay of morally and intellectually ungraded impulses of free individuals competing in the three marketplaces and sharing no values except respect for morally neutral 'rules of the game'. Therefore, when modern Chinese ideologies endorsed freedom, pluralism, and openness, they always guaranteed that these values would be consistent with 'morality' and 'reason', not just procedural regularity, and that therefore capitalism would not lead to serious economic inequality, democracy would be free of the machinations of 'tricky politicians' pursuing selfish interests (*cheng-k'o*), and the competition between ideas would not prevent full moral–intellectual consensus throughout society.[11] *Gesellschaft* would be synthesized with *Gemeinschaft*, *Zweckrationalität* with *Wertrationalität*. Thus while Chinese intellectuals have been enthusiastic about the 'rule of the law', they have typically identified legality with substantive justice in an absolute sense, not merely with formal laws or judicial decisions which may be mistaken but must still be respected. Legality in this morally neutral sense has often been contemptuously identified in modern China with the allegedly mistaken belief that 'even a bad law is still the law' (*o-fa yeh fa*).

The question of civility also entails a ninth issue, that of perspicacity, even though this evaluative term perhaps cannot be applied to specific cases without some disagreement. I have in mind, on the one hand, a way of discussing public issues by trying to obtain information, to be logical, to be serious, and to be reasonable in comparing the gravity of one problem to that of another. This kind of perspicacity has to be cultivated, perhaps from childhood on, through education and the experience of repeatedly arguing about political questions with friends and family members, as opposed, say, to just passionately joining protest movements. In China, so far as I have experienced it, politics is not a staple of dinnertime conversation; testing out arguments about politics is not a

[10] Metzger, 'Modern Chinese Utopianism', pp. 277–82.
[11] Ibid., pp. 305–6.

part of everyday conversation. After all, the chief sage made the remarkable statement that 'One should not discuss the affairs of an office one does not hold' (*The Analects of Confucius*, 8.16). Political discussion is no different from any other activity: practice makes perfect. The reader has to judge for herself whether a 'public sphere' can be formed when the remarks typically made by citizens include the following (these come from my experience in Taiwan): 'Why should I care what happens to the people of Hong Kong? Have you heard that awful dialect of theirs? Who can care about such people?'; 'Taiwan is not an ideal society. So how can you say there has been any progress here?'; 'There is no real difference between the political systems of Taiwan and the Mainland, since neither has established a real democracy'; 'There is no difference between an embezzlement scandal in the Taipei government and the widespread use of illegal drugs by U.S. schoolchildren – these are equally grave matters'; 'So what if President Lee Teng-hui's visit to the U.S. angers Beijing? Why should we care how they feel?'; 'There has been no economic progress here to speak of'; 'Our prosperity is based only on luck, international trade tendencies that happened to favor us.'

'Perspicacity', on the other hand, refers to the propagation throughout society by means of the educational system of a proper philosophy ultimately based on complex, abstruse, intellectual arguments, a cognitive map putting the moral obligations of the citizen into historical and political perspective. To be sure, this idea that civility as an aspect of society requires the propagation of some proper philosophy would be rejected by many. Sceptics would deny that there is any objective standard of proper philosophizing. Many historians and social scientists would doubt that abstruse intellectual ideas can have a serious causative impact on popular orientations and the development of public institutions. Nevertheless, this issue must be kept in mind, since many scholars, though disagreeing about what the right philosophy is, explicitly or implicitly view political behaviour as caused to a large extent by philosophical ideas gradually spreading out from their points of origin in tiny, rarefied intellectual circles. This intellectualistic 'trickle down' theory of historical causation has been basic to modern and pre-modern Chinese thought.[12] It is also illustrated by Robert N. Bellah's argument that Americans can create a 'good society' only by learning to reject 'Lockean individualism',[13] by Christopher Lasch's opposite argument that America's ills can be cured only by returning to Lockean, 'bourgeois'

[12] See e.g. Lin Yü-sheng, *The Crisis of Chinese Consciousness: Radical Antitraditionalism in the May Fourth Era* (Madison: University of Wisconsin Press, 1978).
[13] Robert N. Bellah, Richard Madsen, William M. Sullivan, Ann Swidler and Steven M. Tipton, *The Good Society* (New York: Vintage Books, 1992).

values,[14] by John Dunn's view that a deeply erudite reconstruction of Western political theory can help humankind deal more effectively with the practical problems in its future,[15] by F. A. Hayek's view that wrong theories about the origin of law 'have profoundly affected the evolution of political institutions',[16] by Alasdair MacIntyre's view that the ills of modern society have been caused by the failure of the philosophical effort to demonstrate the existence of objective, impersonal moral norms,[17] or by Kao Li-k'o's concept of a China based on the special philosophical insights that no Chinese thinker succeeded in developing except for Mao (see pp. 229–30 below). James Q. Wilson has largely agreed with MacIntyre in developing his thesis about how 'elites' in the United States propagated a kind of 'scepticism' altering US culture by promoting an 'ethos of self-expression' that undermined 'the "civilizing" process'.[18] S. N. Eisenstadt's sociological thesis regarding 'axial civilizations' turns on the vast 'institutional repercussions' of intellectual or religious visions. Reinhard Bendix, using the idea of 'intellectual mobilization', has analysed the way such repercussions transformed the popular concept of political sovereignty in early modern Europe.[19] In other words, even though so many historians and social scientists insist that the development of a society is caused only by events that directly and materially affect large numbers of people, such as political decisions and economic trends, Leo Strauss's 'attribution of profound practical effects to profound theoretical arguments' accords with the views of a broad array of insightful scholars;[20] thus it should be kept in mind when considering the educational foundation of the civility required by democracies.

If civility can then be seen as an orientation inside and outside the state entailing considerable cultural homogeneity, cordiality between strangers, some political consciousness, the idea that the state is to some extent the vehicle of sacred values, the intention of basing politics on abstract principles, the emphasis on legality and the ruler's accountability, the legitimization of the three marketplaces, and perspicacity, it also seems

---

[14] Christopher Lasch, *The Revolt of the Elites* (New York: W. W. Norton & Company, 1995).

[15] Dunn, *Western Political Theory*.

[16] Hayek, *Law, Legislation and Liberty*, vol. 1: 28.

[17] MacIntyre, *After Virtue*.

[18] James Q. Wilson, *On Character* (Washington, D.C.: The AEI Press, 1991), pp. 28–9, 38.

[19] Reinhard Bendix, *Kings or People* (Berkeley: University of California Press, 1978); Thomas A. Metzger, 'Eisenstadt's Analysis of the Relation between Modernization and Tradition in China', in *The American Asian Review*, vol. II, p. 2 (summer 1984), pp. 1–87.

[20] Strauss and Cropsey, *Political Philosophy*, p. 918. More generally, it used to be a platitude in the Western world that 'The world is largely ruled by ideas, true and false.' See Charles A. Beard's 'Introduction', written around 1931, to J. B. Bury, *The Idea of Progress* (New York: Dover Publications, 1960), p. ix.

inseparable in the Western tradition from a leaning toward a certain 'bottom-up' emphasis, as opposed to a more 'top-down' vision of politics and agency.

This distinction, again, is a matter of degree and may provoke controversy, but it has to be considered if one is to ask whether modern Chinese visions of the civil society have or have not replicated the Western tradition. It is important to note that even when the ideal of the 'civil society' is linked to that of 'rule by the people', conceptualization of 'the people' can still be carried out in a 'top-down' fashion. (Whether this fashion is proper or not is a separate question.)

This distinction between top-down and bottom-up visions of civility can be made by looking at basic assumptions about the nature of knowledge, the social visibility of enlightened persons, human nature, and the nature of history; about the relationship between knowledge, morality, political power, and individual freedom; about the relationship between the state, the various markets, and society's 'ethos' (to use Hayek's terms); about the relationship between official political theory, intellectual political theory, and amateur political theory (slightly to misuse John Dunn's categories); and about the relation between autonomy and heteronomy.[21]

In the top-down framework, an 'optimistic epistemology' posits that the objective public good can be fully known.[22] Even more, the elites who understand it can be reliably identified and can successfully propagate it, and human nature and history include a strong tendency to realize it. Therefore an enlightened elite can work together with history to fuse together morality, knowledge, political power, and an effective concern with individual freedom. Consequently, a good society is created more by making the individual and the government good, rather than, as Hayek recommends, by protecting individuals, bad or good, from coercion inflicted by others.[23] From this standpoint, free intellectual, economic,

[21] This framework comes from Thomas A. Metzger, 'Contemporary China's Political Agenda and the Problem of Political Rationality', a series of lectures given as the 1994 Ch'ien Mu Lecture in History and Culture, New Asia College, The Chinese University of Hong Kong, and being prepared for publication.

[22] The distinction between an 'optimistic' and a 'pessimistic epistemology' refers to the balance in a body of thought between the sense of the obvious ('obviously racism is bad') and the sense of fallibility. The strong epistemological optimism shared by the Confucian tradition with the modern Chinese intellectual mainstream was discussed in Thomas A. Metzger, 'Some Ancient Roots of Modern Chinese Thought', in *Early China*, vols. 11–12 (1985–7), pp. 61–117. So far as I know, Karl R. Popper first devised the terms 'optimistic' and 'pessimistic epistemology', but he used them philosophically to denote wrong ways of thinking, while I use them only to describe historical ways of thinking. See also Thomas A. Metzger, 'Western Philosophy on the Defensive', in *Philosophy Now*, issue 26 (April/May 2000), pp. 30–2.

[23] Hayek, *Law, Legislation and Liberty*, III, pp. 128–31.

and political marketplaces may be allowed to a considerable extent, but the emphasis is on the enlightened elite working alongside or within the state, seeing to it that society is guided by a proper ethos, and putting parameters on these marketplaces. Therefore, amateur political theory (grass-roots opinion) is looked down on, and all hope is placed in official political theory (or, more typically, the theories of intellectuals who feel they should take charge of official theory). Considerable heteronomy is thus combined with the principle of autonomy.

This top-down viewpoint has dominated Chinese thought, liberal as well as Marxist, up to today, being based on the tradition-rooted distinction between ordinary citizens and 'true intellectuals *(chen-cheng-te chih-shih fen-tzu)*' embodying society's conscience, and on the tradition-rooted belief in the state's corrigibility.[24] Thus the agents of political improvement are not ordinary, economically oriented citizens fallibly organizing themselves to monitor an incorrigible state, but certain saintly super-citizens ready to guide society by taking over a corrigible state or at least controlling society's 'nervous system'.[25] This persistent vision of a political centre run by moral virtuosi in turn reflected a tradition-rooted, extraordinary optimistic concept of political practicability (see p. 220 below). Also interesting is that, in China, the traditional word for ordinary members of society, *min* (the people), was not primarily a morally neutral term referring to ordinary folk whatever their moral-political preferences but a morally charged term referring either to 'the people of Heaven' acting as Heaven's 'eyes' and 'ears' by supporting the enlightened elite ('those who are ahead of others in understanding the *Tao*'), or to the morally unsatisfactory masses pursuing profits and rejecting the views of this elite.[26] Yet such a top-down view has also been important in the West, as illustrated even by the thought of the father of modern liberalism, J. S. Mill, who combined his emphasis on liberty with his belief that the sane should control the insane, adults, children, the 'civilized', 'barbarians', and the educated, the uneducated.[27] Thus in his thought too civility entailed a balance between autonomy and heteronomy.

In the bottom-up framework, there is a tilt towards autonomy, what might be called 'the Lutheran bias'. Basic to this tilt is a more 'pessimistic epistemology', as illustrated by Mill's emphasis on 'fallibility'. Also basic

---

[24] Metzger, 'Modern Chinese Utopianism', p. 302.

[25] See e.g. Tu Wei-ming, *Ju-chia ti san ch'i fa-chan-te ch'ien-ching wen-t'i* (Reflections on the Dawning of the Third Period in the Development of Confucian Learning; Taipei: Lien-ching ch'u-pan shih-yeh kung-ssu, 1989), p. 179.

[26] Metzger, 'Modern Chinese Utopianism', pp. 294–6.

[27] Strauss and Cropsey, *Political Philosophy*, pp. 787, 796, 798.

to it is a pessimistic view of human nature and a Popperian or Jamesian view of history as developing indeterminately and failing to exhibit moral guidelines, not to mention lacking any promise that people in the future will be more intelligent and moral than those dominating the present. From this bottom-up standpoint, the very nature of moral–intellectual enlightenment is debatable, and 'the best moral and practical insight of the species cannot be the prerogative of reliably distinguishable or specifiable groups of persons'.[28] Consequently, intellectual political theory, not to mention official, is open to suspicion, and amateur theory deserves respect as not necessarily more fallible than the other two. In this epistemic situation, there is no way to fuse together knowledge, morality, political power, and individual freedom. The proper social order depends more on protecting the freedom of the three marketplaces against the intrusions of the state or of those claiming to have a better understanding of the public good than other citizens have. Therefore the emphasis is not on any enlightened elite working within or alongside the state to promote the proper ethos through education.

Finally, if the Western concept of civility leans toward a bottom-up approach, it is also inherently un-utopian. That is, the social fabric this idea denotes can be identified with either a contemporaneous actual society, as in Hegel's writings, or a kind of social life which a backward society should develop. Either way, however, Western thinkers generally did not expect this social fabric to be morally perfect. In modern Chinese thought, however, 'civil society' has been typically seen as a saintly, utopian *Gemeinschaft* free of 'selfishness', pervaded with 'sincerity', lacking all 'constraints limiting properly free individual desires (*shu-fu*)', free of 'exploitation', without any 'conflicts or feelings of alienation coming between people (*ko-ho*)', and also free of all 'ideological confusion (*fen-yun*)' – a 'great oneness' (*ta-t'ung*). This tradition-rooted *ta-t'ung* ideal – very important in modern Chinese thought, not only in Chinese Marxism – connoted what has been called a state of perfect 'linkage': the resolution of all doctrinal differences (*hui-t'ung*); the oneness of self and cosmos (*t'ien-jen ho-i*); the oneness of the self with the other, that is, with all good people throughout history as well as with all other people in a contemporary world where all bad behaviour and alienation have come to an end, internationally as well as domestically; and the oneness of ideals with the actual world.[29] In such a harmonious social order, all agree on not only the procedures for settling disputes but

<hr/>

[28] Dunn, *Western Political Theory*, p. 116.
[29] The centrality of such 'linkage' in Neo-Confucianism, modern Confucian philosophy, and Maoism has been discussed in my *Escape from Predicament* and other writings, such as 'An Historical Perspective on Mainland China's Current Ideological Crisis', in

also the substantive questions of right and wrong regarding each major public issue (*jen t'ung tz'u hsin, hsin t'ung tz'u li*). Given this utopian outlook, the Chinese have found it difficult even to find a word with which to translate 'civility'. The main word they have used to describe how people should interact outside their families is *kung-te* (the virtue of someone dedicated to the public good), an idea connoting the absolute morality just discussed. One term for 'civil society', *kung-min she-hui*, has a similar connotation, while another, *shih-min she-hui*, just means 'a society formed by city people'.

My argument that modern Chinese thought has to a large extent failed to adopt the Western concept of the civil society is based on the point that Chinese intellectuals have rejected the bottom-up approach and inclined toward utopianism and the *Gemeinschaft* ideal as well as on my view that the Western civil society tradition is, by and large, bottom-up and un-utopian. My argument about 'prudence' (again to steal from John Dunn's lexicon) is twofold. On one hand, this top-down approach is advisable given current Chinese conditions, at least on the Mainland. On the other, with its utopianism, the modern Chinese intellectual mainstream has been disastrously imprudent. For many Chinese intellectuals, prudence has been a morally suspicious concept amounting to an apology for the corrupt vested interests of elites.

The limited development of the civil society in modern and pre-modern China

Few if any scholars have looked for a civil society in China by using the above basically anthropological definition of this term, but the shortage of civility has in effect been deplored not only by modern reformers like the great Liang Ch'i-ch'ao (1872–1929),[30] who called for more *kung-te* (the virtue of someone dedicated to the public good), but also by historians, sociologists, and psychologists discussing the thinness of solidarity ties in China between non-kinsmen. True, a considerable variety of traditional norms legitimized such ties: *pao* (the sense of obligation based on favours received); *jen-ch'ing* (the obligation to be kind to certain people with whom one has interacted); *yuan* (the sense of being predestined to have a good or bad relation with someone); 'face (*mien-tzu, lien*)'; the belief that a tie is created by a variety of shared

---

Proceedings of the Seventh Sino-American Conference on Mainland China (Taipei: Institute of International Relations, 1978), vol. IV: 2: 1–vol. IV: 2: 17.

[30] Huang Ko-wu (Max K. W. Huang), *I-ko pei fang-ch'i-te hsuan-tse: Liang Ch'i-ch'ao t'iao-shih ssu-hsiang-chih yen-chiu* (The Rejected Path: A Study of Liang Ch'i-ch'ao's Accommodative Thinking; Taipei: Institute of Modern History, Academia Sinica, 1994).

experiences, such as being born in the same district or province, having the same teacher, or passing the same imperial examination in the same year; the important Confucian concept of friendship between men of learning and integrity (*i wen hui yu*); various other kinds of friendship, such as the 'sworn sisters or brothers' relation (*chieh-pai*); brotherhoods formed by secret society rituals; and various kinds of religious or semi-religious groups, such as the *I-kuan-tao* society in Taiwan. Despite the importance of the networks based on such norms, China was not and has not become a society emphasizing cordial, trustful relations between non-kinsmen and a social life centring on what Christopher Lasch calls 'the third place' (places like taverns socially located between the home and the place of work).[31] After all, all the above norms presuppose the idea of the exceptional stranger, the person with whom warm relations are appropriate for reasons not applying to fellow citizens generally. Thus they all contradict the idea of a general, diffuse spirit of fellowship shared by all citizens.

This shortage of trust or cordiality outside the family, not only political authoritarianism, has been reflected in the fact that, during all periods of imperial unity, there basically was no form of social coalescence outside the imperial chain of command that was both legal and politically articulate. Even in the twentieth century, institutionalization of legally independent, politically articulate groups outside the head of state's chain of command remained exceptional until 1989, when significant independent political parties apart from the ruling party were legalized in Taiwan.[32] Similarly, in modern Taiwan class consciousness has not been salient. Families and factions have typically cut across class lines. The lack of trust outside the family can also be seen, perhaps, in the great readiness of Chinese to see dark plots behind incidents involving public figures. It is striking that, in the summer of 1997, when Princess Diana died as the result of a car accident, some well-educated Chinese who had long lived in the United States suggested that Prince Charles had had her murdered. Moreover, as already mentioned, modern Chinese political

---

[31] See entries under 'third places' in index of Lasch, *The Revolt of the Elites* and references to the Chinese writing on *pao*, etc., in Metzger, 'Modern Chinese Utopianism', p. 277. I am grateful to Ms. Linda Chao for information about the *I-kuan-tao*.

[32] Recent political developments in Taiwan are discussed in Linda Chao and Ramon H. Myers, *The First Chinese Democracy: Political Life in the Republic of China on Taiwan* (Baltimore: The Johns Hopkins University Press, 1998). Probably the case closest to legal, politically articulated social coalescence independent of the political centre in late imperial times is discussed in William S. Atwell, 'From Education to Politics: The Fu She', in Wm. Theodore de Bary *et al.*, *The Unfolding of Neo-Confucianism* (New York: Columbia University Press, 1975), pp. 333–68.

thought does not focus on society's need for trustful relations distinct from virtue.

This shortage of civility is almost certain to persist, since it is simply the obverse of the distinctive Chinese emphasis on the unique value of ties between me and anyone who is 'one of us (*tzu-chi-jen*)', i.e. kinsmen. After all, Chinese familism not only was basic to the traditional society but also has been vital to all of the successfully modernizing Chinese societies. It is not about to withdraw from the stage of history, however vehement may be the intellectual attacks against it as one of the 'poisons of feudalism'. 'Civility', by definition, differs equally from the social world created by Chinese familism and the tradition-rooted, utopian vision of a harmonious society based on 'virtue'.

While China's domestic community thus displays a shortage of 'cordiality' or 'fellowship' as a middle ground between love for and instrumental use of another person, Chinese conceptualizing the international community similarly find it hard to think in terms not of hierarchy or clashing selfish interests but of foreign policies based on enlightened self-interest and so including a limited commitment to the well-being of foreign nations. In March 1996, the People's Republic of China held military exercises near Taiwan to scare it into abandoning any goal of independence, and the United States sent two aircraft-carrier task forces into the waters near Taiwan to express interest in the peaceful resolution of the differences between the two Chinese governments. Not a few Chinese, however, including a presidential candidate in Taiwan, Ch'en Lü-an, ridiculed the idea that the United States had any intention of helping Taiwan. These naval task forces were sent, Ch'en said, not because the United States 'loves us that much' but because it means to use them as one more 'card to play' in its negotiations with China. Ch'en was described as saying that 'the Western powers do not like the idea that Taiwan and the Mainland could unify and thus become another great power possibly shifting the world balance of power away from the West' (*Shih-chieh jih-pao*, 17 March 1996).

Admittedly, after decades when the American academic and political mainstream regarded Taiwan mainly as an obstacle to good relations with Beijing, there is now some American concern about such a shift in the world balance of power. Yet it is doubtful that Americans regard reunification as aggravating their security or international trade problems. It is also significant that Ch'en did not take into account how Taiwan's democratization had favourably influenced public opinion in the United States, a nation whose leaders often see themselves as promoting democratization throughout the world. Instead, he just depicted the United States as choosing between 'love' for Taiwan and selfish interests. The possibility of some middle ground between these two motivations was precluded in trying to assess what the intentions of this foreign nation were. Moreover, there was nothing strange about this perspective for the Taiwan readers of this newspaper. The parallel with how the Chinese tend to exclude this middle ground in their domestic interactions is undeniable. Presumably in all societies the images used to conceptualize the international arena are continuous with those used to conceptualize the domestic. If 'civil society' refers to the normative culture needed for the effective functioning of a modern, democratic society, it may also refer to norms needed for the consolidation of peaceful, cooperative relations between modern societies.

Scholars asking whether China has had a civil society, however, have usually used the sociological-political definition of the civil society, not the anthropological–philosophical one. They have looked at late imperial China, as well as democratizing Taiwan and the recent liberalization trends on the Mainland, to seek out examples of social coalescence free of state control and aiming to check state abuses or even pursue democratization.[33] From the standpoint of a K. A. Wittfogel or even an S. N. Eisenstadt, the great power of the centralized state essentially precluded such examples during the imperial period. In the recent debate between William T. Rowe and Frederic Wakeman, Jr., however, a fresh approach was evident. Rowe emphasized the existence under the Ch'ing dynasty (1644–1912) of social space largely outside the control of capital offices or even local government offices, the 'substantial degree of de facto autonomy' enjoyed by nineteenth-century Hankow, while Wakeman emphasized that this social space remained fragmented, afflicted by ethnic and other fissures, and failing to crystallize into what Habermas called a 'public sphere'.[34]

Wakeman's point is correct and indeed coincides with the above 'anthropological' considerations about a lack of 'civility', including the lack of legal, politically articulate forms of social coalescence independent of the political centre. But Rowe's point also is important, complementing the thesis that imperial China's political centre, especially by the eighteenth century (when a governmental complex made up of some 3 or 4 million persons ranging from officials to clerks, soldiers, and licensed monopoly merchants was trying to deal with a population of 300 to 400

---

[33] See e.g. Hsin-huang Michael Hsiao, 'The Changing State–Society Relation in the ROC: Economic Change, the Transformation of the Class Structure, and the Rise of Social Movements', in Ramon H. Myers (ed.), *Two Societies in Opposition: The Republic of China and the People's Republic of China after Forty Years* (Stanford: Hoover Institution Press, 1991), pp. 127–40.

[34] Wakeman, 'The Civil Society'.

million), was an inhibited political centre unable to stretch its organizational capabilities beyond a limited scope and leaving the bulk of the economy in the private sector.[35] Throughout the imperial period, each of the vast societal transformations that occurred, whether Mark Elvin's 'revolutions' around the Sung period (960–1279) or the demographic–commercial transformation in the Ming–Ch'ing period (1368–1912), were 'crescive' changes stemming from the grass roots, not 'enacted' ones guided by the state, to use William Graham Sumner's distinction. This point applies *a fortiori* to the various intellectual transformations, such as the rise of Neo-Confucianism in the Sung. Moreover, already in Sung times there was a rising tendency to focus intellectual, educational, and other social energies on the local community, in contrast with the classic effort to influence the emperor's policies.[36] While it was in this period that the civil service examinations began to flourish as the main way of recruiting officials, one of their most crucial effects was the production of huge numbers of highly educated losers, men who had failed to pass the examinations or had passed and were unable to obtain positions as officials. This was at least as important as the examinations' effect on social mobility. Forming a huge supply of cheap teachers, these losers both energized education throughout society and necessarily poured their energies into local communities. Still more, the great expansion of the economy in Ming–Ch'ing times was accompanied by a great increase in the differentiation of the economy from the polity. For instance, as Li Wen-chih showed, it was in the seventeenth and eighteenth centuries that, for the first time in Chinese history, the appropriation of large landholdings became almost totally commercialized, as opposed to appropriation based on the legal or illegal use of political power.[37] At the same time, a great deal of political communication was not vertical but horizontal, that is, not memorials sent up to the emperor and orders sent

[35] The thesis of 'the inhibited centre' was developed as an alternative to Eisenstadt's analysis in Thomas A. Metzger's 'Eisenstadt's Analysis' and also used in Thomas A. Metzger and Ramon H. Myers, 'Introduction', in Myers, *Two Societies in Opposition*, pp. xiii–xlv. It is based on my study of the 'inhibited . . . organizational capabilities' of the late imperial salt monopoly in W. E. Willmott (ed.), *Economic Organization in Chinese Society* (Stanford: Stanford University Press, 1972), pp. 9–45, and of 'accommodative' or 'realistic' political thinking in Ch'ing times in Thomas A. Metzger, *The Internal Organization of Ch'ing Bureacracy* (Cambridge, Mass.: Harvard University Press, 1973), pp. 74–80.

[36] This focus on the local community is basic to many articles in Wm. Theodore de Bary and John W. Chaffee (eds.), *Neo-Confucian Education: The Formative Stage* (Berkeley: University of California Press, 1989). For this point, see Thomas A. Metzger's review of this book in *Harvard Journal of Asiatic Studies*, 54: 2 (Dec. 1994), pp. 615–38.

[37] Thomas A. Metzger, 'On the Historical Roots of Economic Modernization in China', in Chi-ming Hou and Tzong-shian Yu (eds.), *Modern Chinese Economic History* (Taipei: The Institute of Economics, Academia Sinica, 1979), pp. 3–14.

down, but essays and compilations prepared by officials for officials and stimulating one local official to copy the procedure used in another district or province, as illustrated by the spread of fiscal reform (*i-t'iao-pien-fa*) from about 1500 onwards.

Traditionally, Confucian scholars viewed this abundance of centrally uncontrolled activity as one aspect of China's moral decline. Some modern scholars with an etic, sociological view, however, have instead seen a late imperial political order according to which the centre autocratically forbade any political activity challenging its supremacy, while otherwise giving much leeway to a dynamic population viewing it as based on the right teachings but unable to understand and implement them. Thus the legitimization of the inhibited political centre was fragmented, but this centre flexibly persisted for centuries as Chinese civilization dynamically evolved. In modern times, one can argue, this inhibited centre was replicated, not only by the Kuomintang after 1949 in Taiwan but also in China after 1976.[38]

The pairing of the inhibited centre with Confucian utopianism

What was the mainstream, legitimized political outlook associated with this inhibited centre? To what extent, if any, did this outlook resemble any Western concept of the civil society? The Ch'ing centuries have left behind a huge amount of primary material, ranging from local histories and administrative writings to private essays and notes often published in *ts'ung-shu* (collections of various writings) or *wen-chi* (collected writings of one man) (Endymion Wilkinson says there are 'at least 3,000' Ch'ing *wen-chi*). Some scholars are now exploring this universe to find scattered remarks shedding light on important issues, such as Ch'ing attitudes towards commerce. Any attempt to define the Ch'ing intellectual mainstream, however, would have to emphasize the spectrum of views in a famous compilation edited by Wei Yuan (1794–1856) around 1826. This consisted of 2,253 pieces on scholarship and government written essentially during the period 1644 to 1823. It was called *Huang-ch'ao ching-shih wen-pien* (Our August Dynasty's Writings on Statecraft).[39]

Huang Ko-wu (Max K. W. Huang) analysed the first 299 essays in this book, those making up the introductory sections called *Hsueh-shu* (On Scholarship) and *Chih-t'i* (On the Foundations of Government). They

---

[38] For the view of the state in Taiwan under Koumintang martial law as an 'inhibited political centre', see Chao and Myers, *The First Chinese Democracy*.

[39] Ho Ch'ang-ling (ed.), *Huang-ch'ao ching-shih wen-pien* (Our August Dynasty's Writings on Statecraft; 8 vols.; Taipei: Shih-chieh shu-chü, 1964). The figure of 2,253 is taken from the study cited in note 40 below.

express a three-fold outlook.[40] First, these officials and scholars perceived a kind of ideal, saintly, cosmologically grounded moral order or *Gemeinschaft* according to which all society should be based on *jen* (compassionate feeling equating the needs of others with those of ego); people should interact in terms of what Herbert Fingarette called 'the ceremonial act'; and there should be no hierarchy except that based on gender, age, or merit. The most distinctive part of this saintly vision was the central belief that this ideal had been historically realized during The Three Dynasties, centuries before Confucius (551–479 BC). This belief either produced or reflected that extremely optimistic Chinese concept of political practicability which has persisted until today. In other words, this vision of a saintly order strikes many today as utopian; but it was not utopian in traditional Confucian eyes, for in these eyes it had been historically realized and could practicably, even easily, be realized again in the present.

'Chinese utopianism' is a peculiar phenomenon wrapped in a fog of definitional confusion. If 'utopia' denotes a societal ideal regarded as hard or impossible to implement, this idea has been important in the West since Plato but has almost never been expressed in the course of Chinese intellectual history (a possible exception is the poet T'ao Ch'ien (372–427)). If, however, 'utopian' describes the pursuit of an impracticable goal of political perfection by people insisting it is practicable, then the people pursuing it will necessarily deny their goal is utopian. The Chinese intellectual mainstream has been and still is utopian in the latter sense. More precisely, however, what distinguishes this Chinese mainstream is the way it defined the recalcitrance of the present. The Chinese have often been well aware that contemporaneous evils could not be conveniently overcome, but they saw this recalcitrance as an eradicable condition, not as a reflection of permanent human frailties.

Second, as just indicated, this Confucian utopianism was combined with a picture of drastic human frailty comparable to the idea of original sin. Because of selfishness, the inherent elusiveness of moral truth, and their tendency to embrace false doctrines, the Chinese people had been in decline since The Three Dynasties: all the subsequent emperors had been morally deficient; officials had not been properly recruited; bad officials, clerks, and merchants had soaked up the wealth which should have gone

---

[40] This analysis of the outlook in this early nineteenth-century volume is taken from Huang Ko-wu (Max K. W. Huang), ' "Huang-ch'ao ching-shih wen-pien" "hsueh-shu" "chih-t'i" pu-fen ssu-hsiang-chih fen-hsi (An Analysis of the Thought in the "On Learning" and "On the Foundations of Government" Sections of *Our August Dynasty's Writings on Statecraft*)', an MA thesis for the Institute of History, National Taiwan Normal University, 1985.

to 'the state' or 'the people'; governmental offices, fiscal procedures, and land-holding institutions had all been wrongly designed; the 'people (*min*)' were mostly immoral; false doctrines had perverted education; 'barbarians' had repeatedly taken over China; and even the 'will of heaven' sometimes was responsible for bad events. (Because they overlook this pervasive emphasis on 'the historical accumulation of evils (*chi-pi*)', many scholars today assert that Confucian thought identified virtue with the actual hierarchy of power.)

Third, according to this mainstream outlook, this disjunction between the completely practicable ideal order and the actual bad condition of society in the present was accompanied by the moral awareness of the scholarly elite, who defined themselves as super-citizens committed to this saintly ideal even while blaming each other for having proved unable so far clearly to grasp and resolutely to pursue it. To be sure, 'moderate realism' was prevalent in the bureaucracy, whose members mostly worried about local, small-scale reforms.[41] Yet the ideal of bringing absolute morality (*jen*) back into the centre of an organizationally uninhibited polity (the ideal of 'within, a sage, without, a true king', of *The Great Learning's* 'eight steps') remained basic for them. Like the actual political order, their vision of the ideal order was hierarchical, top-down, but it called for a moral transformation at the top of the hierarchy. Their conceptualization of morality, moreover, even included democratic-sounding statements, hardly remarkable in their day, about the fundamental rationale on which government should be based. For instance, in the 1826 compilation noted above, one finds:

At first, people were weak, animals and such strong. Many people were harmed. So a sage appeared and protected the people by repelling these harmful forces. Thereupon the people raised him up to be their ruler and teacher. Therefore the establishment of the ruler is a matter of the people's putting him in that position . . . The ruler and the prime minister, these two are not different from ordinary people. In their case, it's just a matter of some people enlightening and protecting other people, of being used by the people, not using the people. This is what is intended by heaven and earth.[42]

Some scholars have suggested that this scholarly elite calling for the moral transformation of government was part of the popular society outside direct state control.[43] But one can also see a contradiction between this utopian moral consciousness and the popular sectors as they

[41] See ibid. and note 35 above.
[42] Ho Ch'ang-ling, *Huang-ch'ao ching-shih wen-pien*, 1:8b, 1:1b.
[43] Such are Yü Ying-shih's views described in Metzger, 'Modern Chinese Utopianism', pp. 285–91. These views are found in his 28 December 1993 article in *Lien-ho-pao*, a leading Taiwan newspaper.

moved in late imperial times toward commercialization and urbanization. On the one hand, these popular sectors created a kind of *Gesellschaft* society filled with an impersonal, materialistic, morally unpredictable, increasingly complex, urbanized, and decentralized social traffic largely outside state control. Conversely, state power became inhibited. On the other hand, the scholarly elite dominating the society's flow of moral rhetoric, though able to accommodate themselves to such traffic, never dreamed of viewing it the way Adam Smith did, as the vehicle of progress, freedom, and prosperity. On the contrary, they remained morally suspicious of *Gesellschaft*, since the ideal society on which their rhetoric focused was a *Gemeinschaft*, a fundamentally rural, agricultural community bound together by kinship and kinship-like ties, politically ordered in a way fusing together morality, knowledge, political power, and so respecting the true needs of every individual (*ch'eng-chi, ch'eng-wu*). Necessarily, this society would be a hierarchy led by men possessing Confucius's understanding of morality, not by persons trained in the pursuit of commercial gain or skilled in the morally muddy tactics of practical political negotiation (*han-hu*).

If one can speak of a general tension in history between *Gemeinschaft* and *Gesellschaft*, or, as Hayek would put it, between 'tribal' society and a social order based on 'end-independent rules', the history of this tension in China has been different from its history in the West. The popular rise of *Gesellschaft*, as Weber noted, occurred in China as well as the West, but only in the West was the longing for *Gemeinschaft* countered by a decisive moral legitimization of *Gesellschaft*. For the Chinese intellectual imagination, *Gesellschaft* was primarily a moral disaster and has continued to be.

True, in a number of important articles based on his formidable knowledge of Ming–Ch'ing sources, Yü Ying-shih has argued that, from the sixteenth century on, there arose in the Confucian world a 'new, central intellectual theme changing attitudes toward social, political, economic, and ethical issues'. This widespread change, he holds, was provoked by the rise of commerce and the intensification of despotism. It made many people put less emphasis on the policies of the imperial centre, on the leadership of the Confucian scholarly elite, and on containment of the appetite for commercial gain, and more emphasis on efforts outside government to improve the local community, on the importance and dignity of merchants, and on the need to derive the public good from a freer expression of private, even selfish interests.

It seems clear, however, that this new outlook hardly dented the centrality of the traditional Confucian worldview. Indeed, Yü himself, in other writings, has repeatedly treated this worldview as a 'value system' inherited intact by Chinese intellectuals in the twentieth century, who then tried to replace it with Western values.[44] Certainly this new Ch'ing trend did not lead to a decisive legitimization of *Gesellschaft*. The traditional worldview still dominates the 299 essays selected by Wei Yuan around 1826 to sum up the basic principles of scholarship and government with which he wanted to introduce his huge collection of writings on the art of administration. These essays which he selected for his then widely praised compilation did not legitimize and identify as progressive the social interests favouring commercialization, urbanization, reduction of state controls, and increasing sophistication in the bureaucracy, the whole tendency to turn China from a *Gemeinschaft* into a *Gesellschaft* society. Many essays expressed a need to accommodate this tendency, but they still saw it as based on the pursuit of 'profits, selfish interests (*li*)', and they never deviated from the Confucian point that this pursuit undermined the value society most needs, 'righteousness'.

Thus despite some philosophical awareness that the relation between virtue and selfish interests could be construed in a more complex way, the latter were still repeatedly identified with *jen-yü* (material human desires), which almost universally were seen as contradicting 'heavenly principle (*t'ien-li*)'. True, the idea that such 'desires' and the 'selfishness (*ssu*)' they entailed were part of the desirable social order was far from foreign to Chinese thought in Ch'ing times. Yet the idea of selfishness as free, legitimate behaviour violating accepted norms like filial piety did not appear, so far as I know. Who could have dreamed of calling for *wu-te-chih ssu* (selfishness unconstrained by the idea of virtue)? There is no indication that freedom and equality as opposed to virtue became the archetypal norm. It is significant that Ku Yen-wu (1613–82), who came to be one of the most admired Confucians, denounced as immoral precisely those contemporaneous institutional changes central to the increasing ability of people to manage their economic lives free of state control, the popular 'single whip' fiscal reforms. Even more, fully evoking the *Gemeinschaft* ideal, he deeply admired the way society under the terroristic first Ming ruler (1368–98) had been tightly controlled, morally austere, and largely free of commerce. Similarly, when commercialization and urbanization had increased during the Sung period, some six centuries before Ku's time, a major Confucian movement had arisen alongside them (later called 'Neo-Confucianism') seeking a 'return to the past' (*fu-ku*) as a *Gemeinschaft* based on *li* (the rules of moral propriety), on a state-

---

[44] On the new Ch'ing trend, see e.g. Yü Ying-shih, *Hsien-tai ju-hsueh-lun* (Essays on Confucian Learning in the Modern Era; River Edge, N.J.: Global Publishing Co., Inc., 1996), pp. viii, 1–59. On Yü's view of the persisting traditional 'value system', see his book adduced in note 49 below.

controlled land-allotment system (*ching-t'ien*), on regional administration by hereditary lords, not bureaucrats (*feng-chien*), and on local communities each organized as a single, coherent lineage (*tsung-fa*).[45]

During the imperial period, therefore, the dominant moral rhetoric was not that of ordinary people seeking freedom by calling for limits on the power of the centralized state but that of moral virtuosi, super-citizens claiming to embody the conscience of society, looking down equally on the degeneration of state institutions and the private pursuit of economic profits, and continuing to search for some way to restore the ancient saintly *Gemeinschaft*. In other words, the utopian, top-down view of progress as based on the moral dynamism of super-citizens able to influence a corrigible state was never replaced by an un-utopian, bottom-up view of progress as based on the efforts of ordinary free citizens fallibly pursuing their economic interests and organized in a practical way to monitor an incorrigible state. When Chinese intellectuals from the late nineteenth century on started to embrace the ideal of 'democracy' and, later, that of the 'civil society', this utopian, top-down approach remained integral to their thought. Yü himself has repeatedly referred to their 'utopianism'. Far from building on any indigenous notion that the expression of selfish interests is the foundation of the free and prosperous society, intellectual leaders like Chang Ping-lin (1868–1936) anticipated Mao by identifying freedom with the dissolution of distinct, clashing interests. Facing the problems of modernization and the unstoppable tendencies toward *Gesellschaft* which burst forth especially in Taiwan after 1949 and on the Mainland after 1976, China's intellectual leaders retained their belief in the corrigibility of the political centre and their own central role as the conscience of society.

Chinese utopianism and the Western concept of the civil society

After the middle of the nineteenth century, as Western and Japanese imperialism combined with a series of rebellions to shake the foundations of the Ch'ing empire, what John K. Fairbank called 'the great Chinese revolution' unfolded, entailing a process of cultural revision, which included a momentous series of intellectual debates.[46] Basic to these was

---

[45] Metzger, 'Modern Chinese Utopianism', pp. 293–4 and Chan Su-chan, Hsu Shu-ling, Huang K'o-wu, Lai Hui-min, and Mo Tzu-k'o, '*Ching-shih* Thought and the Societal Changes of the Late Ming and Early Ch'ing Periods: Some Preliminary Considerations', in *Chin-shih Chung-kuo ching-shih ssu-hsiang yen-t'ao-hui lun-wen-chi* (Proceedings of the Conference on the Theory of Statecraft in Modern China; Taipei: Institute of Modern History, Academia Sinica, 1984), pp. 21–35.

[46] John King Fairbank, *The Great Chinese Revolution, 1800–1985* (New York: Harper & Row, 1987).

an extremely prompt Chinese enthusiasm for democracy on the part of many mainstream intellectuals and leaders, beginning indeed with the very Wei Yuan who, some years previously, before the Opium War (1839–42), had edited the compilation on 'statecraft' noted above. Like so many Chinese coming after him, Wei Yuan felt that this foreign system whereby 'the discussion of state affairs, adjudication, the selection of officials, the appointment of worthy men to office, all starts from below . . . leaves nothing to be desired'. As Huang Ko-wu (Max K. W. Huang) has shown, the mainstream concept of democracy developed in the next decades coming down to the 1911 Revolution blended distinctly Western procedural ideas, such as the concept of elections or the separation of powers, together with many basic Confucian ideals, such as 'the ruler approves what the populace approves', government is 'devoted to the public good and free of all selfish interests', 'communication between the ruler and the people is opened up', 'superiors and inferiors form one body', and realization of 'the great oneness (ta-t'ung)'.[47]

This ready resonance of the Western ideal of democracy with Confucian values would be hard to explain had Samuel P. Huntington been correct when he described Confucian culture as positing that there are 'no legitimate grounds for limiting power because power and morality are identical'.[48] His view is simply wrong. As already discussed, Confucian culture included a basic tension between political power and moral consciousness, a point which has been made abundantly clear in a large body of secondary literature Huntington prefers to ignore, and which has been obscured by the modern Chinese iconoclastic ideologies polemically denouncing the Confucian tradition as well as by Max Weber's mistaken analysis of Confucian culture. Huntington also overlooks the fact that the Confucian intellectual world, unlike the Moslem, did in fact quickly become enthusiastic about 'rule by the people (min-chu)'. Already by the turn of the century, scholars like Liang Ch'i-ch'ao daring to suggest that China was not yet ready for democracy knew that such 'conservatism' would be rejected by the intellectual mainstream. Distinguished scholars ranging from Hsu Fu-kuan to Yü Ying-shih have emphasized the affinity between the Confucian tradition and the ideal of democracy.[49] Confu-

[47] Huang Ko-wu (Max K. W. Huang), 'Ch'ing-mo Min-ch'u-te min-chu ssu-hsiang: i-i yü yuan-yuan' (The Meaning and Origins of the Chinese Concept of Democracy during Late Ch'ing and Early Republic Times), in *Chung-kuo hsien-tai-hua lun-wen-chi* (Symposium on Modernization in China, 1860–1949; Taipei: Institute of Modern History, Academia Sinica, 1991), pp. 372, 383–4.
[48] Huntington, *The Third Wave*, pp. 300–1.
[49] Yü's view in this regard is illustrated by his *Lien-ho-pao* discussion adduced in note 43 above, while a full interpretation of Confucian culture as a persisting 'value system' according with the main ideals of democracy is in his *Ts'ung chia-chih hsi-t'ung k'an*

cianism is a this-worldly way of thought according to which realization of ultimate values is contingent on fully moral action by the political centre; the standard of political morality transcends the current ruler; and the content of political morality is action in accord with 'what the people regard as beneficial to them' (*The Analects of Confucius*, 20:2). With this viewpoint, many Confucians logically, almost instantly, and quite naïvely perceived Western democratic procedures as infallible means with which to realize their old goal of perfect political morality.

This enthusiasm for democracy, therefore, was little if at all combined with the un-utopian, bottom-up perspective of the Millsian democratic tradition. Just because the Chinese from the start so enthusiastically embraced this Western system of democracy as a completely effective method to make government accord with 'what the people regard as beneficial to them' (the people, that is, as those masses acting in accord with enlightened opinion), they dealt in a distinctive way with the two main Western traditions of democratic thought, the Rousseau–Hegel–Marx tradition and the Locke–*Federalist Papers*–J. S. Mill tradition.[50] While modern Western political thought has been a battle between these two schools, criticism of Rousseau in the Chinese world has been rare.[51] As perfectly illustrated by the thought of Sun Yat-sen (1866–1925), who in this regard was not at all controversial, the Chinese intellectual mainstream has pictured democracy as realized by a moral–intellectual elite (*hsien-chih hsien-chueh*) fusing together knowledge, morality, and political power and then seeing to it that everyone enjoyed what Sun called

Chung-kuo wen-hua-te hsien-tai i-i (Chinese Culture and its Affinities with the Ideals of Modernity: A Discussion from the Standpoint of the Traditional Value System; Taipei: Shih-pao wen-hua ch'u-pan shih-yeh yu-hsien kung-ssu, 1984). Similar views can be found in the English publications of Wm. Theodore de Bary, Tu Wei-ming, and myself (both my books). My refutation of Weber's analysis of Confucianism, found in both these books, as well as in Wolfgang Schluchter (ed.), *Max Webers Studie über Konfuzianismus und Taoism* (Frankfurt am Main: Suhrkamp, 1983), pp. 229–70, has not, so far as I know, been criticized in any publication. See e.g. 'Review Symposium: Thomas A. Metzger's *Escape from Predicament*', in *Journal of Asian Studies*, 39: 2 (February 1980), pp. 237–90. That Confucian thought strongly differentiated political power from morality was first made clear in the monumental writings of the modern New Confucians like Hsu Fu-kuan, T'ang Chün-i, and Mou Tsung-san. In 1995 Professor Huntington and I exchanged letters on this point, but he defended his view that 'in Confucianism Caesar is God' (from his letter of 5 Sept. 1995).

50 This distinction is close to Dunn's between the 'strong' and the 'weak' theories of democracy. See his *Western Political Theory*, pp. 22–4.

51 An exception is Hong-yuan Chu, *T'ung-meng-hui-te ko-ming li-lun* (The T'ung-meng-hui's Theory of Revolution; Taipei: Institute of Modern History, Academia Sinica, 1995). This issue is thoroughly discussed in Huang Ko-wu (Max K. W. Huang) *Tzu-yu-te so-i-jan: Yen Fu tui Yueh-han Mi-erh tzu-yu ssu-hsiang-te jen-shih yü p'i-p'an* (The Raison d'être of Freedom: Yen Fu's Understanding and Critique of John Stuart Mill's Liberalism; Taipei: Yun-ch'en, 1998). Also published in Shanghai by Shang-hai shu-tien ch'u-pan-she, 2000.

'true freedom' and 'true equality'.[52] Easily meshing with Rousseau's theory of the general will, this picture has been basic to the other three modern Chinese ideological traditions as well, Chinese Marxism, Chinese liberalism, and modern Confucian humanism.[53]

Conversely, these four ideologies rejected the Millsian vision of a society as a kind of *Gesellschaft* ultimately dependent on the unpredictable interplay of free, fallible individuals competing in the open intellectual, economic, and political marketplaces and following 'end-independent rules'. Even those prominent thinkers closest to the Millsian view of liberty, Yen Fu (1854–1921) and Liang Ch'i-ch'ao, only partly grasped it, as Huang Ko-wu has shown. What Yen Fu (and indeed all the later Chinese liberals praising his translation of 'On Liberty') missed was not Mill's appreciation for the dignity and freedom of the individual, which easily resonated with Confucian ideals, but Mill's epistemological pessimism, his fervent belief that 'liberty' was needed to pursue 'knowledge' and 'progress' because it was the only way to limit the flood of mistaken ideas stemming from the drastic fallibility of the human mind. From the Confucian standpoint, or from that of a society explicitly viewing itself as 'backward' and taking for granted the goal of catching up to the 'advanced' societies, the basic truths of human life were all too clear. Therefore such fallibility could not be an urgent problem. Because Chinese intellectuals could not appreciate Mill's epistemological pessimism, the energy and passion in his argument could not be even remotely duplicated in the Chinese intellectual world.[54]

At least to a large extent, therefore, the modern Chinese intellectual mainstream has not only embraced a Rousseauistic concept of democracy as control of the government by a rational, morally enlightened citizenry expressing 'the general will' but has also perpetuated the Confucian tradition's epistemologically optimistic, top-down, utopian, *Gemeinschaft* approach to politics. Conversely, the old refusal morally to legitimize *Gesellschaft* has persisted. This approach is evident even in recent Chinese humanistic and liberal thought, not to mention Marxist.[55]

---

[52] Thomas A. Metzger, 'Did Sun Yat-sen Understand the Idea of Democracy?', in *The American Asian Review*, 10: 1 (spring 1992), pp. 1–41.

[53] An overview of these ideologies, with the exception of Marxism, is in my 'The Chinese Reconciliation of Moral-Sacred Values with Modern Pluralism: Political Discourse in the ROC, 1949–1989', in Myers (ed.), *Two Societies in Opposition*, pp. 11–37. See also Thomas A. Metzger, 'China's Current Ideological, Marketplace and the Problem of "Morally Critical Consciousness",' in press as part of the proceedings of the Third International Conference on Sinology organized by the Academia Sinica, Taipei and held 29 June–1 July 2000.

[54] See Huang Ko-wu's *I-ko pei fang-ch'i-te hsuan-tse* and his book mentioned in note 51 above.

[55] The idea that modern Chinese political thought has been 'utopian' is now widely

Princeton's Yü Ying-shih, publishing an essay on 28 December 1993 in *Lien-ho-pao*, one of Taiwan's leading newspapers, offered an understanding of the civil society with which few if any Chinese liberals or modern Confucian humanists would quarrel. In his eyes, 'according to the Chinese traditional outlook, a balance in the relation between state and society should be maintained. This is rather close to the Western views about democracy.' Traditionally, this balance was upset by the excessive power of the state, but the ideal of this balance was reflected in the welcome Chinese intellectuals gave to 'the Western concept of democracy'. They were disappointed, however, as their 'utopian' ideal of perfect freedom and equality clashed with the modern Chinese need for 'an organized, powerful, modern state'. After 1949, the Communists 'destroyed those social sectors traditionally outside state control . . . but the price they paid was destruction of society's vitality'. These sectors thus came back to life again and might eventually turn, as they already have in Taiwan's case, into a 'modern civil society'.[56]

Yü's view seemingly accords with the sociological-political definition of the civil society above. Yet in brushing over the traditional disjunction noted above between utopian intellectual aspirations and the interests of the social strata pursuing economic profits, and in regarding 'intellectuals' as the central agents of progress, he implies a top-down approach. What is missing in his thought is a clear concept of an incorrigible state monitored not by moral virtuosi but by ordinary citizens pursuing their mundane interests and fallibly competing in the three marketplaces. True, were he questioned, he might endorse this concept. It is another thing, however, fully to articulate this concept and use it to sort out the facts regarding China's cultural-political evolution and the role of Chinese intellectuals.

The second example is that of Yang Kuo-shu, an eminent professor of psychology at National Taiwan University who has just retired from his position as associate director of Taiwan's top research centre, Academia Sinica. His many well-known essays in the field of social and political criticism have expressed the ideals of liberalism in a way arousing little if any controversy in Taiwan. According to essays published in 1985, Yang saw a global shift from the agricultural to the industrial stage, which

accepted, as illustrated by Yü Ying-shih's recent writings, and goes back to the new emphasis in the 1970s on its 'optimism'. At that time, this emphasis appeared in the publications of Wang Erh-min, Don Price, and myself. Whether Mainland scholars now discussing 'utopianism' were influenced by these writings, however, is not clear. More controversial, perhaps, is my argument that contemporary Chinese utopianism is rooted in Confucian utopianism, and that the latter was integral to broadly accepted Confucian premises, not just to a few texts like *Chou-li*.

56 Cited in Metzger, 'Modern Chinese Utopianism', pp. 285–91.

necessarily called for democracy, a certain individualism, and all kinds of pluralism. Indeed, Yang, like Yü, is a man as deeply and personally committed to the ideal of personal freedom and dignity as anyone can be. Yang's top-down approach, however, is evident in his strongly teleological vision of history and his – indeed quite uncontroversial – celebration of 'intellectuals' as 'the conscience of society', persons who 'because of the sensitivity of their understanding . . . often can penetrate the outer appearances of things . . . and grasp the basic principles of things'. With their help, society will be based on 'reason', not on the unpredictabilities and injustices of 'the three marketplaces' as defined above.

Thus Yang painted a future for Taiwan and China in which there would be no 'unfair concentration of power', individualism would flourish free of 'selfish efforts to enrich oneself', and society would form a 'circle . . . of mutual respect, cooperation . . . mutually beneficial relations of mutual dependence'. The key would be the 'boundaries' serving as parameters of individual freedom, and these would be justly fixed through 'reason', which would reign because in a free society, if 'some thought is not good, it will naturally fail to survive . . . Legal regulations and moral norms will naturally put obviously incorrect and bad things outside the scope of pluralistic values.'[57] No clearer rejection could be found of the Millsian, epistemologically pessimistic, un-utopian, bottom-up concept of civil society than these passages by a fervently liberal, professionally outstanding, widely admired Chinese intellectual in contemporary Taiwan who obtained his PhD from the University of Illinois.

In mainland China, many writings celebrating the idea of civil society appeared in the 1990s, such as those of Teng Cheng-lai. Here I can only touch on one version of the Marxist aproach, that followed by Kao Li-k'o (b. 1952) around 1990. He was then and still is on the faculty of the Department of Philosophy and Sociology at Chekiang University in Hangchow. I refer here to his 1992 book on modern Chinese thought, a revised version of his 1990 PhD thesis at Beijing Normal University. Maoism is of course basic to the official line of the People's Republic of China, but it is also still today one of the major outlooks pursued by serious intellectuals. Kao's 1992 approach, different from his views in the late 1990s, was based on assumptions that have been central to the modern Chinese intellectual mainstream, not just Marxism. A basic assumption of his was the utopian goal – utopian in my eyes, not his – of

---

[57] Yang Kuo-shu, *K'ai-fang-te to-yuan she-hui* (The Open, Pluralistic Society; Taipei: Tung-ta t'u-shu ku-fen yu-hsien kung-ssu, 1985), pp. 7, 10, 13–14, 18–19, 27, 32–3, 44, 159, 191–2, 196–7. I have tried to analyse Yang's thought in detail in my 'Modern Chinese Liberalism and the Utopian Approach to the Revision of Culture', unpublished.

China as a 'new civilization' unconstrained by the unhappy authoritarianism of traditional times; vibrant with the 'freedom' and 'instrumental rationality' basic to modern life; and, unlike the West, free of the ills of modern life, such as the 'dehumanization' deplored by Jürgen Habermas (a major sage in many contemporary Chinese circles). Thus China would 'transcend the West' by healing the rupture between 'instrumental rationality' and 'the rationality of ends' – Max Weber's distinction – and so, for the first time in world history, making possible the realization of socialism. Kao linked Mao to this blueprint by using Mao's 1940 essay 'On New Democracy'. He equated Mao's 'minimal guidelines' with the 'modernization' programme now being shaped by China's government and Mao's 'highest guidelines' with the 'post-modern' programme of socialism that China's distinctive, superior kind of modernization would eventually make possible.

Much like Yang Kuo-shu, Kao saw this top-down approach as needed properly to steer society away from excessive individualism and selfishness. The key for him was an ethos that would find the elusive balance between the desirable individual pursuit of *ko-t'i-chih li* (what benefits the individual) and the undesirable tendency toward *li-chi chu-i* (putting selfish interests above all else). Mao, Kao held, was the only modern Chinese thinker able to show how China could find this balance and thus 'transcend' the West, because he not only was open to Western thought but also grasped traditional Chinese values and the advantageous nature of China's current situation as a 'latecomer' able to learn from the mistakes of the West and so to profit from the West's current state of cultural enervation. Like the famous Mainland Marxist Li Tse-hou, who at least through 1987 also was enthusiastic about Mao's vision, Kao was proud of his association with Mao's revolution even while admitting that Mao horribly erred after 1949.[58] Kao would no doubt hold that a civil society is integral at least to 'the highest guidelines', the socialism toward which China's modernization is heading, if not to 'the minimal guidelines', but I would argue that his utopian, top-down approach is out of accord with the Western civil society tradition.

In addressing the question of political improvement, therefore, modern Chinese political thought has not turned toward a non-utopian, bottom-up approach. Based on the traditional optimism about political practic-

---

[58] Kao Li-k'o, *Li-shih yü chia-chih-te chang-li – Chung-kuo hsien-tai-hua ssu-hsiang shih-lun* (The Tension between Historical Necessity and the Quest for Humanistic Values: An Essay on the Intellectual History of Chinese Modernization; Kuei-chou jen-min ch'u-pan-she, 1992). I have discussed Chinese Marxism and Kao's thought at greater length in my ' "Transcending the West": Mao's Vision of Socialism and the Legitimization of Teng Hsiao-p'ing's Modernization Program', a 1996 publication in *Hoover Essays*, a series published by Hoover Institution, Stanford University.

ability, it still reflects the traditional paradigm of a morally and intellectually enlightened elite working with a corrigible political centre morally
to transform society, instead of emphasizing the organizational efforts of
free but fallible citizens forming a civil society with which to monitor an
incorrigible political centre. Thus it still tends to be at odds with the
popular impulses actually forming the economically booming *Gesellschaft* worlds in China as well as Taiwan today. True, the prevalent idea
that China is in a period of 'transition' is often used by intellectuals to
accommodate this *Gesellschaft* world. Nevertheless, modern Chinese
intellectual writings lack any explicit willingness to accept the morally
messy world of the three marketplaces as the appropriate medium of
progress. The rise of *Gesellschaft* has only corroborated the sense of
predicament still basic to modern Chinese intellectual discourse.[59] Nor
has there been any decisive shift from the ideal of *kung-te* (the virtue of
people dedicated to the public good) to a formulation of that more
amoral Western concept of civility described above.

Yet one should not hastily assume that Chinese political thought is
'backward'. In fact, it grapples with a problem not yet resolved by any
society: finding the proper balance between the various free markets, the
role of the state working with technical and cultural elites, and the
cultivation through education of what Hayek called the 'ethos' of a
society. The way of achieving this threefold balance, moreover, will vary
depending on cultural traditions. Thus it is far from obvious that any
primarily Western paradigm or concept of political rationality will be
adopted by the Chinese as the key to this problem.[60]

At the same time, however, although not a few scholars argue that
intellectual trends strongly influence societal development in the long
run, such trends are not necessarily decisive. Taiwan's democratization
has been accompanied by many major social changes not obviously
influenced by Taiwan's intellectuals. These changes certainly include the
formation of a civil society according to the sociological definition, but
not necessarily one according to the anthropological one.[61]

---

[59] On the 'sense of predicament', see article on the ROC adduced in note 53 above.
[60] For a current, non-Marxist rejection of the Western combination of capitalism and
democracy, see Thomas A. Metzger, 'Hong Kong's Oswald Spengler: H. K. H. Woo (Hu
Kuo-heng) and Chinese Resistance to Convergence with the West', in *American Journal
of Chinese Studies*, 4: 1 (April 1997), pp. 1–49.
[61] For the formation of this civil society in Taiwan, see Chao and Myers, *The First Chinese
Democracy*.

12   Civil society, community, and democracy in the Middle East

Sami Zubaida

The discourses on civil society in the Middle East follow from the quest for democracy and liberalization of state and society. The state in most countries in the region, whether monarchial or 'socialist', had maintained firm control over politics, the economy, and society, leaving little space for autonomous social or economic power. Connections and networks of advantage and patronage operate between rulers, their bureaucracies, and various social formations and segments, held together by 'primordial' solidarities of kinship, tribe, and locality or just ones formed around powerful leaders and functionaries.[1] These controls, however, depended on the governments' ability to dispense resources in accordance with a political calculus of advantage, and to maintain a welfare system which provides a safety net for growing and mostly impoverished populations. The decline of these resources and the ever-expanding commitments with growing populations, rising expectations at all levels, arms expenditure, and military adventures (such as the two Gulf wars) brought to an end the short-lived equilibrium. From the 1970s and into the 1980s, governments sought to lower their commitments and limit the size of their debts, a process pushed by international demands for 'structural re-adjustment'. It was these pressures which diminished governments' ability to deliver, and which pushed some of them to a programme of liberalization of economy and society which included a measure of 'democratization'.

It is this apparent loosening of government controls over both the economy and political expression which has occasioned the quest for civil society. Civil society is seen as the basis of democracy. The totalitarian state has colonized, controlled, and penetrated society and crippled the forces of social autonomy, the argument runs. To reverse this process it is not enough to hold elections and license political parties: democracy must be based on autonomous and voluntary institutions and associations. These would bring individuals into social and political partici-

---

[1] Olivier Roy, 'Patronage and Solidarity Groups: Survival or Reformation?' in Ghassan Salamé (ed.), *Democracy without Democrats? The Renewal of Politics in the Muslim World* (London: IB Tauris, 1994), pp. 270–81.

pation. They would act as social fortifications for guarding human rights and the rule of law. What then is the nature of this civil society? Is it something that existed historically and is now to be revived? Or is it something to be built anew: 'the birth of civil society'?

Saad Eddin Ibrahim was one of the earliest advocates of civil society as a basis for democracy in the region. He defines civil society in terms of 'volitional, organized collective participation in public space between individuals and the state'.[2] He goes on to list political parties, trade unions, community development associations, and other interest groups. A condition of civil society, he and many others insist, is 'civility', the acceptance of differences, and commitment to peaceful procedures for managing conflict. In an earlier contribution, Ibrahim argued that the volitional associations of civil society stood in contrast to the constraining bonds of political authority (the state) on the one hand, and involuntary bonds of primary and primordial associations such as the family, village, and tribe of historical society, on the other. It is this last specification which proved controversial, as we shall see.

Faced with 'orientalist' denials of the possibility of civil society or democracy in the Arab or Muslim world, many Arab writers, including Ibrahim, defensively cite 'resilient traditional Arab civil formations'.[3] These are the social formations of pre-modern Arab and Middle Eastern cities: guilds, awqaf (trusts and foundations), the ulama, who played a leadership role in the urban communities and sufi orders. The leaders and notables of these civil associations also acted as advisers to the rulers, and as mediators between them and the populace. 'In this capacity, [they] reduced the absolutist nature of the pre-modern Arab Islamic state.'[4]

Interestingly, Gellner (the arch 'orientalist' in this regard) and many others do not disagree. Gellner characterized Muslim urban society as a strong culture facing a weak state. The culture was built, he argued, on the strength and immutability of the sacred law, the shari'a, and the communal leadership of the ulama who upheld it. The state was weak because it lacked legitimacy in terms of this sacred law, and was subject to the regular cycles of disintegration and conquest resulting from strong tribal federations ready to pounce on the weakened state and establish their own dynasty. Gellner, however, did not think of these urban associations as civil society. They were for him examples of historical

---

[2] Saad Eddin Ibrahim, 'Civil Society and Prospects for Democratization in the Arab World', in Augustus Richard Norton (ed.), Civil Society in the Middle East, vol. I, (Leiden: E. J. Brill, 1995) p. 28.
[3] Ibid., p. 30; Ahmad Moussalli, 'Modern Islamic Fundamentalist Discourse on Civil Society, Pluralism and Democracy', in Norton, Civil Society, pp. 79–119.
[4] Ibrahim, 'Civil Society', p. 31.

'segmentary' societies. His definition of civil society, like that of most other Western writers, rested on the field of autonomy and security of the economic sphere, which then generate powers and institutions which bind the state and shape it.[5] In all pre-modern and non-European societies it was/is political and military power which determines wealth, and wealth outside its context is insecure, subject to predatory extortion and confiscation by the holders of power. As such, civil society for Gellner was the 'miracle' of the West. Traditional Muslim civil formations, as Ibrahim's earlier formulations[6] argued, were not voluntaristic or libertarian, but constraining and compulsory social associations which imposed hierarchical and binding authority on individuals.

These 'traditional' social formations differed widely over time and in different parts of the Muslim world, but it would be fair to say that they were almost uniformly patriarchal and authoritarian, often coercive. Positions of authority, such as that of *naqib*, *mufti*, or guild master were in most places held and inherited within families of notables. Guilds were, perhaps, the most participatory of these institutions, with much challenge and bargaining going on, yet they were firmly under the control of the masters, in turn subject to the commands of ruling authorities. Membership of sufi orders coincided with particular families, guilds, and urban quarters, all of which stressed authority, loyalty, and obedience.[7]

These traditional formations have been, for the most part, superseded or destroyed by the processes of modernity. Massive rural migrations have altered the character and forms of solidarity of neighbourhoods and quarters; international trade has destroyed crafts and guilds; sufi orders have declined in size and authority. Yet patriarchal associations and attitudes have persisted, or been reconstituted under modern conditions: tribal and village associations in cities,[8] new religious associations, formal or informal, around neighbourhoods, mosques, and charities, some ruled by modern Islamist organization,[9] and the much less visible

---

[5] Ernest Gellner, *Conditions of Liberty: Civil Society and Its Rivals* (London: Hamish Hamilton, 1994), especially ch. 8, pp. 61–80.

[6] Saad Eddin Ibrahim, 'Al-Mujtama' al-madani wal-tahawwul al-dimuqrati fi-wattan al-'arabi' (Civil society and democratic transformation in the Arab homeland), Pamphlet issued by The Ibn Khaldun Centre, Cairo, 1991.

[7] On urban quarters, sufi orders, and guilds, and their relation to political authority, see Abraham Marcus, *The Middle East on the Eve of Modernity: Aleppo in the Eighteenth Century* (New York: Columbia University Press, 1989), and André Raymond, 'Quartiers et mouvements populaires au Caire au XVIIIème siècle', in P. M. Holt (ed.), *Political and Social Change in Modern Egypt* (London: Oxford University Press, 1968), pp. 104–16, and André Raymond, *Artisans et commerçants au Caire au XVIIIème siècle* (Damas: Institut Français de Damas, 1974).

[8] Ibrahim, 'Civil Society', pp. 42–3; Roy, 'Patronage and Solidarity Groups'.

[9] Sami Zubaida, 'Islam, the State and Democracy: Contrasting Conceptions of Civil Society in Egypt', *Middle East Report* (1992), p. 979.

multiplicity of familistic bonds and authorities. New Islamic and Islamist social and political forces have a special affinity with these social formations, and have sought in many places to control and colonize them; which is why the status of these formations as civil society has become an issue.

Islam, history, and tradition in relation to civil society

The definitions of civil society by Arab writers have been based for the most part on liberal and secular notions, either excluding religion or making a qualified space for it. While wishing to limit the extensions and penetrations of the state, they nevertheless looked to a reformed state for guarantees of civil society, and indeed discerned in the democratization measures of the 1980s the gradual evolution of such a state. These specifications have faced a strong challenge from Islamist and other radical intellectuals, much more forthrightly anti-state.[10] They also underlined social and political Islam as the most active and vital force in modern societies in the region: any account of civil society which ignores this fact, they argue, is unrealistic, to say the least. In addition, it is pointed out, the strongest and most durable associations outside government are precisely the 'neo-traditional' and 'primordial' groupings excluded from civil society by the liberal definitions. I shall now consider in some detail an example of this genre of Islamic writing.

A cautious and nuanced Islamic approach in this direction is made by Sayfuldin Abdelfattah Ismail, a political scientist at Cairo University.[11] Ismail is uneasy about 'civil society': he identifies it as a Western concept which developed historically in Western political experience, and its relevance to the Muslim world as problematic. Whether we like it or not, however, since the beginning of the Arab renaissance, the West has come to live within us, and we must deal with this fact.[12] A further problem is the ambiguity of the term, emerging as it does from the many conflictual and ideological usages, to the extent that it has become a slogan. Nevertheless, he concludes, the concept and the issues surrounding it

---

[10] A notable outspoken writer in this vein is Burhan Ghalyoun, a former secularist and Marxist now aligned to Islamists in denouncing the Arab state. See for example 'bina' al-mujtama' al-madani al-'arabi: dawr al-awamil al-dakhiliyya wal-kharijiyya' (The Structure of Arab Civil Society: The Role of Internal and External Factors), in *Al-Mujtama' al-Madani fi al-Watan al-Arabi wadawruhu fi tahqiq al-Dimuqratiyya* (Civil society in the Arab Homeland and its role in assuring democracy) (Beirut: Markaz dirasat al-wihda al-arbiyya, 1992), pp. 733–82.

[11] Sayfulddin Abdelfattah Ismail, 'Al-Mujtama' Al-Madani Wal-Dawla Fil-Fikr Wal-Mumarasa Al-Islamiyya Al-Mu'asira' (Civil society and the state in contemporary Islamic thought and practice), in *Al-Mujtama'* . . ., pp. 279–311.

[12] Ismail, 'Al-Mujtama'', p. 291.

cannot be rejected by Muslim intellectuals because they have come to occupy a central position in definitions of social and political projects. He then proceeds to transcribe the term into registers of Islamic history and society.

Ismail starts in this task from an operational definition of civil society as advanced by most current exponents as a set of institutions and associations which are public, voluntary, and independent from authority. These include the common list of trade unions, professional associations, political parties, social and developmental projects, and religious associations. Insisting on these specific examples, mostly unique to Western history, argues Ismail, leads some writers to deny civil society in the Muslim world. This insistence, however, makes comparisons impossible. Muslim societies historically have included prominent examples of civil associations independent of and critical of authority. Ismail calls these *mu'assasat al-umma*, institutions of the (Muslim) community. Ismail's main examples of these institutions are those of the *ulama* and the *shari'a*, acting as bases of social autonomy with notions of public rights and duties *vis-à-vis* the rulers. Ismail is aware, however, that these institutions were sites of struggle for incorporation and control by the authorities, which were successful in many instances, notably in incorporating the institution of *ifta'*, the issuing of fatwas (authoritative rulings on religious and social issues) – which was, in most instances, a function of state – with the political appointment of Muftis. For Ismail, however, there remained at the core of these institutions a public and civic function, exemplified in the injunction to command the good and forbid evil-doing.[13]

With regard to 'traditional' forms of association and solidarity, such as tribes and kinship groups, Ismail is sensitive to the definitions of civil society which exclude them. He argues, however, citing the example of the Prophet's dealing with the tribes, that the positive elements in these forms, such as mutual support and security for the individual, can be tolerated if not supported, while the negative elements of factionalism and nepotism can be resisted.[14] It is indeed possible to enlist the positive elements of these social solidarities in the wider project of building social autonomies from the state.

Contemporary Islamic movements, argues Ismail, make a vital input into civil society as defined. They are prominent participants in voluntary associations and institutions, such as unions and syndicates. Their engagement with society and politics has the aim of putting Islamic ideas into practice, finding ways of living the principles of *shari'a*, and

---

[13] Ibid., pp. 296–300.   [14] Ibid., pp. 297–8.

converting others into their way of thinking. They co-exist and engage with other forces and ideas in the democratic process, both in the political arena and the fields of social association. In this task they clash with authorities who seek to deny or limit social autonomies, and in particular the Islamic engagement in these fields.

In his conclusion, Ismail makes a plea for solidarity between civil associations and institutions, whether Islamic or secular, in building up civil society against the interventions and penetrations of authority and to resist incorporation and corruption. The purpose of civil society, it would seem, is to 'marginalize' authority. This plea is oblivious to the existence of social conflicts central to civil society, and the forces that connect the different social factions to elements of the state and its institutions. This follows in part from the associational definition of civil society which neglects the central economic dimensions of social associations and the class and other conflicts which follow from it.

Turkish Islamic utopias

Egyptian Islamic intellectuals, such as Ismail, implicitly accept the framework of the modern nation-state and define their Islamic project within its ambience. Indeed, it has been widely observed that much of contemporary political Islam is statist, and that as an opposition force it aims to conquer the state. The different examples of Iran, Sudan, and Algeria show this clearly. The project of founding an 'authentic' Islamic state is central to the Islamist project.[15] Mainstream Turkish Islamism is no different. Indeed, Turkey is the only country in the region in which a fully fledged Islamic party stands a chance of entering government through electoral contest. It is a group of Turkish Muslim intellectuals, however, who have come out against this statist trend, and have put forward a novel view of the self-governing community. The most explicit statement of these ideas is in the work of Ali Bulac, a sociologist and journalist.[16]

Bulac traces the evil of the modern state to Hegel. While Hegel conceived the state as a secular entity, he also gave it a spiritual

---

[15] Some Egyptian Islamic intellectuals, such as Ismail, are now arguing that the Islamic project is about the *umma*, not the state, and that the *umma* is the civil society of Islam. See Al-Gawhari for an interview with two founders of the proposed new Islamic party in Egypt, *Al-Wasat* (the Centre): Karim Al-Gawhari, ' "We are a Civil Party with an Islamic Identity": An Interview with Abu 'Ila Madi Abu 'Ila and Rafiq Habib', *Middle East Report*, 199 (1996), pp. 30–2.

[16] For an exposition of Bulac's ideas, see Michael E. Meeker, 'The New Muslim Intellectuals in the Republic of Turkey', in Richard Tapper (ed.), *Islam in Modern Turkey* (London: IB Tauris), pp. 189–219, and Sami Zubaida, 'Turkish Islam and National Identity', *Middle East Report* 199 (1996), pp. 10–15.

foundation and made it the ultimate end in itself. This modern state developed into a monster which controls all aspects of social and cultural life: law, education, art, religion. It imposes a common nationality on many ethnicities: the logic of this state is ethnic cleansing internally and nationalist wars globally. God's will on earth is expressed through a community not a state. God's *umma* is *masum* (infallible), without sin and error. The *umma* is the real subject of history. Modernity transformed the *umma* into a state, and therein lie all the problems. Iran, Sudan and other Islamic states have not solved this problem but perpetuated it. The solution lies in the self-assertion of civil society, in the form of multiple communities, against the state. The community(s) must develop their own institutions of law, education, economic forms, and culture, and take these spheres away from the control of the state. The individual, or rather the 'human' (*insan*), must be freed from the clutches of the state, not in accordance with liberal theory viewing the individual as a separate atom, but in accordance with the Islamic view that the human is always part of a community.

This theory has spawned the notion of multiple-law communities, which has a political appeal as a recipe for pluralism. It is argued that law is a function of civil society not of the state. Communities with different beliefs and cultures will wish to abide by different systems of law. Muslims are one such community, which abides by the *shari'a*. This should not be imposed on others, who can choose their own communities and laws.

This system, argues Bulac, is modelled on the example of the Prophet in Medina. The *medina vasikasi* has become a slogan in current Turkish Muslim thought and politics. It refers to the charter drawn up by the Prophet to regulate the relations between the new Muslim community and the existing non-Islamized communities, tribes, and religions of the city. According to this *vasike*, each community followed its own law and custom; matters of common interest to all cohabiting communities were specified and regulated.

These ideas have been taken up by some Islamic politicians as a means of combining the *shari'a* for Muslims with a liberal pluralism for others. It is a Utopian idea, ignoring the intrinsic connections of law to social powers and conflicts, yet it forms an appealing slogan not lost on politicians seeking to establish their liberal credentials while championing Islam. This odd mixture of communal corporatism and libertarianism presents a novel view of civil society, one which is divorced from the nation-state, and indeed aims to abolish it in favour of some 'watch-dog' state with minimal functions of security and coordination.

Secularist worries

Many secularist writers have tried to exclude Islam and Islamism from definitions of civil society. This is partly on the grounds that Islam and Islamism are part of traditional and primordial formations, and partly on the perceived incompatibility of a religious-based society, sought by Islamism, with pluralist democracy. This latter idea is reinforced by the totalitarian and authoritarian manifestations of many sectors of the Islamic movement. The liberal Islamic trend, exemplified by Ismail's work, has sought to challenge both these supposition, and especially to insist on the pluralist democratic commitment. Pointing to the Islamist manifestations which belie these claims, secularist opponents dismiss liberal Islamism as either a-typical of the Islamic current, insincere, or both. Aziz al-Azmeh, a consistent critic of the Islamic current, also points out the affinity of Ismail's conceptions with a populist totalitarian discourse of authenticity which contradicts its liberal pretensions.

Al-Azmeh[17] attacks what he calls a 'democratist' discourse, which postulates democracy as a direct correspondence between the people, conceived as a historical formation with Islam as its essential identity, and a state which expresses that identity. Its diagnosis of the ills of the contemporary state, therefore, is that it is alien to this historically given essence, and as such despotic. The process of democracy, then, is conceived as a rectification. Civil society is identified by this discourse with this historical formation, and is separate from the existing state. The political project is then defined as the mobilization of this civil society against the state which has penetrated, subordinated, and oppressed it. Democracy, then, is the expression of this common popular will in the Islamic state, which must then preserve the identity and unity of the people and the state. Al-Azmeh cites notable exponents of Islamic democracy, such as Rashid Ghannouchi and Hasan Turabi, to illustrate this organic and unitarian conception. Turabi is cited as postulating a plebiscitarian procedure, by which people's consent is sought directly through electronic media, and without the corrupting and divisive intermediaries of political parties.[18]

Political Islam's treatment of women is symptomatic of their basic social concept, argues al-Azmeh.[19] This concept underlines the commitment of Islamic discourse to the society of tribes and cousins, of patriarchy, personal ties, and loyalties, and ultimately of 'private' (*ahli*)

---

[17] Aziz Al-Azmeh, 'Populism Contra Democracy: Recent Democratist Discourse in the Arab World', in Salamé, *Democracy without Democrats?*, pp. 112–29.
[18] Ibid., pp. 124–5.
[19] Aziz Al-Azmeh, 'Comment on Ismail 1992', in *Al-Mujtama'* . . ., p. 314.

society, with its authoritarian structures and emphasis on allegiance and obedience.

Al-Azmeh's critique may seem unfair on Ismail, who is sensitive to these problems and making an effort to tackle some of them. He is, in fact torn between the pull of these key Islamic conceptions of society and government and a commitment to a joint effort, with other national and democratic forces, in a common project. Yet, as we have seen, his emphasis is on unity and consensus between these forces *vis-à-vis* the state. This unitarian and consensual emphasis is typical of Islamist discourses, which relate social cohesion to the unity of God (*tawheed*).

How consistent is Ismail's project with Islamic practice in Egypt and elsewhere? It is important to situate Ismail within one of several different contemporary Islamic currents, a reformist and modernist project. The other, and perhaps dominant, current is the Salafi orientation, much more conservative and 'fundamentalist', more insistent on the literal reading of scriptures and the teaching of the historical authorities of *shari'a*. These ideas are widely held, both in respectable and 'moderate' circles, including prominent *ulama*, and among the radical and violent groups. The ideas of democracy and civil society are either totally rejected by this current, or superficially adapted to their traditionalist and organicist conceptions, in the manner outlined by al-Azmeh. It is this tendency which is dominant in Islamic social projects and institutions. How do these projects relate to conceptions of civil society?

In terms of the associational definitions of civil society, Islamic forces must be admitted to be the most prominent and vital in Egypt and elsewhere. Saad Eddin Ibrahim, the guru of civil society, tells us that Islamic participation is a positive factor. 'So long as such parties and associations accept the principle of pluralism and observe a modicum of civility in behaviour toward the different "other", then they would be integral parts of civil society.'[20] What if they don't? It would seem, then, that the definitional criteria of belonging to civil society are attitudinal rather than organizational or institutional, and inclusion within it is honorific, dependent on good behaviour.

For those secularists who advance the concept and practice of civil society as a path and a basis for democracy and pluralism, there is an acute dilemma with regard to Islamist prominence and vitality in the field they have defined as civil society. Mustafa Kamil Al-Sayyid, an Egyptian political scientist, portrays this dilemma. In surveying civil society in contemporary Egypt, he wrote: 'An essential feature of a civil society is a large measure of respect for freedom of conscience and thought, not only

[20] Ibrahim, 'Civil Society', p. 52.

by state authorities but more importantly by citizens.'[21] He then proceeds to list the many instances and incidents of censorship, intimidation, and assassination by Islamist groups, including respectable and moderate elements, against their opponents.[22] Writers, intellectuals and artists are the main victims of these aggressions. The case of Abu Zayd, a Cairo university professor of Islamic studies who followed modern critical methods in the analysis of Quranic texts and historical sources, is a lamentable example of the convergence of several Islamic personalities and institutions over a period of several years, ultimately with the complicity of a sector of the legal profession and the judiciary, in the intimidation and persecution of an academic, driving him and his wife finally to leave the country or face assasination as an apostate.

Al-Sayyid, then, has to face the fact that civil society as defined institutionally is increasingly under the control of these same Islamists:

The Islamist movement has succeeded in using its resources to gain a large space within civil society. Thus, the movement utilizes its members' knowledge and organizational skills, financial resources, and access to mosques, newspapers, publishing houses, professional associations, and political parties, to mobilize opposition to governmental policies or the state. The movement hopes to transform the social order following its gradual take-over of society's institutions . . . the Islamist movement in Egypt is the most representative and powerful actor in a civil society with contradicting features.[23]

This would contradict Al-Sayyid's insistence on civility and tolerance as essential ingredients of civil society, while Ismail seems to assume (evidently erroneously) that his fellow Islamists share his pluralist outlook. Ibrahim faces the same dilemma with the hope that involvement in the democratic process and pluralistic politics will moderate the Islamists into democrats, on the assumption that democratization will continue. Al-Sayyid makes it quite clear, however, that the Egyptian government has the powers, under 'emergency' legislation in operation for more than twenty years, and with a docile parliament, to control and suppress any association or institution and to violate any human rights.[24] The limitations that the President imposed on his power is largely to do with attempting to satisfy sectors of internal and international public opinion. Since 1992, however, this restraint has been difficult to maintain in the face of mounting challenges and crises, and Egyptian 'democracy' is looking increasingly threadbare, especially after the 1995 parliamentary elections which returned 93 per cent of seats for the government party!

21 Mustafa Kamil Al-Sayyid, 'A Civil Society in Egypt?', in Norton, *Civil Society*, p. 276.
22 Ibid., pp. 276–80.
23 Ibid., p. 289.   24 Ibid., pp. 280–2.

Arbitrary and oppressive government on the one hand, and a civil society increasingly controlled by Islamists with tenuous claims to pluralist democracy on the other, do not appear hopeful for a civil society based on civility and tolerance.

We have to note one important but unremarked feature of the Islamist control of associations and institutions, most notably the professional associations in Egypt. The effects of these take-overs is to politicize these associations beyond their 'civil' functions. They become a field of political contest and conflict. The Islamists, restricted in their access to the political field proper, used these associations as a political platform as well as a vehicle for social mobilization. Their functions as doctors' or lawyers' syndicates then become secondary. The whole idea of civil society is that social institutions and associations pursue and develop interests and activities to do with social and economic functions, part of a social division of labour. In this instance these functions are subverted and subordinated to an inclusive political project. This is another instance of Islamists inheriting the project of the political left, especially the Communists, who pioneered these tactics.

'Neo-traditional' social formations

In the discourses on civil society in the Middle East, these formations constitute a controversial and ambitious category. Liberal writers exclude them from definition of civil society, because they are, for the most part, authoritarian, patriarchal, and their membership is not voluntary, but ascribed. They also tend towards religious affiliations, which is why they are distrusted by secularists and defended by Islamists. Even some liberals, however, seem to waver on this issue: if civil society consists of centres of social power autonomous from the state, then in most Middle Eastern societies neo-traditional formations of tribe, region, or religious association seem to be the most plausible candidates for this role. Many argue that these constitute the reality of Middle Eastern societies, and social scientists as well as political activists have to make the most of them as bastions of social autonomies. Even forgetting the initial definitions of civil society which excluded them, however, the question remains whether these powers promote democracy and pluralism. The answer is that these formations do not constitute a uniform category, but embrace diverse groupings, all transformed by modern processes, some towards alignment with despotic rulers, others towards more autonomous and formalized 'modern' operations.

Many of the ruling cliques are transparently based on such 'neo-traditional' formations, notably in Syria and Iraq. Saddam Hussain, his regime resting on a particular tribal solidarity, sought to bolster his power after the Gulf War debacle by the revival and empowerment of other tribes, restoring their lands and legitimizing their laws and shaykhly authorities, as allies and supporters.[25] The late King Husain sought to modify his democracy by manipulating electoral arrangements to favour tribal and clan solidarities: it is reported that tribal primaries are held in Jordan to decide on agreed candidates. In Yemen, tribal federations, which always lay behind political forces, have come into the open as the Islamic Islah party, fed by Saudi funds, as a Sunni/Wahhabi counterpart to the Zaydis, and a conservative bulwark against the 'progressive' southern forces.

The fact of the matter is that despotic rulers prefer to deal with neo-traditional formations in bargains and deals of patronage and support. The suppression of political and civil associations continues to be an important force motivating individuals to seek security and prosperity through cultivating their primary affiliations of kin, tribe, and region. Olivier Roy[26] shows how many of these formations are modern re-constructions in relation to the power games instituted by governments and authoritative institutions.

Under the right conditions, however, some groups, starting from a traditional basis, can be institutionalized as modern associations with 'universalistic' orientations and open membership. Examples of this trend are to be found mainly in Turkey, where political, legal, and economic conditions have facilitated such developments. Sufi orders, operating secretly since Ataturk prohibited them in the 1920s, re-emerged in the 1980s as charitable foundations instituted under new legislation modelled on American law on foundations but retaining the Muslim designation, *vakif*.[27] Two such foundations now command extensive resources devoted primarily to Islamic education, publishing, and media. Village and regional associations in Ankara and Istanbul have also been transformed into pressure groups in municipal politics, embracing a wider membership than the designated constituency.

Another possible positive input from neo-traditional institutions into democracy is indirect. In so far as such groupings represent alternative power centres to the government (and that is rarely the case), they may provide spaces between the centres for intellectual and cultural activities

---

[25] See Baram Amatzia, 'Neo-Tribalism in Iraq: Saddam Hussein's Tribal Policies, 1991–96', *International Journal of Middle East Studies*, 29 (1997), pp. 1–31.

[26] Roy, 'Patronage and Solidarity Groups'.

[27] See Faruk Billici, 'Sociabilité et expression politique islamiste en Turquie: les nouveau vakifs', *Revue français de science politique* (1993) 43:3, pp. 412–34.

which would be otherwise suppressed. Islamic Iran may be such an example. There, various religious and bazaar institutions and groupings, under powerful molla patrons, and the duality of state power between the presidency and the spiritual leadership, constitute some plurality of power as compared with the neighbouring states. This plurality of power centres and the play between them allowed a free Presidential election in 1997, which elected Khatami, with a reformist programme, and a persistent advocacy of civil society, against the authoritarian ruling mollas. Even though most of the power elites (with the exception of Khatami and his entourage) have no faith in democracy and are mostly despotic and corrupt, yet the fact of diffusion and multiplicity of power does create spaces for intellectual dissent and cultural expression. Such advantages, however, are precarious and can be arbitrarily ended.

The economic sphere: powers and conflicts

Classic Western conceptions of civil society, from Adam Smith to Hegel to Marx, have at their core the notion of a historically emergent economic sphere, 'commercial society', or capitalism, which brings with it sources of powers and conflicts. Institutions and powers generated by this sphere constitute the seeds for further institutional developments in various fields of endeavour, parties, unions, scientific and cultural formations, and so on, which draw upon and sustain these powers and constitute bases of social autonomy. The state itself is transformed by this process, and the modern state, a 'law-state', protects and sustains this civil society which contains the autonomies and powers to confront and limit its own powers. It is this historical formation which Gellner considers to be the unique product of the West.[28]

In the many volumes written on civil society in the Middle East, there is remarkably little said about the economic sphere and its consequences for civil society. Reviews of classic definitions of civil society in the work of Saad Ibrahim and others are accurate in reporting the centrality of the economic in these definitions. Their substantive discussions of contemporary civil society in the region, however, have little to say on this sphere: they concentrate on associations, unions, syndicates, and parties, and when they study business it is typically businessmen's associations and chambers of commerce which concern them. Ismail's essay only mentions the economic sphere in order to dissociate himself and honest Islamists from the shady activities of Islamic investment companies. Almost

---

[28] Gellner, *Conditions of Liberty*.

without exception it is American and European writers on the subject who have highlighted the political economy aspects of civil society.[29]

Everyone, of course, recognizes that government control over the economy, whether 'socialist' or dynastic, is a crucial part of its power over society and its ability to co-opt or suppress would-be opposition, and to prevent the formation of spaces of social autonomy. Many Arab writers on the subject, however, are reluctant to draw an explicit conclusion that the withdrawal of the state from control over the economy is a necessary (if not sufficient) condition for a viable civil society. The legacy of Nasirist socialism, fears of corruption, dependency, and foreign control associated with *infitah* policies predispose many Arab intellectuals, including many Islamists, to distrust solutions based on capitalism. Waterbury[30] notes the close connection between the intelligentsia and the state, which goes beyond material interests of employment and emolument, into a strong sense of identity and shared goals. 'The intelligentsia has frequently been the rhetorician of state mission.'[31] This may explain the neglect of the economic sphere in the Arab writings on civil society.

The link between economic liberalization and civil society/democracy may be challenged with plenty of evidence to show that native capitalism and the private sector have not been champions or facilitators of democracy and social autonomy but have, for the most part, acquiesced – if not thrived on – state control and authoritarian politics. This, the advocates of economic liberalization would argue, is the crux of the matter: state control has created a dependent and weak bourgeoisie, and only state withdrawal from the economic sphere would generate the dynamism which can bring about the vitality of civil society. The question is whether this bourgeoisie can control significant resources beyond the power of the state, and this seems to be doubtful in most countries in the region at present. The private-sector bourgeoisie, argues Waterbury, has entered a pact with the state, an 'alliance for profits', 'the tacit understanding has been that the bourgeoisie would renounce any overt political role and that it would follow the broad economic directives of the state, in exchange for which it would be allowed to make significant profits'.[32]

---

[29] Raymond Hinnebusch, 'State, Civil Society and Political Change in Syria', in Norton, *Civil Society*, pp. 214–42; Alan Richards, 'Economic Pressures for Accountable Governance in the Middle East and North Africa', in Norton, *Civil Society*, pp. 55–78; Roger Owen, 'Socio-economic Change and Political Mobilization: The Case of Egypt', in Salamé, *Democracy without Democrats?*, pp. 183–99; John Waterbury, 'Democracy without Democrats?: The Potential for Political Liberalization in the Middle East', in Salamé, *Democracy without Democrats?*, pp. 23–47.
[30] Waterbury, 'Democracy without Democrats?', p. 27.
[31] Ibid., p. 27.   [32] Ibid., p. 27.

These common interests, often also incorporating official labour leaders, would be threatened by any opening towards democratic processes.

Waterbury goes on to speculate that there may be a logic in the development of capitalism which will transcend this stage. A more developed and confident bourgeoisie may find the alliance for profits too restrictive, and unilateral control by the regime over interest rates, credit tariffs, and prices intolerable.

Private interests may move from lobbying for their specific advantage to trespass into foreign affairs . . . or into the affairs of state . . . The expansion of the private-sector agenda requires no explicit demand for democracy, but it is rooted in a demand for accountability on the part of those who own wealth and capital . . . It may be that someday the Middle Eastern bourgeoisie will work their alleged democratic magic, but it is by no means clear where on the road to the long term the bourgeoisie are now.[33]

Raymond Hinnebusch follows a similar line of reasoning with respect to Syria. Formations and re-formations of the Syrian bourgeoisie since the 1970s have resulted from the Ba'thist state's policies and contingencies. With the decline in revenues in the 1980s the state had to shed many economic responsibilities and patronage spending. Private business had to be given concessions to fill the gap. It has been expanding into greater shares of the domestic and export markets ever since. The bourgeoisie can now mobilize its own capital for investment and job creation. Hinnebusch argues that two sectors of the bourgeoisie, industrial entrepreneurs and expatriate capitalists (wealthy Syrians in Europe and the Americas), have the potential to widen civil society by demanding greater economic and political liberalization in return for investment and expansion. Hinnebusch makes it clear, however, that these are only hopeful signs, and an autonomous bourgeoisie is still a long way off:

[the bourgeoisie] presents no common front in favour of the market since dominant elements of it are still dependent on monopolies in an over-regulated economy and on state contracts and protection . . . The favour or dis-favour of the regime can make or break a business . . . Nor can business yet promote themselves as public figures. Some large merchants who tried to win popularity through press advertisements were broken by the enforcement of currency laws; the regime would tolerate no bourgeois pretensions to political independence.[34]

An independent bourgeoisie with real power over resources as a source of social autonomies and a civil society remains, then, a possible prospect, but remote.

What of the vast and growing 'Islamic economy' in Egypt, Syria, and elsewhere, as a source of social powers and autonomies? There are many

[33] Ibid., p. 29.
[34] Hinnebusch, 'State, Civil Society', p. 232.

different Islamic economic organizations and enterprises. The most visible and official are the Islamic banks, many of them Saudi based and closely related to rulers and princes. In Sudan some branches were associated with social and political projects of the Islamic Front and the government. In Egypt in the 1980s Islamic investment companies were prominent in offering very high returns on deposits, the returns being shares of the profit rather than interest, which is forbidden in Islam. These companies invested in a wide range of commercial and industrial enterprises from car dealerships to food processing to construction, as well as financial dealings on the international markets. Eventually some of these companies collapsed amid scandals and political controversies. It would seem that they were operating on the margins of legality, taking deposits outside the draconian regulations of the Egyptian bureaucracy. They were enabled to operate by co-opting influential figures from the state and religious establishments. When eventually the government moved against them, they were hotly defended by many Islamic intellectuals, who hold them up as an example of Islamic civil society.[35] Subsequently, when their modes of operation were revealed, Islamist intellectuals distanced themselves, and in retrospect branded them as instances not of Islam but of the parasitism encouraged by *infitah*. It is with such examples in mind that Waterbury remarks that 'Islamic business interests are thickly intertwined with state economic interests, state functionaries and the military'.[36]

In general, we can say that there are many businessmen and enterprises, some on a large scale, which are related to the Muslim Brotherhood. They contribute to the projects and charities of Islamist organizations, feeding into the Islamic social networks of patronage, conversion, and mobilization, not least by providing jobs as major employers. They are, then, a vital part of the Islamic civil society discussed by Ismail and Al-Sayyid.

It should also be noted that the provision of social services by Islamic associations in Egypt is welcomed by a government which has largely withdrawn from providing these services. They ameliorate social discontent, and through their organization at local level act as agents of social control. The object of these activities is to Islamize the population in terms of religious observance and ethical conduct, with a heavy emphasis on family morality and 'decency' of women and the young.

---

[35] On Islamic investment companies in Egypt, see Alain Roussillon, *Sociétés islamiques de placement de fonds et ouverture économique* (Cairo: Dossiers de CEDEJ), and Sami Zubaida, 'The Politics of the Islamic Investment Companies in Egypt', *Bulletin of the British Society for Middle East Studies*, 17 (1990), p. 2.
[36] Waterbury, 'Democracy without Democrats?', p. 28.

This only worries the government when it ventures into militancy and opposition. In the words of Roger Owen, 'it makes it more difficult for the regime to maintain its tacit alliance with Islamic groups by which they obtain official toleration for a role in the management of the lives of large sections of the urban poor'.[37]

Conclusions

The concepts and themes of civil society in the Middle East are closely tied up with the quest for democracy. Political differences and contests are expressed in terms of the debates on civil society and democracy. Islamic advocacy and action and secular responses play an important part in these contests. We have seen that in their writings on civil society Middle Eastern thinkers have tended to emphasize forms of association and non-state institutions and groupings as the basis of civil society, containing sources of social autonomy and generating powers which may eventually counter-balance state powers. There is a disagreement on whether neo-traditional groupings can be included in civil society.

Advocates of civil society as associations, however, have to face the problem that these associations, in most countries, seem to be at the mercy of the state. In the countries where political liberalization had been most advanced, such as Egypt and then Jordan, political parties, unions and syndicates, the press and the media have been controlled and manipulated by the governments. Egypt since 1992 has seen a tightening up of government controls: laws were issued to take control of professional syndicates which elected Islamist councils; a press law was passed in 1995 which muzzles opposition and exposés of government corruption on pain of imprisonment for offending journalists and editors; Islamist intellectuals were imprisoned on trumped-up charges. Al-Sayyid[38] gives an account of the awesome, arbitrary powers of the state *vis-à-vis* political and associational life and the media, and the instances of their use. The question, then, is: where are the counter-powers generated or held by non-state associations and institutions? It would seem that this form of associational life can only prosper by the grace of the rulers and at their discretion.

Middle Eastern intellectuals seem to focus on associations, because they regard them as expressions of democratic practice (an assumption which is not always justified) and as a social experience of democracy. In so doing they tend to neglect the sphere of socio-economic processes, not

---

[37] Owen, 'Socio-economic Change', p. 195.
[38] Al-Sayyid, 'A Civil Society in Egypt?', pp. 282–90.

in themselves 'democratic', but which may engender resources of power and autonomy outside the state. That is to say, they concentrate on voluntaristic aspects of organization which are within their sphere of activity as professional intellectuals, and neglect socio-economic *structural* processes, which are unintended consequences of activity and development in the economic sphere. Roger Owen has rightly argued that whereas there is no necessary or direct connection between capitalism and democracy, an autonomous capitalism can be an important condition for democracy:

Opposition politics would be further strengthened by the process of elite fragmentation which, in the longer run, is likely to accompany the development of a mixed and much more market-orientated economy. This will inevitably create conflicts of interest which the regime will find increasingly difficult to manage. It will also create demands for greater freedom and regularity which, in turn, will open up new spaces for political activity. Finally, the development of private sector industry will produce conflicts between workers and employers which the old techniques of labour management will no longer be able to contain. Much will depend on which political forces are best able to anticipate such future trends and to put them to their own advantage.[39]

This line of thought does not seem to come naturally to many Egyptian and other Middle Eastern intellectuals, secular or Islamist, who seem to retain an implicit statist nationalism when it comes to the economy. While recognizing the inefficiency and corruption of state-controlled economies, they still retain a belief in the possibility of better controls. Free capitalism, in this line of thinking, can only lead to parasitism, corruption, greater inequalities, and worst of all, dependence on foreign capital. Associations and groupings have a much more democratic and native ring to them.

[39] Owen, 'Socio-economic Change', p. 196.

13   Mistaking 'governance' for 'politics': foreign aid, democracy, and the construction of civil society

Rob Jenkins

Through a long and uneven process of diffusion, the idea of civil society has entrenched itself within a diverse array of cultural and intellectual settings. One of the contexts into which it has been 'received' is what can loosely be termed 'the development profession'. The community of scholars, consultants, activists, and policy analysts that influences policy-making in national governments, international agencies, and non-governmental organizations has constructed an elaborate discourse around the role played by civil society in the process of social, economic, and political change in post-colonial societies. Because of the influence of this community on foreign-aid[1] priorities – which today encompasses issues of how political life is organized – it occupies a unique niche in contemporary political theory, representing a common locus for both the reception of the idea of civil society and its retransmission to aid-recipient countries.

Scholars attempting to bridge the gap between political theory and development studies have, in general, performed admirably in holding multilateral aid agencies to account for the hypocrisy of their policy statements on civil society. In perhaps the best treatment of this issue, David Williams and Tom Young expose the emptiness of the World Bank's stated commitment to respecting indigenous African political traditions.[2] The Bank's enthusiastic support for civil society, they argue, is nothing less than a backdoor attempt to transform African societies from the ground up by substituting a new understanding of individual political subjectivity – for it is only through such a novel basis for the

---

[1] This term is defined broadly to include all financial transfers (in the form of loans and grants) from governments, international organizations, multilateral financial institutions, or private charities in OECD countries to either governments or non-governmental organizations in economically less-developed countries (LDCs).

[2] David Williams and Tom Young, 'Governance, the World Bank and Liberal Theory', *Political Studies*, 42 (1994), pp. 84–100.

'self' that the accompanying features of an open political sphere and a 'neutral state' can perform the roles assigned to them in liberal political theory and neo-liberal economic policy.

While this has proved a useful exercise, particularly because it also indicts the often sanctimonious community of northern non-governmental organizations as collaborators in the process of social re-engineering, there is less validity in pursuing what some might consider the logical next step – namely, exposing the extent to which the aid agencies' conceptualization of civil society represents a 'misreading' of political theory. The main charge is that the complex ancestry of the term is not acknowledged by practitioners working within the development field. In fact, the multiplicity of meanings behind the term 'civil society' makes it pointless to condemn foreign-aid agencies for failing to adhere to one or another definition. Just as other cultures have developed indigenized versions of the notion of civil society, the aid community has taken this most promiscuous of ideas and fashioned it to suit its own unique culture and purposes. There is as little justification for demanding that the United Nations Development Programme adopt a Lockean rather than a Gramscian conception of civil society as there is for expecting the usage of the term in Chinese political discourse to conform to the meaning ascribed to it by Plato. Different circumstances produce different meanings, and these change over time in response to unpredictable influences. This is one of the main premises of this volume.

There is one crucial difference in the case of aid agencies, however, which is their intentionality. They are deploying considerable economic and political resources to bring about change. Because the notion of civil society is thus employed instrumentally, we are justified in seeking to determine whether the logic which underpins the particular conception aid agencies have developed is consistent with the achievement of their stated objectives, and whether it is compatible with other principles to which they are ostensibly committed. The conclusion reached is that, on both counts, it is not.

The materials on which this critique will be based are not the familiar sweeping statements of the World Bank, which is barred by its Articles of Agreement from engaging in programmes or projects with a specifically political component.[3] (While the Bank effectively skirts this pro-

---

[3] The most important of these are *Sub-Saharan Africa: From Crisis to Sustainable Growth* (Washington, D.C.: The World Bank, 1989), *Governance and Development* (Washington, D.C.: The World Bank, 1992), and *Governance: The World Bank's Experience* (Washington, D.C.: The World Bank, 1994). For more detailed statements, see the publications of the World Bank's Senior Policy Adviser in the Africa Region's Technical Department (written in his 'personal capacity' and therefore expressing views that 'should not be taken as reflecting those of the World Bank'): Pierre Landell-Mills, 'Governance,

hibition by redefining political issues as questions of efficient administration, hence its emphasis on 'governance', its statements on civil society remain for the most part on a fairly elevated plane of abstraction.) The far more active agents in the project of attempting to build civil societies in the south are individual donor governments. It is the foreign-aid programmes of bilateral donors which have seized most energetically upon civil society and attempted to provide substance to the term. We will focus on the detailed programmatic priorities of the most zealous actor, and the one devoting the most resources to this effort – the United States Agency for International Development (USAID) – but the views of other actors in the development community will also feature prominently in the analysis.

Foreign-aid programmes of advanced capitalist 'northern' countries have identified civil society as the key ingredient in promoting 'democratic development' in the economically less-developed states of the 'south'. The logic runs roughly as follows. Development requires sound policies and impartial implementation. These can only be delivered by governments that are held accountable for their actions. Accountability, in turn, depends upon the existence of 'autonomous centres of social and economic power' that can act as watchdogs over the activities of politicians and government officials. Civil society consists of both the associations that make up these 'centres' and the 'enabling environment' that permits them to operate freely. It is an arena of public space as well as a set of private actors. Therefore, aid to the 'democracy and governance sector', as it has increasingly come to be known within the profession,[4] must be earmarked to support both individual associations as well as the political milieu in which they carry out their functions.

With minor variations this story is embedded in the thinking of most bilateral aid agencies and multilateral financial institutions.[5] While the

Civil Society and Empowerment in Sub-Saharan Africa', paper prepared for the Annual Conference of the Society for the Advancement of Socio-Economics, 1992; P. Landell Mills and I. Serageldin, 'Governance and the External Factor', *Proceedings of the World Bank Conference on Development Economics* (Washington, D.C.: The World Bank, 1991); and P. Landell-Mills and I. Serageldin, 'Governance and the Development Process', *Finance and Development*, 29 (1991), pp. 14–17.

[4] This term was used in a number of unpublished papers presented by development practitioners at a workshop on 'Civil Society and Foreign Aid', Institute of Development Studies, University of Sussex, 6–7 June 1996.

[5] Many bilateral donors have not developed fully elaborated positions on the relationship between civil society and good governance. Officials in such agencies often refer to the statements of intergovernmental organizations in which they participate, such as the OECD's Development Assistance Committee (DAC). See, for instance, 'DAC Orientations on Participatory Development and Good Governance', OECD Working Papers, vol. II, no. 2 (Paris, 1994).

preservation of individual liberties is deemed by most agencies to be a good in itself, it is the contribution of individual rights to engendering and maintaining democracy and promoting sound government policy and economic performance that primarily animates aid policy. By funding organized groups within developing countries, aid agencies seek to create a virtuous cycle in which rights to free association beget sound government policies, human development, and (ultimately) a more conducive environment for the protection of individual liberties.

From the standpoint of the role into which civil society has been cast in promoting this equilibrium, there are several problems with this model. The most serious shortcoming is that aid agencies expect too much of civil society. In order to justify its reliance on civil society for so many different missions, USAID has assigned a *range* of meanings to the term. Each use is, in effect, context-dependent. There is nothing inherently wrong in this. The notion of civil society as mutable, something capable of adapting to new configurations of power, might even appear an attractively flexible idea. The problem arises when efforts are undertaken to operationalize these varying conceptions by building (or 'fostering', or 'supporting', or 'nurturing') civil society through the application of foreign aid. It is in their attempts to wed theory to practice that USAID and other donors have effectively stripped the notion of civil society of any substantive meaning. This is not to say that there are no empirical referents to the term in each of these various definitions. In each instance it is clear which types of associations qualify as constituent elements of civil society, and which do not. Rather, the main difficulty is that the definitions are not capable of producing, *in a co-ordinated way*, the three main outcomes that assistance to civil society is designed to produce: (1) transitions to competitive politics, (2) the 'consolidation' of fledgling democracies, and (3) the establishment of market-oriented economic policies, and subsequently positive developmental performance.

To put it slightly differently, in order to make the case for civil society's pivotal role in achieving one of the three objectives, the concept is defined in ways that preclude it from contributing to the other two. This disjunction is remedied by specifying, when referring to the other two objectives, alternative definitions of civil society that render its ability to achieve them more plausible. Unfortunately, the political reality in which events unfold is rather more messy and unpredictable. The dynamics of political contestation are not inclined to change course in order to accommodate the finely crafted theorizing of aid-policy analysts. Since the three objectives are meant to reinforce one another in a self-sustaining system, the USAID conception of civil society is fatally flawed. The instrumental nature of the term cannot contain its multiple meanings.

Above all, donor conceptions of civil society represent not a mis-reading of political theory, but a misreading of history – particularly with respect to the political dynamics which underlie regime change, the entrenchment of a democratic order, and the evolution of economic policy. It is difficult to determine whether, in fact, these misapprehensions have generated the tame (and ineffectual) conception of civil society to which donors have become attached, or whether it has been necessary to portray civil society in such sterile terms in order to justify the expenditure of scarce aid resources in the pursuit of what in fact constitutes an ambitious political agenda; if the former is true, then donor agencies are guilty of extreme naïvete; if the latter, then of extreme cynicism. One can only suspect a partially conscious mingling of the two. The important point is that in either case the vision of civil society on which aid policy is based is incapable of achieving the three desired outcomes.

To understand why this is the case, we must pay particular attention to the ways in which dynamics within one process can have 'spillover effects' for the others. Despite its pronouncements on the need for careful sequencing, USAID's policy, *in effect*, pretends that the three objectives operate in isolation – and therefore that civil society can be represented differently in each case. Political reality makes this untenable. By examining some of the issues that arise in the interaction, first, between democratic transitions and democratic consolidation, and second, between both of these and the making of economic policy, we will be in a position to appreciate the impossible task that aid donors have set for themselves.

From regime overthrow to democratic consolidation: advocates, interests, and the dynamics of political movements

It is at first difficult to grasp the sterility of USAID's conception of the relationship between civil society and democracy because, as we have mentioned, it attributes a range of different meanings to civil society.[6] In its policy statements, these meanings are sometimes given different labels and arranged within matrices to indicate the functional contribution of each to the goals of effecting transitions to liberal politics, consolidating democracy, and ensuring accountable governance. The need to take 'a more operational approach' is the justification for failing to engage with the 'considerable theoretical abstraction and debate in the academic literature'. USAID aims to bypass the widespread 'disagreement about

---

[6] It should be noted that donor agencies are not alone in attempting to define civil society in ways that exclude its less savoury manifestations. See, for example, Naomi Chazan, 'Africa's Democratic Challenge', *World Policy Journal*, 9, no. 2 (1992), pp. 279–307.

how to define "civil society" and set its conceptual boundaries'.[7] Their goal is to assist the decision-makers within USAID 'in designing and evaluating civil society investments in the democracy sector'.[8]

One of the most suspect attempts to reorient the definition of civil society in line with USAID's diverse objectives was a 1996 Program and Operations Assessment Report. This document indicated a conscious shift in terminology, from the term 'civil society organizations' (CSOs) to 'civic advocacy organizations' (CAOs). This was meant 'to highlight the activist and public interest nature of the organizations USAID seeks to support with democracy funds'.[9] Sensibly enough, this definition includes 'labour federations', 'business and professional associations', and 'environmental activist organizations'. But the wider context makes it clear that USAID is interested in these groups only to the extent that they 'engage in or have the potential for championing adoption and consolidation of democratic governance reforms'.[10] What they are attempting to support – through the funding of specific associations – is the acceptable, public-spirited face of civil society. There are two problems with this.

The first stems from the inconsistency between the logics behind economic and political aid. Political aid, in the form of funding for civil society organizations, attempts to locate the 'true democrats' capable of pressing for a 'political opening' – that is, a recognition by a repressive regime that increased participation is justified. In seeking out such committed idealists as strategic allies, however, USAID is violating the sacred neo-liberal logic of allocative efficiency that underlies its economic aid programmes. Northern aid agencies and multilateral financial institutions have spent the better part of two decades attempting to persuade developing-country governments that economic planning, in which state bureaucracies attempt to 'pick winners' from among the range of industries and firms within their national economies, inevitably leads to a sub-optimal allocation of resources, and ultimately to rent-seeking and the creation of powerful interests wedded to the system of preferences. The message was that attempting to second-guess the market would not work. And yet the very same donors are attempting to do precisely the same thing in what they have termed 'the democracy sector'. They are, in effect, distorting the free operation of the 'political market' by funding groups within 'civil society' which *they* consider likely to support democracy.

While it may be possible to justify these interventions by claiming that

---

[7] USAID, Center for Development Information and Evaluation, 'Constituencies for Reform: Strategic Approaches for Donor-Supported Civic Advocacy Programs', USAID Progam and Operations Assessment Report no. 12, February 1996, p. v.
[8] Ibid.   [9] Ibid., p. vi.   [10] Ibid., p. viii.

they are designed to correct the 'market distortions' of authoritarian rule, it is in the course of practical application that they become troublesome. The very existence of funding for 'pro-democracy' advocacy organizations tends to attract other, less altruistic individuals and groups. A recent example of how this can lead to what, from USAID's view, can only be considered undesirable outcomes is the case of the July 1996 *coup* in Burundi. The leader of this revolt, Major Pierre Buyoya, received $145,000 over the previous three years from USAID's 'democracy and governance' budget. It was channelled to Buyoya's Foundation for Unity, Peace and Democracy for seminars and consultations among non-governmental organizations on how to promote democracy and human rights in Burundi.[11] While he may have been motivated by the best of intentions – Buyoya orchestrated the country's first free elections in 1987 – the ousting of the civilian regime of President Sylvestre Ntibantunganya by a military junta is certainly not what USAID's policy documents advocate.

Apart from such blatant power-grabbing, there are other more subtle difficulties with the USAID approach to funding organizations operating within civil society. Most worrying is the extent to which even interest groups that are commited to overthrowing a repressive regime – say, an association of prominent business leaders – may not be particularly concerned with promoting the type of competitive politics to which donors are ostensibly committed. While they may genuinely oppose the way in which the authoritarian regime has governed, there is also a distinct risk that what business leaders prefer is a more efficient oligarchy, one in which they attain a measure of privileged influence, of perhaps the sort they may have exercised before the regime's predatory behaviour reached the point of pathology which fomented widespread dissent. In fact, the establishment of democratic politics may result in a diminution of the influence such interests once enjoyed, and which they might again be enjoying, thanks to considerable sums of foreign assistance. As the political situation becomes more fluid, foreign aid may actually help to place such interests in a privileged position to pursue their self-interest, at the expense of the public interest. USAID and other donors would like us to believe that they have the bureaucratic capacity to filter the genuine advocates of democracy from those who might wish to play the aid game until such time as new circumstances make other, less savoury, options more attractive. Their own neo-liberal logic argues otherwise.

The reason why this is particularly troubling is that the point in time when such interests – they are formed from self-interest, after all, though they might wish to make common cause with other 'principled' groups in

---

11 'U.S. Paid Burundi Coup Leader', *The Observer* (London), 28 July 1996, p. 20.

oppositional activities – is precisely the moment when the question of consolidating democracy arises. Once a transfer of power to an elected government has been effected, there is a great temptation for some interests to throw their support behind a leader, a party, or a coalition of elites in which they will enjoy disproportionate influence. The case of Zambia under Frederick Chiluba, in which powerful interests within civil society have lent support to a newly installed democratic government which engaged in tactics similar to those that discredited his predecessor, Kenneth Kaunda, underscores the importance of this logic. The revised USAID strategy of supporting 'civic advocacy organizations' is an attempt to isolate and support the democratically inclined aspect of individual associations, while ignoring the fact that such groups possess interests of their own that may eventually diverge from those of aid agencies as well as of their one-time comrades in the struggle against despotic rule. Aid agencies want to fund Dr Jekyll, but not Mr Hyde, refusing to acknowledge that they are inseparable. The irony is that this sort of wishful thinking about the motives of political actors should come from a development agency that has built its entire policy framework around unsentimental rational-choice explanations of political and economic behaviour.

The second problem with attempting to 'define-away' the multifaceted nature of actors that operate within civil society is that it leads to a sort of historical amnesia. Explaining this will require a consideration of the wealth of conceptions of civil society available to those responsible for formulating aid policy. Indeed, a notion like civil society eventually reaches a point where it develops such a large corpus of theorizing that there emerges a very considerable secondary literature, consisting of synthetic reviews which attempt a taxonomy of meanings. None of these is capable of doing complete justice to a term as complex as civil society. Gordon White's typology of civil society's meanings, however, is particularly useful for our purposes because it indirectly highlights the extent to which donor thinking relies not on one wrong or inappropriate definition, but on an array of detailed specifications, any one of which can be invoked, depending on which developmental objective it seeks to achieve.[12] (For his part, White sensibly limits himself to one clearly defined usage of the term for his own work, an analysis of the emergence of voluntary associations in China during the period of economic reform.)

White argues that within the intellectual tradition which views civil society as the sphere of associational activity operating between the state

---

[12] Gordon White, 'Prospects for Civil Society in China: A Case Study of Xiaohan City', mimeo, January 1992.

and the family – itself a subset of the vast range of conceptualizations – there are three further subdivisions. First, there is the relatively restrictive definition centred on the version of civil society that Hegel (and in a different sense Marx) had in mind, one linked explicitly with the transition from primordial affiliations to those based on economic interests, consisting of associations 'rooted in an autonomous sphere of economic activity based on private property and regulated by markets'.[13] This would include trade unions, chambers of commerce, professional associations, and consumer lobbies. A second, more inclusive, definition considers any type of association, regardless of its nature, as part of civil society. This can include, in addition to those groups listed above, such elements as religious fundamentalist organizations and ethnic associations centred on perceived kinship links, however distant. White considers such a definition too inclusive to be meaningful, as such a 'usage conflates "civil society" with society'.[14] The third definition takes as its frame of reference a dominating state and a repressed society, and thus includes within the realm of civil society movements which arise in opposition to the state.[15]

The problem for the civil-society promoters is that, unlike White, they are not prepared to limit their claims as to what civil society can achieve, and so they are drawn into the analytical trap of attempting to include too many of these subdivisions within their notion of civil society. This leads to definitional inconsistency. For the purpose of dislodging an authoritarian regime, for instance, USAID is willing to stretch its definition of civil society to include virtually any mass organization that can bring pressure to bear on the government. This even encompasses 'first-tier associations' – that is, those of 'a more ascriptive nature (kin, clan, ethnic, or religious)'.[16] When discussing the later task of consolidating democracy, however, these groups (which correspond to White's second category) are nowhere to be found in USAID's vision of civil society. They have been surreptitiously erased from the 'CAO strategic logic'.[17] But political reality works rather differently. Such mass movements have a tendency to live on beyond the transition phase. As mobilizers of identities that cut across sectoral interests, their actions continue to affect the organizations contained within the more restrictive definition of civil society. Their persistence as agents in the structuring of

---

[13] Ibid., p. 3.   [14] Ibid.

[15] The most thorough elaboration of this conception is Jean-François Bayart, 'Civil Society in Africa', in Patrick Chabal (ed.), *Political Domination in Africa* (Cambridge: Cambridge University Press, 1986).

[16] USAID, 'Constituencies for Reform', p. 2.

[17] Ibid., pp. 5–11.

patronage networks also impinges upon efforts to promote the type of market-affirming civil society that aid programmes would like to see entrenched. While it is possible for USAID to refuse them funding once their usefulness in assisting the transition from authoritarian rule has been exhausted, ethnic associations mobilized for political purposes cannot simply be wished away. Their role in bringing about the demise of a dictatorial regime brings with it a sense of empowerment that can embolden such movements to make further demands for a different type of society and polity. These organizations need to be integrated into the matrix of competitive politics – as they have been in India[18] – rather than cast as obstacles on the road to modernity and good governance.

That donor agencies are not unaware of the downstream implications of an inclusive approach to civil society during the period of democratic transition is evident from their approach to other associational entities. Anticipating the difficulties that emerge when attempts are made to 'consolidate' a newly installed democracy, USAID explicitly excludes political parties from *all* of its definitions of civil society, terming them part of 'political society'.[19] This is an attempt to nip the problem in the bud. While there is ample theoretical precedent for such an exclusion, USAID's stated rationale for doing so – that parties seek to capture, rather than to influence the exercise of, state power[20] – is dubious. It is not until this logic is extended to the point of excluding from its operational definition of civil society those organizations with close links to political parties that it becomes manifestly untenable. To assert that political parties can and ought to remain distinct from the social groups it is their function to reconcile is to assign them a role as dispassionate interest aggregators, shorn of ideology and immune to the pressures of power. There is little empirical justification for such a view in either the recent spate of democratization – the 'Third Wave'[21] – or in the second wave that followed decolonization from the late 1940s to the mid 1970s.

Poland's Solidarity movement, perhaps the greatest single inspiration for the renewed interest in civil society among the donor community during the 1990s, rested upon a complex web of relationships between groups with overlapping memberships, cemented together by charismatic

---

[18] The classic account of how caste identities have adapted to democratic politics in India is Lloyd I. Rudolph and Susanne Hoeber Rudolph, *The Modernity of Tradition* (Chicago: University of Chicago Press, 1967).

[19] USAID, Center for Development Information and Evaluation, Program and Operations Assessments Division, 'Civil Society and Democratic Development: A CDIE Evaluation Design Paper', 24 February 1994, p. 5.

[20] USAID, 'Constituencies for Reform', p. 3.

[21] Samuel P. Huntington, *The Third Wave: Democratization in the Late Twentieth Century* (London: University of Oklahoma Press, 1991).

individuals. While Solidarity did not begin life officially as a 'party', it effectively became one, and well before the transfer of power was complete; and it was the links between the movement's political core and its organizational satellites that transformed it into such a formidable political force. Had USAID's 'strategic logic' criteria been in effect, the party linkages of many of the associations that provided Solidarity with its legitimacy would have disqualified them from receiving funding. What USAID is anxious to avoid is the co-optation of associations by political organizations that are likely soon to gain control of the state. This is an attempt to prevent the re-emergence of authoritarian rule under another banner, to preserve the fragile creation of civil society so that it may go on contributing to the maintenance of the democratic order. However laudable a goal, it in effect puts the 'cart' of consolidating democracy before the 'horse' of effecting a democratic transition. While the current state of relations between the African National Congress and the civic associations that fought apartheid in South Africa is a topic of much concern, no one seriously believes that efforts should have been made to cleanse this branch of civil society of its association with the ANC in the period prior to the ending of white rule.[22]

Not only does this excessively cautious approach to civil-society funding risk robbing pro-democracy movements of their force; in its obsession with maintaining the 'autonomy' of centres of social and economic power, it jeopardizes the healthy development of 'political society'. Even if the realm of parties and the party system is considered beyond the pale of civil society by USAID's policy analysts – better left to organizations like the German political foundations[23] and the funding institutes run by the two main political parties in the United States[24] – they cannot escape the consequences of insisting upon a strict divide between political parties and associations. Where parties become divorced from either organized sectoral interests or 'principled issue'[25]

[22] For an account of the difficulties of this relationship, see Kimberly Lanegran, 'South Africa's Civic Associational Movement – ANC's Ally or Society's "Watchdog"?: Shifting Social Movement–Political Party Relations', *African Studies Review*, 38, no. 2 (1995), pp. 101–26. For an intelligent analysis of how South Africa can reconcile the flaws in both Gramscian and liberal conceptions of civil society (a dilemma which afflicts the aid-agency conception as well), see Mark Orkin, 'Building Democracy in the New South Africa: Civil Society, Citizenship and Political Ideology', *Review of African Political Economy*, 66 (1995), pp. 525–37.

[23] M. Pinto-Duschinsky, 'Foreign Political Aid: The German Political Foundations and their U.S. Counterparts', *International Affairs*, 67, no. 1 (1991), pp. 33–63.

[24] Thomas Carothers, 'The N.E.D. [National Endowment for Democracy] at 10', *Foreign Policy*, 95 (1994), pp. 123–38.

[25] This term is drawn from Kathryn Sikkink, 'Human Rights, Principled Issue Networks and Sovereignty in Latin America', *International Organisation*, 47, no. 3 (1993), pp. 411–41.

associations (environmental advocacy groups, women's organizations), the resulting vacuum can often be filled by less appealing forces. Mobilization around exclusive social identities is certainly not what aid agencies would like to see happen, but in cases such as Kenya and Malawi this is a prominent trend, and has undermined to a significant extent the otherwise welcome ascendancy of civil society. It has been aided by the failure of parties to build strong relations with sectoral interests and principled issue associations.

Developments in Indian politics over the past twenty years represent a similar divergence between high politics and the dynamics of civil society. While this is an extremely complex case, counteracted to a substantial degree by the deep roots that democracy has struck in India over the past half-century, there has been, and continues to be, an alienation of party politics at the national level from specific organized constituencies.[26] The xenophobic, majoritarian politics of the Hindu nationalist Bharatiya Janata Party (BJP) has been a major beneficiary of this trend. Another related phenomenon is what has been termed the 'criminalization of politics'. This is not merely the corruption of high-level elected and bureaucratic officials, but the wholesale entry into mainstream political parties of notorious underworld figures, who are welcomed by established party bosses because of the their hold over formidable political networks. Organized crime syndicates have proved easily adaptable as adjuncts of party machines where party links with trades unions, farmers' organizations and other, more conventional groups in civil society have been weakened. We cannot blame USAID for India's political afflictions. But its sanitized vision of civil society, consisting of public-spirited watchdogs quarantined from political society, indicates a failure to learn from such lessons. It is not a recipe for the establishment of democratic politics in other countries institutionally less well-endowed than India. It is a well-intentioned, but unrealistic, attempt to ensure good governance.

The double-edged sword of autonomy: democracy, accountability, and economic policy

At the root of the tortured attempts of development practitioners to equate civil society with all that is wholesome in political life – citizen involvement, public-interest advocacy, self-help – is a preoccupation with

---

[26] This process can be characterized as a return to the pattern found during colonial rule. As N. B. Dirks has argued, British colonialism – its institutions as well as discourse – transformed caste into an extremely rigid social formation detached from political processes, creating what Dirks calls 'a specifically Indian form of civil society'. N. B. Dirks, 'Castes of Mind', *Representations*, 37, pp. 56–78.

promoting good governance. This is understandable, even admirable. In practice, however, it turns out to be something of a mirage. The problem is with how the conception of good governance is formulated – in particular, the explicit bias towards neo-liberal economic orthodoxy. Market-centred policies, it is everywhere implied, are 'sound', while those that deviate from this logic undermine both efficiency and welfare.[27] There is nothing to prevent USAID and other agencies from pursuing such policies. It is beyond the scope of this paper to dispute either the wisdom of such programmatic priorities or the moral right of development agencies to use aid as a lever with which to effect them. The question is whether the characteristics they ascribe to civil society in democratic transitions/consolidations are consistent with the roles envisaged for it in policy making and implementation.

As this chapter has argued, the dynamics of political movements and the constantly shifting motives which characterize political life bear little resemblance to the sanitized vision of civil society which USAID and other agencies seek to promote. But even if we accept the portrayal of politics as a struggle of ideals, and therefore the conception of civil society as consisting of principled issue advocates, there are logical inconsistencies which undermine any claim to an operational compatibility between the various objectives of organizations like USAID. The initial impetus for investing such great hopes in civil society as an agent of change illustrates this. The flourishing of associational life in many regions, particularly sub-Saharan Africa, was rightly interpreted by many political scientists and development practitioners as representing a force capable of threatening to undermine unresponsive regimes. According to a wide and varied literature, a vast array of collectivities – from associations of peasant farmers to village-level groups demanding greater local control over natural resources – had become 'disengaged' from the state.[28] This disengagement had, in many instances, served as a proxy for overtly political dissent: the ability of civil society thus defined to contribute to regime change, to place democratic politics on a broader footing, and to hold future governments accountable to the rule of law instilled great optimism in the development community.

Many of these communities *are* in fact capable of providing the basis for a more participatory, though mediated, form of politics. They can and do help to broaden the sphere of politics beyond the formation of

---

[27] See, for instance, USAID, Center for Development Information and Evaluation, 'Civil Society and Democratic Development in Bangladesh: A CDIE Assessment', *USAID Working Paper No. 212*, August 1994.

[28] See, for instance, Richard Sandbrook, *The Politics of Africa's Economic Stagnation* (Cambridge: Cambridge University Press, 1985).

elite consensus. Their ability to contribute to good governance is, however, restricted by the way in which this term has been redefined. The goalposts have, in effect, been pushed back. If one reads the small print, the concept of good governance no longer refers simply to authority which is accountable. It is the taking of actions consonant with sound policy, which in turn is construed as market-oriented economics. This raises a fundamental dilemma for the efforts of USAID to promote civil society as the basis for ensuring good governance. The social groups whose associational activities originally made them such attractive allies in the eyes of donor agencies often possess orientations far from harmonious with neo-liberal orthodoxy. Simply because they disengaged economically from particularly rapacious states does not mean that they are uninterested in a strong role for the state in the future. Indigenous environmental groups, for instance, in many cases have ideas about the economic management of natural resources that do not accord with the 'priceist' stance of governments committed to implementing donor-backed structural adjustment policies.

In fact, many of the associations which inspired the original faith in the power of civil society to act as a check on state power arose in opposition to the imposition of such policies by authoritarian regimes. They were formed to bury neo-liberal economics, not to praise it. Governments that are swayed by such voices would, by definition, be providing accountable governance but not good governance – an anomaly that further under-mines the credibility of the aid agencies' conception of civil society. In other words, even advocacy (as opposed to self-interested, potentially rent-seeking) groups in civil society might not desire the policies that aid agencies seek to promote. The assumption that they will is rooted in the logic of the type of democracy that aid agencies envisage.[29] If the government fails to embrace liberal economics, then it is not seen to be operating within the context of liberal politics. The adoption of neo-liberal policies thus becomes the *sine qua non* of civil society.

On a more basic level, what USAID and other donor agencies fail to recognize (or at least openly to acknowledge in their policy statements) is that free-market economics removes many decisions from the purview of not only the state, but also the political community, democratically constituted or otherwise. In their zeal to see dominant social groups stripped of their power to subvert public institutions for private gain, aid agencies simultaneously disempower subordinate social groups: the associations that come closest to the ideal of citizen involvement will find

---

[29] One internal assessment, referring to USAID's support of business associations, argues that '[i]n civil society terms, such assistance could be called a "democratic capitalism" strategy', USAID, 'Civil Society and Democratic Development in Bangladesh', p. 29.

the political basis for pursuing even mildly radical redistributive projects undermined. The most important reason why this fallacy has remained relatively unchallenged is the ability of aid agencies to point to the adoption of market-oriented economic reform in democratic countries. In this respect, India, which is not only democratic but also possessed of a vibrant civil society, has thus become a useful weapon in the rhetorical armoury of donor agencies. Its structural adjustment programme, while less radical than advocates of shock therapy had hoped for, has neverthe-less been far-reaching, greatly exceeding in scope what many commenta-tors had considered politically possible when it was initiated in 1991. The expectation among such commentators was that powerful economic interests threatened by the withdrawal of state subsidies, in alliance with advocates organized on behalf of the poor (who feared that reform would not come with a 'human face'), would join forces to thwart efforts to restructure the Indian economy. The Indian case – in terms of the political sustainability of economic policy reform, if not its economic results – would seem to support the aid-agency view that governments of countries in which civil society was clearly free enough to hold them to account have nevertheless been willing and able to provide good govern-ance (in the form of neo-liberal economic prescriptions). The equation between good governance, accountability, market economics, and civil society was thus maintained.

The details of the Indian case, however, reveal a more complicated picture – one which by no means justifies such facile assumptions concerning how civil society is best conceptualized.[30] One of the main reasons why the Indian reform programme has been able to overcome the political forces arrayed against it is the existence of a federal political system. The logic of economic reform brought many more decisions about economic life to the state level. It removed, for instance, decisions about the siting of industrial ventures from the hands of bureaucrats in New Delhi. Politicians heading state-level governments – representing parties of the left, right, and centre – joined in the competition to lure Indian and foreign capital to their regions. Significantly, these leaders were free to indulge in such activities because the main electoral preoccupation of politicians operating at the state level is with courting the support of organizations engaged in the mobilization of politicized social identities (caste, religion, language, sect, tribe). Sectoral interest groups which, under other circumstances, might have had more success with their efforts to undermine reform found themselves subsumed

---

[30] The arguments that follow are elaborated in greater detail in R. Jenkins, *Democratic Politics and Economic Reform in India* (Cambridge: Cambridge University Press, 1999).

within the matrix of local, primordial politics – a place in which they were relatively powerless. Thus, in this instance, it was the existence of a particular form of civil society – one in which ethnic politics was as organized, competitive, and linked to party politics as were the more conventional functional associations – that allowed the state to avoid 'capture' by powerful interests opposed to the introduction of policies deemed synonymous with good governance. Fixated on promoting the emergence of modern solidarities, USAID's conception of civil society does not allow for the practical utility of such hybrid forms of democratic politics, *even when these are instrumental in effecting their preferred outcomes.*

Another of the reasons why the Indian government was able to succeed in introducing market-oriented reforms also flies in the face of USAID's strategy for promoting civil society. The extremely close relations between trade-union federations and political parties helped to defuse the resistance of organized labour to a number of important reform measures. While, as with other reforms, the Indian government did not take as bold a stance on labour issues as some neo-liberal advocates had hoped for, it did take a number of actions that were previously considered unthinkable given the extent of trade-union power: the partial privatization of public-sector firms; the introduction of numerous changes to work practices in the banking sector; the offering of voluntary retirement schemes; and (in some regions) the turning of a blind eye by state governments to illegal management lockouts by private firms. It was not only the centrist Congress party, but also the centre-left and Communist parties, that reined in their affiliated trade unions, limiting the impact of anti-reform protests by independent labour organizations. While donor-agency rhetoric condemns the establishment of links between civil society organizations and political parties, it fails to recognize the extent to which the ability of governments to achieve policy reforms which donors themselves deem consistent with good governance can rely upon the control of political leaders over such interests.

In their eagerness to protect social groups from the potential for government repression, donors appear at times to have forgotten their earlier concern with insulating policy elites from the exercise of undue influence by powerful interests. Most foreign critics, after all, blamed the persistence of statist economic policies of the type that India followed before 1991 on the excessive power of organizations operating in civil society. Yet, in its elaboration of a five-step procedure 'for determining investment priorities in civil society',[31] USAID advocates supporting

---

[31] USAID, 'Constituencies for Reform', p. 5.

'sectoral' reforms. Though these 'often are not specifically aimed at strengthening democracy, investments in sectoral areas such as environment and natural resources, private sector development and NGOs, may yield substantial multiplier effects for systemic reform in democracy and governance'.[32] The significance of these is that they 'can expand the number and size of autonomous enclaves relatively well insulated from government predations'.[33] This prescription presumes that governments have been the sole predators, when far more often it is alliances between holders of state power and actors in the private sector that are responsible for the great many ills that beset developing societies. The idea that 'increasing sectoral autonomy' will help to 'replace co-optation by government' contradicts neo-liberal logic, in which inordinate influence of interest groups is viewed as the main culprit.

That donor agencies ignore the role played by constraints upon organized interests in effecting market-oriented reforms in developing country contexts highlights an even graver defect in their conceptualization of the relationship between democracy and civil society. The way in which USAID's civil-society assistance programmes are formulated ignores the manifestly illiberal tendencies of many 'actually existing democracies', including the United States. Many (if not most) long-established democracies, as well as those of more recent vintage, exhibit traits that contravene the hallowed principles of accountability, participation, and unrestricted freedom of association. This can be seen quite clearly, though donors fail conspicuously to do so, in complex models of how democracies incorporate fragments of civil society, such as the one elaborated by Philippe Schmitter.[34] Schmitter views modern democracy as an interlocking network of five 'partial regimes', rather than a unified system based upon clear lines of accountability. The nature of each regime is determined by the 'action situations' in which political actors are engaged. 'Electoral regimes' structure relations between legislatures and political parties, while 'concertation regimes' organize the political role of particularized interests, such as capital and labour. Yet, clearly some of these regimes can rely on restrictions upon associational freedom. As Olson famously pointed out, the exit options of trade-union members are often limited by organizational rules sanctioned by law.[35] And the 'clientelist regime', centred on the personalistic networks constructed by local party bosses found in many democracies, is 'formed on

---

[32] Ibid., p. 7.   [33] Ibid.

[34] Philippe C. Schmitter, 'The Consolidation of Democracy and Representation of Social Groups', *American Behavioural Scientist*, 35 (1992), pp. 422–49.

[35] Mancur Olson, *The Logic of Collective Action* (Cambridge, Mass.: Harvard University Press, 1965).

the basis of exclusive instead of inclusive participation of relevant social actors, thereby violating a key constitutive principle of the national democratic regime'.[36]

Rather than revealing a shortcoming of Schmitter's analysis, these features lend authenticity to his model, demonstrating how imperfect is the interface between civil society and democracy as it exists in practice. They also highlight how incompatible is the match between the sanitized version of civil society depicted by aid agencies and the reality of the only functioning examples to which they can aspire in both north and south. Western donors have gone from supporting dictatorship during the cold war to insisting upon an immaculate and idealized form of democracy that exists nowhere but in their imaginations. In order to support that vision of democratic purity, the idea of civil society has been distorted beyond recognition.

In his analysis of why Communism failed to provide the basis for a lasting political order in east and central Europe, Ernest Gellner pointed specifically to the absence of civil society.[37] But what he considered lacking was not what aid-agency policy has created by the same name. The latter vision is too clean-cut and invested with unambiguous virtue to perform the functions to which Gellner was referring. Perhaps the need to spend public funds on promoting civil society requires aid policy analysts to portray it in such noble terms. The UNDP, for instance, equates civil society with 'social movements', which by definition are constructed around ideals.[38] This sort of conceptual *legerdemain* makes it difficult to grasp the contribution of civil society to achieving desirable economic or political outcomes. Gellner depicted a more sensible dichotomy: 'In an important sociological and non-evaluative sense, the Bolshevik system did constitute a moral order. By contrast, and this is perhaps one of its most significant virtues, Civil Society is an a-moral order.'[39] In what should be their moment of triumph, the West's development professionals are in danger of repeating the errors of the Communists by attempting, in Gellner's words, to 'sacralize' the social and political order. To invest civil society with a moral dimension is not

---

[36] James R. Scaritt and Shaheen Mozaffar, 'Toward Sustainable Democracy in Africa: Can U.S. Policy Make a Difference?' *Working Paper No. 171*, African Studies Center, Boston University, 1993, p. 5.

[37] Ernest Gellner, *Conditions of Liberty: Civil Society and Its Rivals* (London: Hamish Hamilton, 1994).

[38] R. C. Riddell and A. J. Bebbington, *Developing Country NGOs and Donor Governments*, Report to the Overseas Development Administration (London: Overseas Development Institute, 1995), 23–4.

[39] Gellner, *Conditions of Liberty*, p. 137.

only to misrepresent its historical role in the regulation of social and political life, but also to deprive it of its capacity to express, and thereby paradoxically to contain, the aspirations for power, influence, and control over truth which are defining features of politics.

The blueprint from which aid agencies are attempting to construct civil societies resembles nothing so much as a textbook of the sort issued to high-school students studying a subject that was once called 'civics'. It uses the term 'governance' as a euphemism for 'politics', in the process grossly underplaying the contingencies which influence the formation of opposition movements, the entrenchment of political order, and the exercise of state power. Civil society emerges as a sort of political ombudsman, reflecting the values of impartiality, fair play, and commitment to public welfare. This niche – its value orientation and functional role – in fact bears a striking similarity to the one which donor agencies see themselves as occupying in relation to the countries to which they give aid. They are 'in' but not 'of', providing guidance, but not asserting interests. Perhaps it should not surprise us, after all, that aid agencies have created civil society in their own image. What we are witnessing in this latest re-export of the notion of civil society is not only its depoliticization and sacralization, but also its bureaucratization.

14   The promise of 'civil society' in the South

Geoffrey Hawthorn

I

It can come conventionally to be said that economic liberalization is desirable, that its political corollary is liberal democracy, that liberal democracy requires a flourishing civil society, and that the opinions which will be expressed in these different spheres will in principle be compatible. Civil society in Locke's sense, 'the state liked', is possible. To be made actual, it requires a civil society in our sense, a lively 'associational realm between state and family'.[1] This is the answer which has been given by liberals in the North and West to the question of how a more responsive and accountable politics might be constructed in the South and East. A free and flourishing associational realm can improve communication between citizens and their governments, raise public morality, create a more satisfactory balance of powers, and in these ways shape an acceptable democracy. It is an answer that misreads the constraints on politics in these places.

II

The governments in Latin America which had begun to industrialize after 1930 (especially those that had benefited from exporting to the United States in the Second World War) and of those territories in Asia and Africa which came to political independence after 1945 accepted what Victor Pérez-Díaz has described as the 'moral project' of the modern

I am grateful to Stefan Collini, Sunil Khilnani, Rama Mani, and John A. Thompson for comments on an earlier version of this chapter.

[1] I take Locke's sense of the term from John Dunn's essay in this collection, the sense widely given to it in the optimistic early 1990s from Gordon White, 'Civil society, Democratisation and Development', in *Democratisation in the South: the Jagged Wave*, edited by Robin Luckham and Gordon White (Manchester: Manchester University Press, 1996), pp. 178–219. This sense is sharply criticized by Lawrence Hamilton, 'Deconstructing "Civil Society": Institutions, Practices, Roles', unpublished paper (Cambridge, 1999). See section III of this chapter.

state.[2] This was for a state ruled by constitutions rather than persons, committed to providing physical protection, representation, and improvements in well-being in what had come to be called 'development'. To celebrate this new civic life, and to ensure that in enjoying their privileges the citizens whose citizenship it was would also acknowledge their duties, governments strove to impart a sense of nationhood for which the state itself, preferably identified with themselves, would be the symbol. But even with the high rates of economic growth in the South and East up to the 1970s, most governments lacked the financial and administrative capacity to redeem their promise. Nonetheless, inclusion, civil and political, was their object, and they were determined that this should be on their terms. Where associations in 'civil society' existed, made demands, and could not be suppressed, they were accordingly co-opted.

By the early 1980s, many of these states were in economic crisis. The causes were complex and are still contested. But few disagree that a steep rise in the price of oil and the sudden availability of cheap credit in the early 1970s, a rise in real interest rates at the end of that decade, sharp falls in commodity prices and after 1981 in international credit also, together with relaxed fiscal policies, played a part. Rates of growth in Latin America and sub-Saharan Africa were negative for the rest of the decade. Short of revenue, and having to implement fierce programmes of financial stabilization and economic liberalization in order to be able to draw on funds from the international financial institutions (the only ones now available to them), governments were forced sooner or later to cut their budgets. In part for this reason, in part as a result of external pressure, this led many by the end of the 1980s to appear to relinquish their monopoly on power and submit themselves to competitive elections. Politically, they found themselves in a position in which, to survive, they had to promise more but were financially forced to promise less. They retreated from their expansive projects, hoping only that they could ride on the promise of democratization itself and continue in some way to control the political spaces that might open up beneath them.

Figures collated by Adam Przeworski and his associates suggest that by the early 1990s, there was widespread disillusion with the new democracies in Latin America and central and Eastern Europe also.[3] This was concentrated in the less educated and less well-off who had experienced no practical benefit from the new nominal extensions of

[2] Victor M. Pérez-Diaz, *The Return of Civil Society: The Emergence of Democratic Spain* (Cambridge, Mass.: Harvard University Press, 1993), p. 61.
[3] Adam Przeworski, and others, *Sustainable Democracy* (Cambridge: Cambridge University Press, 1995), pp. 37, 59.

citizenship. The reasons were in part economic. Even though rates of inflation had come down, foreign trade was more nearly in balance, and fiscal deficits had been reduced, repayments on debt were still high, investment, both private and public, was suffering, unemployment had risen, inequality had increased, and a growth that the deprived could see might benefit them was still in question.[4] But Przeworski also makes the point that with few exceptions, governments in the South and East had made things worse for themselves politically (and for the new regimes under which they were now ruling) by imposing the reforms through decree. They overrode interests that in new democracies might expect to have been consulted. In some cases, in Argentina, for example, in Mexico, and in Venezuela in 1989, they even overrode those to which, in order to get elected, they had promised otherwise. The exceptions, India in the 1990s, Venezuela in its second attempt in 1996, where leaders had the courage to explain and consult, suggest that it might not have been necessary to act in such a peremptory way. Where the purposes of reform have been spelt out and where the governments promoting it have made some attempt to alleviate its social costs, voters have, to an extent, been prepared to accept it.

Yet even the governments that were willing to listen and consult were not always allowed to narrow their project and retreat in peace. 'Civil society' protested. Church leaders and associations of lawyers and other professionals pressed for the real extension of civil and political rights. Street committees, neighbourhood groups and citizens' associations of other kinds emerged in the cities. With greater hesitation, peasant groups also made demands that were more than immediately economic. In some places, these associations extended themselves across their societies. In Mexico in the 1980s, for example, as Merilee Grindle has described, those in the cities came together under a National Urban Popular Movement Co-ordinating Committee, those in the countryside in a National Union of Autonomous Regional Peasant Associations. There was even a National 'Plan de Ayala' Coordinating Committee to connect them all. They valued their autonomy. They tried to press their interests while evading attempts at co-optation by the ruling Institutional Revolutionary Party and resisting the disposition in such associations in the past to let the leaders negotiate with the authorities on the members' behalf. They

---

[4] In 1960, the income of the richest 20 per cent of the world's population was 30 times greater than that of the poorest 20 per cent; by 1997, it was 74 times greater. The greatest increase in inequalities has occurred in the post-Communist states of Eastern Europe and the Confederation of Independent States: United Nations Development Programme, *Human Development Report 1999* (New York: Oxford University Press for the United Nations Development Programme, 1999).

also kept their distance from the Democratic Revolutionary Party on the left (and the National Action Party on the right, the PAN) which had formed to contest national elections in 1988. In Kenya, one of the more liberalized economies in sub-Saharan Africa and Grindle's other case, popular associations were less in evidence. But dissident politicians, actively supported by churchmen and lawyers, did create a Forum for the Restoration of Democracy (FORD) to contest the general election in 1992.

In each country, success was limited. The associations in Mexico were caught between their desire for influence and their wish to remain independent of any party. The opposition parties, although they did win some seats against the PRI, soon either divided or (in the case of the PAN) were themselves co-opted. FORD in Kenya also fell apart. By the early 1990s, both the PRI and Daniel arap Moi's ruling Kenya African National Union had recovered and were again securely in power. The PRI has since turned on its own technocrats to insist that henceforth no-one can be a candidate for high office unless he or she has been a member of the party for at least ten years. Grindle's expectations – that in the course of radical economic reform, the institutional capacity to set new rules of contest and compromise would be weakened, that the technical capacity of governments to implement reform would be strengthened, that their administrative capacities would be reduced, and that their ability to mediate conflict and manage demands for greater participation would (at first at least) be diminished – were confirmed.[5]

These examples are particular. What they indicate, however, is not. Many associations in the South, especially those formed to provide services in towns and villages in the countryside and city neighbourhoods, are irremediably local. Many others, even if they are not so rooted in one place, depend on a narrow constituency. The second sort can find it less difficult than the first, although rarely easy, to form wider networks and increase their influence. But as Grindle's study makes clear, even when they can, they are likely to encounter further difficulties. To acquire the material and organizational resources they need, they can try to ally themselves with a foreign non-governmental organization. These organizations, however, have to be at least as accountable to their overseas donors as to the people whom they are set up to serve, and where they are not already nervous of pressing any case that could be construed by their host government as political, risk a confining restriction or even outright hostility. If the associations avoid foreign control and do succeed in

---

[5] Merilee S. Grindle, *Challenging the State: Crisis and Innovation in Latin America and Africa* (Cambridge: Cambridge University Press, 1996), pp. 155–94, 8, 31.

entering political society by allying themselves with opposition parties, which are themselves often fragile, they risk the fights and fissures that arise in being more overtly political or being taken over. Yet if they decide that the prudent course is to stay away from partisan politics, they can have no wider political effect. As David Lehmann remarked of the 'movements of the base' in Latin America in the 1980s, many grass-roots and non-governmental organizations are expected by those in the wider political society, and indeed often expect themselves, to go 'so far and no further'.[6]

This is not to say that no associations in the South have been able to advance their members' more directly material interests. But where they have, they have done so from conditions in which a wider 'civil society' had been all but destroyed. In most of the countries in sub-Saharan Africa in the 1980s, for example, governments and their institutions of state ceased to be able to sustain even the often minimal levels of support that they had offered before becoming effectively bankrupt and being forced to restructure their economies. Their citizens, deprived of virtually all (in some cases, absolutely all) of the benefits of citizenship in a nominally modern state, had retreated into local self-sufficiency. By the early 1990s, when the governing elites had realized that they could no longer muster the moral and material resources with which to maintain their old projects, and were themselves retreating into a new politics of electoral competition, the new local associations began to connect with each other and press for changes in public policy. A few of these – improvement societies, credit unions, most especially organizations of farmers – appear to have succeeded.[7]

There had also been what Vivienne Shue has described as a pervasive 'miniaturization' of public life in the People's Republic of China. The Maoist government – which had been in difficulties from the early 1960s, under great strain after the Cultural Revolution a few years later, but not in a state of actual collapse – had caused people to recoil and rely on local patrons or the protection afforded by local functionaries. The subsequent economic liberalization galvanized a variety of associations and organizations that came to extend beyond the immediate locality. Shue mentions bodies of producers and traders, including the self-employed, of consumers, lawyers, and journalists, of people with a common faith and senior

[6] David Lehmann, *Democracy and Development in Latin America: Economics, Politics and Religion in the Postwar Period* (Cambridge: Polity, 1990), p. 172.
[7] This is the most recent of what Naomi Chazan has identified as the four phases of 'associational life' in sub-Saharan Africa since the immediately pre-colonial period, 'Engaging the State: Associational Life in Sub-Saharan Africa', in *State Power and Social Forces: Domination and Transformation in the Third World*, edited by Joel S. Migdal, Atul Kohli, and Vivienne Shue (Cambridge: Cambridge University Press, 1994), pp. 255–89.

citizens, technical associations and sports clubs, even discussion groups of the educated, meeting privately to talk about social philosophy, political economy, and culture. Some of these associations are local and all, still, are in declared intent non-political. Some, however, especially those concerned with production, trade and employment, have a regional and even a national reach (Shue mentions the wonderfully named National Internal Combustion Engine Cylinder Cover Trade Association), and have in many cases established close and cooperative relations with the relevant public administrations.[8]

There is an obvious irony in this for the conventional view of the promise of 'civil society'. What Shue has described for two places in China is not a civil society – a term she hesitates to use – acting against the state. Yet the encouragement that the associations and organizations receive from the authorities is strikingly similar to a liberal picture of what, ideally, such a relation should be. In a *People's Daily* piece in 1990 under the headline 'Social groups are actively to develop their role in safeguarding stability', such associations were exhorted 'to support peace and unity consciously, to handle properly the relationship between the particular interests the social group represents and the fundamental interests of the Chinese people at large, and to put particularistic interests at the service of the general interest'. They were 'to solve social problems, alleviate social contradictions, effectively promote the stable development of society, and to create the best possible social climate for economic reconstruction'. This best possible social climate is not, of course, to be thought of as that of liberal democracy; the groups are instructed also to propagandize and implement the lines and policies of the Communist Party.[9] Post-Maoist China, although less disliked, Shue believes, than its predecessor, is not what even the most casual of modern Lockeans would see as a civil society in the older sense of the term. But the glimpse Shue gives of this part of it does suggest that if the object of mobilizing associations outside the state is, as Schmitter and Karl have put it, to provide a 'layer of governance between the individual and the state that is capable of resolving conflicts and controlling the behaviour of members', they succeed.[10] What Shue herself describes as this 'patently state-corporatist line' meets the interest that Northern governments and the

---

[8] Vivienne Shue, 'State Power and Social Organisation in China', in Migdal, Kohli, and Shue, *State Power and Social Forces*, pp. 65–88. This is an excellent paper, of wider interest than its title would suggest for the general question of the relations between 'civil societies', markets, states, and democratization. Shue's first-hand material came from Xinji, a small town in Hebei on the north China plain, and Anxi, a tea-producing county in the Fujian mountains which was officially classed as 'poverty stricken'.

[9] Shue, 'State Power', pp. 6–7.

[10] Philippe C. Schmitter and Terry Lynn Karl, 'What democracy is . . . and is not', in *The*

international financial institutions have in social control without overt coercion. For this reason also, even though their members' interests are thereby met, neither the new Chinese associations nor those in sub-Saharan Africa are what the enthusiasts in central and eastern Europe had in mind at the end of the 1980s when they talked of the liberating possibilities of a 'civil society'.

The irony has force. If those Southern states that are in retreat from their old projects wish nevertheless to continue to be able to respond to the interests of their citizens and secure support for liberalizing economic reform in a democratic framework, they need (like a liberalizing but non-democratic China) to find ways in which institutionally to do so. And the citizens themselves need the means with which to get their interests heard. It may be, as Samuel Huntington once said, that 'the key institution of democracy is the selection of leaders through competitive elections'. But if this is all there is, one has only what Guillermo O'Donnell has called a 'delegative democracy' of leaders who between elections are detached from other institutions and the people they govern.[11] With the policies that most governments are now pursuing, this can subvert their respon-siveness and accountability, frustrate citizens, and threaten the extension of that social justice on which the strength of democracy itself depends. It is not obvious that their responsiveness and accountability will be improved by the kind of incorporation that Shue has noticed in China or the *ad hoc* concessions for producer groups that Chazan has noticed in Africa. There is a considerable variety of alternative institutions in the existing democracies, and if there is a general understanding to be had about which are most effective under any given set of conditions, we do not have it.[12] Nonetheless, assuming that one's objects include trying to counter concentrations of power, which incorporation does not do, and ensuring a degree of representation and accountability, while at the same time not making it too difficult for governments to act, one can still ask what place there might be for 'civil society'.

III

The start of an answer lies in deciding more exactly how to think about what 'civil society' is. There is little disagreement among those who have

---

Global Resurgence of Democracy, edited by Larry Diamond and Marc F. Plattner (Baltimore, Md.: Johns Hopkins University Press, 1993), pp. 39–52.

[11] Huntington quoted by William I. Robinson, *Promoting Polyarchy: Globalisation, US Intervention, and Hegemony* (Cambridge: Cambridge University Press, 1996), p. 50, O'Donnell by Przeworski, and others, *Sustainable democracy*, 63–4.

[12] Przeworski, and others, *Sustainable Democracy*, pp. 40–52.

recently been attracted to the idea about the distinction between associational life and the family.[13] A person is present in the family, Hegel had claimed, 'not as an independent person but as a member'.[14] Gellner extended the thought: 'The general sociological law of agrarian society states that man must be subject to either kings or cousins' (and, one might add, churches also), and not infrequently to all of these.[15] In a 'civil society', by contrast, Pérez-Díaz argues, one is a citizen; to be a citizen is to be 'an autonomous agent', and to be autonomous is to be protected from the intrusions of the state and the family into one's 'reserved domain'.[16] Nor is there any disagreement about including in civil society the great variety of social movements, village and neighbourhood associations, women's groups, religious groupings, intellectuals, and where they are reasonably free, the press and other media, civic organizations, associations of professionals, entrepreneurs, and employees, whose purposes and direction are not controlled by the institutions of state.[17]

It is on the place of economic activity that opinions diverge. For Hegel, as for Marx, economic relations – the relations of what was for Hegel himself the relatively new 'commercial society' – were constitutive. The liberals who celebrated the effervescence of civil society in central and Eastern Europe in the 1980s agreed, demurring only of course with the Marxist belief that bourgeois commerce would be transcended in a truly socialist society. The more recently radical, however, have insisted that a civil society must stand against both state and market. In one of the most extensive discussions, Jean Cohen and Andrew Arato have argued that the idea of civil society can and should be deployed in favour of claims for the 'welfare state' against economic liberalism, for participation against representation, and for 'communitarianism' against a rights-

13 For clear accounts of the many and often contradictory ways in which 'civil society' has been defined and the consequent confusions, see Sudipta Kaviraj's chapter in this volume and the criticisms in Hamilton, 'Deconstructing "Civil Society".'

14 G. W. F. Hegel, *Elements of the Philosophy of Right*, edited by Allen W. Wood, translated by H. B. Nisbet, reprint, 1820 (Cambridge: Cambridge University Press, 1991), p. 199.

15 Ernest Gellner, *Conditions of Liberty: Civil Society and its Rivals* (London: Hamish Hamilton, 1994), pp. 7–8.

16 Pérez-Diaz, *Return of Civil Society*, p. 56. It is this fantasy of 'autonomy' to which Hamilton primarily objects, arguing, very reasonably, that in most modern states it is neither empirically true nor consistent with any coherent conception of freedom.

17 Alfred Stepan, *Rethinking Military Politics: Brazil and the Southern Cone* (Princeton, N.J.: Princeton University Press, 1988), pp. 3–4. Stepan's distinctions have been widely used in the literature on the South. He contrasts 'civil' with 'political' society, by which he means 'that arena in which the polity specifically arranges itself for political contestation to gain control over public power and the state apparatus'. This space is sometimes also described as the 'public sphere', as by Pérez-Diaz, *Return of Civil Society*, p. 57.

based state.[18] Michael Lipton has sharpened the argument for the South. 'Since both state and market must gain power for effective development – and yet tend to destroy each other – that destructive power must be held in check by numerous, peacefully and politically competing individuals, firms and pressure groups.' 'State, market and civil society are *rival* channels for the exercise of power.' They can only increase their powers, Lipton adds, if the networks of family and ethnicity, which presently dominate many decisions in developing countries, are weakened.[19]

One could compromise and agree with Pérez-Díaz that it is only possible to understand the 'peculiar blend of cooperation and competition' within civil society itself and between civil society and the institutions of state if one includes within it those movements and associations that are created by the market. This, however, not only risks presuming the existence of what remains in question for the South. It also risks extending the idea of 'civil society' to include almost everything in public life, outside the family, that is not created by the state, and thereby emptying it of political interest. If the 'civil' in 'civil society' has political force, it is to pick out those associations that are pressing a claim of citizenship. Sports clubs, natural history societies, music groups, and the innumerable other combinations for a particular interest, do of course exercise rights of citizenship. But they do not themselves claim or, beyond the fact of their will to exist, act to press any. Likewise economic agents, which in so far as they act as private economic agents, are exercising a more or less tacit right. Only when associations face a legal obstruction to their activities and persist are they making a claim.

This is a distinction that matters for those who are pressing a material interest. Most governments in the South (and in post-Communist central and Eastern Europe) see no alternative now to attempting to stabilize their finances, open their economies, and make their societies attractive to private investment. To succeed, they reduce public expenditure, tolerate a rise in unemployment, and accept increasing deprivation. If they fail, they try even harder. The interests of a large part of their population suffer, and in the poorer economies, this is the larger part. Much was said in the North in the 1980s about the consequences of 'market failure'. Less, as Lipton points out, has been said about the economic and social consequences of market success.[20] In the post-socialist states of the South and post-Communist Europe, this can lead to

---

[18] Jean Cohen and Andrew Arato, *Civil Society and Political Theory* (Cambridge, Mass.: MIT Press, 1992).
[19] Michael Lipton, 'Discussion', in *Thinking about Development*, by Paul Patrick Streeten (Cambridge: Cambridge University Press, 1995), p. 314.
[20] Lipton, 'Discussion', pp. 315–16.

a loss of many of the rights and privileges of citizenship that their constitutions formally guarantee.

This has institutional consequences. In trying to rescue and sustain their economies, the leaders of mass parties in government or aspiring to it are trapped. Unless there is sufficient revenue to enable it to meet at least some of the demands of the poor without being seen to threaten the interests of the rich, a government cannot readily satisfy both the interests of those within the country and outside who favour reform and the interests of those within who suffer from it. In the conditions that usually obtain in the South, where revenue is scarce, the rich are powerful, and an orthodox social democratic state is impossible, mass parties cannot therefore be a coherent or effective means of connecting those among the governed who are thereby deprived of the preconditions of citizenship to their governments. This is why, in all but rhetoric, the parties will be inclined to withdraw from the attempt to meet people's needs.

They will, of course, fudge the matter. In Mexico, for example, between 1988 and 1993, the President's office made an attempt in its National Solidarity Programme to offset the consequences of its reforms for the poor. Some $12 billion, the office claimed, acquired from the sale of state-owned enterprises, were distributed through 150,000 local Solidarity committees. In this disbursement, officials of the PRI itself were by-passed unless they declared themselves in favour of what the Salinas administration was calling 'modernization'. The increased vote for the PRI in the 1991 elections – it took more than 60 per cent – was widely regarded as a vote for Salinas and the Presidency rather than the party itself.[21] And organizations and associations in civil society that are pressing a material interest do occasionally manage to have their voice heard. But many, as I have said, do not. The protagonists from every side, the agents of the United States and those Western European countries who press for 'democratization', the international financial institutions, and the more radical, will all in their different ways, to their different ends, press the promise of what they call 'civil society'. But the hope that citizenship will thereby be extended, especially to the poor, is vain. It is idealistic in such circumstances, or simply idle, to expect that an adequate democracy, a politics in which every set of interests has at least a chance of being heard when it wishes to be, and of advancing itself, can exist.[22]

---

[21] Grindle, *Challenging the State*, pp. 94, 165–6.
[22] The point is well made by Roberto Mangabeira Unger, *Democracy Realised: the Progressive Alternative* (London: Verso, 1998).

IV

This is not to say that there is any viable alternative. It is to suggest that one has more directly to ask what a democratic politics can be in the sorts of conditions that now obtain in the South (and some parts also of the post-Communist East) and that are likely to obtain for several generations to come. It is also to suggest that if one does ask this question, one should first ask what a politics in such places can now be for.

Most of those who have in recent years pressed the suit of 'civil society' in the North and West have more or less openly hoped to sustain (or revive) the 'moral project' of the modern state. In the United States, where for parts of the population the identification with this wider purpose of politics still exists and intellectuals aspire to extend it, some are even prepared to say that given sufficient liberty and opportunity, a disposition to discursive reciprocity, a readiness to argue on grounds that all citizens can accept, the necessary publicity and accountability, and a willingness to extend discussion to institutions beyond the courts and the legislature, what is at present a merely procedural and constitutional democracy can become a politics of a more properly deliberative kind.[23] In Britain, some find it not impossible to imagine that in entering and transforming what remains of the institutions of social democracy, a more active civil society might revive the project.[24] Others, even in the North and West, have doubts. Accepting the *force majeure* of a liberalized and increasingly privatized structure of the provision of goods and services and of a disempowering and itself now disempowered structure of representation, they suggest that the only practical possibility is for what remains of associational life, what Habermas has called the 'lifeworld', to insulate itself from both, or if they believe this associational life itself to be in decline, speculate only about some yet-to-be-formed cry of rage. A few are simply agnostic.[25]

Not all are optimistic about the South and post-Communist Europe either. Przeworski and others confess to 'a gnawing intuition – no more than an intuition – that something more profound is involved' in the

[23] A thoughtful case is made by Amy Gutmann and Dennis Thompson, *Democracy and Disagreement* (Cambridge, Mass.: Harvard University Press (Bellknap Press), 1996), p. 359.

[24] For example Paul Hirst, 'Democracy and civil society', in *Reinventing Democracy*, edited by Paul Hirst and Sunil Khilnani (Oxford: Blackwell, 1996), pp. 97–116.

[25] Respectively Jürgen Habermas, *Between Facts and Norms: Contributions to a Discourse Theory of Law and Democracy* (Cambridge, Mass.: MIT Press, 1996), Francis Fukuyama, *The End of History and the Last Man* (London: Hamish Hamilton, 1992), pp. 322–39, Perry Anderson, 'The Ends of History', in *A Zone of Engagement* (London: Verso, 1992), pp. 322–39.

difficulties now of effective representation and the wider disillusion with government. 'It is the absence of collective projects, of socially integrating ideologies, of clearly identifiable political forces, of crystallised structures of interests to be represented.'[26] For countries in the South, the usual claim has been that the common project is that of 'development'. Rhetorically, this remains. The World Bank continues to use the word, the regional banks for Latin America, Africa, and south-east Asia (as well as that for central and Eastern Europe) include it in their titles, the United Nations has an active (if hopelessly under-funded) Development Programme, and a host of other institutions exist to define, debate, and promote it. Practically, however, for the reasons I have explained and to which Lipton alludes, 'development' cannot now be a single project.

It used to be spoken of in the same breath as economic and social reconstruction. In practice as well as principle, these two enterprises, one for those industrial economies in Western Europe and non-Communist east Asia which had been weakened by the Second World War, the other for the post-colonial South, were taken to be the responsibility of states which would be supported in the project by the international institutions and foreign aid and expertise. But after the convulsions of the late 1970s, this loose but discernible alliance between states and their international supporters dissolved. 'Development' became 'structural adjustment'. The increasingly influential adjustment division of the World Bank and the International Monetary Fund were in a position to persuade states that the ambition to protect their national economies was now over. And older forms of aid, at least to the South, began to contract.

The change was opposed by national and international non-governmental organizations. Some of the non-financial international institutions, including the United Nations Development Programme, joined the opposition. The Commission on Global Governance, a successor in the 1990s to the Brandt Commission of the early 1970s, even invoked the possibility of a 'global civil society' working through the United Nations to press it; the members of the Commission said that there was still 'a broad consensus on the elements in successful development'.[27] And in the absence of any alternative rhetoric with which to claim support and sustain themselves, most governments in the South have continued to pretend that national 'development' is their commitment still. But even those for which the commitment has been central and which despite everything have been kept to it both by an inability politically to deflect it

---

[26] Przeworski, and others, *Sustainable Democracy*, p. 57.
[27] Commission on Global Governance, *Our Global Neighbourhood* (Oxford: Oxford University Press, 1995), p. 189.

and by the successors of the intellectuals who did so much initially to define it, have been quietly devolving responsibility for it to others.

It is in such a division and devolution of responsibilities for 'development' that a realistic answer lies to the question of what a democratic politics in the South can now be. 'Development' is no longer, and in most countries can no longer be, a single project. It has come to mean too many contradictory things to many different interests. Policies for finance and foreign trade will conflict in the foreseeable future with the extension of well-being to the majority of the population. If states are to survive, their governments must cater to the first. Outside the more prosperous countries in east Asia and one or two (but only one or two) oil-exporting countries, no state has the financial resources for both. For the majority of their populations, the rest can at best try merely therefore to guarantee physical security and sustain a framework of civil law. They have no choice but to pass responsibility for the provision and distribution of more material help to local authorities and institutions of a non-governmental kind.

This is not to suggest that the line between what states can and cannot do is being, will be, or can be drawn in the same place in every Southern country. Nor is it to suggest that this line will always be sharp. Some governments are willing to consult NGOs, for example, on how to act on some of their commitments – the government of Colombia's extensive consultations on supporting education in indigenous languages is a recent instance – and in the course of doing so will from time to time accept advice that crosses the line between the technical or administrative and the political. What have come to be called 'advocacy NGOs', the new pressure groups in the South, will also continue.[28] It is merely to suggest that for most countries in the South now, there is no future in perpetuating what is now the fantasy of an integral modern state that can act as the agent of inclusion for all its citizens and provide them with means for improvements in their well-being. The model must be of a different kind.

It would not be a model of a politics which would reject all hope in the power or influence of what has come to be thought of as 'civil society'. Nor would it be one in which associations would cease to expect ever to engage the state; if only in law, there are always conditions of success that only the state can guarantee, and if the state fails in this, it has, where possible, to be challenged. But it would be a politics that ceased to see the ultimate purpose of 'civil society' to be that of shaping the direction of the state itself. The power of 'civil society' would consist rather in its

---

[28] I owe the general points here to Rama Mani, the Colombian example to Stephen Hugh-Jones.

associations and organizations being able more directly to meet the interests of those for whom they exist. Such associations and organizations, as I have said, are generally particular in their purpose, often local, and most energetic and effective in meeting particular interests in particular places. Given this, and given the political compromises they would otherwise find themselves having to make, the risks of being subverted or overridden, above all, the impotence of government itself to give them any substantial and enduring support, they do better to remain apart from political parties and the other agents of a national politics. Political peace and practical benefit lie in acknowledging a separation of spheres. For its more particular purposes, 'civil society' does well to give up on the state, in return for which the agents and institutions of state do well to acknowledge its separation and cease to regard it, as they often have, as a threat to its existing powers or an opportunity to extend these powers. And states themselves can benefit from the distance. As Chazan and Shue both conclude in their accounts of the negotiations between associations and states in parts of sub-Saharan Africa and the People's Republic of China in the 1990s, the relative autonomy and effectiveness of the one may be served by the relative autonomy and effectiveness of the other.[29]

V

For such a politics, the politics of what one might describe as a free republic of divided and autonomous powers within the law, two questions remain. In pursuit of their old 'moral project', modern states have been good at constraining, incorporating or, where they have had to, destroying powers that lie beyond them. Can they now be expected to create such powers? And if they cannot, what can?

The answer to the first question is clear. Governments will only allow powers with a freedom under the law that they cannot themselves direct if they believe that the alternatives will, for them, be worse. Most of the ex-colonial governments in Latin America in the years of political reconstruction between the 1930s and the 1970s and in Africa or Asia in the 1950s and 1960s did not at first believe that they would be. Most, it turned out, were wrong. In order to avoid being subverted by their own impotence, even some of the seemingly most powerful saw that they had eventually to concede. Geisel in the *abertura* to which he was committed in Brazil after 1974, the Gandhis in India after the political mistakes of Emergency Rule in the 1970s and the failure to maintain the party in the

[29] Chazan, 'Engaging the State', p. 275, Shue, 'State Power', pp. 82–4.

1980s, the Kuomintang in Taiwan after 1986, the military government and its civilian successor in Korea after 1987, the Rawlings administration in Ghana after 1988, are only a few of the more obvious examples. Yet although each may have had to trim its ambitions, none need politically to have feared. Most state governments and village councils in India have tended to reproduce the hierarchical, exclusive, and often brutal relations of power in their areas. Rawlings was careful not to let the District Assemblies escape the supervision of his ruling party. The revived local governments in Korea do much to strengthen the regional bases of the national parties. Local patronage was actually enshrined in the fiscal powers given to the Brazilian states in the 1988 constitution. And it remains a powerful force in Taiwan. In each case, the political class at the centre has continued to try to contain any opposition to its powers.

In answer to the second question, of how lively and effective associations might be sustained against such constraints, it has become fashionable to invoke the importance of 'social capital'. Robert Putnam, deploying the notion to explain the varying quality of 'institutional performance' in regional governments in Italy since the early 1970s, followed James Coleman and others in distinguishing between 'norms of reciprocity' and 'networks of civic engagement' and argued that the second serves to reinforce the first. Civic networks construct reputations, raise the costs of defection, make communication and co-operation easier, reduce uncertainty, enhance security, and are more humanly satisfying than the miseries of social distance, dislocation, dependence and distrust. The central difference between civic and uncivic communities is that in the one, people follow rules in which they believe they have a stake, and in the other, since they have no stake, they do not.[30] The mystery is not therefore why, once established, such habits should persist, but why they should be so difficult to form in the first place. Putnam's contrasts in Italy, he argued, push the question back to the reasons nearly a thousand years ago for the creation of self-governing republics in the centre of the peninsula. Grindle remarked on the interesting re-emergence in Kenya in the 1980s, recalling Mau Mau and other such associations in the 1950s, of a secret society.[31] But other contrasts, like Shue's between the 'parcellization' and particularity of

---

[30] Robert D. Putnam, Robert Leonardi, and Raffaella Y. Nanetti, *Making Democracy Work: Civic Traditions in Modern Italy* (Princeton, N.J.: Princeton University Press, 1993). Coleman's definition of 'social capital' in James S. Coleman, *Foundations of Social Theory* (Chicago, Ill.: University of Chicago Press, 1990), pp. 300–9. It might be thought that Putnam and his associates are better at describing where and how civic life is and is not active than in showing how it affects the performance of local government.
[31] Grindle, *Challenging the State*, pp. 169–70.

relations in China under Maoism and the emergence of some civic-like associations there in the 1980s and 1990s, have suggested (in this case against Fukuyama, who detects a pervasive, anti-civic 'familism' in Chinese life)[32] that one might not always have to resort to such a deep history. Government itself can have an effect. Malabar, joined with Travancore and Kochin to form the new state of Kerala in south India, was initially more backward, but forty years later was exhibiting the same relatively high levels of publicly provided health care and education as the other two. Putnam and his associates themselves detected a possible effect of a similar kind in Italy in those places in which there had been local rule by the Italian Communist Party.[33]

What does seem clear and agreed – not surprisingly, since it is all but tautologous – is that 'an effective norm of generalised reciprocity is likely to be associated with dense networks of social exchange'.[34] Local associations, once they do arise, can meet this condition. But this does not necessarily mean that once the condition is met, politics will benefit. To connect the associations with political parties and government itself, which is what the advocates of an active 'civil society' hope to see, can actully destroy their civic virtues: the relations between political parties and various kinds of non-governmental organizations cannot be dense, and the party politics themselves, however 'democratic' they may be in name, are often predicated on presumptions of inequality and proceed on legacies of distrust.

VI

It might nevertheless be said that this picture of a political society of independent powers under the law in the kinds of conditions that obtain in the South, pessimistic as it is, still takes too optimistic a view of the nature and capacities of the associations that already exist or are likely to; that it is too confident of the possible security of such associations under the law; and that it is too careless of the wider prospects of 'democracy' in the state. It could be said that the existence and effectiveness of private associations will depend on private and local initiative, the existence perhaps of 'social capital', or on action from donors, and that this will vary. Some people and places will be favoured, others will not. It

---

[32] Francis Fukuyama, *Trust: The Social Virtues and the Creation of Prosperity* (London: Hamish Hamilton, 1995), pp. 69–82.

[33] Jean Drèze and Amartya Sen, *India: Economic Development and Social Opportunity* (Delhi: Oxford University Press, 1995), pp. 200–1, Putnam, Leonardi, and Nanetti, *Making Democracy Work*, pp. 200–1.

[34] The phrase is from Putnam, Leonardi, and Nanetti, *Making Democracy Work*, p. 172.

could be said that there is no guarantee that such associations will not themselves be hierarchical and so reproduce the distrust they exist to overcome. Indeed, their initial if not lasting dependence on outside support, as many have noticed, makes that all the more likely, and many have dissolved for this reason. Governments, moreover, might either not recognize a right of association or, if they do, insist that associations are in no way political; and if the associations accordingly pursue their purposes in a separate sphere, they could reduce rather than enhance the prospect of a national politics in which each set of interests has a chance of being heard and advancing itself.

The only alternative to the inevitable inequalities of associational life, however, is likely to be a dismal equality of impotence without public support or the advantages of private co-operation. The answer to a lack of protection under the law or active interference by the government can only be the courage that associations of lawyers and churchmen have occasionally shown – and, where that is foolish, prudence. The reply to the charge that separate spheres preempt the extension of a wider democracy is that in keeping a distance from the state and its politics and doing something for the well-being of those they exist to help, such associations are more likely to achieve for material needs what democracies should do but under the conditions, political and economic, that now obtain in much of the South, will not. And if they do achieve this, they are more likely also to make it possible for people actually to be able to exercise some of the rights of citizenship to which they are formally entitled.

VII

The 'new structure of normative thought' in the name of modern liberty that Giuseppe di Palma was not alone in believing he could see in the events in central and eastern Europe in 1989, the conviction that 'the proper constitution of civil society' was central to democracy, was neither new nor true.[35] The thought that what we now think of as an independent civil society is essential to a 'moderate' or liberal politics, in which powers respect each other and are in balance, dates at least from Montesquieu.[36] The thought that an active and independent civil society in this sense is

---

[35] Giuseppe di Palma, 'Why Democracy Can Work in Eastern Europe', in *The Global Resurgence of Democracy*, edited by Larry Diamond and Marc F. Plattner (Baltimore, Md.: Johns Hopkins University Press, 1993), p. 267.

[36] 'Moderation' was Montesquieu's own term, *The Spirit of the Laws*, translated and edited by Anne M. Cohler, Basia Carolyn Miller, and Harold Samuel Stone, reprint, 1748 (Cambridge: Cambridge University Press, 1989), pp. 10–20.

essential to a constitutionally and procedurally acceptable democracy is simply mistaken. The nature of democracy in the United States, the most insistent model now – at least in the United States – for the South and East, makes that plain. The more interesting questions are whether a democracy that is constitutionally and procedurally acceptable can be made more acceptable still through wider deliberation, whether a lively civil society can contribute to that, and whether such deliberation can enhance the actions of the state. Advocates of 'deliberative democracy' in the United States itself suggest that the answer to each question is 'yes'. For states in the South, I have been suggesting here, whose capacities are now constrained, it cannot be so straightforward. Associations concerned with civil rights can press issues of a constitutional kind, those concerned with political rights for improvements in political procedures. And both are likely to be able more effectively to do so if there are opportunities for discussion and debate, opportunities that these associations, with others, might be able to do something to improve. But it is unrealistic to suppose that the associations can act greatly to extend the scope and powers of public policies to improve the well-being of the majority of the population. To be clear about the point of 'civil society' is first to be clear about what citizenship can be, about what the state can do, about the point of politics itself. In the South, all three have changed.

15   In search of civil society

Sudipta Kaviraj

To understand political modernity in the non-Western world is impossible without Western social theory; it is equally impossible entirely within the terms of that tradition. It is essential to formulate a more complex orientation towards the current resources of political theory to achieve that objective. This is simply because of the nature of the affair we call modernity. I would like to suggest that the entire body of what we call Western political theory is a peculiar intellectual response of modernizing societies of the West to the strange cognitive challenge of their own history; in that sense, to put it somewhat grandly, they constitute the self-reflexive thinking of European modernity. It emerges out of a paradoxical sense that this history was self-created, but at the same time, it was startlingly changeable, because all social forms were made impermanent, and therefore this phase of history was specially cognitively disorienting.[1] As the processes of modernity are universal, but these processes are realized through a trajectory of historical events which are specific to each society, we must learn from Western social theory, but not expect it to tell us about our precise future. Therefore we must climb this essential and edifying ladder, but learn to dispense with it when the time comes; that time comes precisely when historical sociology begins.

Accordingly, this chapter is divided into three sections in which I hope to do three distinct things. In the first, I will follow the career of this complex and elusive idea in various Western theoretical traditions (the plural is essential): I will not do that, however, in a strictly textual or contextualist spirit: i.e., not by trying to understand the internal coherence and consistency of a set of concepts, nor to establish with reasonable

I wish to thank Sunil Khilnani, Donal Cruise O'Brien, Stephen Hopgood, Edward Keene, and Tom Young for discussions which have helped me clarify various aspects of this argument.

[1] One of the best expressions of this sense of paradox – about a history which was more than ever 'made' by men, and was also unusually difficult to master cognitively – comes in the last section of Alexis de Tocqueville's *Democracy in America*, where he claims 'the past has ceased to throw light on the future' and as a result 'the mind of man wanders around in darkness'. Similar remarks can be found in other modern thinkers like Marx or Hegel.

certainty what exactly the writers/theorists might have intended by these arguments. Clearly, it is impossible to do anything with theoretical ideas without following these methodological procedures to a minimal extent. But the primary purpose is not to be either philosophically exacting or hermeneutically exact/reliable; but constantly to read Western texts with an eye on non-Western history – to be on the look out for an argument or a sketch that might illuminate aspects of non-Western political history, and to try to inventorize them in order to build on them later. Secondly, I will try to see how ideas of civil society have been used in the context of analyses of non-Western politics. In the final part, I will try to suggest whether we can glean serious theoretical lessons from this exercise, and how this can feed into a theoretically informed understanding of the role of politics in the larger chronicle of modernity outside the West.

I

In modern Western social theory, the concept of civil society seems to have three main meanings, determined by the precise manner of their general use in a particular theoretical language game. All three meanings are based on dichotomies or contrasts: it is a minor curiosity that 'civil society' appears to be an idea strangely incapable of standing freely on its own: it always needs a distinctive support (i.e., support by being one half of a distinction) from a contrary term. It is defined through its opposition to 'natural society' or '*state of nature*' in early modern contract theory (for instance, in Hobbes's and Locke's use); against the *state* in the entire liberal tradition, and contrasted to *community* (*Gemeinschaft*) in a theoretical tradition of modern sociology (particularly Tönnies). There exist other, less conventionalized, but often extremely interesting, modern uses which I shall entirely neglect for parochial reasons.[2] This contrastive language is hardly surprising, since political arguments and concepts often develop through intellectual and practical opposition to established structures perceived as oppressive. To set them in their appropriate political 'game', therefore, would be to understand the setting in which that exact inflection of the concept was thought and used. Even the exegesis of the idea in the Western tradition would be deliberately lopsided: out of the various aspects of the concept of civil society in the

---

[2] For fairly exhaustive accounts of traditions of 'civil society' in the West and their current status, see John Keane, *Democracy and Civil Society* (London: Verso, 1988), and Jean Cohen and Andrew Arato, *Civil Society and Political Theory* (Cambridge, Mass.: MIT Press, 1992). For two very interesting arguments about what the meaning of civil society can possibly be in the context of current Western debates see Charles Taylor, 'Modes of Civil Society', *Public Culture*, 3, no. 1 (Fall 1990), and Michael Walzer, 'The Idea of Civil Society: A Path to Social Reconstruction', *Dissent* (Spring 1991).

West, I would try to highlight those whose which appear to have a
bearing on non-Western politics. This is driven by the conviction that
Third World politics is based on an unavoidable paradox. The language
of modern politics is astonishingly and misleadingly universal. Wherever
we go in the Third World, we meet socialists, liberals, a suspiciously high
number of democrats of all kinds, nationalists of all varieties, federalists,
and centralists. Yet, much of the time, their actual behaviour is quite
substantially different from what we are led to expect by the long-
established meanings of these terms in Western political and social
thought. In studying Third World politics, therefore, we face an
additional problem of linguistic reference – a serious mismatch between
the language which describes this world, and the objects which inhabit it.
To get a grip on this world, in which not single isolated ideas but entire
languages seem to be composed of systematically misleading expressions,
we must start from an understanding of what civil society means in the
Western tradition, and then move on to try to capture what it might seek
to express in the language that describes and evaluates political possibilities in that other world.

The three dichotomies of civil society

Civil society and natural society

The first dichotomy is between civil society and a 'state of nature', or
natural society, used in theories of social contract which show how
rational human beings exchange their insecure 'natural rights' for civil
rights secured by a state. At first sight this particular contrast appears
unlikely to offer much with any serious bearing on non-Western situations, except the appropriateness in conditions of state collapse, of the
metaphor of Hobbesian anarchy. But it does emphasize a relevant point.
At this stage of conceptual elaboration the reference to 'nature' carries
two slightly different significations. First, in Hobbes's case, the state of
nature is simply a condition of unrestricted competitiveness leading to a
condition in which everyone becomes equally vulnerable to violence and
uncertainty. As Hobbes makes clear, it is not actual violence that is
required for the success of his doctrine, but the constant tendency
thereto.[3] The state of civic order, irrespective of its actual constitutional
form, provides more security than the state of nature, crucially, not
merely to those who are weak or unsupported, but even to the strong. It

---

[3] Thomas Hobbes, *Leviathan*, chapter 13: 'So the nature of war consisteth not in actual
fighting but in the known disposition thereto, during all the time there is no assurance to
the contrary', ed. C. B. Macpherson (Harmondsworth: Penguin, 1968), p. 186.

is an essential part of Hobbes's argument to provide a rational motive for even those who are in a condition of relative strength in a stateless situation – for example, warlords well-stocked with military supplies – to contract out of such insecure dominance into stabler security shared with other citizens.

However, the Hobbesian rejection of Aristotelian teleology supplies a further, probably more relevant, argument. If we read Hobbes through Oakeshott's famous interpretation, which emphasizes the idea of the state as a 'civic association', this can offer a highly significant angle for thinking about political construction in the Third World.[4] In Oakeshott's reading, Hobbes suggests a way of looking at the state radically different from the Aristotelian reliance on the idea that a state was a natural institution, lodging the requirement of the formation of states in the *natural* sociability and interdependence of human beings, making them teleologically destined to live in the *polis*. By emphasizing the non-instinctual expedient of the contract, Hobbes wishes to stress the radical un-naturalness of the political association. The Hobbesian argument stresses the indispensability of the state, but removes the reassurance that the ability to construct it is somehow teleologically implicit in men's biological constitution (nature). Rather, it should be viewed as a massive *civic* achievement, unassisted by nature, at least in the Aristotelian sense. Hobbes's argument also emphasizes that the rational achievement implicit in producing a civil government is not derived from the pre-eminent virtues of individuals. It must rest, however passively, subtly, or underlyingly, in a truly collective rational decision, an ability of members of a society to imagine an essential non-natural institution. The state, according to this startling argument, is the most essential and inclusive product of the associational capacity of human beings. Translated into Third World terms, this might deliver a certain basic warning/cautionary idea with particular clarity. Of course, in non-Western societies it would be fruitless to search for an exact intellectual equivalent to Aristotelian teleology; but we can detect quite similar strands of thinking which neglect the collective–rational achievement underlying a political community.[5] Hobbes's argument in this slightly 'foreign' reading simply advises us against relying on a benign fatalism which suggests that the political order of the state does not have to be deliberately created and

---

[4] Michael Oakeshott, *Hobbes on Civil Association* (Oxford: Blackwell, 1975), introduction to Leviathan, especially pp. 29ff.

[5] In fact, the interest in the Oakeshott interpretation of Hobbes lies precisely in the fact that Hobbes shows that it is false to apply the language of community in the sense of our third dichotomy to the state. It is a community as essential as others; but it is not produced by the same instincts.

protected, but can be left to the innate goodness of either human beings or their maker. Aristotelian teleology might be unavailable outside the intellectual contexts of the Western intellectual tradition, but the cultural worlds of Asia and Africa are full of strands of thought marked by highly intellectualist fatalism which de-emphasizes the constructedness of the world of the state, and our utter dependence on our own collective resources of rational foresight, compromise and institutional imagination. The Hobbesian argument is also significant in another sense: it brings into relief with unprecedented clarity the depths of suffering that the lack of political order can bring upon a society. No earlier writer painted such a frightfully compelling picture of the chilling consequences of political chaos.

Civil society and the state

Charles Taylor has shown, in an excellent analysis of the intellectual origins of the concept of modern 'civil society', how two rather distinct lines of anti-absolutist reflection come together in the classical dichotomy between the civil society and the state.[6] The first of these comes from early English liberal theory, particularly Locke, the second from the different conceptual arguments of Montesquieu. As John Dunn's chapter in this volume shows, for Locke 'civil society' means a legitimate political order centred on a 'state liked'.[7] Locke is also a convenient starting point for a second, distinct argument about the nature of political power in which the conceptual contrast is between the state and civil society. Translated into sociological terms, Hobbes's theory underlines the requirement of political order as a precondition for all other achievements of a modern or 'commodious living'. Locke's argument presciently suggests that this great collective achievement can turn into a particularly intractable danger to liberty if the potential power of the modern sovereign state is not brought under reliable restriction. It is true that the sovereign state, which has a monopoly of legitimate violence in a society,[8] is a precondition for all other activities in modern civilization. Yet, that state itself can become a strangely uncontrollable phenomenon if it starts behaving irresponsibly and in its own narrow self-interest,

---

[6] Taylor, 'Modes of Civil Society', especially p. 107. Interestingly, Taylor's treatment analyses the Western traditions of political theory in the narrow sense, to a relative neglect of the contrast between civil society and community that fascinates the sociological tradition. Partha Chatterjee's criticism of Taylor focuses on the relation between capital and community. *Public Culture*, 3, no. 1 (Fall 1990), pp. 119ff.

[7] This volume, p. 55.

[8] Weber's idea appears to be a sociological translation of the point that contract theorists were trying to make in a language of traditional natural law.

defined against the interests of others, particularly of property and a new kind of commerce. It is precisely the surrender of other resources of violence or coercive power to the state which makes it essential that the state must be made to function in a way that does not systematically injure individuals or groups. By the purely technical expedient of the double contract, a social contract prior to and distinct from the governmental one, Locke opens up the conceptual possibility of distinguishing between the conceptual spaces and functions of society and the state. This qualifies the priority of political order over other social activities; logically, at least, the death of a government does not instantly imply a dissolution of society.[9] Locke's treatment is so central to liberalism precisely because it shows that the state is both essential and needs to be limited.

How is the state to be limited? What does the limitation of the state mean? It means in Locke at least two related things. First, it means that the state should not have the material resources to overwhelm all other sections of society if it so wishes. Secondly, this can be done by clearly laying down moral principles which distinguish the function of the state from that of other social bodies. Social life has an illimitable number of potential ends, for each one of which human beings require social organization of interrelated action. The state is not the proper association for these substantive ends of human life; it is the indispensable instrument for securing an order in which ordinary individuals can pursue these activities unmolested – producing a civilization. Interestingly, this argument makes the state both indispensable and limited.

The crucial point here is to observe that this line of thinking, taken to its logical limits, could make the achievement of a liberal state a precondition for the creation of a modern civilization. It is important therefore to appreciate clearly what this distinction involves, because most non-Western societies trying out modern states would not necessarily have an exactly equivalent intellectual distinction ready at hand. This critical conceptual development in the West has come about primarily through two complementary theoretical traditions: first in political theory of the kind contract theorists produced, and subsequently through the rise of sociology. In Locke, writing before the ideas of national monarchies or of popular sovereignty, the sovereign or government is quite distinct from the body of the people; and thus there is no difficulty in distinguishing between the society constituted by the entire population and the sovereign or government composed of those who rule

---

[9] John Locke, *Two Treatises of Government*, ed. Peter Laslett (New York: Cambridge University Press, 1960), chapter xix, pp. 454 ff.

over them. Although he does not use the concept of civil society in the more modern dichotomous form, against the state, the fundamental distinction of principle is well articulated. The government performs a specific function of producing and maintaining order which is a pre-condition for all other types of activities that make human life; but this function is distinct from them. If the government is not put under restraints by legal rules – constitutionalism – its unrestrained power might become a threat to other civilizing activities of which commerce, based on property, is of primary importance. By the technical ingenuity of his detailed argument, as we know, Locke makes property antecedent to the creation of government,[10] and makes it the primary task of civil government to protect it. What is crucial in all this is that we can already see the outlines of a new ontology of society integrally connected to the liberal political imagination. The state, or government, is conceived here as one sphere which exists against another sphere composed of all other associations. It is this space of other associations which is collectively called 'civil society' in later stages of the liberal tradition, and it is this mass of associations in civil society which keeps the state in check by keeping it within its limits, and not allowing it, by their alertness, to encroach on activities not legitimately within its sphere. There are two aspects which are still missing from this emerging discourse of civil society: the social ontology is not entirely clear, and it is still not influenced indirectly by some powerful ideas about science and its responsibility of discovering laws of particular 'fields' of reality. This Lockean vision of a society distinct and prior to government can have, as Taylor explains, radical popular applications when the society is equated with the people – who have a common will opposed to their government, and the government can be legitimately defied in its name.[11]

Commercial society and civilization

Another clear intellectual stage offering a distinctive theoretical argument intervenes between the Lockean stage of this contrast and the form it eventually gets in Hegel.[12] At the time of the rise of modern capitalism,

[10] John Locke, *Second Treatise*, chapter v, pp. 325 ff.
[11] Taylor, 'Modes of Civil Society', glossing Thomas Paine and American revolutionary use of this idea.
[12] I accept Taylor's view that the ideas about 'civil society' received their most complex formulation in Hegel; though that evident complexity of the concept's theoretical meaning does not make it more acceptable to all types of opinion. Taylor believes that Marx's use of the concept impoverished it by making it one-dimensionally economic. Marxists would argue that this makes the argument better because it refuses to accept the ideological surplus in the concept.

focused on the primacy of production and commercial activity, some strands of social theory soon recognized this social form as being distinctive and different from the feudal societies which preceded it. As Albert Hirschman has shown, certain arguments were commonly used to justify this new kind of society, but some of these assertions were not in fact true about capitalism once it gained ascendancy and developed its fully grown features. These intellectual justifications, as Hirschman demonstrates, worked from an earlier, traditional theory of passions, but brought in a major innovation in portraying money-making as a 'cool' passion that required rational calculation, unlike lust or military glory which destroyed agents' ability to act rationally.[13] Not surprisingly, what began as a justification of commercial activity centred on moral defence of money-making slowly developed into a full-grown theory of 'civil society', which began to formulate a certain relation between unrestricted commercial activity and the jurisdiction of a limited state as being central to this new, higher stage of civilization; that the term could now be read as a society of civility or civilization. It was a society of high civilization since it cultivated the arts and the sciences, but also because it fulfilled two other basic functions particularly well. First, it offered its members a material life of unprecedented fullness and choice, driven primarily by the production of goods which was itself induced by the constant production of more sophisticated wants. Secondly, it was a society of civility, in the sense of social order, pacification, and restraint. It was a society of civility in the sense of gentle manners, opposed not merely to the wildness and violence of primitive or warlike peoples, but also to the great volatility caused by the passions of military aristocrats or conquering rulers.

Taylor's essay shows carefully that the eventual, fully blown meaning of the term civil society was infused with an argument coming from Montesquieu, which emphasized several important elements of this kind of socio-political formation.[14] More sceptical about the capacity of associations in non-political society to restrain the powers of absolute monarchies, Montesquieu saw the internal division of the powers of the agencies of the state as a major guarantee of citizens' freedom. If there are no other agencies in society sufficiently powerful to restrict the state, much the best arrangement against absolutism was to divide the power of the state by law, to use it, as it were, against itself, by creating checks and balances among political institutions themselves, such that the jealousies between them kept the power of the state under control. If one agency of the state restricted another, it reduced the likelihood of the full powers of

13   Albert Hirschman, *The Passions and the Interests* (Princeton: Princeton University Press, 1977).
14   Taylor, 'Modes of Civil Society'.

a modern state being used against any section of the society. In Montesquieu's theory, there was a clear preference for the increasing complexity of social organization expressed in a still traditional language, expressed as a preference for a 'mixed' constitution in which various social elements brought different types of virtues and initiatives, contributing to a more complex and sophisticated civilization which writers had not yet started calling modern. Montesquieu also joined other theorists of capitalism 'before its rise' to extol the virtues of commerce, in particular its preference for social order and legality. In this way, a significant shift of inflection occurs in the meanings of the idea of civil society. The agonistic virtues of republican activism, which carried forward the tradition of the forum, of a keen and vivid sense of collective freedom and perceptions of threats to civic liberty gradually recedes from the liberal tradition.[15] The subtle preferences and social structures of commercial society undoubtedly contribute to this slow decline. The Rousseauian admiration for republican citizenship, which valued the virtues of the political collective life above all else, is gradually seen, even by its admirers, to be unpracticable in large modern states. Simply by their size, modern states made the 'freedom of the ancients', in Constant's language, unworkable.[16] Several historical developments lead to a new thinking about representative institutions. The activity of making decisions had to be given over to representatives in place of the more intense agonistic enjoyments of direct democracy. Parallel to this was another movement which contributes to the liberal emphasis on legality. Serious conflicts of interest in traditional societies were settled eventually by a recourse to violence, by military means, a high price for living in a society of 'blood and roses'. Conflicts of interest did not necessarily diminish in commercial society; indeed, due to the principles of competitiveness and individuation which were central to its functioning, these increased and intensified. But a legal system ensured that interests of aggrieved parties could be pursued by specialized lawyers through a trustworthy legal system, rather than by the parties themselves and whatever support they could rally to their cause. By this powerful impulse to avoid violent conflict, commerce contributed to legality and a *rechtstaat*. Commercial people did not have either time or the inclination to pursue their own

---

[15] For an account of this tradition of thinking about liberty, see Quentin Skinner, *Liberty before Liberalism* (Cambridge: Cambridge University Press, 1998).

[16] It is important however to distinguish between two different arguments: the first would still consider the value of public life paramount but despairingly concede that it could not be practised; a second line would undermine its paramount value by suggesting that human life was enriched by the emergence of a large range of alternatively valuable ways of leading a life, and this contributed to the superiority of modern civilization to earlier ones.

conflicts; they appointed legal representatives to settle them through the arena of the judicial system. Spread of the commercial society, therefore, was meant to contribute to the development of a culture of legality in place of a culture of violence. European historical novels chronicle, sometimes with nostalgia, often with irony, this slow replacement of the ethic of heroism by an entirely unheroic ethic of business.

Ironically, the principled lack of heroism in the bourgeoisie, which Marx never forgot to remember, thus contributed to a great development of civilization, and a picturesque decline of the warrior. This is an interesting aspect of the discussion, as some of the admirers of the idea of civil society in the Third World, especially militant activists in some NGOs, appear to be indifferent to this shift of nuance. They seem to confuse the ideal of civil society with the conceptually quite distinct ideals of civic republican activism. Actually, these are two very different ways of defending liberty. In the republican tradition, the permanently active citizens grab a weapon and fight for the defence of their freedom, a strand of thought and political action that flowed down various channels of libertarian theory before it became domesticated by liberalism. The other sees freedom being defended not by active citizens constantly taking collective decisions, but by a structure of secure and reliable legality which leaves citizens free to pursue other vocations, thus enhancing and complicating the collective civilizational life of the society.

This mode of thinking about civil society is predicated upon a less explicit movement of thought, one that is crucial to the Western modernity, and particularly alien to other traditions. As capitalist economic relations matured, it seemed evident that there was something ontologically distinct called the *economy*, the congeries of all economic relationships going on in a particular society, most commonly seen as a field, or a terrain. Activities in this sphere were governed by its own intrinsic laws which it was the task of a specialized science of political economy to discover. In addition to other arguments, it was because of its ontological specificity and distinctiveness that the economic realm was entitled to autonomy from state control. If the state interfered with its autonomous, distinctive laws, that was bound to harm the prospects of commercial prosperity and thus the well-being of society in general. This argument drove through decisively the new kind of ontology of social 'fields', starting with the decisive distinction between the political and the economic, and later with the rise of sociology, recognizing a special sphere of 'the social'.[17] It is hardly surprising that thinkers who endorsed

---

[17] In this volume, Keith M. Baker's chapter charts the invention of society in the French Enlightenment. For a more general treatment see Johan Heilbron, *The Rise of Social Theory* (Cambridge: Polity Press, 1995), chs. 3–5.

this idea of separation between levels or fields of society, either as subsystems, or through a depth ontology, as with Marxists, often tended to minimize the significance of the political.[18] Although this third strand of theory gradually sets up a systematic distinction between civilized societies of modern Europe and all other civilizations as rude or primitive, leading to the subsequent equation of 'civil society' with early capitalism,[19] it brings into focus two important ideas. The first is that the *social* side of capitalist economy, unrestricted individuation and decline of all communitarian practices, is celebrated as unequivocally progressive.[20] Sometimes this idea takes a specific form analysed in great detail in Marx's critiques of bourgeois ideology: the substitution of communal social forms by individualist ones is not seen as a replacement of one way of doing things by another. It is seen as a process of falling away of unnatural restrictions on the natural inclinations of human beings. This manner of portrayal celebrated capitalist forms as not merely more progressive than others, but simultaneously as more 'natural'. Thus, it was possible for less sophisticated admirers of bourgeois society to expect a spontaneous irruption of capitalism anywhere in the world as soon as unnatural restrictions like religious beliefs, social habits, or political despotism were taken away. This made it appear that the 'natural' condition of man was to live under capitalist social relations; it was their absence which required explanation. Secondly, this line of thought establishes a strangely uncriticized orthodoxy about the supposed link between democracy and the capitalist class. In the European context of absolutism and its rivalry with early capitalist mercantile enterprise, capitalist classes followed a broadly consistent anti-absolutist political strategy. This purely local fact is often generalized into a universal theory which asserts a mysterious essentialist tendency in bourgeois classes everywhere to support democratic movements. As a consequence, political analysts have looked at capitalist classes all over the world with an entirely unreasonable eternal hope – that they would side with popular forces instead of an oppressive state, and support restrictions on state power rather than cosy backroom arrangements with its possessors. This was a classic example of a significant but contingent occurrence of European history being turned into a metaphysical truth.

---

[18] See again Taylor, 'Modes of Civil Society', on this point.

[19] The clearest example of this is Adam Ferguson's *An Essay on the History of Civil Society*, ed. Fania Oz-Salzberger (Cambridge: Cambridge University Press, 1995).

[20] This remained a common presupposition of liberal and most forms of Marxist theory, until challenged recently by communitarian critics.

Hegel on family, civil society, and the state

Hegel's theoretical reflection on civil society offers a more complex position than the previous traditions because it runs several distinctions through this field of ideas. By introducing a tripartite division of forms of sociability in place of a dualistic one, Hegel brought the narrower dichotomy between state and civil society into a complex connection with another significant opposition – between the public and private spheres. Clearly, however, in Hegel's treatment the private/public distinction does not map simply on to the state/civil society distinction.[21] The family represents the domain of the private life; and by contrast, both civil society and state spheres would represent public or universal ideas. The market, which is an arena of unrestrained pursuit of private or sectional interests, and the state are both 'public' spheres, but in quite different ways. In the Hegelian re-statement of the argument about civil society, therefore, two separate arguments are brought into contact, and rendered into an innovative, internally consistent doctrine about the forms of sociability possible under modern conditions. It could be called a theory of reconciliation of forms of sociability.[22] In the theory of *sittlichkeit*, first the family is seen as a precondition for the growth of sociability in modern man, the deepest part of his cultural and social habitus. Next, it shows the limitation or unsuitability of the spirit (in Hegel's sense) of the family for large-scale impersonal practices required by modern societies: its principle of trust, based on immediate reliability of biological ties, is too intense and too close, and unrelated to rational judgement, to be applicable to the large-scale operations of the modern economic and social life. The sphere of the civil society allows unrestricted differentiation, and is therefore a field of innovation, energy, and initiative – which is one of the major advantages of modernity over the intensely agonistic public life of ancients. More well known, of course, is the recognition of civil society as a field of competitive economic enterprise which adds complexity and refinement to the material civilization of modern capitalism. Despite its impermanence, its mutability, and its non-universality,

---

21 'This congeries of ideas about the economy and public space constituted one of the strands in the new notion of "civil society" which was distinguished from the state. It comprised a public, but not politically structured domain. The first feature was essential: civil society was not the private sphere . . . any definition of civil society which identifies it simply with the existence of autonomous associations free from state tutelage, fails to do justice to the historical concept. This defines a pattern of public social life, and not just a congeries of private interests'; Taylor, 'Modes of Civil Society', pp. 110–11.

22 See M. Hardimon's interesting interpretation of Hegel's theory as a project of reconciliation. M. Hardimon, *Hegel's Social Philosophy* (Cambridge: Cambridge University Press, 1994).

the life of the civil society also requires skills in development of trust – but of a kind very different from the family: to use a later term, the trust among strangers. It is this peculiarly modern form of trust – among strangers – which underlies the ability of modern firms and economic corporations to manage large industrial activity. Although Hegel does not directly point to this similarity, this is also obviously the skill or the social aptitude required effectively to run bureaucratic impersonal political institutions. This is mainly traceable to the common submission of individuals, irrespective of their personal inclinations or interests, to a set of impersonal rules to which there exists a kind of social precommitment. But this sociability of civil society is marred by its primary principle of competitiveness in the economy. Hegel shows radical scepticism about the idea of the reliability of the hidden hand. If we do not take the invisible hand idea on trust – because its supporters do not offer a rational explanation of how it works, but merely, dogmatically assert that it does – we face an unprecedented problem of social construction. Modern society would be threatened with disruption not merely because of the selfishness of natural individuals, the strictly Hobbesian problem, which is bad enough; in addition, it faces the problem of dealing with interests which are settled, partial, sectoral, deeply entrenched, and which have much greater resources under their control than ordinary Hobbesian individuals. The ineradicable fractiousness and conflictual trends of the civil society, therefore, threaten modern society with dissolution through a logic of segmented rationalities.[23] It is because of this that modern societies necessarily require another level of sociability, or a distinct plane of their settled moral order asserting the overriding nature of some common interests. This is represented by the abstract idea of the state and the concrete work of the bureaucratic 'universal class'. The differentiation of civil society is simultaneously an economic and a moral principle. It liberates and encourages the economic impulse of infinitely diversified productivity driven by consumer wants; but it is also the field in which individual autonomy and ethical differentiation is achieved. As this constitutes a major achievement for collective ethical life, it shuts off irreversibly the nostalgic route to the ancient agonistic life of political activism. A return to this past is not only historically unfeasible, it would be an impoverishment of ethical life. The greatest quality of Hegel's theory is that it shows the underlying dilemmas of modern ethical life – the rational impossibility of either uncritical celebration or total rejection. Hegel's picture of modern capitalism is, in one sense, more truly contra-

---

[23] This line of thought clearly develops further in some aspects of Marxism, for instance in Lukács's celebrated thesis about the conflict of rationalities between powerful economic corporations and the economy as whole.

dictory than the Marxist one. Hegel clearly understands the costs involved in choosing modernity, but his theory offers rational grounds for being 'reconciled' to the form of life it offers.[24] By distinguishing between three spheres and their distinctive principles: of the immediacy of the family or the cosiness and warmth of the small community to which people return for emotional sustenance, of the civil society with its two forms – of the market and the public sphere of ideas – and its power of moving society forward through endless competition of commerce and intellectual life, and the global community of the state which in its ideal form re-establishes the idea that despite discord and competition modern societies must have commitment to some common interests, Hegel shows the enormous richness of the possibilities of ethical life under the arrangements and forces of modernity.

But this enormously subtle and complex picture can be read in two different ways. It recognizes, first of all, the distinctiveness of the three principles, and therefore at least the theoretical, if not the historical possibility of their conflict. The competitiveness and partiality of civil society can in principle corrode the intimacy of the circles of friends and family (i.e., the first principle). Carried to an extreme intensity of blindness, people who are driven by their own partial or sectional interests might intellectually deny, or practically undermine by their unheeding actions, the requirement of any universality in the state. Additionally, the speculative nature of Hegel's theory makes its socio-logical translation always peculiarly difficult, as most interpreters recognize. These elaborations of family, civil society, and the state are openly recognized as ideal forms. Although sympathetic Hegel scholars can argue with some plausibility that this makes it possible to criticize actually existing institutions, by saying that if families or states do not conform to their 'essence' we can withhold recognition from them as a true family or state, in a sociologically interested political theory this is a frustrating disability. We can withhold our recognition to a particular state, as falling short of what a true state should be; but that is unlikely to be fatal to the state or its unworthy behaviour.

Marx's critique of bourgeois society

Indeed, Marx's critique of Hegel is in part at least of this kind: he mistrusts the power of the state to correct and balance by its universality the sectional over-enthusiasm of civil society's class strife. Marx is convinced that the competitive principles of civil society (now read as

---

[24] Hardimon, *Hegel's Social Philosophy*, ch. 3.

bourgeois society without the benign associations of the public sphere) would either openly or secretly overwhelm the universalistic principles of the state, and in fact the class which is dominant in the economic sphere would use the state's machinery in its own interests. Indeed, that domination would be cognitively more difficult to understand and rectify because it would not be immediately apparent due to the universalistic form of legal rules. Thus in Marx's reading the distinction of spheres – between the society and the polity – creates a possibility of intellectual confusion or estrangement. Recently, Marx's line of thought about civil society, which is more sceptical than others', separating an ideology of civil society quite apart from its real principle, has come under heavy criticism. Taylor argues, quite rightly, that Marx's version represents an impoverishment of the richer one in Hegel: Marx, in his view, reduces its effectiveness only to the capitalist market and its limitless competition.[25] Gellner criticizes Marx for believing civil society was 'fraudulent'.[26] In retrospect, after the historical failures of Soviet communism, it is easy to see that Marx's position on the relation between civil society and the state under conditions of capitalist modernity was too extreme to be of explanatory or normative effectiveness. Perhaps one of Marx's false moves was to link the problematic relation between civil society and the state to the unpromising metaphor of the base and superstructure, and the more significantly misleading distinction between appearance and reality. To see political relations as superstructure was to withdraw from them any serious causal powers, and to reduce them misleadingly into 'epiphenomenal' insignificance; and this tied nicely in with the tendency to see the inequalities of the economy as real and the purported equality of the state and its rights as being ineffective or close to illusory.

However, Marx saw a really important distinction, but probably misread its form or its operative significance. Marx's political writings constantly refer to the ironic dissonance between the 'bourgeois' and the 'citizen', influenced by the Hegelian distinction between partial or selfish interest and commitment to a collective interest of the entire political community. The irony arises from the paradoxical relation between two principles which appear equally central to modern societies: how can an individual specialize in sacrificing others to his own interests, and himself to theirs? The ethical requirements of being bourgeois and being citizen in this not entirely implausible reading of the matter, appear to run in such directly contradictory directions that it appears impossible to

[25] Taylor, 'Modes of Civil Society', p. 108.
[26] Ernest Gellner, *Conditions of Liberty* (London: Hamish Hamilton, 1994), ch. 7 and pp. 55ff.

cultivate the two types of ethical behaviour at the same time. Hegel's speculative reconciliation of these two ideas was not fraudulent but followed a different line. Crucial to Hegel's argument was the idea of a realm of needs: the modern economy and its division of labour not merely tended to intensify individuals' and particularly groups' disposition to advance their interests fiercely against competing ones, but in a manner similar to Durkheim it also made it obvious how satisfaction of needs created an economy of complete interdependence.[27] Thus living in civil society was an education in the perception of some minimal common interests. For Hegel, given this slightly benign thought, which obviously overestimates the subtlety of cerebration of the average bourgeois individual – that he would feel both his specificity and his limitedness – living in the capitalist economy is a philosophical preparation for citizenship. Unfortunately, it is equally plausible to assume that such subtlety would escape individuals working under the fierce pressures of survival in a capitalist economy, which would increase the vividness of their sense of self-interest instead of their interdependence. One of the main innovations of modern life is the general application of two principles, which are both 'universal', to two different spheres. The capitalist market is based on some principles of universality, and is no respecter of privilege in the traditional form. As it expands and brings under its domination all spheres of economic production, the market subjects its participants to some universal laws. Yet the universality of insecurity of a market economy produces great inequalities as an end result, although these are generally defended by the morally mitigating circumstance of these being entirely just deserts for enterprise and in any case impermanent. The universality of the state runs on entirely different principles. In constitutional–legal terms, modern states usually confer legally equal rights on its citizens, and in most cases where the state is based on a sense of nationalism, that too accords a kind of equal sense of cultural privilege to all its members. Democracy, the third important element of political modernity, reinforces political egalitarianism by giving equality of weight to electoral rights. But, taken as whole – i.e., when we try to fit into our cognitive picture both the state and market principles and emphasize their different universalities – this condition leads to difficulties in understanding the way the society works precisely because the two universal principles act in opposite ways. Marx's argument could be seen to be useful, especially in non-Western political contexts, if it is rescued from its extreme onesidedness, a result of his

---

27 G. W. F. Hegel, *Elements of the Philosophy of Right*, trans. H. B. Nisbet (Cambridge: Cambridge University Press, 1991), sections 187–96, pp. 227–31.

mistrust of democratic institutions. Marx identified a discord between the two most significant principles of modern social life; however, he read its consequence wrongly by thinking one side of this conflict was merely illusory.

Civil society and community

A discussion of Marx naturally leads to the third contrast through which the meaning of civil society is established: its opposition to a community (*Gemeinschaft*). Although Marx's mature writings do not develop this aspect systematically, underlying his elaboration of the capitalist economy there is evidently a distinction of this kind. This also underlies his eventual ambivalence about the relation between socialism and pre-capitalist forms of community life which might survive in places like Russia in spite of a weak growth of capitalism. It is clear that Marx deplored the tendency of the capitalist economy to corrode all forms of non-individualist or communal relations, and the fact that the only type of sociability that capitalism left standing was the famous unsocial form.[28] To understand more clearly why the concept of civil society attracts some analysts of the Third World and troubles some others, it is essential to explore this particular contrast more fully.

First, this comes from the different theoretical tradition of modern sociology which at times self-consciously tried to distinguish itself from political theory (in fact, by means of an argument which extends the differentiation of spheres, now positing a distinction between separate and autonomous realms of the polity, the economy and *society*). Secondly, the literature on the contrast between community and civil society (*Gesellschaft*) poses the problem with a striking and powerful simplicity, linking it to the general sociological concern with the nature of transformation from tradition to modernity. The current discussions about the role of civil society in Third World politics derives the content of this term simultaneously from these two theoretical traditions : the primary contrast between civil society and the state drawn from Western political theory, and the one between community and civil society from the sociological tradition. This is particularly appropriate, because in Western societies, where the conceptual discussions primarily happen, political processes do not usually involve appeals to and deployment of communitarian forms of belonging. Quite clearly, in some cases, like long-running nationalist, irredentist, or separatist struggles, there are

---

[28] Engels, in his interpretation of the genealogy of Marxist thought, emphasizes this connection between Rousseau and modern socialism. Friedrich Engels, *Socialism: Utopian and Scientific* (Moscow: Progress Publishers, 1978).

exceptions; but even in these cases, people accept a primarily individualist conception of their social life. Nationalism can take very intense, at times ugly forms, in Western societies;[29] still, it is safe to say that these nationalisms operate over a more fundamental substratum of individualistic sociability. Contemporary communitarian theory seeks to use the historical memory, or vestigial practical capacities of community relationships in a critical engagement with individualistic liberalism.[30] But this is a nostalgic, historical, or critical invocation of the lost skills of practising communities, rather than a direct sociological engagement with the power of non-individualist sociability working through state institutions and forcing them into unfamiliar shapes. In the analytical literature on Third World politics, therefore, there is often a desire for civil society instead of a communal nostalgia. In discussions of non-Western politics, however, it is essential to understand first the deep attraction of *gesellschaft* sociability as distinct from community.[31] Secondly, it is essential to understand the dual society – somewhat like the dual economy – this gives rise to and the manner in which the state responds to these distinct forms of sociability and their demands on its resources.

The sociological argument on the distinction between community and civil society takes its purest, most systematic, and perhaps excessively elaborate form in the work of Ferdinand Tönnies.[32] In Tönnies's stark opposition, these represent two basic forms of coming together of human wills. Using contemporary imagery, Tönnies called these 'real or organic' life and 'imaginary or mechanical' structures – *Gemeinschaft* and *Gesellschaft*. Tönnies's explication of the two principles of *verbindung* or bonding is illuminating because of its precision and forcefulness.

Gemeinschaft is old; *Gesellschaft* is new and as a name as well as a phenomenon.[33]
. . . all praise of rural life has pointed out that the community among people is stronger there and more alive; it is the lasting and genuine form of living together.

---

[29] Racism or other forms of exclusivistic nationalisms of course exist in Western societies, and sometimes have large followings.

[30] The most celebrated examples of this kind of argument are found in the later works of Macintyre, Charles Taylor, or with some modification, Martha Nussbaum.

[31] For a clear posing of the problem, see Partha Chatterjee, 'A Response to Taylor's "Modes of Civil Society"', *Public Culture* (Fall 1990), and a revised version, which connects this discussion with modern Indian political history in his *The Nation and Its Fragments* (Princeton: Princeton University Press, 1993), ch. 11, and especially pp. 226 ff.

[32] Ferdinand Tönnies, *Community and Association (Gemeinschaft und Gesellschaft)*, trans. Charles P. Loomis (London: Routledge and Kegan Paul, 1955).

[33] Ibid., p. 39: however, embedded within this passage is a quote from Bluntschli which calls the community natural, and connects it firmly with rural life, and *Gesellschaft* by contrast with urban life and most interestingly with the 'folkways, mores and ideas of the third estate'.

In contrast to *Gemeinschaft*, *Gesellschaft* (society) is transitory and superficial. Accordingly, *Gemeinschaft* (community) should be understood as a living organism, *Gesellschaft* as a mechanical aggregate and artifact.

In enumerating the great laws of the *Gemeinschaft*, Tönnies refers to the family whose members think along similar lines, as do neighbours and friends. Those who love each other have an understanding, and those who understand and love each other dwell together and produce a common life. 'A mixed or complex form of common determinative will, which has become as natural as language itself and which consists of a multitude of feelings of understanding which are measured by its norm, we call concord (*eintracht*) or family spirit (concordia as a cordial allegiance and unity).'[34] Tönnies's elaboration of the principle of *Gesellschaft* is equally sharply delineated: '*Gesellschaft*, an aggregate by convention or laws of nature, is to be understood as a multitude of natural and artificial individuals, the wills and spheres of whom are in many relations with and to one another, and remain nevertheless independent of one another and devoid of mutual familiar relationships.' In Tönnies, this distinction between community and society is seen as a general historical contrast between two principles of sociability which interact and predominate in different historical periods,[35] but there is no doubt that the triumph of modernity meant a general move towards *Gesellschaft*, a condition in which every man becomes in some measure a merchant,[36] because of the gradual tendency to replace communal types of relations of trust with contractual ones.

Is there a certain connection between the two dichotomies: state and civil society on the one hand, and civil society and community on the other? There are significant connections between these two separate arguments in several types of analyses of Third World politics. It has been argued that the proper working of a modern constitutional state requires a distinction not merely between state and other organizations in society, but the sphere of non-state organizations being governed by *Gesellschaft*-like principles. Besides, argument about civil society in the context of the Southern states is generally a reflection about democracy. Democracy is connected to the idea of a 'civil society' in two ways. Historical experience of democratic governance clearly demonstrates that for democracy to function properly, it is not enough to have procedures of majority rule, but these majorities must be of a certain kind. Communal majorities generate a kind of totalizing commitment which, if

---

[34] Ibid., p. 55.
[35] Ferdinand Tönnies, 'Gemeinschaft und gesellschaft' (1931), reprinted as Introduction to Tönnies *Community and Association*.
[36] Ibid., p. 87.

effective, would render formal institutional rules of democracy meaningless for minorities. A second argument sometimes elaborates the first:
for commitments to be partial or fragmented people should see themselves as modern individual selves whose lives are lived in different arenas
and whose selves can be altered by willed decision.[37] The enquiry about
civil society is then actually an interesting discussion about the unstated
subtle sociological preconditions for the success of formal democracy.
The main problem is simple. Democracy as a matter of formal institutions can be constructed by an explicit act of political elites, but the more
underlying norms of social behaviour cannot be similarly brought in by
legislation. If the proper functioning of explicit forms depends on these
inexplicit patterns of belief in everyday sociability, this constitutes an
intellectually serious problem to be addressed independently. In the
Third World context, at least, the arguments about civil society are
related but distinct, and cannot be entirely substituted or subsumed into
the discussion about the politics of democracy.[38]

II

The search for civil society in the Third World

To understand the modern interest in civil society in the Third World, it
is important to remember its intellectual context. How were Third World
societies seen conventionally – after the retreat of colonial power in the
1950s and 1960s? Analysis of politics was dominated by three governing
ideas: the first was an extreme form of political constructivism about
institutions of the state; the second, a kind of unthinking functionalism
which went with this – an expectation that transformation towards
modern social forms would be internally symmetrical between various
aspects of social life – in politics, economy, social habits, etc; thirdly,
these were accompanied by a form of crass evolutionism which simply
assumed that Western or Communist societies showed to post-colonial
societies images of their only possible futures. Fifty years of political
history has shown the fallibility of these theoretical attitudes. It has
shown with terrifying clarity that democracy is not just a matter of
constructing a legally preferable, rationally justifiable constitution; these
constructions could collapse pitifully in the face of determined hostility

---

[37] For an excellent elaboration of this view, and criticisms against it, see Stephen Hopgood,
'Constructing the Unencumbered Self: Eradication of Pre-modernity in Global Civil
Society', unpublished paper, 1999.
[38] Krishan Kumar, 'Civil Society: An Inquiry into the Usefulness of an Historical Term',
British Journal of Sociology, 44, issue no. 3 (September, 1993), pp. 390–1.

from well-organized modern social groups, like armies or state bureaucracies, or from traditionally minded communities. Still more appalling
was the lesson that even authoritarian regimes could not produce reliable
governance, any serious form of *rechtstaat*, however iniquitous. Democracies could with frightening ease collapse into authoritarian regimes,
which in their turn could decay and degenerate into a complete decline of
political order, a very malign form of statelessness. This in turn makes
the pursuit of all modern activities difficult, if not impossible. Current
'civil society' discussions arise out of a critical engagement with this set of
problems. I interpret them as exploring, probably through an inappropriate concept taken from a different intellectual culture, an essential
question of historical sociology of power in the non-Western societies of
today. To be fruitful, a discussion of this kind must be better informed
about at least three aspects of non-European societies. It must not be
ignorant of their specific cultural intellectual histories, and must understand the theoretical concepts and ideas which structure each intellectual
tradition. It must also be sensitive to the existing structures of practice
relating to the use of and opposition to power specific to each society.
Finally, analyses of Third World politics should not confuse the normative with the empirical and believe that simply by accosting, or to use
Althusser's famous term, 'interpellating' people as individuals, they can
be successfully turned into 'unencumbered selves'.

Colonial states and colonial 'civil society'

It appears safer to argue that the introduction of modern political
practices to non-Western societies began as a result of the combination of
colonialism, liberalism, and capitalism in the eighteenth and nineteenth
centuries rather than attributing it to the sole universalizing force of
capital.[39] The coming of colonialism began the long historical process of
political transformation which has led to the present predicaments in the
Third World. In most parts of the non-European world, the institution of
the modern sovereign state played a central role in two ways. In a
majority of cases, European power defeated an established political
regime and introduced colonial control through the defeat or conquest of

---

[39] See for this view, Chatterjee, *The Nation and Its Fragments*, p. 235. 'If there is one great
moment that turns the provincial thought of Europe to universal philosophy, the
parochial history of Europe to universal history, it is the moment of capital – capital that
is global in its territorial reach and universal in its conceptual domain.' This seems to
restrict the argument down to the problems of traditional Marxist ones; though if the
term 'capital' is taken, somewhat arbitrarily, to refer to a more complex constellation of
modern forces, I have no disagreement with this argument.

political power.[40] Once European colonial power was established, however, it almost always set about the establishment of a state as close to the modern kind as possible. It is this signal fact of non-European history which ought to be analysed properly if we wish to have a clear idea of the problem of 'civil society'. Other societies might not have had developed legal languages of highly differentiated legal subjectivity (i.e., the legal existence of different types of bodies or persons starting from natural individuals to cities, municipalities, or guilds), or a highly developed conceptual language of natural rights, based on an idea of what human beings in general *naturally* are. Hindu religious traditions, for example, developed an intellectual argument which ran in the opposite direction, in tune with the social practices of the caste system. Its idea of discrete natures or *svabhava* (literally, characteristics constituting the self) of different types of social castes, as of animals, etc., was radically opposed to the European conception of a human nature shared by all human individuals by virtue of their creation by the same Christian God. Hindus would regard the fact that individuals are born into caste-determined heredities as the explicit mark of God's will to fix people into separate destinies by giving them separate natures.[41] However, this culture certainly had a conception of society distinct from its political structure, precisely because of the relatively marginal existence of the state in relation to the primary legislative function of producing binding norms for society. It can be suggested that perhaps in traditional societies both Hindu and Islamic – where political authority's legislative competence was strictly restricted, and the norms that produced social discipline were considered natural/divine (i.e., not created by political rulers) – society has a sharp definition against political rulers; and certainly the whole society and its life was never defined or determined by the structure of political power. In such cultures, society does not need to protect itself from encroachments of the state, which is restrained by overriding religious rules of conduct. Threats to the well-being of society are seen to arise from non-observance of social norms – by deviance in conduct rather than from the power of the state. Since all political authority is not gathered into a single centralized state which could override all other authorities, a society does not need a collective definition of all other groups *defined against* the state. To make the same

[40] I argue elsewhere that India is an exception to this general trend, since European power in Bengal was established without a clear conflict with established political authority, and this was possible because Indian pre-colonial society was not dependent on provision of social discipline by political authority. The second argument seems to be more generally applicable.

[41] For a brief discussion of the idea of *svabhava* in Hindu thought, see Bhikhu Parekh, *Colonialism, Tradition and Reform* (Delhi: Sage Publications, 1989).

point historically, societies which did not go through the specific experience of absolutism and its imperialistic claims against all other social organizations, would not require a typical 'civil society' type of argument, in the manner of our second dichotomy. Segmentation of political authority, a fairly widespread feature of all pre-modern religious agrarian societies, pre-empts absolutist claims of political power.

Colonial states, by contrast, were always driven by an ideology of sovereign power,[42] and when their power was established they revelled in the unlimitedness of the control they wielded over these societies. In the case of many Third World societies, therefore, it is the colonial state that functions as a close local/regional equivalent to absolutism. Colonial sovereignty, then, gave rise to some early ideas of 'civil society' in at least two different ways. European states themselves accepted and took for granted the new social ontology after the eighteenth century – a story recounted in detail in this book.[43] In some specific cases, as in India, Orientalist knowledge systems introduced a healthy scepticism against an excessively unheeding transference of European concepts and practices, and made colonial regimes wary of an attempt to bring all parts of life under their control. Colonial administrations themselves occasionally worked on an implicit understanding of the division between the true province of state control and a province of society which could be left unregulated. In large parts of the colonial world, educational reforms produced a new Europeanized elite skilled at fluent use of practical concepts of European social life. By imitative enthusiasm they usually developed a literary public sphere; with the growth of newspapers a public arena of discussion on common issues came into existence, and even an attitude of mendicancy towards the colonial state encouraged the formation of associations based on interests. Development of modern economic processes like mining and extractive industries usually contributed to the growth of commercial classes, who showed astonishing subtlety in appreciating opportunities of enrichment created by the modern market. This was normally accompanied by the creation of a labour market and growth of a colonial working class – though the actual behaviour of neither the bourgeoisie nor the proletariat followed European models – causing utter confusion particularly among Marxist intellectuals. Thus the colonial administrations themselves, partly out of their own conceptual habits, partly out of convenience, allowed a

---

[42] I am indebted to Edward Keene for showing me the internal variations in European legal theory on this question. See Edward Keene, 'The Grotian Law of Nations and the Westphalian System', Paper presented at the Arrabida Conference on the 350th Anniversary of the Peace of Westphalia. (Unpublished).

[43] See especially Keith M. Baker's essay, but also corresponding points in Oz-Salzberger's paper in this volume.

substantial part of social life to be free of their direct control – creating an inchoate, early 'civil society'.

Nationalism and claims of 'civil society'

Subsequently, with the stirrings of nationalist ambitions among the modern elites, political groups began to claim certain aspects of social life to be the proper province of decisions by the indigenous people, particularly its elites, rather than the foreign state authority. European colonialism of course produced regimes of extreme diversity: at times the same metropolitan power, e.g. Britain, followed substantially divergent policies towards their colonies, producing in each case a specific, highly divergent form of political exchange with the indigenous society. India is an interesting case, precisely because it comprised such a huge segment of Western colonial empires, but also because the political exchange between Indian nationalism and British colonial authorities showed levels of political 'civility' that were relatively rare in the generally violent history of colonial empires. The politics of Indian nationalism showed all the marks of 'civility' with rare purity: growth of associations, respect for a certain kind of legality within the colonial state, a general politics of restraint, accommodation, and rule-following, even a great predominance of lawyers in the Indian nationalist elite. Even the bourgeoisie, more developed than elsewhere in the colonial world, behaved impeccably, and supported democratic nationalist politics. In many other colonies, such development of colonial civil society was perfunctory or absent, the imitation of colonial rulers limited to externalities like accents, manners, dress codes, a taste for cricket and Shakespeare. Imitativeness of the indigenous elite did not often extend to a serious attempt to replicate the rules of Western institutional life. Not surprisingly, after independence, many of these colonies did not attempt an import-substituting strategy in institutions but continued their extreme and pathetic reliance on universities, economic firms, and other modern institutions of the West instead of trying to establish these themselves. But the Indian case was exceptional in another sense: the transfer of power was generally an orderly constitutional affair; while in most colonies the retreat of European colonialism was ugly and brutal, without any semblance of such civility. Yet, even in India, as Chatterjee's chapter in this volume demonstrates, this civil society and its tacit acceptance of liberal individualist premises of social existence were partial and limited: in his interesting case, not all poets approved of a condolence meeting and some considered the public sphere an inappropriate stage for expressing feelings of personal grief. More significantly, those who did formed a rather small, privileged circle, with understanding of such modern rules hardly extending into the lives of poorer city-dwellers or the masses of the peasantry. The purity of the practice of this colonial civil society was thus as striking as its limitedness.

Careful observation of the actual operation of this restricted 'civil society' shows another interesting feature, with long-term implications for post-colonial politics. The associational life that burst forth in colonial Calcutta comprised associations of two distinct types, only one of which had a pure *Gesellschaft* character. Numerous societies were established for the cultivation of science, or the establishment of Western-style education, or for setting up journals and newspapers – which all used a principle of open access on the basis of economic or intellectual interest. However, there were also other, extremely powerful associations which were based on ascriptive loyalties of either caste or homeland or language. These associations aspired to a certain kind of universal membership: the Kayastha Sabha, a highly successful caste association, would not have relaxed its efforts at recruitment until the last Kayastha had joined its ranks; but by its very principles of membership, it could not be open to anyone else. Tönnies's formal distinction would have broken down entirely in the face of such ungrammatical organizations:[44] they were associations, artificially created to petition and pressure the colonial state, to influence its public policies; yet they were based on entirely ascriptive, *gemeinschaftlich* criteria. Or, from a somewhat different angle, they used a strange complex of the opposite principles of universality of access and a particularity of membership. Obviously, elite inhabitants of colonial Calcutta led a culturally amphibian existence. Functionalist theories believe that such ambidexterity has limits, and eventually people have to choose between consistently traditional or consistently modern forms of behaviour. But surprisingly large sections of mankind, like the Bengalis or Chinese or Japanese, seem to live in defiance of such functional rules.

But the much larger problem for Indian politics, in the longer term, was the fact that large masses of the peasantry and country-dwellers were mainly untouched by these activities, since they lacked the English education which gave the elites these concepts and associated practical orientations. As long as politics remained within the confines of the colonial state – an exchange between the colonial administration run by Westerners and their Indian subordinates on one side and the modernist Indian elites on the other – these rules of both liberal politics and

---

[44] This is strikingly similar to the line of argument in Thomas Metzger's chapter in this volume.

etiquettes of civil society and legality were observed punctiliously. Such habits of politics continued for about two decades after independence. By the 1970s, however, the meaning of democracy had communicated itself to the predominantly peasant electorate who were less practised at seeing themselves as monadic individuals grouped into transient constellations of interests. Consequently, *gemeinschaftlich* behaviour started emerging into the democratic political arena, altering the meanings and conse-quences of all democratic procedures and occasionally creating tension between the individualistic premises of the legal–constitutional structure and the predominantly community-oriented self-understandings of large electoral groups.

It can be argued however, and indeed this is strongly implied in cases where Western observers, scholars, donors, or activists argue with well-meaning impatience about the creation of a civil society, that it simply does not matter whether Southern societies had traditions of conceptual separation of society from the state, or conceptions similar to natural rights. These are irrelevant to this robust, businesslike constructivist argument. Although they do not usually put their arguments in this shape, its advocates could draw upon a widely acknowledged modern view that concepts can be formed not merely by explicit intellectual traditions, but also, probably with greater insidious compulsion, by entanglement in practices. If they are subjected to state practices which assume the existence of that ontology, people must develop a practical understanding of what these involve. Every successful transaction with the state on matters relating to property claims, inheritance, civil marriage, litigation about infringement of rights, freedom of newspapers, habeas corpus, etc., constantly forces people to *act* these concepts. Any successful and repetitive transaction in the modern context, therefore, must produce this conceptual understanding. Despite its plausibility, this theory of forcible conversion of peoples into unknowing users of Western political theory is unrealistic. Societies of the Third World have had experience of modern institutions sitting thinly over their traditional structures for close to two centuries, with admitted variations, but do not show signs of either a firm conceptual grasp of these ideas, or of a natural preference for these over more traditional ones. This raises all the difficult questions of the transfer of political concepts, and the seemingly inevitable displacement or slide that accompanies cases of institutional graft.[45]

---

[45] For a collection of papers on these questions, see Jean François Bayart (ed.), *Le greff de l'Etat* (Paris: Karthala, 1997).

Failures of the state in the post-colonial era

All successful states are alike, i.e., liberal, but each unhappy one is unhappy after its own fashion. Though this Tolstoyan insight should be kept in mind to avoid overgeneralization, the post-colonial states' assorted miseries can be divided into three types. Post-colonial states have often begun by giving themselves unpractically extensive projects which not merely overextended the state's capacities but took it into areas where in principle it could not be very effective. A typical example can be taken from the usually practical thought of Gandhi who, in a moment of typical nationalist sentimentality, said overexpansively that he expected independence 'to remove every tear from every eye'. This is an appropriately lyrical presentation of the idea of a 'moral project' of the new nation-state common to anti-colonial thinking. Since such ideas came from the depths of nationalist thinking and emotion, and since present states in the South are products in some measure of anti-colonial nationalism, it is important to explore the relation between the modern state in the South and the nationalist imagination.

Because in pre-colonial times most of these societies were not centred on the state, if not acephalous,[46] the astonishing power of the sovereign states of the modern West created an enormous impression on them. But this was to create difficulties for principles of 'civil society' after independence. It was entirely natural for native elites initially to accept and subsequently to advocate an idea of civil society distinct from the legitimate province of the state when it was subjected to colonial power. It was, under the usual conditions, equally convenient for the colonial state to maintain this distinction, though these demarcations and even basic civilities tended to break down when nationalist struggles slid into colonial wars. As nationalism evolved and gained strength, it had to speak increasingly in the name of the entire society against the colonial state, and question its moral right to rule. Not surprisingly, it was not the colonial administration which thought of introducing modern disciplinary techniques into Third World societies, because of its perceived alienness, but nationalist elites embraced them with great enthusiasm. Thus the relation of the state with the society at the moment of nationalist success was crucially different from the anti-absolutist phase of European history. Absolutist states faced suspicion and hostility from social groups, such as merchants and nobility, as they feared that these could constitute themselves as a partial interest which had the power to override all others. The practical ingenuity and theoretical reflection of

---

[46] See the argument about Africa in Jack Goody's chapter in this volume.

European societies were thus focused on finding an answer to this problem, and restraining its power from all sides – the political context for the growth of civil society.

The situation in the post-colonial societies was entirely different. Nationalist movements successfully persuaded their followers that development of their societies required the removal of colonial rule; freedom was not simply a matter of recognition. Colonial states kept their remits restricted, but were immensely powerful within those confines; nation-states[47] in the South happily inherited that coercive apparatus, complete with some habits of gratuitous barbarism.[48] The secret of the immense power of the nation-states was not the inheritance from colonialism but from their nationalist mobilization. Through the national movements, these elites laid claim to a right to mobilize all sections of society, and extended the state's influence over all spheres of social life. This is one significant paradox of post-colonial 'civil society' or rather its absence. Nationalism created a situation in which, after its triumph, the nationalist elite dominated not merely the state but also the other spheres of social life which it had, till then, assiduously protected from the control of the colonial state. Nationalism, making colonialism responsible for everything wrong with colonial societies, was making an insidious preparation for its own title to dominate all domains with unquestioned legitimacy. Its seemingly democratic and egalitarian ideology – because it spoke for everyone against colonial rulers – contributed to this impression. Thus the historical circumstances in which colonial nationalism laid hold of the state and became the state of the nation – its rare combination of power and utter dominance over the moral imagination of its people – were not propitious for the continued growth of a 'civil society' after independence. Any group or interest which spoke about restricting the new nation-state's power could be suspected of betrayal. Only in some exceptional cases, like India, the elite which constructed the institutions of political life adhered sufficiently to liberal ideas to accept, almost to create, limits on its own power; but even there such understandings were muddied as electoral politics became increasingly frantic.

Under such circumstances, it was only natural for the state, and the

---

[47] I use this to mean the post-colonial nationalist state: i.e., a state which is produced by colonial rule, and which carries over many of its structural characteristics, but is animated and legitimized by a nationalist ideology.

[48] Again, to take an Indian example, the nationalist elite in the Congress party bitterly complained about the lack of consideration and brutality of the police in British India, in other words, a lack of civility/moderation. Yet, after coming to power, they did nothing to alter this culture of alienation from the common people and to punish its occasional slide into brutality. Apparently, when used in support of the nation-state, this was reinterpreted as greater effectiveness.

elites who controlled it using the nation's name, to have unrealistic expectations about its project. Materially, in terms of economic development, these new states were expected to bring a modern economy into existence in a short time. The natural corollary of this was for the state to take on large measures of responsibility in running the economy directly. In some cases, where nationalism was more radical, and infused by leftist economic theory, the state nationalized enterprises run by ex-colonials, and undertook to run them in their place. Usually, nation-states also gave themselves unusually large responsibilities in the cultural sphere, especially in education. Responsibilities for health and providing infrastructures often fell by default on the new states. It is not surprising under these conditions that the state's area of operation would become grossly over-extended. In part, precisely because of the aloofness of the colonial regimes and their lack of interest in development of the economy, this expectation fell on the nationalist elite; and when they realized political power, they naturally used the ubiquitous instrumentality of the state to solve these problems and provide services. Within a short time, this contributed to a process of bureaucratization, with the state bureaucracies constituting themselves as a strong interest group. Quite often, their natural allies were the military, the second social group to have pronounced self-definition, a clear structure of organization and leadership and with enormous access to the increasingly centralized resources of the state. Since these societies had no previous history of associational activity, very few institutions independent of the state existed. More significantly, the modern elites, who had the intellectual, organizational, and financial capacity to set up structures with independent strength, were themselves in control of the state, and preferred the use of its well-entrenched machinery instead of organizations of 'civil society'. Not surprisingly, in the early stage of post-colonial nation-states, nationalism often created an illusion of consensus and an active 'civil society' distinct from the state was not considered necessary; after several decades of the state's unresisted expansion, it was considered impossible. The state had over-extended itself in several senses. Financially, it sometimes did not have revenue to perform all its expected activities; this was very often compounded by extensive corruption of the political or military elites. It had taken on tasks for which the state was not the best instrument, as in education. At times, it had also created a culture of utter reliance on the state among ordinary people, extending people's expectation from it and its own areas of activity beyond all reasonable limits. Its initial success was in fact the distant cause of its subsequent failure.

In some cases, the state failed more directly and signally – not in providing services, but in providing minimal political order. Especially in colonial Africa, the process of colonization was such a frantic scramble for territory that its administrative settlements were even more arbitrary than elsewhere, setting down lines of political control without regard for any pre-existing cultural or social faultlines. With the withdrawal of colonial rule, these territorial conglomerations automatically turned into post-colonial states, often with egregiously illegitimate pretence of homogeneous nationalism. Not surprisingly, after the state structure was entrenched, either single ethnic groups or personal cliques and military cohorts came to establish exclusive control of its revenues, defended fiercely by its coercive apparatus. Its treatment of other groups was so entirely arbitrary and exclusionary that this often led to demands either for overthrow of these governments irrespective of constitutional modalities, or for secession from the state's fraudulent claims of a national identity. Since the incomes of the military, bureaucratic, or quasi-commercial elite depended heavily on control of territory, particularly its natural resources, these elites invoked disingenuous arguments of moral betrayal to justify the use of armed power to stamp out dissidence. During the cold war, these often produced stalemates, in a few rare cases bloody conclusions; but after its end, such conflicts usually resulted in a complete collapse of the state. In such cases, actually, a Hobbesian argument of 'civil society' is entirely applicable; unfortunately there are few social groups left around which can translate a civil association into reality.

A third case of political experience should not perhaps be termed a straightforward failure, but it presents perplexing questions to the theoretical imagination. In cases like India, the state has not entirely failed in either of these two ways. Despite persistent criticism from advocates of liberalization, although the state is certainly over-stretched, it has not crumbled under its responsibilities. In fact, it now shows signs of an internal redistribution of functions through which it might successfully shed some of the functions which it performed spectacularly badly. It still provides a minimal civil order in most of its territory, though it is impossible to ignore large pockets which periodically descend into statelessness.[49] However, in India's case, the crisis is also partly because its politics are spinning out of all recognized trajectories charted by Western political theory – which is not necessarily a disaster in itself. Probably, it is more a crisis of theory rather than a crisis of the state: the state and the politics around it are becoming increasingly important in

---

[49] Examples are the states of Jammu and Kashmir, Assam and Bihar where for entirely different reasons, political order is entirely insecure.

the life of society, but it is doing things for which no precedents are found in Western history or theory. Since our theoretical imagination is almost entirely confined to these horizons, this creates a peculiar anxiety among modern elites and interpreters. In fact, this calls for new theoretical efforts to understand its nature and find concepts adequate for its description. Partha Chatterjee's chapter in this volume suggests a solution to at least one part of this predicament by a distinction between civil and *political* society.[50] The duality of sociability expresses itself in political life. Elite groups, educated in Western style, understand the advantages of social individuation and have the skills of association – i.e., the subtle and in some ways culturally unfamiliar art of getting together and committing themselves partially and transiently to others with the same sectional interests. People belonging to other social groups do not. They live in a world of more complete commitments. However, the European tradition of civil society emphasizes a most significant point: the whole reason for existence of these associations is not to turn their backs on the state, but to produce constant transactive relations with it. In fact the pleasant peculiarity of a liberal-democratic state is precisely that it explicitly respects this division and allows associations in civil society to form public opinion and allows its own decisions to be shaped by them. Even though the associationism of civil society is not highly developed in the case of the majority of poor citizens in India, the need to influence the state does not go away. The poor in particular need constantly to interact with the state in positive and negative ways. For example, when they are evicted from slums, they need to influence politicians to restore their illegal 'right' to remain; they depend more intensely on state provisions where these are available – cheap food distribution through the subsidized rationing system, supply of municipal water, cheap electricity, primary education for children, minimal provisions for health in state hospitals. For the lowest strata of Indian society associational channels, which depend on education and a certain lack of desperate necessity, are not easily available: their repertoire, which has considerable range, stretches from acceptance of patronage from politicians to wary support to local toughs; from political mendicancy to spontaneous violence. All elements of this repertoire lie outside the definitions of associational 'civility'. Chatterjee calls this relationship with the state – which is more tenuous and more intimate at the same time, and anyway more urgent – 'a political society':[51] and he views the rise of various forms of populism within Indian democracy in terms of

---

[50] Chatterjee's chapter in this volume, especially its last part.
[51] Ibid.

this distinction. It helps in part to explain the curious mixture of success and failure of Indian democracy: its great success in increasing popular participation, coupled, ironically, with its increasing difficulty in maintaining norms of democratic restraint.

Civil society and community in opposition to the state

Some of the turbidity of the meaning of civil society in the South comes from conceptual unclarity, some from the enormous variety of circumstances which await serious classificatory exercises. For example, much of the discussion about civil society simply uses a strangely undifferentiated idea of the post-colonial state; but the actual variety of states in the Third World is probably more extensive than in the North. It is essential to move beyond the outrageously undifferentiated use of 'the state' or the careless taxonomy of democracy/authoritarianism which involves the misleading and indolent conflation together of S. Korea and Zaire as suffering from similar troubles. However, as in the case of the West, in the South, too, political discourse is a response to strongly felt perceptions of problems, primarily of peoples' dissatisfaction about the performance of local states, and the use of civil society arguments are here invariably adversarial or critical. To understand with precision what political imagination each particular use of the term/slogan carries within itself, we must identify what exactly it criticizes in the functioning of state power in the local, regional, or national context. That cannot be done with any degree of intellectual precision until we produce a more intellectually acute taxonomy of non-European states. We cannot do that unless we recognize that in these continents the state, despite its European provenance, has begun a life of its own.

Some preliminary clarifications can be made even in this parlous state of our knowledge. These arguments emerge out of shortcomings of the state, which is seen as repressive, ineffectual, or unresponsive. The slogan for a revival of civil society is to rally forces in society to correct these shortcomings. If the state is repressive and interferes with all aspects of social life, a pitifully imitative totalitarianism in the Southern context, writers want 'civil society' to come out of its suffocating control: in this case, the argument is remarkably similar to that concerning Eastern Europe or post-Communist Russia. If the state is overextended but ineffectual, civil society means a demand for the creation of other bodies in society which can provide essential services instead of the faltering bureaucracies. If the state is unresponsive, and the democratic party system appears too disorderly or otiose, civil society is a call for the regeneration of grassroots organizations of marginal and dispossessed groups who cannot usually make their aspirations break through the regular format of political parties.[52] The slogan 'civil society' rings out in all three cases, but its precise significance is quite different and specific.

Two uses of civil society

If it is true that all civil society arguments stem from some deep disillusionment with the state and its mode of functioning, and writers who call for a re-assertion of 'civil society' are basically calling for people to gather up all resources of sociability to form their own collective projects against the states', we face another conceptual difficulty. In a sense, this is an application in the Third World context of Tocqueville's idea that the modern centralized state was so immensely powerful that it could not be resisted by individuals, who are in any case systematically atomized by economic processes of capitalism, and can be resisted or influenced by collective bodies – the *corps intermédiaires* which fill the space between the state and the individual. It seems straightforward up to this point: what can be more uncomplicated than the suggestion that if people find the state oppressive, they should try to mobilize what social resources they have to try to oppose, correct, or limit it? However, the serious trouble with this idea is the uninflected homogeneity of the two terms: the state and 'civil society'. The state, as I have already argued, has to be distinguished in terms of civilian and military, secular and religious, democratic and authoritarian, with finer distinctions within each of these broad types. This is essential because although all these states can cause concern or repression, the exact kind of crisis or repression or dissatisfaction depends on what kind of state it is, and what adventitious mischief it is doing at the moment. More important for our argument, in these anti-state arguments 'civil society' can mean two different things. It can mean *all* social organizations apart from the state – which would include not merely those based on *gesellschaftlich* principles, but also those of *Gemeinschaft*. Alternatively, there can be a more cautious and restrictive use of the term which implies that the powers of the state should be restrained – not by any possible form of social organization, but only by those of the right sort, i.e., the *Gesellschaft* ones. Just the statistical difference between these two conceptions is enormous: in the first case, civil society would simply mean the rest of society and would include potentially powerful communal collectivities. In the second case, it would mean a substantially smaller segment of social associations and

---

[52] See in particular arguments by Rajni Kothari about the failures of Indian democracy, in his *State Against Democracy* (Delhi: Ajanta Publications, 1981).

groups, and in some Third World societies their collective power against the state would be negligible.

Why should we make this distinction at all in this context? Why not use all types of social bodies to curb the power of the state rather than only those of a special type? This connects back again with the principle of autonomy and individuation. The demands of the state are often peremptory and unbearable precisely because they are compulsory; that is the reason why particular groups or classes, if they get control of the state, can present their sectional interests – to use Marx's language – fraudulently as the 'general interests' of the whole society. Associations act on the basis of voluntary and retractable membership; and since these are normally associated with a part of individuals' lives, these cannot in principle make such large and comprehensive demands on their commitments. The voluntariness of the associational principle is thus fundamentally linked to a conception of the individual or the self.[53] This is a self constituted by an individual by his own rational and deliberate choices, and since such choices are provisional and revisable, so is this individual self. In a different context, this Kantian view of a radically autonomous individual has been called the 'unencumbered self',[54] because the self in this view does not consist of any intrinsic attributes; all its attributes are self-chosen. To his own self, the individual stands in a relationship of possession; and the attributes he has can be altered by his own choice. Autonomy therefore implies that commitments are not either comprehensive or final. The trouble with the oppressive state is that it does not allow individuals this space for autonomy. If the trouble with the state is this intensity of commitment and its comprehensiveness, so that it can demand even the highest sacrifice from its citizens, the conflict with its unreasonable demands or intrusions into individuals' lives can be seen in terms of a dichotomy between compulsoriness and choice, mandatory controls and voluntarism, autonomy and compulsion. Evidently, this is the classical liberal critique of the state played out in the unfamiliar terrain of modern Southern societies. The trouble with *Gemeinschaften* is precisely that their claims on the commitment of their members are quite similar. The use of *Gemeinschaften* against the state would not be appropriate precisely because it might lead to the replacement of one kind of compulsory membership by another. Individual autonomy is smothered as much by a state with totalitarian pretensions as by religious groups, or community identities which require total commitment, and

[53] I am indebted to Tom Young for showing me that this ideological move is still alive and frequently used in much contemporary political discourse about the Third World.

[54] Michael Sandel, 'The Procedural Republic and the Unencumbered Self', *Political Theory*, 12, no. 1 (1984).

provide injunctions for all of life's activities, not just some of them. In fact, the major problem lies in the fact that if *Gemeinschaft* identities are used to fight against the state successfully, the political order these are likely to produce after their victory would be similarly opposed to autonomy and principles of choice. There is no doubt that this is a serious argument on the theoretical plane; sociologically, it has still greater force, as sometimes individuals in situations of crisis might be forced across this analytical line from *Gesellschaft*- to *Gemeinschaft*-type resources. If a journalist or a lawyer enters into a conflict with the state, he would expect support from the press or the lawyers' associations. If these associations are weak, states would tend to ignore their pleas and threats on his behalf. He might then be thrown back on his religious or linguistic community or tribal group, which might decide to do the right thing (to protect him) for the wrong reasons (not because the state action was illegal, but because he is a member of their community). Thus the original classification of Tönnies's sociology, regarding these communal sociabilities as 'primary', calling them 'the most natural' or 'organic' forms of human solidarity contains an important secondary insight. It is a truism that human beings carry numerous identity attributes. To call *Gesellschaften* mechanical, non-organic, secondary, suggests that the *Gemeinschaften* are identities of the last resort: under stress, or situations of crisis, other solidarities might fail; and as they do, individuals have no recourse but to turn to the primary ones. Sociologically, this indicates one of the major problems for Third World societies and their struggle to bring their states under control. In the South, most often the only social groups which have sufficient numbers, historical cohesion, and sheer collective force are identity-based collectivities. Although these have often generated or have been vehicles for movements against mistreatment or discrimination, once successful, because of their fundamental principles, they have rarely contributed to creation of democratic states.

Although this critical point can be made easily, it takes us into another theoretical difficulty of comparative sociology. Tönnies's distinction between *Gemeinschaft* and *Gesellschaft* suffers from a difficulty common to much of classical Western sociology. Like Weber's or Marx's conceptual distinctions, its primary cognitive object was to render analysable and find a language for the unfamiliar transformations Western societies were going through in the modern age. The point of all these dichotomies was to understand clearly and without any serious cognitive loss the social systems of the modern West by emphasizing its distinction from all others in the European past or in non-European history. Such dichotomies, while illuminating the specificity of Europe and modernity, has the considerable disadvantage of clubbing together into a single artificial sociological type social forms of radical diversity. An example from Marx can illustrate this point. Marx generally insisted that social formations like feudalism and slavery were entirely distinct, and it was a fundamental historical error to treat them indiscriminately. Yet in some parts of the *Grundrisse* he clearly works with a dichotomous opposition between capitalist and pre-capitalist societies.[55] While a capitalist society, in Marx's terms, referred to a real social formation, the designation 'pre-capitalist' did not point to any distinct type of society, but to a *logical* type created by the requirement of the specific argument. Tönnies's use of *Gemeinschaft*, and the current uses of community which are deeply indebted to him, seems to suffer from the same sociological error. Comparative sociology does not have a sufficiently inflected and complex map of pre-modern sociabilities. While it is true that all 'communities' share some characteristics in opposition to *Gesellschaft*, they need not be identical. In other words, all communities are different from civil society, but each might be different for a different reason. Certainly, Hindu caste society and Islamic conceptions of the *umma* give rise to senses of community; yet the first is as strictly hierarchical as the second is egalitarian. The question of how traditional practices might change its repertoire, and whether these can generate indigenous traditions of 'civility' if not 'civil society' must depend significantly on this kind of internal structure of existing practices of community. Ironically, it might transpire that what we call 'community' is as internally differentiated as the idea of 'civil society'; and some of the conceptual confusions and practical difficulties in creating political tolerance might arise from the first confusion, not just the second.

Civil society and the language of liberal desire

There is a certain tendency in the theoretical literature on international relations which shows an evangelical impatience about these questions, and suggests, in effect, that people of repressive cultures must be mildly forced to be free.[56] Civil society might not already exist; but a coalition of forces can try to bring it into existence. In fact, the assorted power of such a 'civil society' oriented coalition can be considerable, in some cases probably overwhelming. Taking a generous view, the indigenous middle classes have a natural taste for liberty; the modern working class, if not

---

[55] Karl Marx, *Pre-Capitalist Economic Formations*, ed. E. Hobsbawm (London: Lawrence and Wishart, 1971). Hobsbawm notes in his introduction this oddity of conceptual use.

[56] For a thoughtful and critical exploration of the subject, see Tom Young, ' "A Project to be Realised": Global Liberalism and Contemporary Africa', *Millennium*, 24, no. 3 (Winter 1995), pp. 527–46.

deluded by Communist ideology, wants rights of trade unionism; women desire liberation from patriarchy; children deliverance from parental repression. In this best of all possible worlds, especially after the collapse of Communism, international forces of liberalism like Western governments and international financial agencies are all interested in the growth of a civil society.[57] The prospects of this would appear quite different, depending on whether we see liberal individuation as natural or cultural. If we reject the thesis that this transformation is 'natural', we are left with the slow and unreliable process of cultural transference. In current moral philosophy, there is a powerful argument which asserts that moral persuasion is less successful by the invocation of an Archimedean point; it is more effective when the argument acknowledges the existence of a moral sense in the interlocutor and seeks to persuade him to alter that. Advocates of civil society must then look for ideas bearing some resemblance to these in other cultural traditions, and begin to build arguments from some intelligible points of connection, rather than from the moral 'outside'. Will, not force, must constitute the durable basis for civil society outside the West.

It is in the nature of the problem that the debates about civil society remain inconclusive; but these are not, for that reason, fruitless. After all, these debates form parts of a collective reflection on the nature of the conditions which political democracy requires to take root and flourish. Precisely because of its elusiveness and intractability the idea of civil society in the Third World forces us to think about the social terrain behind explicit political institutions and to try to explicate what happens in that essential but relatively dark analytical space.

[57] Robert Jenkins's chapter in this volume deals in detail with the literature on international development.

Index

absolutist states, 309
acephalous societies/polities, 161–4
Addison, Joseph, 64, 76
Aesthetic Education of Man (Schiller), 79, 111
Africa, 26–7, 160, 250–1, 256–7, 282, 316
African National Congress, 260
Ahmedabad, 159
Al-Azmeh, Aziz, 239, 240
Al-Sayyid, Mustafa Kamil, 240, 241, 247, 248
Alsted, J. A., 62, 80
Althusius, 34
Althusser, Louis, 196–7, 307
Analects of Confucius, 226
Ancient Constitution, 56
Ancient Greece, 149
Angkor Wat, 152
Angostura, Congress of (1819), 187, 188
apartheid, 260
Aquinas, 38, 150
Arato, Andrew, 17, 276
Aristotle, 17, 34, 70, 77, 82, 149, 150, 151, 290
Argentina, 189, 190, 201, 271
artificiality (of social forms), 167
Asante, 163
associations/associational life, 172
Athens, 152, 183
Augustine, Augustinianism, 33, 103–4, 206
Austin, John (1790–1859), 163
Avineri, Shlomo, 116

Balazs, Etienne, 159
Bandiagara (Mali), 161
Bangladesh, 170
Barbeyrac, Jean, 62
Bayart, Jean-François, 27, 258
Bellah, Robert N., 207, 209
Bendix, Reinhard, 210
Bengalis, 311
Bentham, Jeremy, 184

Berlin, Isaiah, 15
Bernier, François, 159
Bernstein, Richard J., 204
Betancourt, Romulo, 194, 198
Bharatiya Janata Party, 261
Bobbio, Norberto, 17, 141, 142, 185
Bolívar, Simón, 181, 183–6, 189, 191, 195, 202
Bolsheviks, 140
Bosnia, 57
bourgeois society, 15
bourgeoisie, 245, 246
Brahmins, 156
Brandt Commission, 280
Brazil, 189, 190, 282, 283
Britain, 279
British pluralism, 2
Bruni, Leonardo, 35
Bryce, James, 189
Buddhism, 155, 156
Buffier, Claude, 90
Bulac, Ali, 237–8
Bürger, 80, 82
Bürgerliche Gesellschaft, 3, 62, 78–81, 107, 108, 172, 196
Burlamaqui, Jean Jacques, 90–1
Burundi, 256
Buyoya, Pierre, 256

Calcutta, 311
Carmichael, George, 62
Castro, Fidel, 197, 198
Central Europe, 270
Chamorro, 198
Chang Ping-lin, 224
Chapelier Law (1792), 125
Chatterjee, Partha, 317
Chattopadhyay, Bankimchandra, 165, 166, 169
Chazan, Naomi, 275, 282
Ch'en Lü-an, 216
Chile, 183, 189, 190, 198

324

Chiluba, Frederick, 257
China, 153, 154, 156, 157, 159, 160, 202,
  204–31, 273–5, 282, 311
Christianity, 19, 111, 170, 174
Cicero, 33–5, 39, 70, 82, 185, 202, 206
citizens, 137
citizenship, 277
city, 157
The City (Weber), 158
civil, meanings of the term, 64
civilisation, 294, 296
civilitas, 36
civilité, 86
civility, 28–9, 180, 294, 310
civitas, 62, 79, 80, 86, 195
Clinton, President, 39
Cohen and Arato, *Civil Society and Political
  Theory*, 17, 32
Cohen, Jean, 17, 276
Coleman, James, 283
Colombia, 189, 201, 281
colonial 'civil society', 4
Comintern, 182, 193, 194, 195
Commission on Global Governance, 280
commercial society, 14, 20, 99, 244
Communist parties, 16, 194, 196, 197, 265,
  274
Communist societies, 1–2, 306
communitarianism, 276, 304
community, 176, 177, 288
comparative analysis, 5–6
Comte, Auguste, 60
Condition of the Working Class in England
  (Engels), 128
condolence meeting (as public event),
  166
Condorcet, 125
Confucius, 207, 209, 220, 221–2, 223, 227
Congresso Constituyente de Bolivia, 186
Constant, Benjamin, 60, 184, 185, 295
constitutionalism, 186, 190, 293
Copernicus, 131
'corporations', 124, 125, 134
corps intermédiaires, 319
Cotgrave, Randle, 86
Cousin, Victor, 60
Cuba, 183, 189, 195, 196
Cultural Revolution (China), 273
Czechoslovakia, 196, 197

D'Alembert, Jean le Rond, 84, 88
Dahrendorf, Ralf, 13
Dante, 36
De Pradt, Dufour, 184
De Tocqueville, Alexis, 319
'deliberative democracy', 286

democracy, 152, 177, 178, 189, 198, 232,
  239, 279, 302, 305, 306, 307
Descartes, René, 100, 151
development, 280, 281, 315
di Palma, Giuseppe, 285
Dickens, Charles, 129
Dickey, Lawrence, 113
Diderot, Denis, 84, 88
*Discourses on the Origins and Foundations of
  Inequality among Men* (Rousseau), 66, 69
Division of Labour in Society (Durkheim),
  162
Dogon, 161
Domat, Jean, 103
'domestic society', 167
Dumont, Louis, 95–7, 99, 100, 104
Dunn, John, 18, 19, 192n, 207, 210, 211,
  214, 291
Durkheim, Emile, 162, 302

earth priests, 161
Eastern Europe, 16, 270, 277, 318
Eberhard, 159
Economic and Philosophical Manuscripts
  (Marx), 110
economic determinism, 141
economy, 296
Edo (Japan), 157
Egypt, 30, 240–2, 246, 247
Eisenstadt, S. N., 207, 210, 217
Elvin, Mark, 159, 218
Encyclopédie, 84, 85, 88, 94
Engels, Frederick, 128
England, 126, 127, 128
Enlightenment, 149, 151–3, 174, 195
Enquiry concerning Human Understanding
  (Hume), 63
Enquiry concerning the Principles of Morals
  (Hume), 63
Erasmus, 37
Essai sur le despotisme (Mirabeau), 84
Essay on the History of Civil Society
  (Ferguson), 59–78
Essays on the Laws of Nature (Locke), 46–7
Esprit des lois (Montesquieu), 185
Estienne, Robert, 86
etic/emic views of society, 205
Evans-Pritchard, E. E., 162

Fable of the Bees (Mandeville), 70, 97, 122
Fairbank, John K., 224
family, 35, 173, 216, 298
Federalist Papers, 226
Ferguson, Adam, 25, 58–83, 111, 112
feudalism, 135
Feurwerker, 159

Fichte, J. G., 116, 117
Filmer, Robert, 96
Fingarette, Herbert, 220
Fletcher, Andrew, 59
Fortes, M. and Evans-Pritchard, E. E., 161, 162
Foucault, Michel, 28, 173
France, 158
Frankfurt School, 15
French Enlightenment, 3, 17, 135
French Revolution, 107, 112, 113, 125, 135
friendship, 22
Fukuyama, Francis, 284
Furetière, Antoine, 87–8

Gandhi, Mahatma, 175, 176
Gandhis, the (Indira and Rajiv), 282
Gans, Edouard, 129
Garve, C., 78, 82
Gauchet, Marcel, 98–100, 104
Geisel, 282
Gellner, Ernest, 233, 244, 267, 268, 276, 301
Gemeinschaft, 208, 213, 220, 222–4, 227, 288, 303–5, 311–12, 319–22
general will, the, 227
German Ideology (Marx and Engels), 108
Germany, 78, 158
Geschlossene Handelstaat (Fichte), 116
Gesellschaft, 208, 222–4, 227, 230, 303–5, 311, 319, 321
Ghana, 283
Ghannouchi, Rashid, 239
Gillion, Kenneth L., 159
Gierke, Otto von, 95, 98
'good governance', 262, 263
Gorz, André, 144, 145, 146
gradualism, 13
Gramsci, Antonio, 16, 139–43, 192, 251
Gravina, G. V., 66
Grindle, Merilee, 271, 272, 283
Grotius, Hugo, 58, 102, 103
Grundrisse (Marx), 322
Gonja, 163
Goethe, 152
Guilds, 36, 125, 234
Guangxi, 162
Guangdong, 162
Gupta, Rajanikanta, 165

Haiti, 39, 189, 190
Habermas, Jürgen, 150–1, 153, 160, 168, 206, 217, 230, 279
Hamann, G., 78, 106
Hankow, 157, 158, 159, 217
Hangzhou, 157, 158
Hardenberg, 125

Harneker, Marta, 197
Hawthorn, Geoffrey, 31, 202, 203
Haya de la Torre, Victor R., 194
Hayek, Friedrich A., 207, 210, 211, 222
Haym, Rudolf, 108
Hegel, G. W. F., 3, 14, 16, 17, 23–24, 40, 60, 78, 79, 105–30, 133–4, 136, 137, 141, 171, 172, 185, 226, 237, 258, 276, 293, 298–300, 302, 303
hegemony, 139, 141
Heinecius, 62
Held, David, 206
Herder, 78, 82, 106
Hinduism, 308
Hinnebusch, Raymond 246
Hirschman, Albert, 25n, 26, 294
History and Class Consciousness (Lukács), 110
Hobbes, Thomas, 23, 48, 55, 104, 132, 155, 288–91, 299, 317
Holbach, Baron de, 60
Holy Roman Empire, 83
Horkens, Henri, 86
Hont, Istvan, 102
Hsu Fu-kuan, 225
Huang Ko-wu, 219, 225, 227
Huguenots, 52
human rights, 153
Humboldt, Alexander von, 125
Hume, David, 58, 59, 60, 61, 62, 71, 76, 77, 81, 82, 101, 102
Huntington, Samuel P., 207, 225, 275
Hussain, Saddam, 242
Hutcheson, Francis, 62, 64, 65, 72
Hard Times (Dickens), 129

Ibrahim, Saad Eddin, 233, 240, 241, 244
Ilting, Karl-Heinz, 120
India, 2, 27, 154, 156, 160, 174, 259, 261, 264, 265, 271, 282, 309, 310, 314, 317
Indian National Congress (Congress Party), 176, 265
individualism, 96–7
infrastructure, 140, 301
Inkeles, Alex, 207
Institutes of Moral Philosophy (Ferguson), 76, 78
Institutional Revolutionary Party (PRI), 271, 273, 278
International Monetary Fund, 280
Iran, 244
Iraq, 242
Iselin, I., 78
Islah party, 243
Islamic banks, 247
'Islamic economy', 246

Islamic Front, 247
Islamism/Islamist, 235–7, 239, 242, 245, 247, 248
Ismail, Sayfuddin Abdelfattah, 235–7, 239, 240, 241, 244, 247
Italian Communist Party, 284
Italy, 140, 283

Jacobi, F. H., 78, 83
Jacobinism, 195, 202
Jains, Jainism, 154, 155
Jansenists, 103–4
Japan, 157, 311
Jefferson, Thomas, 184
Jesuits, 154
John of Salisbury, 35
John of Viterbo, 37
Jordan, 248

Kant, Immanuel, 23, 78, 81, 101, 106, 113
Kao Li-k'o, 210, 229, 230
Karl, Terry Lynn, 274
Kaunda, Kenneth, 257
Kaviraj, Sudipta, 25n, 26n, 29n
Kayastha Sabha, 311
Kenya, 261, 272, 283
Kerala, 284
Khatami, 244
Khilnani, Sunil, 207
Khmer, 152
Kshatriya, 156
Kohli, Atul, 25n
Korea, 283, 318
Kuomintang, 283
Ku Yen-wu, 223

Lasch, Christopher, 209, 215
Latin America, 16, 179–203, 269, 270, 282
League of Nations, 193
Lee Teng-hui, 209
Leca, Jean, 28–9
Lehmann, David, 273
Leibniz, 62, 80
Lessing, G. E., 60, 78, 113
Li Tse-hou, 230
Li Wen-chih, 218
Liang Ch'i-ch'ao, 214, 225, 227
liberalism, 227
liberty, 75
Lipton, Michael, 277, 280
Locke, John, 3, 14, 17, 18–20, 40–57, 58, 60, 91, 96, 97, 100, 102, 104, 131–2, 134, 150, 155, 226, 250, 269, 274, 288, 291, 292, 293
London, 128
Low Countries, 158

Luddites, 118
Lukács, Georg, 16, 110, 112, 114, 115
Luther, Martin, 35, 103, 113
Lycurgus, 186

MacIntyre, Alasdair, 204, 210
Machiavelli, N., 35, 59, 70, 184
machines/mechanization, 118
Malaysia, 26
mahajans (guilds), 160
Maine, Henry, 190
Maitland, F. W., 190
Malawi, 261
Mali, 161
Mandeville, Bernard, 70, 71, 96, 97, 103, 122
manly virtues, 67–9
Mao Ze Dong, 210, 224, 229, 230, 284
Marcuse, Herbert, 16
Mariátegui, José Carlos, 194
markets, 11, 13
Marx, Karl, 3, 60, 78, 108, 109, 115, 131–46, 141, 154, 155, 160, 172, 192–3, 212–13, 226, 258, 276, 300–3, 322
Marxism, 16, 192, 193, 194, 195, 198, 199, 202, 213, 227
Medieval Cities (Pirenne), 158
Medina, 238
merchants, 154
Mendelssohn, 78
Mesopotamia, 153
Mevs, G., 39
Mexico, 189, 190, 201, 271, 272, 278
Mill, John Stuart, 60, 212, 226, 227
Milner, A. C., 26
Mirabeau, 84
Mitra, Dinabandhu, 169
modernization theory, 14, 172
modernity, 287
Montesquieu, 17, 22, 65–6, 71, 76, 104, 112, 181, 185, 187, 190, 285, 291, 294, 295
Müller, Adam, 116
Muslim Brotherhood, 247
Muslims, 163
Mayhew, Henry, 129

NGOs, 12, 281, 296
Nagarseth, 160
nationalism, 304, 310–12, 313–15
Natural Law and the Theory of Society (Gierke), 95
natural law, 180
natural rights, 180
Neo-Confucianism, 223
new social movements, 145–6, 151
Newton, Isaac, 100

Nicaragua, 183, 190, 195
Nicole, Pierre, 103
Nicot, Jean, 86
non-Western modernity, 172, 178
Novalis, 78
Nozick, Robert, 39
Ntibantunganya, Sylvestre, 256
Nuer, 162

Oakeshott, Michael, 290
O'Donnell, Guillermo, 275
Old Regime (in France), 89, 189
Olsen, Mancur 266
Oriental Despotism (Wittfogel), 156
Orme, Robert, 154, 156
Owen, Roger, 248, 249

Paine, Thomas, 179n
*Paraphrase and Notes on the Epistles of
   St Paul* (Locke), 48
Parsons, Talcott, 151, 162
Pascal, Blaise, 101
People's Daily, 274
Pérez-Diaz, Victor, 269, 276, 277
Peru, 190, 200
Phenomenology of Mind (Hegel), 109, 110,
   114
Phillipson, Nicholas, 64
Philosophy of Right (Hegel), 105, 108–9,
   111, 116–18, 126, 131, 141, 171
Pirenne, Henri, 158
Plant, Raymond, 115
Plato, 33, 121, 220
Poggi, Gianfranco, 138
Poland, 16, 259
Polanyi, Karl, 98–9
political society, 173, 175, 176, 177, 260
political romanticism, 188
Polybius, 77
Popkin, Richard, 100
Popper, Karl, 15, 115, 204
population, 173, 176
Portugal, 154
post-colonial state, 313–18
post-Marxism, 144, 146
post-modernism, 16
Poulantzas, Nicos, 197
poverty, 123, 126–31, 132–3
Principes des droit naturel (Burlamaqui), 90
Principles of Moral and Political Science
   (Ferguson), 68
Principles of Political Oeconomy (James
   Steuart), 109
Prison Notebooks (Gramsci), 139–43, 192
Przeworski, Adam, 270, 271, 279
public sphere, 168, 169

'publicity' (*Öffentlichkeit*), 150
Putnam, Robert, 283–4
Pufendorf, Samuel, 17, 58, 62, 79, 80
pyrrhonism, 100, 102

'rude nations', 73
'the rabble'/Pöbel, 119, 120, 126, 127, 128,
   129
rationality, rationalization, 5, 151, 152, 153,
   208
Rawlings, Jerry, 283
Raynal, Guillaume-Thomas-François,
   Abbé, 99
Rechtstaat, 30, 295, 307
Reason, 45, 106
Reasonableness of Christianity (Locke), 47
recognition, 24
Reformation, 100, 131, 138
Reid, Thomas, 63–4
Reidel, Manfred, 23
religion, 90–4, 112, 113
Religion within the Limits of Reason Alone
   (Kant), 106
representation, 152
Republic (Plato), 121
republicanism, 59, 156, 179, 180, 181, 190,
   193, 194, 202, 203
Res publica, 108, 180, 182, 183, 190–1, 202,
   203
revolution, 193, 195
Richelet, Pierre, 86–7
right to revolution, 53
Ritter, Joachim, 119
Rochefoucauld, La, 103
Rochefort, César de, 87
Roman law, 33, 34, 95
Romano, Egidio, 36
Rome, 183, 184
Rosenkranz, Karl, 109, 117
Rousseau, Jean-Jacques, 23, 65, 66, 67–70,
   72, 94, 155, 181, 183, 184, 187, 190, 202,
   226, 227, 295
Rowe, William T., 159, 217
Roy, Olivier, 243
Ruge, Arnold, 108
Russia, 140

'social', meaning of the term, 85
'society', 84–5
s'-Gravesande, 101
Sādhanā (journal), 166
Salafi, 240
Sandinistas, 198
Sarajevo, 152
Schelling, 107
Schiller, F., 60, 78, 106, 107, 111–12, 113

Schlosser, G., 82
Schmitt, Carl, 188n
Schmitter, Philippe, 266, 267, 274
Scott, James C., 157
Scottish theorists of commercial society, 18,
    20–2, 58–83
self, conceptions of, 28
Seligman, Adam, 145, 146
Sen, Nabinchandra 165, 166, 169, 170, 175
Shakespeare, 310
Shanghai, 159
Shari'a, 233, 236, 238, 240
Shastri, Haraprasad, 165
Shue, Vivienne, 273–4, 282, 283–4
Silver, Allan, 21, 25
Singapore, 155
Sittlichkeit, 23, 111, 114, 132, 298
Skinner, Quentin, 76, 207
Skinner, William G., 159
Smith, Adam, 20, 58, 60, 61, 71, 77, 81, 82,
    110, 111, 116, 117–18, 125, 133, 134, 222
social capital, 283, 284
Social Contract (Rousseau), 67, 94, 186
social contract, 92–3
socialism, 16, 183
societas, 33, 37, 95
societas civilis, 17, 59, 62, 79, 108, 180, 185,
    202
Solidarity (Poland), 259, 260
South Africa, 260
Sparta, 183, 185
Spencer, Herbert, 162
state of nature, 43, 67, 132, 288
Stein, Lorenz von, 129
Steuart, Sir James, 109, 111, 116, 117, 118
Stewart, Dugald, 60, 71
Strauss, Leo, 150, 210
Stedman Jones, Gareth, 23
Subaltern Studies, 176
sub-Saharan Africa, 262, 270, 273, 275, 282
Sudan, 247
Sue, Eugène, 129
Sumner, William Graham, 218
Sun Yat-Sen, 226
Sung, 159
superstructure, 139, 141, 146, 301
svabhava, 308
Syria, 242, 246

Tacitus, 154
Tagore, Rabindranath, 165, 166, 167, 168,
    171, 174
Taiwan, 209, 215–16, 228, 283
Talmon, J., 15
T'ao Ch'ien, 220
Taylor, Charles, 170, 291, 293, 294, 301

Teng Cheng-lai, 229
Texier, Jacques, 141
Thebes, 183
Thomasius, 80
Tocqueville, Alexis de, 319
Tönnies, Ferdinand, 288, 304–5, 311, 321,
    322
towns, 35, 37
transfer of concepts, 312
tradition/traditional, 154, 172
Traité de la société civile (Buffier), 90
transitions to civil society, 13
Treatise of Human Nature (Hume), 63, 102
Treitschke, 115
Tuck, Richard, 102, 103
Turabi, Hasan, 239
Turgot, 125
Turkey, 237–8
tributary state, 160

ulama, 236
umma, 238
'uncivil' society, 149
unintended consequences, 25, 69
United Nations, 280
United Nations Development Programme,
    251, 267, 280
United States of America, 180, 181, 183,
    184, 186, 210, 266, 278–9, 286
universitas, 95
universities, 37
universal male suffrage, 129
Uruguay, 189
USAID, 252, 253, 254, 255, 256, 257–66
utopia, 142, 143, 220, 229

Venezuela, 189, 201, 271
Voltaire, François-Marie Arouet, 101
Von Haller, Carl Ludwig, 108

Wakeman, Jr., Frederic, 217
Walch, J. G., 80
Washington, George, 184
Waterbury, John, 245, 246, 247
The Wealth of Nations (Smith), 125
Weber, Max, 138, 151, 153, 154, 156, 157,
    158, 159, 160, 222, 225, 230
Wei Yuan, 219, 223, 225
West Bengal, 170
White, Gordon, 257, 258
Wieland, C. M., 82
William of Ockham, 48
Williams, David, 250
'withering away of the state', 142
Wittfogel, Karl, 156, 217
World Bank, 250, 251, 280

The Young Hegel (Lukács), 110
Yao, 162
Yañez, Francisco Javier, 180, 181
Yang Kuo-shu, 228, 229, 230
Yen Fu, 227
Young, Tom, 250
Yü Ying-shih, 222, 224, 225, 228

Zaire, 318
Zambia, 257
Zayd, Abu, 241
Zaydis, 243
Zubaida, Sami, 30